# Repentance in Christian Theology

*Mark J. Boda*
*and*
*Gordon T. Smith*

Editors

A Michael Glazier Book

**LITURGICAL PRESS**
Collegeville, Minnesota

www.litpress.org

A Michael Glazier Book published by Liturgical Press

Cover design by David Manahan, O.S.B.
Photo by Ryan KC Wong, iStockphoto.com.

1     2     3     4     5     6     7     8

**Library of Congress Cataloging-in-Publication Data**

Repentance in Christian theology / Mark J. Boda and Gordon T. Smith, editors.
        p.     cm.
    "A Michael Glazier book."
    Includes bibliographical references and index.
    ISBN-13: 978-0-8146-5175-9 (alk. paper)
    ISBN-10: 0-8146-5175-5 (alk. paper)
    1. Repentance—Christianity.   I. Boda, Mark J.   II. Smith, Gordon T., 1953– .   III. Title.

BT800.R47 2006
234'.5—dc22

                                                    2006009150

# Contents

**Section Two: Historical Perspectives**

**Section Three: Theological Traditions**

**Section Four: Reflection**

# Preface

There are many whom we want to thank for their assistance in bringing this volume to press. We are grateful to the sixteen writing participants for their eager engagement in the project from its inception. In addition, there were many other scholars who attended the sessions and enriched the conversation with comments and questions. We are thankful for those who helped us capture the oral reflection around the table and put it into written form. There are some inherent challenges to working with such a large group, but the final results have exceeded our expectations and whetted rather than dulled our appetite for further collaboration.

The management team at Liturgical Press, especially Linda Maloney and Mark Twomey, provided encouragement in the early stages by believing in the project and offered wise counsel as we shaped the project. The final stages of production were ably superintended by Linda Maloney, Susan Hogan/Albach, and Colleen Stiller. We are thankful to faithful graduate assistants at McMaster Divinity College, first Darren Lampson, who learned the Liturgical Press publishing style and then transformed penultimate drafts into chapters of the book, secondly David Beldman, who meticulously corrected the proofs, and finally James D. Dvorak, who produced the indices.

The chapters of this book were first presented in draft form and discussed at two colloquia held in 2003 (Atlanta) and 2004 (San Antonio) at the joint American Academy of Religion/Society of Biblical Literature National Meetings. We are grateful to these two scholarly organizations for providing a venue to foster critical dialogue which has enhanced the quality of the present volume. We are thankful for the support of our own institutions (McMaster Divinity College and reSource Leadership International), who have supported us in this venture by offering administrative assistance as well as funds to attend the conferences and complete the manuscript.

Finally, we are grateful for the opportunity that this project has afforded us to work together—to bring together our mutual passion for scholarship in the service of the Christian community and any others who might want to understand better this particular dimension of the Christian tradition. It has been an example for us of how a collaborative working project can deepen a friendship.

Mark J. Boda and Gordon T. Smith, Lent 2006

# Abbreviations

| | |
|---|---|
| AB | Anchor Bible |
| ACW | Ancient Christian Writers |
| AOTC | Abingdon Old Testament Commentaries |
| *AUSS* | *Andrews University Seminary Studies* |
| *Bib* | *Biblica* |
| BSLK | *Die Bekenntnisschriften der evangelisch-Lutherischen Kirche, herausgegeben im Gedenkjahr der Augsburgischen Konfession 1930* (repr. Göttingen, 1976) |
| BZAW | Beihefte zur Zeitschrift für die Alttestamentliche Wissenschaft |
| *CBQ* | *Catholic Biblical Quarterly* |
| CBQMS | Catholic Biblical Quarterly Monograph Series |
| CCSL | Corpus Christianorum: Series Latina |
| ConBNT | Coniectanea biblica, New Testament Series |
| ConBOT | Coniectanea biblica, Old Testament Series |
| CRINT | Compendium Rerum Iudaicarum ad Novum Testamentum |
| CS | Cistercian Studies |
| *CTM* | *Current in Theology and Mission* |
| CWS | Classics of Western Spirituality |
| ER | Hans J. Hillerbrand, ed., *The Oxford Encyclopedia of the Reformation*, 4 vols. (New York: Oxford University Press, 1996). |
| *ExpTim* | *Expository Times* |
| FC | Fathers of the Church |
| GCS | Die griechische christliche Schriftsteller der ersten [drei] Jahrhunderte |
| *HBT* | *Horizons in Biblical Theology* |

| | |
|---|---|
| HUCA | *Hebrew Union College Annual* |
| Int | Interpretation |
| JBL | *Journal of Biblical Literature* |
| JECS | *Journal of Early Christian Studies* |
| JPSTC | Jewish Publication Society Torah Commentary |
| JSOR | *Journal of the Society of Oriental Research* |
| JSOTSup | *Journal for the Study of the Old Testament,* Supplement Series |
| LCL | Loeb Classical Library |
| LThK | *Lexikon für Theologie und Kirche* |
| LW | *Luther's Works,* American Edition, eds. Jaroslav Pelikan and H. T. Lehmann, 55 vols. (St. Louis: Concordia Publishing House; Philadelphia and Minneapolis: Fortress, 1955– ) |
| n.s. | new series |
| NCB | New Century Bible |
| NICOT | New International Commentary, Old Testament |
| NIDNTT | *New International Dictionary of New Testament Theology* |
| NPNF | *Nicene and Post-Nicene Fathers* |
| NSBT | New Studies in Biblical Theology |
| OBT | Overtures to Biblical Theology |
| OrChrAn | Orientalia Christiana Analecta |
| OTL | Old Testament Library |
| OtSt | *Oudtestamentische Studiën* |
| ParOr | *Parole de l'Orient* |
| PETSE | Papers of the Estonian Theological Society in Exile |
| PS | Patrologia Syriaca |
| RAC | *Reallexikon für Antike und Christentum* |
| RB | *Revue Biblique* |
| RevExp | *Review and Expositor* |
| SBEC | Studies in the Bible and Early Christianity |
| SBLAB | Society of Biblical Literature Academia Biblica |
| SBLDS | Society of Biblical Literature Dissertation Series |
| SBLEJL | Society of Biblical Literature, Early Judaism and its Literature |
| SBLSP | *Society of Biblical Literature Seminar Papers* |
| SBT | Studies in Biblical Theology |
| SBTS | Sources for Biblical and Theological Study |
| SC | Sources Chrétiennes |

| | |
|---|---|
| *ScC* | *La scuola cattolica* |
| SEAug | Studia Ephemeridis Augustinianum |
| Sehling | Emil Sehling, ed., *Die evangelischen Kirchenordnungen des XVI Jahrhunderts*, Vols. I–V (Leipzig: O. R. Riesland, 1902–1913), vols VI–VII, XI–XV (Tübingen: J. C. B. Mohr [Paul Siebeck], 1955–1963) |
| SHR | Studies in the History of Religions |
| SJLA | Studies in Judaism in Late Antiquity |
| *SJT* | *Scottish Journal of Theology* |
| SP | Sacra Pagina |
| *ST* | *Studia Theologica* |
| STDJ | Studies on the Texts of the Desert of Judah |
| STL | Studia Theologica Lundensia |
| *StPatr* | *Studia Patristica* |
| TB | Theologische Bücherei: Neudrucke und Berichte aus dem 20. Jahrhundert |
| *VC* | *Vigiliae Christianae* |
| VCSup | Supplements to *Vigiliae Christianae* |
| WA | *D. Martin Luthers Werke, Kritische Gesamtausgabe*, 127 vols. (to date) (Weimar, 1883– ) |
| WBC | Word Bible Commentary |
| WC | Westminster Commentaries |
| *WW* | *Word and World* |
| *ZAW* | *Zeitschrift für die alttestamentliche Wissenschaft* |
| *ZKT* | *Zeitschrift für katholische Theologie* |
| *ZNW* | *Zeitschrift für die neutestamentliche Wissenschaft* |

# Introduction

# Creating Space for a Theological Conversation

## Mark J. Boda*

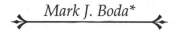

From the moment of Johann Philipp Gäbler's proverbial shot across the theological bow in the late eighteenth century, seeking to create some *Lebensraum* for the investigation of the Bible as a historically rooted and conditioned document, if not long before, the relationship between the theological disciplines has been one of creative tension. On one level this is natural, for those engaged in the study of the particular, which is often called exegetical theology, will always have opportunity to call into question the results of those engaged in the study of the general, which is systematic theology, and also vice versa. However, when such tension results in relational disintegration, or worse yet, disregard, the conversation is indeed the poorer.

Most scholars engaged in the study of theology (in its broadest sense) could probably cite anecdotal evidence of such disregard. A conversation I had with one of my professors during my doctoral studies made this clear. Studying the literature of the early Persian period and the sociological fracture of the Jewish community during this era (itself already

---

* An earlier and slightly different form of this chapter appeared as part of my contribution to "Penitence in Christian Tradition," *Canadian Evangelical Review* 29 (2005) 45–54.

an indication of the ample *Lebensraum* "enjoyed" in that department), I asked about the current work of a particular Old Testament scholar whose research had dominated an earlier decade. The response was simply that he had moved out of biblical studies and of late was involved in "theology."

This incident highlights the uneasy relationship between biblical and systematic theology since the time of the Enlightenment. Those involved in biblical studies focussed their agenda on the recovery of the meaning of the biblical texts within their original context and were suspicious of the imposition of theological traditions onto the biblical corpus. Freed from these "oppressive" theological constraints many within the biblical guild adopted a largely historical strategy with lessened interest in the theological content of the biblical texts. As already noted, this historical and particularistic agenda was laid out by J. P. Gäbler as early as 1787 as he sketched out the difference between biblical and dogmatic theology.[1] The former was an analytical task describing the thought of the biblical writers, while the latter was a constructive task of interpretation tracing how the church had appropriated the Bible. By the end of the nineteenth century this analytical agenda had led most biblical scholars to the writing of *Religionsgeschichte* (history of religions) rather than biblical theology.

During the twentieth century, although diachronic aspects *(Religionsgeschichte)* were never completely abandoned, there was a return to theological reflection within the biblical guild. In particular during the period from 1930 to 1970 the writing of biblical theology was resurrected among biblical scholars.[2] This move toward the "theological" was encouraged by

---

[1] John Sandys-Wunsch and Laurence Eldredge, "J. P. Gäbler and the Distinction between Biblical and Dogmatic Theology: Translation, Commentary, and Discussion of his Originality," *SJT* 33 (1980) 133–58; Ben C. Ollenburger, Elmer A. Martens, and Gerhard F. Hasel, eds., *The Flowering of Old Testament Theology: A Reader in Twentieth-Century Old Testament Theology, 1930–1990,* Sources for Biblical and Theological Study 1 (Winona Lake, IN: Eisenbrauns, 1991); Loren T. Stuckenbruck, "Johann Philipp Gäbler and the Delineation of Biblical Theology," *SJT* 52 (1999) 139–55.

[2] The evidence cited will focus largely on this phenomenon from an Old Testament perspective (for obvious reasons): Walther Eichrodt, *Theology of the Old Testament* (Philadelphia: Westminster, 1961); Gerhard von Rad, *Old Testament Theology* (Edinburgh: Oliver and Boyd, 1962); Theodorus Ch. Vriezen, *An Outline of Old Testament Theology* (2nd ed. Oxford: Blackwell, 1970); Walther Zimmerli,

a shift in broader literary studies to more synchronic approaches (New Criticism, Structuralism) in the latter half of the past century. Many biblical scholars strove for a more integrative approach to biblical studies, one that illuminated final literary forms in the Hebrew and Christian Bibles rather than tracing the history of religions alone.[3] This shift provided an avenue for biblical scholars to again speak theologically rather than merely historically, as Brevard Childs encouraged the guild "to avoid dogmatism on the right and historicism on the left."[4]

With the rise of postmodern epistemologies has come a plethora of new approaches to biblical texts and subsequently a shift from biblical theology to biblical theologies that are expressive of particular interpretive communities (defined by tradition, ethnicity, gender, etc.).[5] This new awareness that biblical theology is not merely a "descriptive," but rather a "constructive" enterprise has opened up a new opportunity for dialogue between the biblical and theological guilds, a dialogue that has been showcased over the past decade and a half in various collections of essays[6] as well as individual works.[7]

---

*Old Testament Theology in Outline* (Atlanta: John Knox, 1978); cf. Robert C. Dentan, *Preface to Old Testament Theology* (rev. ed. New York: Seabury, 1963); Gerhard F. Hasel, *Old Testament Theology: Basic Issues in the Current Debate* (4th ed. Grand Rapids: Eerdmans, 1991).

[3] E.g., Brevard S. Childs, *Old Testament Theology in a Canonical Context* (Philadelphia: Fortress Press, 1985); John Sailhamer, *An Introduction to Old Testament Theology: A Canonical Approach* (Grand Rapids: Zondervan, 1995).

[4] Childs, *Theology*, 9.

[5] E.g., Phyllis Trible, "Overture for a Feminist Biblical Theology," in Ben C. Ollenburger, E. A. Martens, and Gerhard F. Hasel, eds., *The Flowering of Old Testament Theology: A Reader in Twentieth-Century Old Testament Theology, 1930–1990*, Sources for Biblical and Theological Study 1 (Winona Lake, IN: Eisenbrauns, 1992) 448–64.

[6] E.g., Ben C. Ollenburger, ed., *So Wide a Sea: Essays on Biblical and Systematic Theology* (Elkhart, IN: Institute of Mennonite Studies, 1991); *Journal of Religion* 76 (1996); *Biblical Interpretation* 6 (1998); Joel B. Green and Max Turner, eds., *Between Two Horizons: Spanning New Testament Studies and Systematic Theology* (Grand Rapids: Eerdmans, 2000); Craig Bartholomew, Mary Healy, Karl Möller, and Robin Parry, eds., *Out of Egypt: Biblical Theology and Biblical Interpretation*, Scripture and Hermeneutics Series 5 (Grand Rapids: Zondervan, 2004).

[7] E.g., Ben C. Ollenburger, "Biblical Theology: Situating the Discipline," in James T. Butler, Edgar W. Conrad, and Ben C. Ollenburger, eds., *Understanding the Word: Essays in Honor of Bernhard W. Anderson*, JSOTSup 37 (Sheffield: JSOT,

This does not mean, however, that postmodern sensibilities have made biblical and theological studies identical disciplines. The results are often different because of the primary focus of energy and starting point of each discipline. The biblical guild still focuses more attention and energy on the interpretation of the text rooted in its context (historical and/or literary), while the theological guild expends more energy on the history and interpretation of the faith community. Neither, however, can operate in isolation, as text and community are partners in the production of meaning and significance (if they can be distinguished). This hermeneutical shift has brought a new opportunity within religious and theological studies to create avenues for dialogue.

The literature cited in the preceding footnotes highlights clarion calls to the theological disciplines and traditions to enter into a deeper and broader conversation for the mutual benefit of church, academy, and society. Such calls have prepared the ground hermeneutically, but now it appears to be time to allow this hermeneutical reflection to bear fruit and to engage in the conversation proper. It is for this reason that three years ago the editors of this volume spearheaded a project designed to assemble biblical scholars, systematic theologians, and church historians around a common "table" at the American Academy of Religion/Society of Biblical Literature Annual Meetings (2003, 2004) to research a common theological theme. The theme that was chosen, "Repentance/Penitence," was first of all (to be honest), one of enduring interest for the editors as individual scholars[8] as well as a point of contact for our own conver-

---

1985) 37–62; Brian D. Ingraffia, *Postmodern Theory and Biblical Theology: Vanquishing God's Shadow* (Cambridge: Cambridge University Press, 1995); Francis Watson, *Text, Church and World: Biblical Interpretation in Theological Perspective* (Grand Rapids: Eerdmans, 1994); Francis Watson, *Text and Truth: Redefining Biblical Theology* (Grand Rapids: Eerdmans, 1997); Walter Brueggemann, *Theology of the Old Testament: Testimony, Dispute, Advocacy* (Minneapolis: Fortress Press, 1997); J. G. McConville, "Biblical Theology: Canon and Plain Sense," Finlayson Memorial Lecture 2001, *Scottish Bulletin of Evangelical Theology* 19 (2001) 129–33.

[8] Mark J. Boda, *Praying the Tradition: The Origin and Use of Tradition in Nehemiah 9*, BZAW 277 (Berlin: Walter de Gruyter, 1999); Mark J. Boda, "From Complaint to Contrition: Peering Through the Liturgical Window of Jer 14,1–15,4," *ZAW* 113 (2001) 186–97; Mark J. Boda, "Zechariah: Master Mason or Penitential Prophet?" in Bob Becking and Rainer Albertz, eds., *Yahwism After the Exile: Perspectives on Israelite Religion in the Persian Era*, STAR 5 (Assen: Royal Van Gorcum, 2003) 49–69; Mark J. Boda, "The Priceless Gain of Penitence: From Communal Lament

sations across the theological disciplines.[9] It is this second aspect that convinced us that this theme was one shared by the various theological disciplines: biblical, historical, systematic, practical, and thus would be useful to showcase the interdisciplinary conversation. Additionally, it was a theme that was closely related to the life and rhythms of the church as a community of grace. How a community deals with "sin" in its midst can be easily described while at the same time it offers insights into a whole constellation of theological themes.

In this project, therefore, we sought to showcase the wealth of theological resources within the Christian tradition for reflection on the theological theme and practice of repentance and penitence. Seven biblical scholars were invited to the table, each focussing her or his attention on a particular corpus within the Christian canon: Mark Boda (Torah), Terence Fretheim (Former Prophets), Carol Dempsey (Latter Prophets), Richard Bautch (Writings), Guy Nave (Synoptic Gospels/Acts), Edith Humphrey (Johannine tradition), and Stanley Porter (Pauline, Petrine, and General Epistles). Seven theologians were invited also, each rooted in a particular tradition within the Christian global and historical community: Michael Battle (South African/African American traditions), John Chryssavgis (Eastern Orthodox traditions), Ralph Del Colle (Roman Catholic traditions), Cheryl Bridges Johns (Pentecostal traditions), Andrew Purves (Reformation traditions), Gordon Smith (Evangelical traditions), and Wafik Wahba (Middle Eastern traditions). Two church historians were invited to offer perspectives from two eras within Christian history that were key to the development and diversity of penitential theology within the church: Cornelia Horn (Early Church period) and Ronald Rittgers (Reformation period). Finally, two scholars were invited to offer their reflections on the process and results of the project. Biblical scholar Walter Brueggemann was to offer his insight from a life of biblical study with theological sensibilities, while liturgical theologian Marva Dawn

---

to Penitential Prayer in the 'Exilic' Liturgy of Israel," *HBT* 25 (2003) 51–75; Gordon T. Smith, *Beginning Well: Christian Conversion & Authentic Transformation* (Downers Grove, IL: InterVarsity, 2001); Gordon T. Smith, *On the Way* (Colorado Springs: NavPress, 2001).

[9] See now Mark J. Boda and Gordon T. Smith, "The Recovery of Confession," *Faith Today* 22 (2004) 32–34; Gordon T. Smith and Mark J. Boda, "Confession as Essential Practice: An Evangelical Perspective," *Conversations* 3 (2005) 43–48.

was to offer her thoughts drawn from a life spent studying the worship of the church.

Each of these scholars offered extensive scholarly presentations based on their expertise and made these available to the various participants prior to our meetings. The reason for this was that the project was designed to enter into a conversation that would mutually enhance our own reading within our academic disciplines and Christian traditions. One goal was to show the potential of a conversation across and among the theological disciplines to enhance a biblical scholars' reading of the biblical text. Biblical scholars can gain insights into their own section of the canon by listening to reflection on other sections. Furthermore, viewing this theme from the vantage point of past and present communities of faith can highlight certain streams in the biblical text that are otherwise missed. Another goal was to see how such a conversation can also enhance a theologian's reading of a particular tradition, that is, as one listens afresh to the canonical witness, are there streams in the biblical text that provide a basis for the practice of theology within a particular theological community or that challenge such practice within that community? Finally, our goal was also hermeneutical, reflecting on the conversation itself and discerning how reading together across disciplines and traditions enhances and enriches our reading of the Christian narrative, whether that is the biblical text, the historical experience, the theological creeds, or the contemporary life and practice of the church. While Walter Brueggemann was charged with the duty of an elongated hermeneutical reflection, each member of the project was required to produce a one-thousand-word reflection on how the project shaped his or her own perspective on penitence and the way she or he now approaches her or his discipline.

The hope was first and foremost that the volume you now hold in your hand would be a resource for the interpretation, theology, and practice of penitence within the Christian tradition. As will become obvious in the volume, the church is in desperate need today of reengagement with this rhythm so foundational to all Christian traditions.

It is hoped, second, that the shape of the volume and the hermeneutical insights expressed will also be a catalyst for more interdisciplinary and ecumenical conversation. This is essential because on a practical level the church has always been sustained by the various resources represented abstractly by the "disciplines" of the theological guild. Those engaged in pastoral ministry (in all its forms) live as "interdisciplinarians," drawing on biblical, systematic, and historical resources as they seek answers to the pressing questions that confront them in culture today. In addition, those engaged in pastoral ministry are learning increasingly how to communicate across traditional boundaries, entering ecumenical conversations and sustaining interdenominational friendships with Christians in their local ministry contexts.

What is true on the practical level in the church is increasingly true in the academy (and happily so). The past climate of animosity between disciplines can hardly be sustained in most contexts in which biblical, theological, and religious studies are taught. In universities, colleges, and seminaries those who teach these disciplines are often isolated from colleagues within their limited fields and thus must build relationships across the classic disciplinary divisions. What was true on the practical level, however, has now become hermeneutically necessary in the integrative climate of twenty-first-century culture.

Members of the theological guild thus carry several identities as they approach the vocation of "theologian" (used in the generic sense). Obvious at first is that each represents one of the classic theological disciplines: exegetical theology, biblical theology, historical theology, church history, systematic theology, practical theology, spiritual theology, liturgical theology, ethics, apologetics, missiology, etc.[10] It is true that some even live increasingly and legitimately among and between these disciplines, but for most the key foundation for any career (that is, "job") in the academy was the mastery of a classic discipline. But there is more. Scholars represent a diversity of theological traditions, including Christianity within the mainline Protestant, mainstream evangelical, charismatic, Catholic, Orthodox traditions, and beyond. Furthermore, there is an increasingly global character to this guild, reflecting the multicultural richness of a global village. Finally, scholars represent a diversity of reflective purposes, ranging from interest in the practices of particular Christian communities to the hermeneutical implications of theology within broader ecumenical and cultural contexts.

In light of these various identities it strikes me as odd how often academics come to the academic table sporting only the identity of their theological discipline. Indeed, there is security in wearing this identity alone, but it appears that it is time for new approaches and practices.

---

[10] James I. Packer, "The Preacher as Theologian," in Chris Green and David Jackman, eds., *When God's Voice is Heard: The Power of Preaching* (Leicester: Inter-Varsity, 1995) 79–95.

In light of this and in closing let me advance the words of two scholars, representing Old and New Testament studies, as well as those of a systematic theologian, wisdom that encourages us to the grand task of theology across the disciplines:

> The genuine theological task can be carried on successfully only when it begins from within an explicit framework of faith. Only from this starting point can there be carried on the exegetical task which has as its goal the penetration of the theological dimension of the Old Testament. Approaches which start from a neutral ground never can do full justice to the theological substance because there is no way to build a bridge from the neutral, descriptive content to the theological reality.[11]

> . . . that biblical interpretation should concern itself primarily with the theological issues raised by the biblical texts within our contemporary ecclesial, cultural and socio-political contexts . . . biblical interpretation should no longer neglect its theological responsibilities . . . .[12]

> As presented here, biblical theology is that approach which describes the "world views" and literary shapes of the Bible, and especially that "thick" description of the canon as a divine communicative act. Biblical theology is a description of the biblical texts on levels that display their theological significance. Accordingly, biblical theology is nothing less than a theological hermeneutic: an interpretative approach to the Bible informed by Christian doctrine. The biblical theologian reads for the theological message communicated by the texts taken individually and as a whole collection.[13]

---

[11] Brevard S. Childs, "Interpretation in Faith," *Interpretation* 18 (1964) 259–71.

[12] Watson, *Text, Church, and World*, vii.

[13] Kevin J. Vanhoozer, "Exegesis and Hermeneutics," in T. Desmond Alexander and Brian S. Rosner, eds., *New Dictionary of Biblical Theology* (Downers Grove, IL: InterVarsity, 2000) 63.

# Section One

# Canonical Texts

One

# Renewal in Heart, Word, and Deed: Repentance in the Torah

*Mark J. Boda*

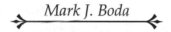

Although only five books in length, the Torah has exerted inordinate influence on theological reflection within its reading communities. In light of this it is an important source for reflection on the theme of repentance and penitence in Christian theology. Not only does the Torah examine the fundamental cause and universal extent of human sinfulness, it reveals the foundational phases of the redemptive story of Israel, a story that is placed within the broader narrative of the world (Genesis 1–11).

## 1. Text

### a. Penitence and Repentance

#### (1) Genesis–Exodus

Interestingly, however, repentance does not play a dominant role in the books of Genesis and Exodus. Sin is accentuated in stories from Adam and Eve through Cain and Abel, Sodom and Gomorrah, to the Nadab-Abihu incident. In each of these cases, however, repentance does not play a role, although there are warnings and treatments of the shame and consequences of sin, all highlighting the crisis of the human condition and the need for avenues of renewal for the relationship between God, humanity, and creation.[1]

Three incidents in the first two books of the Torah, however, are worthy of mention.[2] First of all, the Joseph Novella concludes with the powerful scene of remorse by Joseph's brothers after the death of their father (Gen 50:15-21). There are legitimate reasons for questioning the authenticity of the brothers' remorse (based on their fear of Joseph repaying them for their earlier abuse; 50:15), as well as the authenticity of their quotation of the instructions of their father (50:16-17).[3] Although appearing to highlight the importance of confession for receiving forgiveness for sin, the narrator places the accent on the grace of the offended party.

The second incident is found in the book of Exodus and again on the lips of a character whose genuineness in confession is explicitly questioned in the narrative itself. In Exodus 9:27-30, after the plague of hail, Pharaoh summons Moses and admits: "I have sinned," that is, "the Lord is in the right, and I and my people are in the wrong" (9:27). The Pharaoh declares his willingness to let the people go (9:28), even though Moses denies that the Pharaoh and his court fear Yhwh (9:30). Here we see an admission of culpability by Pharaoh, suggesting a rhythm that is key to the restoration of relationship with an offended party, but discover that this is not always equated with true renewal.

---

[1] This point has been noted succinctly in Jacob Milgrom, "Excursus: Repentance in the Torah and the Prophets," *Numbers*, JPSTC (Philadelphia: Jewish Publication Society, 1990) 397, who writes: "wherever repentance occurs in the early narratives, it is a human virtue. God does not call upon man to repent or upon his prophet to rouse him to repentance" (cf. Exod 32:11-13, 31-34; 34:9; Num 12:11-13; 14:13-19; Deut 9:16-29; "other intercessors turn to God for pardon but do not urge man to repent" (cf. Gen 18:23-33; 1 Sam 7:5-9; 12:25; 1 Kgs 17:17-23; 2 Kgs 4:33; 6:15-20; Job 42:7-9).

[2] None of these passages is linked to either the Priestly or Deuteronomic traditions in the Torah; see Antony F. Campbell and Mark A. O'Brien, *Sources of the Pentateuch: Texts, Introductions, Annotations* (Minneapolis: Fortress Press, 1993).

[3] The narrator could have provided the appropriate citation in his account of the death of Jacob in Gen 49:29-33 to back up the brothers' story, but does not do this. Their lack of sincerity is evident in the words of Judah to Joseph in 44:20 and, according to Coats, is a regular motif in the Joseph Novella (cf. 37:31-32; 43:3-5); George W. Coats, *Genesis With an Introduction to Narrative Literature*, FOTL 1 (Grand Rapids: Eerdmans, 1983) 291, 312; cf. Robert Alter, *The Five Books of Moses: A Translation with Commentary* (New York: Norton, 2004) 294.

The third incident occurs in the quintessential passage on sin and forgiveness in the Torah, the great Golden Calf complex in Exodus 32–34. The people, facilitated by Aaron, participate in idolatry as Moses is on Mount Sinai receiving the Torah from Yhwh. Yhwh initially judges the people through the Levites who slay three thousand. Moses returns to Yhwh to implore his mercy, but Yhwh promises to reject the guilty. In Exodus 33:4 the people "began to mourn" when God said he would not go with them. The narrative makes it clear that it is not the penitence of the people that causes God to relent, but rather, first of all, the mediator who pleases him (33:17, although see 32:30-34) and, second, Yhwh's character (34:5-7).

The lasting legacy of this narrative is clearly its presentation of the "name" of Yhwh (Exod 34:6-7): "Yhwh, Yhwh, God who is merciful and gracious, slow to anger and abounding in covenant loyalty and faithfulness, who keeps covenant loyalty until the thousandth generation, who forgives guilt, rebellion and sin, who surely does not leave unpunished, who visits the guilt of the parents upon the children and upon the children's children, upon the third and the fourth (generation)." This creedal statement, which Katharine Doob Sakenfeld calls "the Exodus 34 liturgical formula," is echoed throughout the literature of the Old Testament (cf. Num 14:18; Neh 9:17; Pss 86:15; 103:8; 145:8; Joel 2:13; Jonah 4:2; Nah 1:3; cf. Ps 111:4; 2 Chr 30:9).[4] It demonstrates the priority of grace in the character of Yhwh, while at the same time reminding us of the seriousness of sin. First of all, the declaration that Yhwh is one who "forgives guilt, rebellion and sin" *(nōśē² ᶜāwōn wāpešaᶜ wĕḥaṭṭaᵓâ)* is based on the fact that he is "Yhwh, Yhwh, God who is merciful and gracious, slow to anger and abounding in covenant loyalty and faithfulness, who keeps covenant loyalty until the thousandth generation" *(Yhwh Yhwh ᵓēl raḥûm wĕḥannûn ᵓārēk ᵓappayîm wĕrub-ḥesed wĕᵓĕmet nōṣēr ḥesed lāᵓălāpîm)*. It is instructive that when this ancient creedal statement is echoed elsewhere in the Old Testament it usually occurs in contexts related to sin, and that the quotation is

---

[4] Cf. Gerhard von Rad, *Gesammelte Studien zum Alten Testament*, TBü (Munich: Kaiser, 1958) 9–86; von Rad, *The Problem of the Hexateuch and Other Essays* (London: Oliver and Boyd, 1966) 1–78; G. E. Wright, *God Who Acts*, SBT 1/8 (London: SCM, 1952) 85 n2; Katharine Doob Sakenfeld, *Faithfulness in Action: Loyalty in Biblical Perspective*, OBT 16 (Philadelphia: Fortress Press, 1985) 49; Mark J. Boda, *Praying the Tradition: The Origin and Use of Tradition in Nehemiah 9*, BZAW 277 (Berlin: Walter de Gruyter, 1999) 50–51; Boda, "The Priceless Gain of Penitence: From Communal Lament to Penitential Prayer in the 'Exilic' Liturgy of Israel," *HBT* 25 (2003) 51–75.

restricted to the first few characteristics (merciful, *raḥûm;* gracious, *ḥannûn,* slow to anger, *ʾārēk ʾappayîm;* abounding in covenant loyalty, *rab-ḥesed*).

Although the creedal statement is focused on the grace of God, one cannot avoid the fact that it does warn that God does not leave guilt unpunished and that the stain of such guilt has ramifications for the "third and fourth generations." The relationship between this punishment and the immediately preceding statement that God is one who forgives guilt, rebellion, and sin has been a matter of debate. One may say that it is claiming that although God does forgive the guilt, rebellion, and sin of a particular generation, this sin does have implications for future generations, an aspect that we will discuss more fully below. Another option is that there is a difference between those forgiven of guilt, rebellion, and sin and those who will not be cleared of guilt. This latter approach can be discerned in one stream of later Jewish tradition as seen in *Yoma* 61a, which "interprets the sentence to mean 'He remits punishment for the penitent, but not for the impenitent.'"[5] However, as we have seen, there is nothing in this context that suggests a motivation for forgiveness linked to human response. Furthermore, in the foreshadowing of the declaration of the name in Exod 33:19 the mercy is rooted entirely in the mysterious character of YHWH: "I will proclaim my name, the LORD, in your presence. I will have mercy on whom I will have mercy, and I will have compassion on whom I will have compassion."[6]

The Golden Calf incident offers the reader an important theological foundation for the theology of penitence in the Torah. Sin's seriousness is rooted in God's careful attention to justice; God will not let the guilty go unpunished. At the same time, the only hope for a sinful people is the gracious character of YHWH and the participation of his mediatorial figure. Noteworthy is that, after YHWH's self-revelation in Exod 34:5-7, Moses highlights his role as mediator and then implores God's forgiveness for the people ("forgive our wickedness and our sin," 34:8-9). That YHWH has heard is evident from his response: "I am making a covenant with you . . ." (34:10). Terence Fretheim has noted that no human penitential act is highlighted as the motivation for divine forgiveness, but only God's unilateral initiative of grace secured through the mediatorial

---

[5] Nahum M. Sarna, *Exodus-Shemot,* JPSTC (Philadelphia: Jewish Publication Society, 1991) 216.

[6] Although it is possible that this is actually not filling out the proclamation of the Name (33:19a), but rather the fact that Moses will be able to survive this divine encounter where the name is proclaimed (33:20).

work of Moses.[7] Furthermore, he notes the contrast between the original Sinai covenant in Exodus 20–24 (especially 20:6 and 24:3) and this
renewal of covenant in Exodus 34, where the conditional clause "those
who love me and keep my commands" is now absent (see 34:6-7) and
no response from the people is narrated, as it is in 24:3.[8]

These three initial passages in some ways fail to create great expectations for the human side of a penitential theology. The first two cases
highlight the unreliability of expressions of human remorse and culpability, and the third illustrates the lack of divine response to human
remorse. Instead, in all three cases the accent is placed on the grace of
the offended party (whether human or divine), and in the last case on
the importance of the mediator for securing a gracious response.

### (2) Deuteronomy

The book of Deuteronomy has long been recognized as the key locus
for penitential theology in the Torah. It was Wolff who expressed this
long ago when he concluded that "the theme of 'return' appears at important highpoints of the Deuteronomic presentation of history, and it
thereby demonstrates through different examples what Israel should
hear and do under judgment in the exile."[9] This theme he identified
not only in the Former Prophets (Judg 2:1; 1 Sam 7:3; 2 Sam 12; 1 Kgs
8:46-53; 2 Kgs 17:13, 15; 23:25) but also in the book of Deuteronomy itself
at 4:29-31 and 30:1-10. Wolff's conclusion was that the close affinities
between these two passages suggest that they were part of an editor's
strategy to mesh Deuteronomy together with the Deuteronomic History
by repeating the call to return both before and after the incorporation of
Deuteronomy into the narrative.[10]

---

[7] Terence E. Fretheim, *Exodus*, Int (Louisville: John Knox, 1991) 308; see also
304.

[8] However, Fretheim does not explain adequately the fact that there is an
enduring warning of punishment on future generations, simply stating that this
is evidence of "a continuing recognition of the moral order" (ibid. 302).

[9] Hans Walter Wolff, "The Kerygma of the Deuteronomic Historical Work,"
in Walter Brueggemann and Hans Walter Wolff, eds., *The Vitality of Old Testament
Traditions* (Atlanta: John Knox, 1975) 83–100, at 90; originally published in German as Hans Walter Wolff, "Das Kerygma des deuteronomistischen Geschich-
tswerk," *ZAW* 73 (1961) 171–86.

[10] Wolff, "Kerygma," 83–100, at 96–97. See, however, Moshe Weinfeld, *Deuteronomy 1–11: A New Translation With Introduction and Commentary*, AB 5 (New York:

Wolff was wise to highlight the key role these passages play in the book of Deuteronomy as a whole. The opening narrative in chapters 1–3 consistently reminds the people of the serious nature of rebellion against their God. The failed venture at Kadesh Barnea showcased this, for there God disciplined the wilderness generation, refusing their entry into the land. Even when they declared words of remorse ("we have sinned against YHWH") in 1:41, there was no change in the divine plan, something made clear in 1:45: "You returned and wept before YHWH, but he did not pay attention to your weeping and turned a deaf ear to you." Similarly, even the great mediator himself, Moses, is refused a divine change in plan, as he is denied entrance into the land (3:21-29).

This theme of God's disciplinary immutability comes to a climax in chapter 4 as the speech looks to the day when the people will violate the very core of the covenant relationship by worshiping idols. Such an action will lead, according to 4:26-27, to the people's expulsion from the land and dispersion among the nations, divine discipline linked to the description of YHWH in 4:24: "for the LORD your God is a consuming fire, a jealous God." Ironically, it is here that the Deuteronomic tradition presents the first sign of hope, shaping the people's response "from there" (4:29), that is, from their position "among the peoples . . . among the nations" (4:27).[11]

The exilic response in these "later days" is identified clearly in 4:29-30: to "seek (bāqašᴾⁱ) YHWH your God," a seeking (dāraš) that involves "all your heart" and "all your soul." Such seeking involves a full engagement of the inner affections of the penitential community, as Tigay says of this collocation: "To do something with all the heart and soul means to do it with the totality of one's thoughts, feelings, intentions and desires."[12] Such depth of seeking is defined in v. 30 with the vocabulary of repentance: "return (šûb) to YHWH your God and obey (šāmaᶜ + bĕqôl) him."[13]

---

Doubleday, 1991) 217–21, who traces the ancient roots and ubiquitous influence of the penitential theology found in Deuteronomy 4 and 30.

[11] It is this that has led many to distinguish Deuteronomy 4 from the preceding three chapters, which for many represent the introduction to the Deuteronomic History as a whole. However, as we shall soon see, repentance is only envisioned after expulsion from the land.

[12] Jeffrey H. Tigay, *Deuteronomy*, JPSTC (Philadelphia: Jewish Publication Society, 1996) 77.

[13] Rodney A. Werline, *Penitential Prayer in Second Temple Judaism: The Development of a Religious Institution*, SBLEJL 13 (Atlanta: Scholars, 1998) 12–18, calls these

Such "turning" is explicitly stated as a returning "to" (ʿad) God, without any explicit mention of turning "from" unfaithful covenant relationship, an aspect that is restricted to passages outside the Torah.[14] Such "turning" is an example of Holladay's "covenantal" *šûb*: "expressing a change of loyalty on the part of Israel or God, each for the other."[15] Such "turning" must involve obedience (*šāmaʿ + běqôl*), that is, this seeking and turning is expressed in changed action.

The subject of these verbs is always "you," that is, the humbled community in exile. The mood of the verbs, however, is indicative, stating what will happen within the exilic community. Indeed, there is a conditional nuance in the phrase: *kî tidrěšennû běkôl-lěbābkā uběkol-napšekā* ("when/because/if you seek him with all your heart and with all your soul"), showing that such repentance will not be mere lip service. However, the Deuteronomic vision is for a future day of repentance among God's people that will usher in the restoration. Such a response is made possible because "a God of mercy (*raḥûm*) is YHWH your God" who "will not fail you nor destroy you nor forget the covenant which he swore to your forefathers" (Deut 4:31), a declaration that contrasts with the earlier description of YHWH in 4:24.[16] One needs to look to the end of the book of Deuteronomy to discover the role this God of mercy will play in the production of such a day of repentance.

---

stages of repentance (self-examination, repentance, and pledge of obedience), but they appear to be various nuances of the same penitential act. The last stage or nuance, however, seems to be more than just a pledge, but actual proof in action that obedience is being practiced.

[14] William Lee Holladay, *The Root ŠÛBH in the Old Testament: With Particular Reference to its Usages in Covenantal Contexts* (Leiden: Brill, 1958) 78–80, lists instances of "turning to" (using the prepositions ʾel (25x), ʿad (13x), ʿal (2x), and lě (1x). Deuteronomy 4:30 and 30:2 use ʿad, while 30:10 uses ʾel. One may conclude that "turning from" is implicit in a context that has been preceded by covenant infidelity.

[15] Ibid. 2. Although he sees this as covenantal, Holladay concludes that the "idea [of repentance] never seems to come into focus" (p. 156). This fails on two fronts. First, it appears to inappropriately limit "idea" to "vocabulary." Second, it presupposes a definition of repentance rather than allowing the biblical vocabulary and texts to shape that definition.

[16] So also A. D. H. Mayes, *Deuteronomy*, NCB (Greenwood, SC: Attic, 1979) 157; Richard D. Nelson, *Deuteronomy: A Commentary*, OTL (Louisville: Westminster John Knox, 2002) 68.

The same motifs found in Deuteronomy 4 reappear near the end of the book in chapter 30.[17] Deuteronomy 27 and 28 focus attention on the blessings and curses that attend the Torah covenant. Chapter 29 begins a literary complex that will extend into the following chapter in which Moses is cast as an agent of covenant renewal.[18] In this renewal he reminds them again of the dire consequences of idolatry, a sin that will lead to their expulsion from the land (Deut 29:25-29). As in Deuteronomy 4, this introduces a discussion of penitence.

Penitence begins, according to Deuteronomy 30, with deep reflection. The collocation used, $šûb^{Hi}$ + $^{\circ}el$ + $lēb/lēbab$, usually appears without a direct object. On the one occasion in which it does have an object (Lam 3:21), the accusative is that upon which the person is to reflect. On another occasion this object of reflection is introduced by the word $kî$ (Deut 4:39). In most cases, however, the object is omitted, but appears to be implied in the surrounding context: in Isaiah 44:19 what is reflected on is the folly of bowing down to an idol made from wood used for other mundane purposes (cf. Isa 46:8) while in 1 Kgs 8:47//2 Chr 6:37 what is reflected on is the discipline of God that resulted from their sin. So in Deut 30:1 what is reflected on appears to be not only the circumstances that have befallen them, but in particular the divinely promised blessing and curse.[19] Thus deep reflection is demanded at the outset of the

[17] Duane L. Christensen, *Deuteronomy 1–11*, WBC 6A (Dallas: Word Books, 1991) 95, notes the close relationship between Deuteronomy 4:29-31 and 30:1-10 and further that they introduce and conclude the two brackets around the inner frame of the book (chs. 4–11 and 27–30). It is interesting that the term $šûb$ is only used in these two passages in its religious sense. This evidence has led, for example, Mayes, *Deuteronomy*, 156, 367–69, to link these chapters to later deuteronomistic editing rather than to the preexilic Deuteronomic editor; see also idem, "Deuteronomy 4 and the Literary Criticism of Deuteronomy," *JBL* 100 (1981) 23–51; Norbert Lohfink, "Recent Discussion on 2 Kings 22–23," in Duane L. Christensen, ed., *A Song of Power and the Power of Song: Essays on the Book of Deuteronomy*, SBTS 3 (Winona Lake: Eisenbrauns, 1993) 36–61, at 48 n57.

[18] Many see ch. 29 as a later insertion separating chs. 27–28 from their continuation in ch. 30; cf. Wolff, "Kerygma," 83–100, at 94–95; Alexander Rofé, "The Covenant in the Land of Moab (Deuteronomy 28:69–30:20): Historico-Literary, Comparative, and Formcritical Considerations," *A Song of Power*, 269–80, at 272; Nelson, *Deuteronomy*, 348.

[19] See also Nelson, *Deuteronomy*, 348, who links this reflection to the blessings and curses; contra Peter C. Craigie, *The Book of Deuteronomy*, NICOT (Grand Rapids: Eerdmans, 1976) 363, who translates this as "return to your senses."

Deuteronomic penitential response according to Deut 30:1, and this deep reflection is to fix the penitent community on the promises of both blessing and curse that are essential to the covenant arrangement. Here one can discern an echo of the quality of seeking that is encouraged in Deuteronomy 4, a seeking with all one's inner affections, but this seeking is now defined more carefully as a reflection on the grace and discipline of God exemplified in the covenant agreement and known in the community's experience.

Such depth of reflection is linked in Deut 30:2 to turning *(šûb)* and obeying *(šāmaᶜ + bĕqôl)*, echoing chapter 4, an echo confirmed with the use of the same declaration that began the treatment in Deuteronomy 4: *bĕkôl-lĕbābkā ubĕkôl-napšekā* ("with all your heart and soul"). These latter two phases are repeated again in 30:8-10, arranged in chiastic fashion: *šûb . . . šāmaᶜ + bĕqôl . . . šāmaᶜ + bĕqôl . . . šûb* ("turn . . . obey . . . obey . . . turn") and again ending with *bĕkôl-lĕbābkā ubĕkôl-napšekā* ("with all your heart and soul"). This shows that they lie at the core of the Deuteronomic theology of penitence.[20]

Clearly one can discern echoes of the penitential rhythms and vocabulary of Deuteronomy 4, but Deuteronomy 30 is not identical. First, in both 30:8 and 10 obedience is defined specifically as doing *(ʿāśah)* and keeping *(šāmar)* commands *(miṣwôt)* linked to the direct revelation of Yнwн (v. 8) now encased in the book of the Law (v. 10). This aspect is not completely absent from Deuteronomy 4, but it is not emphasized in the immediate context of the description of repentance and obedience (cf. 4:30).[21]

Second, while Deuteronomy 4 expressed a future hope that the exilic community would repent, focusing on the necessity of seeking with all one's affections, Deuteronomy 30 brings greater focus on divine activity. This is seen initially in the fact that the human penitential response, at the core of which is the term *šûb*, will be met with the reciprocal divine action of *šûb* as Yнwн restores *(šûb)* them (30:3)[22] and returns *(šûbᴴⁱ)* them

---

[20] Nelson, *Deuteronomy*, 347, notes two interlaced concentric structures in Deut 30:1-10, one based on *šûb* (return/turn) and the other on *bĕkôl-lĕbābkā ubĕkôl-napšekā* (with all your heart and with all your soul). See Weinfeld, *Deuteronomy 1–11*, 216, who emphasizes the continuity between the two passages.

[21] So also Robert Polzin, *Moses and the Deuteronomist*, A Literary Study of the Deuteronomic History 1 (New York: Seabury, 1980) 70.

[22] On the idiom here, *šub + ʾet-šĕbût*, see Tigay, *Deuteronomy*, 284, 399 n3, who notes the link of this collocation to *šûb + qadmâ* (former state) in Ezekiel 16:53, 55; cf. also the review of the problem and versional evidence in Holladay, *ŠÛBH*, 110–15.

to the land (30:5).[23] To return to God opens the way to one's return to the Promised Land lost through disobedience. This divine activity also is seen in the greater emphasis in Deuteronomy 30 on the role played by YHWH in the penitential process.[24] Whereas in Deut 10:16 the people of Israel are called to circumcise their hearts, in Deuteronomy 30 it is YHWH who will perform this on the people and their descendants.[25] This image is a metaphor for "radical, interior renewal that makes love and obedience fully possible."[26] In Deuteronomy 30 we thus see an important development in the penitential theology of Deuteronomy. The future penitential response of the people described in Deuteronomy 4 is based on a work initiated and facilitated by YHWH. The Deuteronomic stream within the Torah thus envisions repentance as something that follows serious disciplinary action of a jealous YHWH in response to idolatry and results in exile. What should not be missed, however, is that penitence is not seen as a regular rhythm within the life of the community, but rather as an important phase in the history of salvation, a phase that will bring an end to the exile of the community.[27]

[23] Rofé, "Covenant," 269–80, at 270. Nelson, *Deuteronomy*, 348 notes the progression of 30:1-10 beyond 4:29-31 in this vision of restoration. See further on *šûb* as leitmotif in Deut 30:1-10 in Mayes, *Deuteronomy*, 368.

[24] See especially M. Z. Brettler, "Predestination in Deuteronomy 30:1-10," in Linda S. Schearing and Steven L. McKenzie, eds., *Those Elusive Deuteronomists: The Phenomenon of Pan-Deuteronomism*, JSOTSup 268 (Sheffield: Sheffield Academic Press, 1999) 171–88, and J. G. Millar, *Now Choose Life: Theology and Ethics in Deuteronomy*, NSBT (Grand Rapids: Eerdmans, 1999) 174–76, although Brettler takes it too far when he says of 30:1-10: "this passage, which looks Dtr, is really pseudo-Deuteronomic, while being anti-Dtr" (at 185–86). A major plank of Brettler's argument is that vv. 1b and 2 and 10 need not be taken as conditional clauses (although he does admit they can be taken as such). However, even if they are not, they do set out an agenda of repentance that is an essential component of the transition from exile to restoration, even if YHWH enables such.

[25] See Craigie, *Deuteronomy*, 364 for this key contrast.

[26] Nelson, *Deuteronomy*, 348–49, who also notes the similarity to Jer 31:31-34 and 32:37-41.

[27] Tigay, *Deuteronomy*, 54, notes the distinction between the visions of repentance in Torah, as opposed to the Prophets, in this way: "In the Torah [repentance] is mentioned only as something that occurs after punishment has taken place: if the people take their punishment to heart and return to God, He will terminate their punishment . . . [the prophets] called upon people to repent before it was too late, and to thereby avert punishment altogether." This claim by Tigay needs to be carefully nuanced. The description of Torah relates to the Deuteronomic

This repentance, based on the merciful character of Yhwh and ultimately enabled by this merciful God, begins with sincere reflection on God's gracious promises and stern warnings, followed by turning back to God in obedient covenant relationship, displayed through observance of Torah.

### (3) Leviticus–Numbers

While the Deuteronomic stream within Torah has drawn the attention of those interested in penitential theology, the Priestly stream has been largely ignored. This may be related to the dominant Christian view of the sacrificial system: that it became a means by which Israel avoided obedience, opting instead to cover their misdeeds by sacrifice. While this view may be justified in light of certain abuses of the sacrificial system in Israel's history highlighted by the prophetic stream in Israel (1 Sam 15:22; Isa 1:10-17; Jer 7:21-26; Hos 6:6; Mic 6:6-8; cf. Pss 40:6-8; 51:16-17), it does not do justice to several aspects of the sacrificial system. Key for the consideration at hand is that at least some sacrifice was to be accompanied by a penitential disposition, a point that was not lost on the ancient rabbis and that has been recovered in more recent considerations of the sacrificial system.

While the vocabulary of penitence in Deuteronomy is anchored by the key verb *šûb* ("return/turn"), in the Priestly tradition this central role is played by the verb *ʾāšam*.[28] Milgrom has argued cogently that this verb when used without a personal object should be translated not as (traditionally) "be guilty," but rather as "feel guilty," that is, "the self-punishment of conscience, the torment of guilt."[29] This verbal form then

---

stream within Torah for, as we will see, the Priestly tradition does speak of penitence as a regular rhythm in life as well as something needful to avert exile. In relation to the prophets it must also be pointed out that there are cases among the prophets, especially as represented in the book of Jeremiah (under Deuteronomic influence), in which opportunity for repentance has clearly passed; cf. Mark J. Boda, "From Complaint to Contrition: Peering Through the Liturgical Window of Jer 14,1–15,4," *ZAW* 113 (2001) 186–97.

[28] Holladay, *ŠÛBH*, 78–81, 127; Moshe Weinfeld, *Deuteronomy and the Deuteronomic School* (Oxford: Clarendon, 1972) 334–35. However, we are careful to note with Holladay (pp. 126–27) the presence of the Priestly idiom, *šûb* + *mēʾaḥᵃrê* (turn away from; Num 14:43; 32:15; 22:16, 18, 23, 29; 1 Sam 15:11). This, however, is an idiom of apostasy, not of repentance.

[29] Jacob Milgrom, *Cult and Conscience: The Asham and the Priestly Doctrine of Repentance*, SJLA 18 (Leiden: Brill, 1976) 11; see idem, "Further on the Expiatory

highlights the internal dimension of the sacrificial system, even if it is clear in the Priestly tradition that sacrifice remained mandatory.[30]

Milgrom also demonstrated the intimate link between the *ʾāšām* offering and the word *maʿal*, a term denoting sins against deity. Such sins belong to two categories: inappropriate physical contact with the holy (Lev 5:14-19; 14:10-14, 21-25; 22:14-16; Num 6:12; Jer 2:3; Ezra 10:19) and violation of God's name sworn on oath (Lev 5:20-26; Num 5:6-8). It is this second category and in particular the introduction of the term *hitwaddāh* (to confess) into Numbers 5 that leads Milgrom to the conclusion that for "involuntary sin, *ʾšm* or remorse alone suffices; it renders confession superfluous. But for deliberate sin there is the added requirement that remorse be verbalized; the sin must be articulated and responsibility assumed."[31] Such remorse *(ʾāšām)* and confession *(hitwaddāh)* have the

---

Sacrifices," *JBL* 115 (1996) 511–14, and idem, *Leviticus 23–27: A New Translation with Introduction and Commentary*, AB 3 (New York: Doubleday, 2001) 2446–52, as he meets the challenge of Adrian Schenker, "Interprétations récentes et dimensions spécifiques du sacrifice *ḥaṭṭāt*," *Bib* 75 (1994) 59–70. He notes especially that the "distinction between intentional and presumptuous sins is nonexistent. All deliberate sins are presumed presumptuous unless they are tempered by subsequent acts of repentance" (Milgrom, "Further on the Expiatory Sacrifices," 514). Nobuyoshi Kiuchi, *The Purification Offering in the Priestly Literature: Its Meaning and Function*, JSOTSup 56 (Sheffield: JSOT Press, 1987) 31–34, challenges Milgrom's position, concluding in the end that *ʾāšām* has both objective and subjective aspects. He proposes "realize guilt" rather than "feel guilt"; see Milgrom's response in Jacob Milgrom, *Leviticus 1–16: A New Translation with Introduction and Commentary*, AB 3 (New York: Doubleday, 1991) 338.

[30] So Milgrom, "Excursus: Repentance," 396–98, who contrasts the prophetic tradition, where repentance was identified as sufficient.

[31] Milgrom, *Cult*, 109–10. This contradicts a longstanding interpretation of Num 15:30b, that there was no forgiveness for those who brazenly violated God's law: "A more correct understanding of this Priestly postulate would be that sacrificial atonement is barred to the *unrepentant* sinner, to the one who 'acts defiantly (*byd rmh:* TO *bryš gly,* 'publicly'; *byd rmh ʾw brmyh,* 'brazenly or deceitfully', 1QS8:23), reviles *(mgdp)* the Lord . . .' (Num 15:30), but not to the deliberate sinner who has mitigated his offense by his repentance"; see further Jacob Milgrom, *Numbers*, JPSTC 34, who claims there that actually God compromises his justice. Baruch A. Levine, *Leviticus*, JPSTC (Philadelphia: Jewish Publication Society, 1989) 28, takes the focus entirely off the confession: "The requirement of making confession is not the main thrust of this statement. The verb *hitvaddah,* 'to confess' is more likely indicative rather than subjunctive; it

effect of reducing "intentional sin" to "an inadvertence" and so render it "eligible for sacrificial expiation."[32] As Samuel Balentine, in his affirmation of Milgrom's work, has so aptly written:

> Confession is the cotter pin that joins contrition to reparation and reparation to a public commitment to change. Without confession, sin seeks the camouflage of secrecy, the status remains quo, and brokenness continues to diminish the "very good" world God has created.[33]

This understanding of the key role that confession plays in Priestly treatment of deliberate sin brings clarity to the other two appearances of the term *hitwaddāh* (to confess) in the Priestly corpus: Lev 16:21; 26:40. The first case relates to the event on the Day of Atonement when the high priest confesses unrepented intentional sins among the community that threaten the sanctity of the sanctuary.[34] In this we see the Priestly practice of penitence on the communal level as the people enter into the experience by "denying themselves" (16:21), even as the priest sacrifices and confesses on their behalf.

The final case of *hitwaddāh* (to confess) in the Priestly stream, Lev 26:40, looks to a people living in the wake of the exilic punishment precipitated by Israel's deliberate idolatrous violation of their covenant

---

is conveying a fact rather than expressing a statement." The reason why confession is introduced at this point is that it is "material to the judicial process," for here "we are dealing with private acts and the failure to act, which might never have come to light had the offender himself not come forth to confess." Gordon J. Wenham, *The Book of Leviticus*, NICOT (Grand Rapids: Eerdmans, 1979) 100, characterizes the sins in Lev 5:1-6 as sins of omission, those that slipped one's memory: "In each case, when conscience smites the forgetful person, he must confess his sin and bring a purification offering" (p. 93).

[32] Jacob Milgrom, "Priestly Doctrine of Repentance," *RB* 82 (1975) 117. Milgrom (pp. 119–20) makes an interesting note that repentance in these early narratives is not the same as repentance in the prophets: it is ineffectual prior to judgment. It can mitigate or postpone it, and in the case of exile it can only terminate the punishment, but not prevent its onset; also, repentance is a human virtue, not a divine imperative, that is, people interceded for others (like Moses) to annul judgment, but not once are they expected to bring their people to repentance; against this backdrop one can see the innovation of P.

[33] Samuel E. Balentine, *Leviticus*, Int (Louisville: Westminster John Knox, 2002) 57.

[34] Milgrom, *Leviticus 1–16*, 1034, 1042–44; idem, *Cult*, 109 n406.

oath (Lev 26:27-30).[35] As in Leviticus 16, confession is operative on the communal rather than individual level. In this passage the key turning point that moves the people from a state of discipline (vv. 28-39) to one of grace (v. 42) is a confession both of their own sins and of the sins of their ancestors (see further below), an act that is linked to the humbling of their hearts *(kānaᶜ ᴺⁱ + lēbab)*. Each part of the long list of covenant curses in Leviticus 26 is introduced by the conditional particle ʾim (26:15, 16, 18, 21, 23, 27), highlighting that throughout the history of their rebellion Israel would be given the opportunity and would be expected to respond to God in repentance. Thus this emphasizes the importance of penitence to covenant relationship. However, we should not miss that after v. 27 there is a long string of verb constructions (*waw*-relative + verbs in the suffix conjugation) that describe the future of the people in exile and beyond. The ultimate turn is not seen as conditional, but a promise from God. That this truly involved the human participants is evident, but how it will be accomplished is not clarified as it is in Deuteronomy 30.

The Priestly stream within Torah has a place for penitence; however, such expression is not cast in terms of obedient behavior, but rather in terms of internal remorse and humility *(ʾāšam; kānaᶜ ᴺⁱ + lēbab)* as well as verbal confession *(hitwaddāh)*, on the individual as well as communal levels. Such expression will play a role not only, as the book of Deuteronomy notes, in the ending of exile and inauguration of restoration, but also in the regular rhythm of life in a fallen world. As in the Deuteronomic tradition, this exilic experience is not cast in the conditional mood ("if"), but rather is described as an expected future event.

## b. Sin and Solidarity in Torah

### (1) Priestly Sin and Solidarity

One aspect of the Priestly doctrine of repentance that must be considered more closely is that of the intergenerational character of sin, especially because it shapes the particular expression of penitence in the Torah. We have seen that on two occasions the term *hitwaddāh* is used in corporate contexts. First, the description of the Day of Atonement in Leviticus 16 stipulates that the high priest will confess the sins of the entire community even as they participate through rites of "denial." In this we see what is understood by many to be the theology of *intragenerational* culpability, the belief that sins committed among the community have

---

[35] See further Boda, *Praying,* 47–55; idem, "Complaint," 186–97.

implications for the community as a whole. Second, Lev 26:39 declares that the remnant left in exile will "waste away" in the lands of their enemies both because of their sins and also because of the sins of previous generations. This informs, then, the type of penitential confession that is demanded of a generation hopeful to see an end to the exilic experience: "they will confess their sins and the sins of their fathers" (26:40). In this we see what is often articulated as the theology of *intergenerational* culpability, the belief that sins committed by one generation have implications for future generations. Such expressions of culpability and penitence are based on the doctrine of collective responsibility, an ideology that Milgrom has shown to be "a cardinal plank in the structure of Priestly theology."[36]

Many have noted that the root of the theology of intergenerational culpability is ancient in Israel, expressed in the Decalogue (Exod 20:5-6//Deut 5:9-10) and in the Character Creed (Exod 34:6-7), where the sins of the fathers will be visited upon the children. Tigay highlights a slight difference, however, between these two ancient passages, distinguishing between what he calls "cross-generation retribution," which involves the transfer of an ancestor's sins (Exod 34:7b), and compound retribution, which involves the addition of an ancestor's sins to the children's sins (Decalogue). [37] Leviticus 26:39-40 represents this latter compound form of retribution theology, noting that the exilic community suffers for its own sins as well as the ancestors' sins, and that its members will confess their sins as well as their ancestors' sins.[38]

Thus the Priestly stream contains evidence of corporate solidarity in its doctrine of sin. This ideology has in turn shaped penitential expressions.

---

[36] Milgrom, *Leviticus 23–27*, 2331.

[37] Tigay, *Deuteronomy*, 436–37.

[38] In this I depart from Milgrom, *Leviticus 23–27*, 2327, who sees in Leviticus 26 nothing that "implies the cancellation of vertical retribution if the children are virtuous." Leviticus 26 states that the remnant lives in exile because of the sins of the ancestors as well as their own sins, and safe return will mean confession of their ancestors' sins and their own sins. This is a clear example of compound ideology. See further Mark J. Boda, "Confession as Theological Expression: Ideological Origins of Penitential Prayer," in Mark J. Boda, Daniel K. Falk, and Rodney A. Werline, eds., *Seeking the Favor of God: The Origin, Development and Impact of Penitential Prayer in Second Temple Judaism*, SBLEJL (Atlanta: Society of Biblical Literature, forthcoming).

### (2) *Deuteronomic Sin and Solidarity*

The picture is more complicated, however, in the Deuteronomic stream. Both Jacob Milgrom and Joel Kaminsky have argued cogently that Deuteronomy does incorporate the Decalogue with its intergenerational theology of collective responsibility (Deut 5:9-10).[39] In addition, however, Deuteronomy also develops a retributive principle that restricts punishment and culpability to the offending generation only (Deut 24:16; cf. 7:9-10).[40] While some have sought to explain the presence of these two theological streams in Deuteronomy on evolutionary grounds, Kaminsky sees this as oversimplifying the relationship between the two ideas (individual versus corporate), encouraging us to read the two conceptions as "complementary" rather than "contradictory."[41] What is interesting about the penitential passages we have considered in the book of Deuteronomy (Deut 4:29-31; 30:1-3), is that they place little emphasis on distinctions between former and present generations. The "you" who is addressed

[39] Milgrom, *Leviticus 23–27*, 2328; Joel S. Kaminsky, *Corporate Responsibility in the Hebrew Bible*, JSOTSup 196 (Sheffield: Sheffield Academic Press, 1995); cf. idem, "Joshua 7: A Reassessment of Israelite Conceptions of Corporate Punishment," in Steven W. Holloway and Lowell K. Handy, eds., *The Pitcher is Broken: Memorial Essays for Gösta W. Ahlström* (Sheffield: Sheffield Academic Press, 1995) 315–46; idem, "The Sins of the Fathers: A Theological Investigation of the Biblical Tension between Corporate and Individualized Retribution," *Judaism* 46 (1997) 319–32; Baruch Halpern, "Jerusalem and the Lineages in the Seventh Century BCE: Kinship and the Rise of Individual Moral Liability," in Baruch Halpern and Deborah W. Hobson, eds., *Law and Ideology in Monarchic Israel*, JSOTSup 124 (Sheffield: JSOT Press, 1991) 11–107, traces this transition from corporate to individual ideology to the social forces set in motion by the renewals under Hezekiah and Josiah, monarchs who sought to break clan social power by creating individual links to the crown.

[40] Milgrom also notes the presence of this same diversity in the DtrH (cp. 2 Kgs 14:5-6 with 21:10-15; 23:26-27; 24:2-4) and Jeremiah (cp. Jer 15:4; 32:18-19, 30-31 with 18:1-12; 31:29-31). Only with Ezekiel does one find individual generational retribution alone (Ezekiel 18, 33); see also Halpern, "Lineages," 12.

[41] Kaminsky, *Corporate Responsibility*, 178. Contra Gordon Matties, *Ezekiel 18 and the Rhetoric of Moral Discourse*, SBLDS 126 (Atlanta: Scholars, 1990) especially 145–46. See also Halpern, "Lineages," 12, who is careful to note that, at least for Torah material, views of corporate responsibility were never universal but existed alongside legal material that "stipulat[ed] individual punishments for infractions." However, Halpern does echo the classic view for Jeremiah and Ezekiel (pp. 14–15).

in exile is not distinguished from the "you" upon whom the punishment of God has fallen. It is this rhetorical technique that may explain the presence of both ideologies within the same tradition stream. The focus of attention does not appear to be on issues of culpability, but rather on the opportunity for the exilic generation to respond to Yhwh and begin anew, unshackled by sinful patterns of previous generations.

## c. Summary

The Torah thus contains several key sources for penitential theology in the Old Testament.[42] At the outset we saw how the books of Genesis and Exodus do not place much hope on the ability of the offending party to initiate or secure forgiveness through penitence. The accent is clearly placed on the grace of the offended party alongside a role that may be played by a mediatorial figure.

In the remainder of the Torah we find two key streams of penitential theology, the Priestly and the Deuteronomic. On the one side we find the penitential theology of the Priestly tradition, which identifies the key role repentance will play to bring an end to exile (Lev 26). In the Holiness Code this priestly ideology is connected to the most serious form of *ma'al* (idolatry), which led to the exile. Ultimately a penitential confession would be necessary to restore covenant relationship and bring about a return to the land. The Priestly tradition also creates space for penitence in the rhythms of ritual law, whether that was in the regular sacrifices (Lev 5:5; Num 5:7) or the yearly rhythm of *Yom Kippur* (Lev 16:21). Expressions of penitence in the Priestly tradition have also been influenced by an underlying view of sin and culpability that extended beyond the individual. The Priestly stream highlights contrition that expresses the sorrow of the entire community over sins committed within its midst (Leviticus 16, intragenerational) as well as sins committed in generations past (Leviticus 26, intergenerational).

On the other side we find the penitential theology of the Deuteronomic tradition with its concern for a return to the observance of Torah as covenant document, which fosters the eternal relationship between God and his people. Key to this tradition is the reorientation of the affections of the community toward God and Torah. Repentance in Deuteronomy, however, is not presented as a human response to avoid judgment, but rather as a human response to bring an end to judgment, that is, the exile. Based

---

[42] See further Boda, "Confession," forthcoming.

firmly on the mercy of God, ultimately this repentance is only possible through internal divine work. While the Priestly doctrine of repentance emphasizes the external component of verbal confession flowing from an internal disposition of remorse, the Deuteronomic doctrine of repentance emphasizes the external component of active obedience flowing from an internal disposition of self-examination. The Deuteronomic tradition assuredly shared with the Priestly tradition a similar underlying view of sin and culpability that extended beyond the individual. Such theology, however, was not to be used as a way of avoiding one's own culpability in the present circumstances, an abuse that is confronted by key texts beginning in the book of Deuteronomy and further developed in the Deuteronomic History and prophets like Jeremiah and Ezekiel.

Clearly the accent in these two key Torah traditions of penitence is not placed on human response as much as on divine grace expressed both through God's acceptance of penitential expressions and God's enablement of such expressions. It is this emphasis on the grace of God that brings us full circle to the initial passages we considered in Genesis and Exodus. There hope was placed on the potential of the grace of the offended party and in particular the grace of YHWH as revealed at Sinai, rather than on the potential of human penitential expressions.

## 2. Implications

How, then, does the Torah contribute to a Christian theology of penitence? Here we do not have time to develop the broader hermeneutic for the relationship between the Old and New Testaments in general and the Torah and the New Testament in particular.[43] It is sufficient to say that the New Testament draws on the Torah (both narrative and legal materials) as relevant to Christian faith and witness, relevant to foreshadow New Testament themes, to point to the need for Christ, as well as to shape our response to God.

*A. Redemptive History:* Penitence is presented in the Torah as a signal of the end of exile, something that provides theological orientation for the importance of penitence to the rest of the Old Testament, in particular those texts that struggle with the exile and hope for restoration (Ezra, Nehemiah, Daniel). It also has significance for our understanding of the

---

[43] See the introduction to Mark J. Boda, *Haggai/Zechariah* (Grand Rapids: Zondervan, 2004).

New Testament witness, as has been highlighted by individuals like N. T. Wright. The preaching of John the Baptist, Jesus, and the early church, especially in their calls to repentance, must be understood first and foremost as a sign of the inauguration of the restoration of God's people.

*B. Spiritual Theology:* Indeed, penitential expressions signaled the beginning of a new era of redemption, but they were also to become normative for the message of the gospel throughout the ages as each new generation encountered the story of Christ. Such is true not only for what is often called initial repentance, but also for the rhythms of penitence that would characterize Christian experience. Such rhythms were nourished in the Priestly tradition, which describes penitence as a regular component of covenant faithfulness. This may help us to understand why confession and penitential rites endured in the experience of the church from its earliest era until today.

*C. Character of God:* The Torah consistently bases penitence on the grace and mercy of God. This trend is continued into the New Testament witness as Romans 2:4 reminds us that it is "the riches of his kindness, tolerance, and patience" that lead us to repentance, and 1 John 1:9 assures us that confession of sin will lead to pardon because "God is faithful and just." Both passages echo the Character Creed of Israel, so important for the forgiveness of Israel's sin. In many Christian theological traditions, especially those within holiness or revivalistic streams, penitence has been linked almost exclusively to the theology of God's justice and wrath. Interestingly, however, the Torah places the emphasis on the theology of grace and love when speaking of repentance. This has implications not only for how we proclaim the gospel, but also how we explain the life of discipleship.

*D. Pneumatology:* The Torah presents penitence as accomplished through a circumcision of the heart by God. The influence of this tradition can be discerned in the promise of Jer 31:31-34 that in the new covenant God would put his law on the people's minds and write it on their hearts. Ezekiel echoes and advances this theology in declaring that after the exile God would cleanse his people and give them a new heart and spirit, placing his Spirit within them in order that they might obey his laws (Ezek 36:24-28; cf. 37:14). Such divine work is clearly linked in Ezekiel to the work of the Holy Spirit, a theological theme that is developed significantly in the New Testament (e.g., Rom 8; 2 Cor 3; Gal 5; Eph 3:14-19). This theological emphasis reminds us of our utter need for the Holy Spirit for repentance to become a reality in our lives.

*E. Community:* Although not univocal in expression, the Torah is a catalyst for reflection on the corporate dimension of penitence, both intra- and inter-generationally. It reminds us that we are deeply connected to one another within the community of faith, but also within our broader familial and cultural communities. The Western church in particular has become adept at focusing on individual confession of sins committed in secret. The communal dimension of sin and of confession found in Torah challenges us to consider ways we have offended God's values as members of communities and ways we can confess and confront such sinful patterns.

# 3. Futher Reading

Boda, Mark J. "Confession as Theological Expression: Ideological Origins of Penitential Prayer." In Mark J. Boda, Daniel K. Falk, and Rodney A. Werline, eds., *Seeking the Favor of God: The Origin, Development and Impact of Penitential Prayer in Second Temple Judaism.* SBLEJL. Atlanta: Society of Biblical Literature, 2006.

Brettler, M. Z. "Predestination in Deuteronomy 30:1-10." In Linda S. Schearing and Steven L. McKenzie, eds., *Those Elusive Deuteronomists: The Phenomenon of Pan-Deuteronomism.* JSOTSup 268. Sheffield: Sheffield Academic Press, 1999, 171–88.

Kaminsky, Joel S. *Corporate Responsibility in the Hebrew Bible.* JSOTSup 196. Sheffield: Sheffield Academic Press, 1995.

_____. "The Sins of the Fathers: A Theological Investigation of the Biblical Tension between Corporate and Individualized Retribution," *Judaism* 46 (1997) 319–32.

Mayes, A. D. H. "Deuteronomy 4 and the Literary Criticism of Deuteronomy," *JBL* 100 (1981) 23–51.

Milgrom, Jacob. *Cult and Conscience: The Asham and the Priestly Doctrine of Repentance.* SJLA 18. Leiden: Brill, 1976.

_____. "Priestly Doctrine of Repentance," *RB* 82 (1975) 186–205.

Millar, J. G. *Now Choose Life: Theology and Ethics in Deuteronomy.* NSBT. Grand Rapids: Eerdmans, 1999.

Weinfeld, Moshe. *Deuteronomy and the Deuteronomic School.* Oxford: Clarendon, 1972.

Werline, Rodney A. *Penitential Prayer in Second Temple Judaism: The Development of a Religious Institution.* SBLEJL 13. Atlanta: Scholars, 1998.

Wolff, Hans Walter. "The Kerygma of the Deuteronomic Historical Work." In Walter Brueggemann and Hans Walter Wolff, eds., *The Vitality of Old Testament Traditions.* Atlanta: John Knox, 1975, 83–100.

## 4. Hermeneutical Response

It was a statement that Walter Brueggemann somehow slipped into an interchange between Terry Fretheim and me over the Deuteronomic tradition in one of our sessions that awakened me to what was going on: "Well, of course . . . he's a Lutheran." He reminded me what Terry brought to the text from his Lutheran tradition, especially related to the Deuteronomic tradition in which we overlapped in our presentations, and what I brought to the text from my Holiness tradition. This is what I heard Yale's Nicholas Wolterstorff once call (in an oral lecture at my university) "Privileged Cognitive Access," that is, an ability shaped by our ideology, theology, and experience to see things in a text that are indiscernible to others. Of course, I had my concerns that appeals to grace were merely cover for the oft-cited Lutheran declaration: "Go and sin boldly," an aspect of the Protestant church that the Holiness tradition sought to rectify in its call to the deeper Christian life empowered by the Holy Spirit. Nevertheless, you will see the impact of that Lutheran Fretheim on my essay as I returned to the text to discover the lack of imperative language when it came to the theology of penitence in Deuteronomy and the accent on future expectation. Maybe it was my Holiness tradition that emphasized the need for a deep change in our lives, or the fact that when my parents said "you will do this or that . . ." this was code for "Do this or that," but I found that I did impose this faulty "deep structure" onto Deuteronomy. In the end, however, I didn't completely throw out my Holiness sensibilities. Although shifting the accent more strongly onto divine grace in Torah, deemphasizing human ability, I did find that there is in some way an expectation that divine grace does produce real human penitential remorse and change on a deep affective level. This is in keeping with the later uses of this Torah penitential tradition in the early Persian period Jewish community and exemplified in the powerful prayers of penitence now recorded in Ezra 9, Nehemiah 1, Nehemiah 9, and Daniel 9 (see Richard Bautch's essay). Such a conclusion leads me back to Paul's call to "continue to work out your salvation with fear and trembling, for it is God who works in you to will and to act according to his good purpose" (Phil 2:12-13), a call that addresses the tension between Lutheran and Holiness traditions by encouraging us to embrace both.

One (among many) unresolved aspect of our conversation is related to what I think is one of the most powerful contributions of the Torah to the present day and age. Ron Rittgers' essay on private confession as well as several of the essays on the Western Protestant traditions reminded me of the highly individualistic approach to penitence within the West. However, it was comments by both Michael Battle and Guy Nave around the table in both years that resonated with the intra- and intergenerational character of penitence within (especially) the Torah traditions and in some ways emboldened me to affirm even more strongly the contribution the Torah had to offer a Christian theology of penitence. What does it mean to repent and confess as a community of faith, a theological tradition, a religion, or even a nation? In what way is our repentance and confession linked to the sins of former generations? How does this then relate to contemporary situations related to historically abused groups, for example in South Africa, Australia, the United States, and Canada? How does it relate to global abuse by dominant nations and groups of people? In all of this, however, I think it is important to consider the ways in which this relates to the New Testament theology of justification. There is obvious room for a deep dialogue between the Torah, Paul, and the contemporary context.

After the sessions of our second year were over, and just outside the book room at the American Academy of Religion/Society of Biblical Literature meetings, I overheard comments of an individual who was not a contributor to the Penitence study group, but did come to the sessions to listen and interact. He was expressing his frustration over the inability of our group of theologians to truly answer the searching question he had raised in one of the sessions about the relevance of repentance to a key contemporary issue. It is this frustration that I also shared as we came to the end of our deliberations. It reminded me that the dream we had in bringing this study group together could never be realized in such a short period of time and in the particular venue of a scholarly conference. It would take a diverse community of conversation willing to struggle with the wealth of Christian tradition and experience over an extended period of time to discover theological and practical solutions to the kinds of issues we face in our world today. This experience, however, has not dulled my appetite or dimmed my vision for such conversations, but rather increased my vision and heightened my desire to create spaces for such conversation in the future.

Two

# Repentance in the Former Prophets

*Terence E. Fretheim*

## 1. Text

Regarding Deuteronomy 29–30, Dennis Olson writes: "A delicate dialectic exists in this liturgy between the promise of *God's* creation of obedience (30:6-9) and the exhortation and command to the *people* to be obedient (30:10-20). . . . Somehow the liturgical promise of God and the persuasive call to obedience in worship combine to become active speech that generates and empowers."[1]

The Former Prophets (plus Deuteronomy)—commonly called the Deutcronomic History (DtrH)—do not comprise a narrative in praise of Israel; rather, they are "a kind of confession of Israel's sin."[2] This theological and didactic literature understands that disaster came upon Israel again and again because they had rejected the word of God spoken by

---

[1] Dennis Olson, *Deuteronony and the Death of Moses* (Minneapolis: Fortress Press, 1994) 132.

[2] Ralph Klein, *Israel in Exile: A Theological Interpretation* (Philadelphia: Fortress Press, 1979) 23; so, similarly, Gerhard von Rad, *Old Testament Theology*, Vol. 1 (New York: Harper, 1962): The Deuteronomist's "work is to be understood as a comprehensive confession of Israel's guilt" (p. 337).

the prophet and refused to repent (see 2 Kgs 17:9-23).[3] The destruction of Jerusalem is fully justified, given Israel's idolatrous unfaithfulness to the relationship with God. Israel's calamitous end is due to its own sin, not to divine inattention or failure.

This assessment suggests that repentance is at the heart of the purpose of this body of literature.[4] On the one hand it is a narrative act of repentance. In its very telling, it constitutes a repentant act. On the other hand it is an invitation to readers (exiles initially) to confess this story of unfaithfulness as their own story, to take personal responsibility for the sin that has brought this calamity upon them and to turn back to God.[5] Such an understanding would seem to make the Former Prophets direct descendants of the prophets of 2 Kgs 17:13, who called for Israel to "Turn from your evil ways." Yet inasmuch as this text is the only explicit call to repentance in the entire history, and retrospective at that, some pause is in order.[6] Is a positive response to a call to repentance so beyond human possibility that only a decisively new act of God will enable a restoration

---

[3] A typical, if problematic, formulation is that of Richard D. Nelson, *The Historical Books* (Nashville: Abingdon, 1998). The most characteristic of the theological themes of DtrH is "a doctrine of divine punishment and reward derived from Deuteronomy. Apostasy and disloyalty to the Lord inevitably bring wrath and punishment, but return, repentance, and fidelity to the law written in Deuteronomy bring salvation and blessing" (p. 73). The language of "punishment" is deeply problematic in this formulation and the relationship between repentance and blessing is too mechanistically conceived.

[4] Sometimes repentance is equated with conversion. But such an *equation* would violate the very important place that repentance has *within the life of faith* (believers are both saints and sinners). So it is probably best to understand repentance in two ways, as conversion and as a faithful response within an existing relationship. At one level most Old Testament texts speak of the latter; that is, Israel has a history of a covenant relationship with God and so repentance would refer to renewal within the relationship. At another level it is possible that the relationship with God has been so violated that only conversion language truly conveys what repentance entails.

[5] See Martin Rose, "Deuteronomistic Ideology and the Theology of the Old Testament," in Albert de Pury, Thomas Römer, and Jean-Daniel Macchi, eds., *Israel Constructs its History: Deuteronomistic Historiography in Recent Research* (Sheffield: Sheffield Academic Press, 2000) 424–55. Raymond F. Person, Jr., *The Deuteronomic School: History, Social Setting, and Literature* (Leiden: Brill, 2002).

[6] Ralph Klein, *Israel in Exile*, 43, warns that this theme should not be exaggerated.

of the relationship? The necessity of repentance remains, but finally it is a (resistible) gift of God. We will turn to a fuller discussion of these issues, but first some comment about the origins and character of the Deuteronomic History.

## a. The Deuteronomic History and its Themes

Taking their cue from the literary and theological Deuteronomic imprint on the Former Prophets, many scholars have come to see Joshua–Kings as an independent historical work, with Deuteronomy as an introduction.[7] In the classic formulation by Martin Noth,[8] an author living in the exilic period gathered a variety of oral and written traditions and wove them into a comprehensive whole (the exilic context is evident in several texts, 1 Kgs 8:34, 46-53; 9:6-9; 2 Kgs 21:8-15). The resultant narrative is punctuated with formal speeches at key junctures in Israel's history, providing historical retrospect and theological perspective at transitional moments (Joshua 23; Judges 2; 1 Samuel 12; 1 Kings 8; 2 Kings 17; 2 Samuel 7 has been added by other scholars).

While this hypothesis has gained wide acceptance in its general form, certain problems have occasioned significant refinements in its formulation. Foremost among these issues is the absence of the typical theological reflection upon important events at the end of 2 Kings—in this case, the destruction of Jerusalem.[9] In view of this observation (and other factors), a hypothesis has emerged that posits two major stages of editing (a "dual redaction") of the historical work.[10] The first is a major edition

---

[7] For a convenient and clear summary of the critical issues see Steven L. McKenzie, "Deuteronomistic History," *ABD* 2:160–68; Gary N. Knoppers, *Two Nations Under God*, Vol. 1 (Atlanta: Scholars, 1993) 1–54; Person, *The Deuteronomic School*. For my own perspective see my *Deuteronomic History* (Nashville: Abingdon, 1983) 15–27; more briefly, *First and Second Kings* (Louisville: Westminster, 1999) 6–10.

[8] Martin Noth, *The Deuteronomistic History* (Sheffield: JSOT Press, 1981), originally published 1943.

[9] That there is no major theological assessment relating to the fall of Jerusalem means that, in effect, the statement of 2 Kings 17 regarding the Northern Kingdom is understood to apply also to the south.

[10] E.g., Frank M. Cross, *Canaanite Myth and Hebrew Epic: Essays in the Religion of Ancient Israel* (Cambridge, MA: Harvard University Press, 1973) 274–89; Richard D. Nelson, *The Double Redaction of the Deuteronomistic History* (Sheffield: JSOT Press, 1981). For other important critical developments see McKenzie, *ABD*, and Person, *The Deuteronomic School*. From my perspective it is important to note that while

by an apologist for the reform of Josiah (ca. 620 B.C.E.); the second is a minor exilic edition that brought the work up to date, stressing the just judgment of God (2 Kgs 25:31-34 reports an event from ca. 561 B.C.E.). Other hypotheses have been developed, but for our purposes this general sketch is sufficient.[11]

The purpose of this historical work is basically hortatory, and in that sense it is continuous with the book of Deuteronomy, often described as "preached law." While key themes recur throughout, giving a certain overall perspective to the work, cautions are in order. Stress on one major theme would force the work into a mold for which it was not designed. With its hortatory agenda various and diverse themes are expressed, corresponding to complexities of the communities for which

---

an exilic redactor (or redactors) may have supplemented an earlier work, that was not the only editorial strategy available. He could also have omitted and rearranged traditions to reflect the concerns of the era in which the edition was produced. It is also clear that the redactor(s) of this work inherited a variety of traditions from the past. Considerable diversity in perspective was characteristic of these inherited traditions—which make up the bulk of the history—and the redactor(s) worked them over in different ways. Some of these sources are explicitly referred to in the narrative (cf. Josh 10:13; 1 Kgs 11:41; 2 Kgs 16:19). Some materials appear to be self-contained and isolable from their context, and hence may well have come to the redactor's hand in a form much like what we now have (e.g., the ark narrative in 1 Samuel 4–6; the tribal allotment list in Joshua 13–21). Certain periods were virtually ignored (e.g., the reign of Omri), while others were described at length (e.g., Elijah and Elisha). Certain materials were edited in recognizable regularity (e.g., the reigns of the kings), while others were given little redactional attention (e.g., 1 Samuel 13–31). This diversity may suggest that several editors (a school) were at work on the material over time, having a common perspective overall but working with different editorial principles. In this light, it is my view that the dual redaction hypothesis is too simple, as if there were two theoretically discoverable dates on which the editions of the total history were published. It seems more likely, especially in view of this diversity, that this school was at work on these traditions over a number of generations, perhaps from the time of King Hezekiah onward and even into the postexilic period. Thus the concerns of a number of eras are reflected in the completed work, while the most basic stamp is probably exilic.

[11] We cannot be certain whether the editors were country preachers (Levites), a prophetic school, or leaders standing within the Jerusalemite tradition but influenced by northern interests (the last seems most likely). Whether the final redactor lived in Palestine or Babylon is uncertain.

it was intended and the variety of the inherited traditions. These various themes are not in competition with one another; taken as a group, they give theological direction to the work as a whole. A brief survey of key thematic studies is important, not least because of the role repentance has played.

For Martin Noth the Deuteronomic History has a pessimistic perspective, designed only to show that God's actions leading to the destruction of Israel and Judah were justified. Sharper and sharper warnings of the disastrous effects of idolatry/infidelity had been voiced, with occasional interims; finally, God could only move toward disaster. From such a perspective the past was used only in order to explain the present, with no hope articulated for the future. Such a bleak picture is seldom maintained today, although the dark elements in the narrative cannot be dismissed.

A more balanced picture emerged with the work of Gerhard von Rad.[12] He understood these traditions to be woven into an account of the word of God functioning within the ongoing life of Israel, not an effort to write the history of Israel as such. Thus "Yahweh's word is active in the history of Judah, creating that history, and that in a double capacity: (1) as law, judging and destroying; (2) as gospel, i.e., in the David prophecy, which was constantly being fulfilled—saving and forgiving."[13] The law is largely derived from Moses and the prophets; their clear and unmistakable warnings were ignored, which led to the death of both southern and northern kingdoms. Judgment has come "according to the word which Yahweh had spoken by his servants, the prophets" (2 Kgs 24:2). Given Israel's sin, God's judgment was justified. At the same time, interwoven with this word of judgment is God's covenant with David (see especially 2 Samuel 7); this divine promise provided hope for Israel in times of difficulty, even in the death of exile; to this end the release of the Davidic heir (Jehoiachin, 2 Kgs 25:27-30) had theological significance. Yet about "any goal to which this saving word was coming he had nothing to say; the one thing he could do was . . . not to close the door of history, but to leave it open."[14] The corpus left room for God's promises to remain alive and for God to begin anew with this people.

---

[12] Gerhard von Rad, "The Deuteronomic Theology of History in I and II Kings," in idem, *The Problem of the Hexateuch and Other Essays* (Edinburgh: Oliver & Boyd, 1965) 205–21; idem. *Theology* 1:334–47.

[13] Gerhard von Rad, *Studies in Deuteronomy* (London: SCM Press, 1953) 89.

[14] Ibid. 343 n22.

In this formulation a fusion of the Mosaic and Davidic traditions takes place: Turn from your wicked ways and trust God's promise, which will not fail.[15] "The determinative thing which Jahweh was now waiting for from Israel was 'turning.'"[16] This hortatory language makes sense only if a future for Israel with God is actually possible.

Of the various overarching perspectives proposed, von Rad's remains the most satisfactory. For the historian to take up the telling of this story is a sign of hope in itself; he or she is not resigned to a history of despair, but believes that a future for this people will be made possible by God. This means that, finally, the historian values Davidic promise over obedience to Sinaitic law; God's promise assures that Israel's future will be positive.

The work of Hans Walter Wolff is deserving of fuller attention.[17] He seeks to show that repentance *(šûb)* plays a central role in key texts (e.g., Judg 2:16-18; Deut 4:30-31; 30:1-10; 1 Sam 12:13-35; 1 Kgs 8:33-50). The Judges text features a key pattern: apostasy, judgment, repentance, deliverance.[18] This pattern reveals that, even in the face of apostasy, Israel's history continues, for again and again "Israel implored Yahweh anew and . . . Yahweh was moved to pity."[19] This repeated pattern encourages a repentant response on the part of readers in every generation, including the exiles. In the wake of Israel's apostasy and the resultant judgment, repentance was now necessary if exilic Israel was to recover its relationship with God.

Wolff disagrees with Noth, asking why an author would even write (and at such length), if the point was only a negative one. Wolff also

[15] See von Rad, *Theology* 1: The "Deuteronomist sees the main problem of the history of Israel as lying in the question of the correct correlation of Moses and David" (p. 339).

[16] Ibid. 346. Von Rad adds: "The form to be taken by the turning is remarkably spiritual. It is in the heart. It was not therefore cultic. And its chief means was prayer."

[17] Hans Walter Wolff, "The Kerygma of the Deuteronomic Historical Work," in Walter Brueggemann and Hans Walter Wolff, eds., *The Vitality of Old Testament Traditions* (Atlanta: John Knox, 1982) 83–100. This article was originally published in 1961.

[18] It is not unimportant to note that Judges only uses *šûb* in its negative sense ("relapse," 2:19). Its positive sense may be implied, but should that fact not make it a less central theme than Wolff suggests?

[19] Wolff, "Kerygma," 87.

disagrees with von Rad, stressing that certain passages (e.g., 1 Kgs 2:3-4; 9:5-7) make the Davidic covenant conditional upon obedience and hence subordinate to the Sinaitic covenant.[20] Because of apostasy, the Davidic covenant was no longer in force. In the absence of any *specific* hope, Israel could only trust that, given God's past response to a repentant people, a comparable response by the exiles means that God would hear and forgive (1 Kgs 8:33-50). In summary, these texts constitute a program of repentance, designed to meet the needs of a devastated community so that it might proceed into the future with hope and confidence.

### b. Moving beyond Wolff

In response to Wolff one must ask whether he makes Israel's future too much dependent on actions taken by the people, as if Israel had the wherewithal within itself to return to God. Wolff gives insufficient attention to this issue. He correctly speaks of the historian's "stress upon Yahweh's agency" and claims that "the return is plainly part of the promise" (especially Deut 4:29-31; 30:1-10). Circumcision of the heart is a *divine* action (30:6). Hence "Dtr preaching lacks the character of legalistic urging."[21] But Wolff does not move far enough along this line of thought, placing too strong an emphasis on the (rare) call to return. Indeed, Wolff considers the divinely *promised* repentance only a matter of "eschatological salvation."[22]

Several texts suggest that "eschatological" may be too "big" a word for the repentance God promises, evident most clearly in Deut 4:29-31; 30:1-10. God *promises* that Israel *will* repent, not least in view of the promises to Abraham (Deut 29:13). The reason is that the Lord is merciful and will not renege on promises made (4:31). That provided a promissory undercurrent in the life of both North (2 Kgs 13:23) and South, enabling a hope beyond exile to be voiced (Deut 4:31). For another example, Samuel's call for Israel, "serve the Lord with all your heart, and do not turn aside after worthless things" (1 Sam 12:20-22), is immediately followed by a "for," which speaks a strong promise: "For the Lord will not cast

---

[20] Ibid. 86. The conditioning of the Davidic covenant has now been demonstrated to be limited in scope; the ending of Kings voices an uncertainty only with respect to the shape fulfillment might take (see, e.g., Richard D. Nelson, *Dual Redaction,* 1981).

[21] Ibid. 98–99.

[22] Ibid. 99.

away his people, for his great name's sake, because it has pleased the LORD to make you a people for himself." In effect the articulation of this unconditional promise *enables* Israel's response: human repentance is *possible* only because the divine promise is fully in view; at the same time the call to repent can be resisted and rejected (1 Sam 12:25). Another key text (1 Kgs 8:14-59) makes clear that repentance is not presented as a naked demand. The repentance called for in 8:47-48 is possible only because it stands in the wake of a strong reiteration of unconditional promises to David (8:22-26), followed by reference to the promises given to Moses (8:51-53). Indeed, the encouragement to repent is specifically grounded in God's faithful promises to Israel (8:56) and the speed of divine mercy often in evidence through Israel's history.[23] From within this promissory context *God* will "incline our hearts to him, to walk in all his ways, and to keep his commandments" (1 Kgs 8:58).

The consequence of these texts is well stated by Heinz-Josef Fabry:[24]

> God himself will orient Israel's thinking and actions toward him, creating thereby the prerequisites for the people to turn to him in an undivided and unqualified fashion. Hence, what initially seems to be the condition for ending the exile (30:3). . . . all this can now be seen as God's own work, which is why at the end it can be expressed as a promise for the future" (30:8). . . . Israel is incapable of repenting and returning on its own . . . and must be enabled for such through a profound transformation of its very essence.

The work of Walter Brueggemann is also important in this connection.[25] He observes a recurring concern for "the good" in the history, understood primarily in terms of the faithfulness and graciousness of God that serve to draw the people to repentance. For him, the call to repentance "is governed and informed by the more fundamental statement

[23] See 1 Kgs 18:37, where God turns the heart of the people back to God.

[24] Heinz-Josef Fabry, "Shub," *TDOT* 12:501. See also p. 498, about Hosea: "Calls to repent and return appear first in oracles of salvation, where one finds that conversion is not the condition for the reception of salvation; rather, the promised salvation is itself the presupposition or grounding of conversion. As such an invitation, the admonition [to repent] is clearly dependent on the oracle of salvation."

[25] Walter Brueggemann, "The Kerygma of the Deuteronomistic Historian," *Int* 22 (1968) 387–402. Brueggemann builds on the work of Wolff but his articulation of the relationship between repentance and promise is more sharply and helpfully stated than that of Wolff.

of Yahweh's intention for Israel. The first word to the exiles is not imperative but declarative, not talk about Israel's responsibility but Yahweh's
intention."[26] With particular reference to 2 Samuel 7, he states:

> There will be a future because of this promised word which does not
> fail. . . . The punishment (correction) is for a moment. The promise
> of fidelity is forever. . . . The kerygma of "good" places the call to
> "turn" (*shuv*) in a context which can evoke repentance in Israel, enable
> her to change . . . [God's] faithfulness makes repentance possible and
> attractive.[27]

I would concur that the former prophets understand that repentance
is possible, finally, only because of God's promise. Human repentance
constitutes a *gift* of God in view of the promise; indeed, repentance is not
possible without the promise being understood as directly applicable to
the one who would repent.[28]

The extent to which the narrative is punctuated with unconditional
promises signals their import for reflections regarding repentance. For
example: "the Lord your God is a merciful God; he will not fail you or
destroy you or forget the covenant with your fathers which he swore to
them" (Deut 4:31; see 29:13; 2 Kgs 13:23); "I will never break my covenant
with you" (Judg 2:1); "For the Lord will not cast away his people" (1 Sam
12:22); "Your throne shall be established forever" (2 Sam 7:16). To these
texts might be added the references to the Davidic covenant in 1–2 Kings
(1 Kgs 8:20, 25; 9:5; 11:5, 13, 32, 36; 15:4; 2 Kgs 2:4; 8:19; 19:34; 20:6).

These divine promises will not fail; they will never be made null and
void as far as God is concerned. While a rebellious generation might not
live to see the fulfillment of the promise because they have rejected God,
the promise can be relied on. The divine promise is an everlasting one,
though participation in its fulfillment is not guaranteed to every person
or generation. Thus for all of its character as gift, the call to repentance
can be resisted and rejected (2 Kgs 17:13). In Wolff's words, "It is not so
much the total apostasy which makes the judgment final as the contemp-
tuous disregard of the call to return."[29] Positively, Israel's only activity
is a kind of "let it be." The promise is always there for the believing to

---

[26] Brueggemann, "Kerygma," 393.
[27] Ibid. 399, 401–402.
[28] On faith being created by the promise see Gen 15:1-6.
[29] Wolff, "Kerygma," 91.

cling to, and they know that God will ever be at work to fulfill it. Only within such a promissory context is repentance possible.

How, then, does God create repentance? Israel's repentant response is created in and through the announcement of judgment (e.g., 2 Sam 12:10-12; 2 Kgs 22:11-13; cf. 2 Kgs 20:1-6) or the experience of judgment, accompanied by the continuing articulation of the salvific promises of God. In other words, judgment is necessary for forgiveness and salvation. No theological contradiction exists between the themes of death-dealing judgment and promise, and the presence of the latter theme does not mean optimism that judgment can be avoided. In several texts (e.g., Judges 2–3) this rhythm is reiterated as a basic way of God with this persistently unfaithful people: Israel must pass through death in order to receive life. At the end of 2 Kings death has been experienced, and this reality nearly overwhelms the narrative. Yet no final rejection is stated; the promises articulated are understood to continue in place.

### c. The Language of Repentance

The *NRSV* translates "repent" only twice in the entire corpus, Deuteronomy–Kings (1 Kgs 8:47-48), though other language carries the idea. Even more, the word "forgiveness" is rarely noted (generally, only 1 Kgs 8:30-50; cf. 2 Sam 12:13). For the surface reader of the text, the language of repentance and forgiveness will commonly remain a minor theme. I here look at three expressions that expand the conversation: divine repentance, the confession of sin, and the use of the metaphor "turn, return."

#### (1) Divine Repentance.

While divine repentance (usually *niham*) is seldom related to human repentance (2 Sam 24:16 may be an exception), a few notes are in order.[30] This theme is infrequent in the history (Deut 32:36; Judg 2:18; 1 Sam 15:11, 29 [bis], 35; 2 Sam 24:16; it is implied in 1 Kgs 21:27-29 and 2 Kgs 20:1-11). In a few texts *šûb* is used for *divine* (not) turning away from wrath (Deut 1:45; 13:17; 30:8-9; Josh 7:26; 2 Kgs 23:26; cf. Deut 30:3; cf. Josh 24:20; cf. *sûr* in 1 Sam 28:16). In 1 Sam 15:11, 35 the word has reference to the divine rejection of an already accomplished act (Saul; cf. Gen

---

[30] I have dealt with this theme at length, especially in "The Repentance of God: A Key to Evaluating Old Testament God-Talk," *HBT* 10 (1988) 47–70.

6:6-7).[31] The claim of 1 Sam 15:29 (cf. Num 23:19; Ps 110:4) that God "is not a mortal, that he should change his mind" pertains to God's faithfulness to promises made (see Hos 11:9, where God *does* change his mind, because he is not a mortal!).

With respect to these and other deuteronomic texts (Deut 32:36; Judg 2:18; 2 Sam 24:16), divine repentance is *not* a reference to divine forgiveness, but to the alleviation of the judgment being suffered or to the prevention of it altogether, either on God's own initiative or in view of human groaning (Judg 2:18; cf. 1 Kgs 21:27-29; 2 Kgs 20:1-11). In some texts intercession on behalf of a sinful people is based on the character and promises of God, not on anything that the people have done or said (Exod 32:7-14; Num 14:17-20). An important point for our study: because God does repent, no fixed relationship exists between sins, repentance present or absent, and the determination/cancellation of a judgmental future.

Inasmuch as divine repentance is associated especially with prophecy, a few words about this important deuteronomic theme are in order. Many texts can be cited wherein the prophetic word of judgment is fulfilled later in the history (e.g., 1 Sam 2:31 with 1 Kgs 2:27). Yet fulfillment is not the only story to tell about prophetic words of judgment. Now and again the judgment word of God is not (literally) fulfilled. Isaiah announces to Hezekiah (2 Kgs 20:1-6) that he will die and not recover. Yet in response to Hezekiah's prayer the prophetic word is reversed through a direct word from God. Similarly, when Ahab repentantly responds to God's word through Elijah, God delays the fulfillment of the word (1 Kgs 21:27-29). Or God's word to Elijah in 1 Kgs 19:15-18 is only partially fulfilled in his ministry; aspects of this word remain for others to accomplish (2 Kings 9–10). In addition, God's ongoing merciful interaction with the people affects the course of Israel's history, even in the face of contrary prophetic words (cf. 2 Kgs 13:4-5, 23; 14:26-27).

The fact that *some* prophetic words are not (literally) fulfilled means that in *every* such case the future is understood to remain open until fulfillment actually occurs. Israel's future is not absolutely determined by the prophet's word. In other words, prophetic words of judgment do not function mechanistically, as if the word were some autonomous power beyond the reach of God's continuing attention. Even more, this "play" in the time between the word and its (potential) fulfillment gives room

---

[31] For a study of these Samuel texts see my "Divine Foreknowledge, Divine Constancy, and the Rejection of Saul's Kingship," *CBQ* 47 (1985) 595–602.

for the promise to be at work even in the midst of judgment. Indeed, finally, God *uses* judgment, not as an end in itself, but as a refining fire for salvific purposes—in the service of the word of promise.

### (2) *The Confession of Sin*

Specific reference to a verbal confession of sin by individuals or the people of Israel occurs sixteen times.[32] This may or may not be used in association with the verb *šûb* (see below). The confession may be accompanied by certain rituals, including prayers, weeping, rending clothes, wearing sackcloth, sprinkling with ashes, and fasting (1 Sam 7:3-6; 2 Sam 12:16; 1 Kgs 8:33-35, 47-48; cf. 1 Kgs 21:27-29, where Ahab's ritual actions may imply a confession of sin). Sometimes the confession of sin issues in forgiveness (2 Sam 12:13; 1 Kgs 8:30-50) and sometimes it does not. Sometimes repentance serves to ward off the consequences of sin, but in a surprising number of cases it only ameliorates the effects or has no reported positive effect whatsoever. In what follows I offer a basic outline of the texts and then present several different, but not contradictory, theological interpretations. One evident point here is that mechanistic understandings of sin and consequence are not in order.

*(a) Instances where the confession of sin has no stated positive effect:*

- Deuteronomy 1:41 (Israel; their confession does not turn away God's wrath, 1:45);

- Deuteronomy 3:23-26 (While Moses may not voice a confession of sin, all of his words and deeds are of no avail; he will not be allowed to enter the land of promise);

- Joshua 7:20 (Achan confesses, but he is then stoned to death, 7:25);

- 1 Samuel 15:24-25, 30 (Saul confesses his sin *three times,* but it has no positive effect on God's decision to reject him, 15:28-29, 35).[33]

It is apparent that certain sins are understood to be irreversible, and for several reasons (e.g., 2 Kgs 23:26; 24:4 [the sins of Manasseh]; Deut

---

[32] The translation "penitent" (*rak,* be soft, tender) is unique to 2 Kgs 22:19; 2 Chr 34:27.

[33] On this text see my "Divine Foreknowledge."

29:20; 1 Sam 3:13-14). While there is hope for forgiveness, it is not an automatic divine response to repentance, even if sincere (as, apparently, in Saul's case or in Jeremiah 14). In such cases prayers of repentance are too late. "The effects of the people's sins, both historical and natural . . . had been so pervasive that the situation could not be turned around," even by God. It was too late, even for God. The judgment had to fall.[34] While Samuel would have sinned had he not interceded on behalf of Israel (1 Sam 12:23), Jeremiah was explicitly told by God not to do so, chiefly because it was too late and, moreover, the lack of intercession would intensify the negative effects and hasten the judgment (Jer 7:11; 11:14; 15:1). There is, finally, a "who knows?" or a "perhaps" with respect to such a divine response (see 2 Sam 12:22; Jer 26:3; Joel 2:14; Jonah 3:9).

*(b) Instances where the effects are mixed:*

- Judges 10:10, 15 (Israel confesses twice; initially God determines not to deliver them any more, 10:13, but finally does, because persistence counts and God could "no longer bear to see Israel suffer," 10:16);

- 2 Samuel 12:13 (David confesses, and though forgiven, still suffers many adverse effects, many of them pronounced *before* David confessed, 12:10-14);

- 2 Samuel 19:20 (Shimei confesses, and David responds by saving his life, 19:23; but Solomon kills him for his deeds, 1 Kgs 2:44-45);

- 2 Samuel 24:10, 17 (David confesses twice; after the first, the plague still ravishes Israel; after the second, the plague is averted; in between God relents regarding the judgment with no apparent reference to the confession, 24:16).

Some texts (e.g., 2 Samuel 12) show clearly that a distinction must be made between forgiveness and the elimination of sin's adverse effects. Another way of stating the matter is that repentance may have personal effects (on, say, the relationship between God and the repentant one), but sin's effects will have rippled out across the social and even cosmic fabrics and will wreak their negative effects. The act of repentance with

---

[34] For detail see Terence Fretheim, *Jeremiah* (Macon: Smyth & Helwys, 2002) 230. See also "Is Anything Too Hard for God? (Jer 32:27)," *CBQ* 66 (2004) 231–36.

the divine response of forgiveness does not immediately "gather" all those effects and cut them off in their tracks; dealing with them takes time, even for God (in the contemporary world, witness the distinction between forgiving a child abuser and the ongoing effects on the child that take time to heal). Salvation has to do not simply with the forgiveness of sin, but also with the healing of the reverberating effects of sin.[35]

This perspective may also be a way of thinking through Josiah's reform and his personal turning to the Lord (2 Kgs 23:24-25). Not only does the Josianic reform not halt (or perhaps even delay) Judah's destruction, but also Josiah himself is killed in battle (Huldah's positive word about his future, 22:18-20, is at best partially fulfilled). The forces that make for destruction had so gotten out of control (voiced in terms of the sins of Manasseh, 23:26; 24:3-4), that no amount of repentance or reform could stop Judah's demise. It is not that Josiah's reform was irrelevant (many long-term positive effects may have been generated), but that it was too late (or too little, too late), even for God. As for Josiah's death, it could also be considered the result of an accident or undue risks taken.

From another perspective, prayers of repentance may only bring a delay. Delay means that repentance is understood to have some positive effect, but it does not turn the situation around, for the "evil" is so deep and profound. And so Ahab's confession has limited effect; it delays the consequence only by a generation (1 Kgs 21:27-29). Jehu's removal of the Baals from Israel extends his line for only four generations, because he did not "turn aside" *(sûr)* from the sins of Jeroboam or follow the law (2 Kgs 10:26-30).

In some texts (Judges 10; 2 Samuel 24) another angle is presented: no report of divine forgiveness follows upon confession of sin, but Israel is delivered from the consequences of its sins anyway. In 2 Samuel 24 a greater intensity of repentant conduct by David seems to have an impact on God and the plague is averted (though the link with the prayers is not altogether clear). This scenario seems also to be the case in the Judges 10 texts, except that here God is moved not only by repeated repentance but also by Israel's suffering.

These various texts imply that a mechanistic notion of sin-consequence, or a fixed theory of retribution, cannot be ascribed to the Deuteronomic History. These texts do not introduce a contradictory element into an

---

[35] For this more comprehensive understanding of salvation see my "Salvation in the Bible vs. Salvation in the Church," *WW* 13 (1993) 363–72.

otherwise basic teaching regarding retribution; rather, they show considerable complexity of understanding regarding the relationship of sin to consequence. In addition, the witness to divine repentance (noted above) clearly indicates that no clear relationship exists between sins that have been committed, repentance (present or absent), and the determination of a judgmental future.

*(c) Instances where the effect is positive, or potentially so:*

- 1 Samuel 7:6 (associated with *šûb*, see below);

- 1 Samuel 12:10, 19. A retrospective confession is associated with worship of other gods (v. 10); the people addressed by Samuel respond in comparable ways (v. 19), reversing the judgmental effects. This confession is followed by Samuel's word to the people, including both charge and promise (12:20-22).

- 1 Kings 8:30-50. Israel's anticipated confession of sin is explicit only in 8:47 but is implicit in various expressions throughout this section (prayer; pleading; turning to God; turning from sin). These various elements are used as a motivation to argue for divine forgiveness and compassion.

- 2 Kings 5:18 (Naaman, to which Elisha responds with a word of peace).

A brief study of *šûb* will lift up the key elements in these texts that witness to the positive effects of the confession of sin.

### (3) (Re)turning to the Lord (šûb).

"Repent" is not a common translation of *šûb* because the verb is often followed by a prepositional phrase (e.g., turn "to the Lord") while "repent" is not.[36] The phrase "(re)turn" to the Lord uses the analogy of walking on a way; the people have turned away from God and turned elsewhere, namely, to the worship of other gods (Josh 22:16, 18, 23, 29; 23:12; Judg 2:19; 8:33; 15:11; 1 Kgs 9:6; 2 Kgs 21:3).[37] The positive sense

---

[36] For dictionary articles see especially the extensive study of Heinz-Josef Fabry, "Shub," *TDOT* 12:461–522.

[37] Cf. also the use of *sûr*, "turn away/put aside," (Deut 9:12, 16; 11:16, 28; 17:17; 28:14; 31:29; 1 Sam 12:20-21; 2 Sam 22:22-23; 1 Kgs 11:2; 2 Kgs 10:29; 17:22; 18:6).

of *šûb* is to return to the point of departure, to the original relationship with Yahweh (for exiles, the return to the land is also in view, Deut 30:2-3). This return should not, however, be understood in a cyclical sense; the situation upon return to God is not identical to that from which one turned to the worship of other gods. The intervening experience has its continuing effects (both positive and negative) and there is genuine newness in the divinely reestablished relationship. The importance of this theme may be signified by the placement of such words in the mouths of leading characters—Moses (Deut 4:29-31; 30:1-10), Samuel (1 Sam 7:3-6), Solomon (1 Kgs 8:33-53), and the prophets (2 Kgs 17:13). Whatever the role of repentance over the course of Israel's history, these texts renew its importance for the exiles (and other readers).

The contexts in which *šûb* appears with a human subject are infrequent (on *God's* turning, see above). The people will turn to God or turn from their sin *in the future* (Deut 4:30; 30:2, 8, 10) or it is anticipated that they will (1 Kgs 8:33-35, 47-48) and, as noted, this turning will be possible only because the promise is explicitly in view. Elsewhere Israel is asked whether they are "returning" to the Lord wholeheartedly (1 Sam 7:3), so it is possible to return with less than a whole heart. This action commonly entails "putting away" *(sûr)* foreign gods (Josh 24:14, 23; 1 Sam 7:3-4; Judg 10:16; 2 Kgs 10:31). This language *(šûb)* is also used to evaluate kings negatively (Jeroboam, 1 Kgs 13:33) or positively (Josiah, 2 Kgs 23:25). Whether or not the people have turned is used to evaluate the Northern Kingdom as a whole (2 Kgs 17:13). This last is the only text in the Former Prophets that refers to the people being called to return to the Lord, and it is retrospective (cf. Deut 30:2).

What does turning entail? Initially it should be noted that it does not entail that Israel obey commandments (except for the first/second, which is, at its heart, not a matter of obedience, but of faith).[38] Rather, again and again the turning texts involve the putting away of other gods and turning to the Lord with a whole heart (e.g., 1 Sam 7:3-4). The issue is faith, not obedience. Hence, to make a key point: repentance for the historian is defined fundamentally in terms of a turning (back) to YHWH, not a detailing of commandments now (to be) obeyed.

The opening section of the Former Prophets, Josh 1:1-9, helps us draw out some concluding reflections. These verses show that notions

---

[38] For an extensive effort to show that the Deuteronomic History is most basically concerned with the first commandment see my *Deuteronomic History*, 21–26.

of gift and promise provide the context for any talk about commandments. It is, first of all, God's electing and saving action that *constitutes*
the relationship with Israel. Obedience to commandments is a concern
that derives from an already established relationship rather than being
the basis for establishing it. Hence a call to obedience, including the
call to repentance, invites the people to a life that will be true to that
already existent relationship or do justice to it. Moreover, obedience
cannot maintain or preserve (or reestablish) the relationship, since it was
not constitutive of the relationship in the first place. While one can more
fully realize the existing relationship through obedience, because of sin
one cannot finally preserve it. Disobedience, on the other hand, is a *sign*
(not the substance) that something has gone wrong with the relationship
with God. Because of Israel's lack of faith and trust in God alone (which
would issue in disobedient actions of various sorts), the relationship with
God is endangered and, finally, capable of fracture. But such a result is
not inevitable, since God in mercy and patience could preserve the relationship in spite of such disloyalty (and did so again and again). All of
the hortatory language in this opening to the Deuteronomic History is
repeatedly undergirded by the divine promise: God "will be with you,
will not fail you or forsake you" (Josh 1:4, 9). Obedience, including obedience to the call for repentance, is understood to be possible for Israel
only because such unconditional promises of God are the very ground
of their continuing life.

## 2. Implications

### a. Repentance and Promise

The unconditional promises of God punctuate the narrative. The
Former Prophets understand that human repentance is possible, finally,
only because of God's word—of judgment and promise. Only the proclamation of this unconditional promise to the sinner who stands under
judgment enables Israel's response, for human repentance is *possible*
only because the divine promise is fully in view and is understood to
be directly applicable to the sinner's life, enabling a new future with
God. Human repentance constitutes a *gift* of God in view of such a
word. One practical implication of this reality for contemporary read-
ers/hearers: they should not be called to repent, indeed cannot truly be
called to repent, independent of the implicit or explicit articulation of
the unconditional promises of God. The promises do not *guarantee* the

repentance, however, for the call to repent can be successfully resisted and rejected.

## b. The future is both open and settled

Another implication for contemporary reflections relates to a strict form of retribution that the Former Prophets are often thought to have. These texts, however, cut against any such understanding. We have seen the confession of sin to have various effects, with no singular divine response that shapes the person's future. Moreover, the absence of a strict relationship between a prophecy of judgment and its fulfillment shows that God is free to act "outside the box" (including acts of divine mercy and divine repentance); consequently, the future for individual/community has a certain amount of openness rather than a strict predictability. These texts that exhibit such openness show considerable complexity regarding the relationship of sin to consequence and constitute an important witness to Israel's God.

## c. The image of God

God is revealed as anything but locked into a retributionary scheme. Rather, God has proven faithful to promises given and is the source of blessings without end, though the people have often proved faithless (cf. 1 Kgs 8:26, 56). God has been willing to make adjustments in working with people, always taking new initiatives in dealing with negative situations (e.g., the monarchy). Warnings of the consequences of unbelief are often given, particularly through the prophets whom a merciful God has raised up to speak (2 Kgs 17:13). God has been "moved to pity" time and again, mercifully giving Israel another chance to turn from its disloyalties (Judges 2). And even, finally, when disaster must fall, this divine move is cast in terms of death, but not annihilation, for judgment is perceived as a refining fire, a means by which life might finally come again (cf. Deut 4:26-31). No final rejection of Israel is ever pronounced. The persistent pattern of prophetic word and fulfillment throughout the narrative makes it clear to exilic readers that this kind of God—one who keeps promises—is the only basis for hope. All of God's actions are directed to one goal: "That you might know that the Lord is God; there is no other besides him" (Deut 4:35, 39; 30:6). This promise and purpose of God with and for this people is the interpretive key to the history of Israel.

# 3. Further Reading

Brueggemann, Walter. "The Kerygma of the Deuteronomistic Historian," *Int* 22 (1968) 387–402.

Fabry, Heinz-Josef. "Shub," *TDOT* 12:461–522.

Fretheim, Terence F. *Deuteronomic History*. Nashville: Abingdon, 1983.

Klein, Ralph. *Israel in Exile: A Theological Interpretation*. Philadelphia: Fortress Press, 1979.

Nelson, Richard. *The Double Redaction of the Deuteronomistic History*. Sheffield: JSOT Press, 1981.

Noth, Martin. *The Deuteronomistic History*. Sheffield: JSOT Press, 1981. Originally published in German in 1943.

Olson, Dennis. *Deuteronony and the Death of Moses*. Minneapolis: Fortress Press, 1994.

Person, Raymond F., Jr. *The Deuteronomic School: History, Social Setting, and Literature*. Leiden: Brill, 2002.

Rad, Gerhard von. *Old Testament Theology*. Vol. I. New York: Harper, 1962.

Rose, Martin. "Deuteronomistic Ideology and the Theology of the Old Testament." In Albert de Pury, Thomas Römer, and Jean-Daniel Macchi, eds., *Israel Constructs its History*. Sheffield: Sheffield Academic Press, 2000, 424–55.

Wolff, Hans Walter. "The Kerygma of the Deuteronomic Historical Work." In Walter Brueggemann and Hans Walter Wolff, eds., *The Vitality of Old Testament Traditions*. Atlanta: John Knox, 1982, 83–100. Originally published in 1961.

# 4. Hermeneutical Response

I highlight two major issues that surfaced in our conversations and seem to call for further reflection on my part and on the part of other participants.

One, among the matters discussed regarding repentance (see n. 4) was whether it referred to renewal in an existing relationship or to conversion, that is, whether the relationship with God has been so violated that only conversion language will convey the issue at stake for Israel. The more I think about this, the more it seems likely that both understandings are present in the Former Prophets. On the one hand an example of repentance as a renewal in relationship is the response of an adulterous David in the wake of the judgment of Nathan (2 Samuel 12). On the other hand I think the overall perspective of the history exhibits a more radical understanding of repentance. Israel's relationship with YHWH has diminished to such an extent that, at least for most people in Israel, they have become adherents of another religion. This would account for the emphasis, in every central text, upon the first/second commandment (Deut 6:5), which has fundamentally to do with faith itself. Again and again Israel has turned away from Yʜᴡʜ and turned toward other gods, worshiping them. In other words, the issue for Israel is not fundamentally that of obedience and disobedience, but faith and unbelief. This reality may explain the concern at the heart of the book of Deuteronomy; the tradition is not only to be taught *(fides quae)*, but to be inwardly appropriated *(fides qua;* see Deut 6:2-9). The very relationship with God is at stake. Radical repentance is the only way into the future.

Two, the question then becomes how Israel, standing *outside* a relationship with Yʜᴡʜ, can move again into a relationship with Yʜᴡʜ. This issue has generated most of the oral and written response to this paper. Perhaps it was prompted by my less-than-clear statement that the issue in the Former Prophets has to do with conversion and *not* (except for isolated individuals) renewal in relationship. If the latter were the case, then repentant actions from within the existing and ongoing relationship might be considered more in terms of human response prompted by God's word of judgment (e.g., David to the word of Nathan).

But if conversion is the need, then a more radical divine action seems to be in view. Recall that the only call to repent in the entire corpus is found in a retrospective word (2 Kgs 17:13), except perhaps more indirectly. It is intriguing to me that the narrative as a whole, in its very telling, can be called a repentant act (rather than a call to repentance). The purpose, it would seem, was to enable the readers/hearers to confess this story of unfaithfulness as their own story, to take personal responsibility for their own sin that has brought about this sad state of affairs.

Is this a more subtle call to repentance? The rhetoric is certainly of such a nature that readers would not be able to claim innocence or argue that God or even life itself had somehow been unfair to them; any finger they point should be back at their own selves. A central text revealing of at least some exilic readers is 1 Kgs 9:8-9 (essentially the same as Deut 29:24-26, only there voiced by the nations; cf. Jer 5:19, etc.). The readers ask: "Why has the Loʀᴅ done such a thing to this land and to this house?" The answer given is that they have forsaken the Lord and turned to other gods. If the readers are asking this question, this suggests that they are *unrepentant* and clueless about the theological import of these disastrous events. They will need to be caught up in this story, realize that they have brought this judgment upon themselves, and turn back to God. But how can they do that?

The narrative witness to sixteen differing confessions of sin on the part of both individuals and community will be a somewhat ambiguous read for these readers. Will the exiles be more like Saul, who confessed his sin three times and it brought no forgiveness or hope for a new future? Are they but another Saul? Or are they like the people in the time of the judges who cried out, and God responded with deliverance even though there was no repentant act? Or are they more like David, who did confess his sin, but also experienced devastating effects on his family and his people? Yet, in the midst of tragedy, God continued the promises to David—and God will faithfully keep promises. Or will they be more like the people in Solomon's prayer (1 Kgs 8:14-59)? God's promises to David and Israel (1 Kgs 8:22-26, 51-53, 56) surround and ground the statement of potential repentance (8:46-53), made possible only by divine action (8:58).

This variety suggests that it is not some pattern of repentance that will enable them to live again; acts of repentance in themselves are shown to have ambiguous effects. The only words to which they can cling are the promises, and the God who is committed to those promises. They can continue to reject the promises and the promise-giver. But nothing that they do, no human action, even acts of repentance, will enable a positive future. They can only rest back in the promises of God and let those promises wash over them and, from within that promissory wash, God will circumcise their hearts (Deut 30:6), gifting them with the repentance necessary for their future.

My personal response to this kind of theological project is that it has been very helpful for my own work and continuing reflection. The gatherings of participants were important in fostering interdisciplinary conversation and giving us a good sense for the range of scholarship regarding the topic. In this conversation it became evident how our personal theological commitments shape our work. It was made evident to me that my Lutheran convictions shape my exegetical work. But I also became more fully aware of the theological commitments of others, and that knowledge will no doubt enable me to engage in a fuller and more nuanced conversation in the future.

Three

# "Turn Back, O People":
# Repentance in the Latter Prophets

*Carol J. Dempsey*

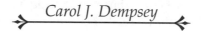

## 1. Text

To reflect upon and write about the theme of "repentance" in the Latter Prophets is no small task, and to try to discuss this theme in relation to selected passages from the prophetic texts is to do a disservice to the theme itself since repentance, both as a call and a theme, is central to the prophets' preaching and the message of their writings. That much being said, I propose in this study to approach the prophetic texts synchronically. Material is organized thematically in an attempt to capture the subtle nuances of "repentance" as a dynamic virtue that played itself out in the tumultuous yet passionate relationship that existed between God and God's people, and between God and ancient Israel in particular. Various sub-themes structure the discussion and move readers through not only the prophetic corpus but also the life of a divine and human relationship that continues to provide a vision of hope for today. The writings of the prophets show that the God of creation, the Lord of history remains faithful to love and to covenant despite the people's infidelities, transgressions, and impenitence. Throughout the prophetic texts we see the role that the heart plays in relation to repentance, fidelity, reconciliation, and transformation.

## a. Setting the Stage: Repentance in the Context of Torah

The Torah creates the backdrop for the mission and ministry of the Latter Prophets. The creation account heralds humanity as having been created in God's image, according to God's likeness (Gen 1:27). The first humans procreate (Gen 4:1); civilizations form (Gen 4:17-22); genealogies take shape (Genesis 5); ancestral families develop (Genesis 12); and nations emerge (Genesis 17), all of which exist in the midst of divine presence, blessing, and promise. Abraham does become the ancestor of a multitude of nations through Ishmael, Hagar, Isaac, and Sarah. Through Isaac, an everlasting covenant is established (Genesis 17), and in David and his successors this covenant continues down through the ages and into the Christian era (1 Samuel 16; 2 Samuel 7; Matt 1:1-17).

Of significance in the book of Exodus is the Sinai covenant. Israel becomes God's treasured possession out of all the peoples (Exod 19:5). For Israel's God, the covenant was an affair of the heart. According to the biblical text God had set God's heart in love on Israel (Deut 7:7; 10:15) and in return, God wanted Israel's heart as well (Deut 10:12). As one sees from the biblical text, singleheartedness was and continues to be a gradual process, highlighted by Moses' encouragement that the Israelites circumcise the foreskins of their hearts (Deut 10:16). Centuries later Jeremiah repeats this word of exhortation to his community (Jer 4:4), and although circumcision of the heart seems as if it might be something that humans and communities of believers might be able to accomplish over the course of a lifetime, the writers of Deuteronomy and later Pauline literature remind us that the circumcision of the heart comes to fruition through God's own work (Deut 30:6) and presence within the human community as a whole (see, e.g., Rom 3:20; 4:1-12).

As part of the Sinai covenant Israel becomes entrusted with God's law, meant to help preserve and safeguard covenant relationship (Exodus 20). The keeping of the law ensured right relationship with God and with one's neighbor and creation in general. Old Testament law with its many stipulations and ordinances was later simplified to reflect the law's essence as recorded in Deut 10:12-16 (cf. Deut 6:4-6; Matt 22:34-40). Common to both Old and New Testament law was wholehearted love. Forgetfulness of God, infidelity to covenant relationship characterized by apostasy and idolatry, along with the breaking of the law, led to the raising up of many prophets during Israel's most difficult years between the eighth and fifth centuries B.C.E. The biblical text suggests that unless the people repented of their ways they would be made to suffer horrific consequences at the hands of a jealous God. The drama of the prophets with their repetitive plea to "repent" now unfolds.

### b. The Prophetic Mission and Word: "Turn Back," "Return," "Repent"

One of the many tasks of the prophets as part of their mission was to warn both the wicked and the righteous about iniquity and its consequences. The text of Ezek 3:16-21 brings this dimension of the prophetic vocation to the fore. Here Ezekiel makes known to his listeners the message God had declared to him:

> Mortal, I have made you a sentinel for the house of Israel; whenever you hear a word from my mouth, you shall give them warning from me. If I say to the wicked, "You shall surely die," and you give them no warning, or speak to warn the wicked from their wicked way, in order to save their life, those wicked persons shall die for their iniquity; but their blood I will require at your hand. But if you warn the wicked, and they do not turn from their wickedness, or from their wicked way, they shall die for their iniquity; but you will have saved your life. Again, if the righteous turn from their righteousness and commit iniquity, and I lay a stumbling block before them, they shall die; because you have not warned them, they shall die for their sin, and their righteous deeds that they have done shall not be remembered; but their blood I will require at your hand (Ezek 3:17-20).

Hence the prophets have to proclaim repeatedly *šûb*, "repent," "return" (see, e.g., Ezek 14:6; 18:30). This call to repent included a call to amend one's ways (Jer 26:13).

From what should Israel repent? All of the books of the Latter Prophets mention the transgressions of Israel and Judah. The two kingdoms are guilty of excessive land appropriation (Isa 5:8), the perversion of justice (Isa 5:20), self-centeredness (Isa 58:3a), oppression of laborers (Isa 58:3b), infidelity and disloyalty (Hos 4:1), swearing, lying, murder, stealing, adultery (Hos 4:2), false prophecy (Mic 3:3-5), political and religious depravity and arrogance (Mic 3:9-11), social injustices of every sort (Amos 8:4-6), idolatry (Mic 1:7; Ezek 6:4, etc.), apostasy (Jer 2:19), among other transgressions. A people guilty of having broken covenant relationship, they have refused to turn back to God (Jer 5:1; Isa 9:13) despite the prophets' preaching and pleas.

The texts of the Latter Prophets identify the root of such transgressions, namely, a false, devious, perverse, stubborn, rebellious, and proud heart (see, e.g., Hos 10:2; 13:6; Jer 5:23; 17:9; 49:16; Ezek 28:7; Obad 1:3). Israel has taken its idols into its heart (Ezek 14:4). Thus the people's hearts have not remained one with the heart of their God; they have fallen out of covenant relationship with their God and consequently, right relationship with all other people as well. Although they fast and offer sacrifices (Isa 1:12-15), such acts of atonement are rendered unacceptable to their God who asks for acts of justice and righteousness (Isa 1:12-15; 58:6-14), who desires "steadfast love and not sacrifices, the knowledge of God rather than burnt offerings" (Hos 6:6).

The texts of the Latter Prophets portray God continuing to desire a mutual relationship based on both parties' returning to each other, despite infidelities on the people's part from which they are also encouraged to return:

> Return to me, says the LORD of hosts, and I will return to you, says the LORD of hosts. Do not be like your ancestors, to whom the former prophets proclaimed, "Thus says the LORD of hosts, Return from your evil ways and from your evil deeds." (Zech 1:3; see also Jer 15:19; cf. Mal 3:7)

The call and desire for a rekindling of a relationship with God extends to both the wicked and the righteous, with the caveat that repentance brings with it the promise of continued life. If, however, the people do not turn from their transgressions there will be serious repercussions, which the biblical text ascribes to God and God's ways (see, e.g., Ezek 18:21-24; cf. 33:11-15).

### c. "Turn Back," "Return," "Repent": The Prophets' Call to Repentance

As the people of Israel and Judah totter between transgression and repentance, between peril and promise, their fragile state makes their repentance and return to God ever more tenuous. Given the state of the people and the condition of their hearts, the call to repentance becomes ever more poignant on the part of the prophets, especially on the part of Hosea and Jeremiah.

With robust energy and graphic imagery Hosea declares to the people of Israel and Judah their transgressions and the painful consequences that are about to befall this apostate, idolatrous people who are guilty of wickedness and monstrous crimes (Hos 5:1–7:16). The prophet's message can be subdivided into three units that present readers with a blistering picture of the kingdoms' depravity (5:1-7; 5:8-15; 6:4–7:16). Israel's and Judah's religious and political leaders are profaned; the people have played the whore and are defiled (5:1-15). The spirit of whoredom within this proud and guilty people prevents them from returning to their God (5:4). The people stand accused of apostasy, idolatry, and wickedness—they rob, murder, and deal falsely with their own, among other crimes (6:4–7:16).[1] In the midst of the prophet's scathing divine message comes a divine word of encouragement and assurance. Hosea calls the people to "return" (6:1-3).

As a literary art form Hos 6:1-3 is a song of penitence that includes a double summons. Here God, speaking through the prophet, quotes what the people will say when calamity befalls them. As the text shows, this call to repentance will go forth from some Israelites only after they have experienced divine wrath (Hos 5:8-15). Hence these verses foreshadow what Israel will do, and what God will do for Israel.

Verse 1a begins with an imperative, "come," followed by a cohortative, "let us return to the LORD." These two phrases are followed by four successive statements of assurance. God will heal, bind up, revive, and raise up. Verse 3 begins with a double cohortative: "Let us know," and "Let us press on to the LORD." Following these two cohortatives is a double statement of confidence in God, whose appearance will be "as sure as the dawn," and who will come to them "like the showers, like the spring rains that water the earth" (v. 3aa-bb). In the context of Hos 5:1-15 and Hos 6:4–7:16, Hos 6:1-3 responds to the former and sets the tone for the latter.[2] The three verses offer a message that stands in

---

[1] For an extensive treatment of Hos 5:1–7:16, and especially for a comprehensive outline and discussion of Israel's and Judah's transgressions, see Francis I. Andersen and David Noel Freedman, *Hosea*, AB 24 (New York: Doubleday, 1980) 380–480.

[2] Bruce Birch, *Hosea, Joel, and Amos*, WC (Louisville: Westminster John Knox, 1997) 67, asserts that the voices in vv. 1-3 seem to be either those of the people or of unidentified speakers. He then proceeds to outline two possibilities for understanding Hos 6:1-3. On the one hand, the double summons may be a report by Hosea that sheds light on the people's response to the prophet's perishing and the catastrophic events the people have already endured. On the other hand, the penitential song could be a parody of the people's response that serves to shed light on the sentiments of the following verses that depict God's frustration with the people's impenitence. In the context of Hos 5:8-15 and Hos 6:4–7:10, Birch's two suggestions seem possible, but with closer attention

stark contrast to what has been heard in Hos 5:1-15 and 6:4-16. At the heart of the exposition of sin is a call, a plea to repent that includes becoming reacquainted with God: "Come, let us return to the LORD . . ." (Hos 6:1), "Let us know, let us press on to know the LORD . . ." (Hos 6:3; cf. 6:6).[3]

The call to return to God amid one's sinfulness continues in Hos 12:2-5. Here the prophet outlines Israel's duplicity by calling to mind Jacob's story. The prophet's final suggestion to Judah, against whom God has an indictment, is to return to God, hold fast to love and justice, and wait continually for God (v. 6). Hence the prophet encourages the people to continue in relationship with their God despite their sinful state. The act of waiting continually for God suggests that God will indeed remain in relationship with the people as well, which points up God's fidelity to covenant relationship despite the people's wayward state.

For a third time in the book of Hosea the prophet calls the people to repentance as heard in Hos 14:1-3. Here the prophet urges the people of Israel to return to the Lord their God (v. 1a). He also points out to them that they have stumbled because of their own iniquity (v. 1b). In vv. 2-3

---

to detail one can determine the speaker and function of Hos 6:1-3, as I have already suggested.

[3] For further discussion on Hos 6:1-6 and the theme of repentance see Thomas G. Smothers, "Preaching and Praying Repentance in Hosea," *RevExp* 90 (1993) 239–46, especially 243–44. Smothers views Hos 6:1-3 as a sincere call to repentance and a statement of confidence in God's ability to heal and restore the people of Israel and Judah. In the context of Hos 6:1-6, however, Smothers argues that the expression of repentance is unacceptable because it lacks a confession of sin. Smothers' contention is similar in vein to Mark J. Boda's argument that essential to the prayer of penitence "is the admission of the sins of the community both past and present (Ezra 9:6-7, 10, 13-15; Neh 1:6-8; 9:33-35, 37; Dan 9:5-11, 13-16, 18)." (See Boda, "The Priceless Gain of Penitence: From Communal Lament to Penitential Prayer in the 'Exilic' Liturgy of Israel," *HBT* 25 [2003] 51–75.) Smothers argues further that "repentance, to be genuine, had to be lived consistently, not just stated at the sanctuary" ("Preaching and Praying Repentance," 244). While I agree with Smothers and Boda, I would suggest that a return to "knowing the Lord" is the first step toward confession of sin that can lead to conversion and the transformation of one's life, with repentance, forgiveness, and reconciliation at the heart of transformation (Hos 6:6; cf. Jer 31:34; Isa 1:2-4; 5:4; 8:2). See also the article by Jeremiah Unterman, "Repentance and Redemption in Hosea," *SBLSP* 21 (1982) 541–50, and Michael L. Barré, "Hearts, Beds, and Repentance in Psalm 4,5 and Hosea 7,14," *Bib* 76/1 (1995) 53–62.

the prophet urges the people to acknowledge their sin and repent of their ways.[4] Then God will heal the people and love them freely (Hos 14:4-7).[5] Hence God's compassion seems to be contingent on the people's returning to their God and on their repentance. But is it?[6]

The call to repentance is also part of the fabric of several other texts of the Latter Prophets.[7] In some instances it is complemented by the prophet's encouragement to make lamentation that would take the form of various penitential exercises such as the donning of sackcloth.[8] This call to repentance and to outward penitential expressions of mourning and atonement extended to the nations as well (see, e.g., Ezek 27:1-36, especially v. 30). Amid all the calls to repentance found in the Latter Prophets, however, perhaps the most poignant one is heard in Jer 3:6–4:2.[9]

---

[4] In his article on repentance in Hosea ("Preaching and Praying Repentance in Hosea"), Smothers succinctly outlines what Israel must do: "Israel was to acknowledge her guilt in three areas: her dependence on foreign alliances which provided the potential for religious syncretism, her trust in military might to provide security, and her idolatry" (p. 244). These three sins serve as umbrellas for all the other transgressions of which the people were guilty.

[5] See, e.g., Jer 4:1. Smothers (ibid.) rightly points out that Hos 14:1-3 stands in contrast to Hos 6:1-3 insofar as the former passage emphasizes the confession of guilt whereas the latter does not.

[6] In his discussion on "The Theological Significance of the Root *SWB* in Jeremiah" (*AUSS* 39/2 [2001] 223–32), George Ossom-Batsa makes this point about the invitation to return in Jer 2:1–4:2: "The invitation to return in these chapters is not in the physical sense of motion, but concerns an interior change initiated by the grace of God through [God's] potential forgiveness. This leads to true confession of sin and actual divine forgiveness. In consequence, the covenantal relationship is reestablished" (p. 230). Ossom-Batsa's point about the Jeremiah material has implications for the theme of divine healing and repentance in the book of Hosea. I would argue that even though the people's return to their God and their repentance are essential to the restoration and renewal of their relationship with their God, this restoration and renewal does not begin through the people's initiative; rather, it begins with divine initiative—with God's grace that invites one's heart to a change, to a conversion of ways and manners. In this regard this gift of divine initiative and divine grace are themselves expressions of divine compassion that is freely extended.

[7] See, e.g., Isa 31:6; 55:7; Jer 3:6–4:18; 35:15; Ezek 18:30; Joel 2:12-14, etc.

[8] See, e.g., Isa 32:11; Jer 6:26.

[9] In his commentary on Jeremiah (*A Commentary on Jeremiah: Exile and Homecoming* [Grand Rapids: Eerdmans, 1998] 41), Walter Brueggemann points out the three

Spoken by God through the prophet, this call to repentance can be divided into eight units (vv. 6-10, 11-14, 15-18, 19-20, 21, 22-23, 24-25; 4:1-2). As a whole, the passage sheds light on several points: (1) the Judahites' sinfulness, which is worse than the Israelites' sinfulness (vv. 6-11); (2) God's anger, which is passing and not a lasting emotion (vv. 11-12); (3) the need for the people to acknowledge their guilt and sin, especially their hardness of heart toward their God and divine instruction (v. 13); and (4) the overarching divine compassion of God, who will intercede on Judah's behalf (vv. 15-16). Judah will be restored to God and to the land as a result of God's intercession (vv. 17-18). Even though God's people have been ruthless, faithless, and stubborn of heart, their lives remain "graced." They live in the midst of divine promise of redemption, restoration, and renewal, not contingent upon their repentance but as a result of God's enduring compassion and fidelity to covenant relationship.[10] This theme of enduring divine compassion and fidelity to covenant relationship continues through the texts of the Latter Prophets and serves as a complementary theme to repentance. The Judahites are called three times to return to God (vv. 12, 14, 22), and then are given a divine promise that is contingent upon their return (Jer 4:1). As a whole community, however, the people do not return to their God. Their return is only wishful thinking on God's part (vv. 22b-23), and their admission of guilt remains but a rumination in God's heart (vv. 24-25).[11] History bears out that even when God does intercede as promised in vv. 15-18,

---

layers of this text that offer a "sequenced reflection on Judah and Jerusalem." The three layers reflect Judah and Jerusalem addressed as (1) a "community of faith," (2) a community "more fickle than the north," and (3) a "restored community." Brueggemann's observation of the three layers of text "as a sequenced reflection on Judah and Jerusalem" allows one to see the movement of the theme of repentance within the text of Jeremiah which, I would argue, mirrors the movement of the dynamic relationship that exists between God and God's people.

[10] Both themes culminate in the New Testament, specifically through Jesus, and continue to come to deeper fulfillment in the life of the Christian community and other believers down through the ages.

[11] For a detailed exegetical study of Jer 3:6–4:2 that gives attention to the text's theological dimensions, see Ossom-Batsa, "The Theological Significance of the Root *SWB* in Jeremiah," as well as Victor J. Eldridge, "Jeremiah, Prophet of Judgment," *RevExp* 78 (1981) 319–30, especially 327–28, and Robert M. Paterson, "Repentance or Judgment: The Construction and Purpose of Jeremiah 2–6," *ExpTim* 96 (1985) 199–203. For additional reading on the theme of penitential prayer in the book of Jeremiah as it relates to the theme of lament see also Mark J. Boda,

full reconciliation to God and the transformation of the human community into God, along with all creation, is an ongoing and evolutionary process that has begun but has yet to reach its fulfillment.

### d. A Divine "Reaction" to Israel's Impenitence

The texts of the Latter Prophets show that because neither Israel nor Judah repented of their transgressions, both kingdoms were devastated, the Temple was destroyed, and the kingdoms' peoples were either deported or exiled. From within the texts of the Latter Prophets a vivid picture emerges of how God was envisioned to have reacted against the people's impenitence despite repeated efforts of the prophets to get the people to "turn." One can glean from the writings of the prophets a general impression of God's reaction to Israel's and Judah's sad state.

First, because of the people's impenitence God threatens to be a lion to Ephraim and Judah. God will "tear" and go away. God will return to God's own place until the people acknowledge their guilt, seek God's face, and beg God's favor (see, e.g., Hos 5:14). God will distance God's self from Israel. Second, God threatens to turn the people back on the way they came, namely, Israel shall return to Egypt, and Assyria will be Israel's king (Isa 37:29; Hos 11:5). Third, God threatens to create a day of lamentation among the Israelite people. Their feasts will be turned into mourning, their songs into lamentations. Sackcloth will be on all loins, and baldness on every head (Amos 8:10). Furthermore, because of the threat of the disaster that God promises to bring upon the people, the people themselves will go into mourning (Ezek 7:7-27, especially v. 18). To be noted is that the foreign nations are also encouraged to lament for their own deeds as well (Jer 49:1-6). Finally, with disaster imminent, Israel is encouraged to put on sackcloth, to lament and wail (Jer 5:8; cf. Jer 18:11). The people are warned further that God's anger will not be turned back (Jer 4:28; Ezek 24:14).

Thus God threatens to act violently toward the people, to respond coldheartedly to them by means of distancing God's self from them, and to change their jovial, assured spirit into gloom and fear. The texts of the Latter Prophets also attest to the weariness of God and the frustration of the prophets who repeatedly have tried to persuade the people to turn back, to repent.

---

"From Complaint to Contrition: Peering through the Liturgical Window of Jer 14, 1–15,4," *ZAW* 113/2 (2001) 186–97.

### (1) Divine and Human Response to Israel's Impenitence

Two texts in particular, Jer 15:5-9 and Jer 18:19-23, provide readers with an insight into the toll Israel's and Judah's impenitence took on both God and the prophets who preached God's word and acted on God's behalf. In Jer 15:5-9 the prophet serves as God's spokesperson to deliver a message that captures not only the terrible fate of Jerusalem but also the sentiments of God's heart. The poem opens with a series of three rhetorical questions that foreshadow the dire state in which Jerusalem is soon to find itself. The vocative "O Jerusalem" adds a despairing tone to an already bleak picture, and the reference to Jerusalem is a collective personification of the people in the capital city, a personification that extends to the entire populace of Judah. No one will pity, console, or inquire about the well-being of Jerusalem, of the Judahites (v. 5). In v. 6a God makes a direct accusation against Jerusalem—against the people of the land: "You have rejected me . . . you are going backward." Rejection of God has led to Jerusalem's worsening ethical condition. Jerusalem's lamentable state is ironic since it is God's holy city and home of the Temple, wherein lies the ark of the covenant and the Torah. The remaining verses describe the ravages of war and exile encapsulated in metaphorical language that refers to harvesting and the desperate conditions of various women, namely, widows and mothers who symbolize Jerusalem. The verse of greatest import in Jer 15:5-9 is v. 6b, where God confronts the people directly with the forthright statement: "I am weary of relenting." The people's impenitence has indeed tried God's patience.

Similarly, in Jer 18:9-23 the text portrays the prophet crying out to God from a desperate state. In response to his life being threatened by his enemies—the people he has been trying to turn from their transgressions—the prophet prays in anguish to God. Frustrated Jeremiah does not want God to forgive the people's iniquity (Jer 18:23). He has reached his limit of patience with stubborn-hearted people who now turn on him. In sum, the texts of Jer 15:5-9 and Jer 18:19-23 present readers with a picture of a God and a Jeremiah who have become wearied by the people's impenitence. One thing remains for the people to do, and that is to return to God with a penitent heart and an expression of remorse that acknowledges their sin, their guiltiness. Earlier texts show that a penitent heart evokes divine compassion (see 2 Kgs 22:19; cf. 2 Chr 34:27).

Elsewhere in the Latter Prophets one sees that a penitent heart, coupled with an expression of guilt and remorse, can, according to the biblical text, effect a change in God as the prophet Jonah describes so well in relation to the conversion of Nineveh (Jonah 3).[12] As the Ninevites turn from their evil ways, so God turns toward them favorably by turning away from the divine plan of calamity being concocted for them.[13]

Although weary, neither God nor the prophet forsakes the people. Just as God remains faithful to covenant love, so the prophet remains faithful to the people and faithful to God and God's mission of reconciliation. The prophet becomes the people's hope insofar as he embodies God's writhing heart and God's faithful love. In Mic 7:8-10 the prophet relates the indignation that must be born because of the people's refusal to repent, but here he also expresses his confidence in his God, the God he believes will vindicate him and his people. In Isa 63:15–64:12 the prophet pleads with God for God to turn back from doing all the impending divine disasters that are about to befall the people. What the people cannot admit to, the prophet confesses, and thus the prophet becomes both intercessor for and servant of the people, a preacher of a

---

[12] In his article on "'The Repentance of God' In the Books of Samuel, Jeremiah, and Jonah," *HBT* 16 (1994) 156–75, John T. Willis addresses the Bible's use of metaphorical and anthropomorphic language in relation to God. He deals with the Bible's affirmation of whether or not God can grieve, repent, and even have a change of heart and mind. He lays out clearly the function of anthropomorphic language as it is used in the Bible, and argues that such language is humanity's attempt to make known who God is and how God responds and reacts to the human condition. While a four-point objection can be made against God's ability to "repent," an argument that Willis outlines in his article, he concludes that "the biblical writers saw no conflict between God's living in an eternal state of happiness and his grieving over and repenting of things he had done or announcements of doom he had proclaimed" (pp. 170–71). In essence, then, according to the biblical text and tradition there can be a change of mind and heart on the part of God, but this "change" needs to be understood in the context of the Bible's use of anthropomorphic language, which cannot be used to make definitive claims about the nature of God.

[13] The repentance of the king of Nineveh, the Ninevites, and God parallels Jer 26:16-19, where Hezekiah repents after hearing Micah preach, and where God repents of the evil divinely planned against Hezekiah and Jerusalem. For further discussion on repentance in the book of Jonah see Beate Ego, "The Repentance of Nineveh in the Story of Jonah and Nahum's Prophecy of the City's Destruction—A Coherent Reading of the Book of the Twelve as Reflected in the Aggada," in Paul L. Redditt and Aaron Schart, eds., *Thematic Threads in the Book of the Twelve* (New York: de Gruyter, 2003), and Sandor Goodhart, "Prophecy, Sacrifice and Repentance in the Story of Jonah," *Semeia* 33 (1985) 43–63.

word that becomes for the people a source of grace despite their rejection of it.

### (2) *The Dawn of "Justice":*
### *A Portrait of Divine Wrath and Compassion*

Despite all the prophets' preaching, exhorting, encouraging, and acknowledgment of the people's transgressions and guilt, God's people of Israel and Judah will be made to suffer for their apostasy, idolatry, and rampant social injustices, all indicative of infidelity to covenant relationship. Inevitable historical events come to pass and are attributed to the "ways of God" by people of faith. Not only are the kingdoms of Israel and Judah destroyed, but also the power of many of the other nations' rulers (see, e.g., Isa 26:1-21; Isa 29:4). Such a time of devastation becomes the impetus for lamentation. The prophet wails over daughter Zion (see Lamentations 2–4), and grieves over the ill-fortune of other nations as well: "My heart cries out for Moab" (Isa 15:5a; see also Ezek 27:30; 28:18). The people will also lament (see, e.g., Isa 3:24; Jer 48:37; Amos 8:10). To be noted, however, is the fact that nowhere in the course of the people's suffering do they as a community or nation confess to their sin, nor is there evidence of a repentance that speaks of change of heart evidenced by their turning from their wicked ways.[14] Surprisingly, ill-fortune brings

---

[14] Jeremiah 14:12 makes reference to the people's fasting, crying, and sacrifices of burnt offerings and grain offerings in response to impending divine judgments. Although these expressions may be signs of penitence and lament, they do not seem to indicate repentance in the sense that the people have "turned away from" their wicked deeds. Mark J. Boda, in his examination of Jer 14:1–15:4, makes convincing connections between Jer 14:19-21 and Leviticus 26. He concludes that Jer 14:19-21 is drawing on Leviticus 26, and thus "the conspicuous correspondences between Lev 26 and Jer 14:19-21 suggest that prior to the fall of Jerusalem, Jeremiah was cognizant of a confession of sin that reflected the agenda set out in Lev 26" (see Boda, "From Complaint to Contrition," 196). In Jer 14:20 a clear admission of the people's sin and guilt is expressed but it is made by the prophet on behalf of the people. It is not made by the people themselves. The speaker of the poem (Jer 14:19-22) is the prophet; cf. Walter Brueggemann, *A Commentary on Jeremiah* (Grand Rapids: Eerdmans, 1998) 138–39, and J. A. Thompson, *The Book of Jeremiah* (Grand Rapids: Eerdmans, 1980) 386, *contra* Louis Stulman, *Jeremiah*, AOTC (Nashville: Abingdon, 2005) 144, who asserts that "the community cries out in sorrow, acknowledges its wrongdoing and pleads for God's mercy and help (14:19-22)." Thus while Jeremiah may be cognizant of a confession of sin, as Boda argues, the biblical text itself has Jeremiah confessing

pain and suffering and lamentation, but not an expression of repentance, though the call to repentance and prayer remains constant on the part of the prophets (Joel 1:8–2:17). In Jer 31:15-22, however, a different perspective is offered. In Jer 31:15 it is not the prophet who expresses repentance on behalf of the community; rather, it is Mother Rachel who is lamenting and weeping bitterly, as the prophet makes known to his listeners when he delivers the message he received from God. Rachel's lamentation and bitter weeping evokes a response from God, who invites her to cease crying (cf. Isaiah 25) because her children will indeed come home. The divine response offers a word of hope in the midst of inconsolable agony and grief (Jer 31:16-17). Verses 18-19 continue God's response to Mother Rachel, in which God quotes one of Rachel's forlorn children, Ephraim. The words of the child express sorrow, regret, and repentance. The contrite one yearns to return to God. In v. 20 God offers a further response that begins with two questions highlighting the steadfast love God has toward Ephraim. The key phrase in this verse is at 20b: "As often as I speak against him, I still remember him." To be remembered by God is to be graced by God (see, e.g., Gen 8:1; Num 10:9; Ps 136:23). The remainder of v. 20 expresses God's heartfelt sentiments. God is deeply moved on behalf of Ephraim and will have mercy on him. In the final two verses of the poem the focus shifts from Mother Rachel and Ephraim to Israel, who is invited to return, to set out for home. The final metaphor that speaks of a woman encompassing a man symbolizes the new relationship the people and God will enjoy at God's initiative, for God has "created a new thing on the earth" (vv. 21-22).[15]

Looking at Jer 31:15-22 in the context of the Latter Prophets as a whole, one sees that God's mercy—God's compassion—blossoms into promise: the people will be returned to the land; mourning will be turned into singing (Isa 51:11); God will return to Zion (Isa 52:7-10); and nations will no longer be a threat to Israel (Isa 49:22-23). God's heart has recoiled; God's compassion has grown warm and tender; God promises not to come in "wrath" again (Hos 11:8-9). Jubilation resounds (Isa 52:2; 61:4; Zeph 3:14), and the promise of restoration goes forth: Jerusalem shall

---

on behalf of the people and not the people themselves confessing and acknowledging their sinfulness.

[15] For an insightful discussion of the newness, the hope, and the transformation that await Israel and that these verses suggest, see Walter Brueggemann, *A Commentary on Jeremiah: Exile and Homecoming* (Grand Rapids: Eerdmans, 1998) 288.

never be uprooted or overthrown again (Jer 31:38-40). Hence repentance provides fertile ground for not only restoration but also transformation, and readers see in Jer 31:15-22 the relationship between repentance and restoration. As the people repent, so they are restored to their God, and as they are restored to their God and their God to them, so they are restored to the land.

### e. Conclusion: Moving from Repentance and Restoration to Transformation

As has been demonstrated, the texts of the Latter Prophets have embedded within them overtures to the theme of repentance. Throughout the discussion thus far there has been allusion to the importance of Israel's heart. Israel's stubbornness of heart kept the people from repenting and changing their ways, and because of such stubbornness of heart the people had to endure great pain and suffering. The prophets as characters within the texts of the Latter Prophets show readers that even though prophets acted and interceded on the people's behalf, their preaching, their intercession, their prayers and acts of penitence could not effect a total and lasting change within their respective communities. While new expressions of righteousness did take root, injustice and infidelity continued to flourish alongside justice, despite all the prophets' efforts. Although some of the people of the prophets' day may have turned back to God, many probably did not, and thus the holy preaching of the prophets remained constant.

One cannot understand "repentance" in the Latter Prophets aside from the theme of divine promise. Central to the texts of the Latter Prophets are two divine promises that, as we have seen in the life of the Jewish and Christian communities, have already come to fulfillment, and yet the promises have not reached their total fulfillment. Thus they remain eschatological. The first divine promise, heard in Ezek 11:14-20, speaks of a new heart.[16] This is complemented by a second promise, a new covenant, implied in Ezek 11:20 but explicit in Jer 31:31-34:

> The days are surely coming, says the LORD, when I will make a new covenant with the house of Israel and the house of Judah. It will not be like the covenant that I made with their ancestors when I took them by the hand to bring them out of the land of Egypt—a covenant

---

[16] Cf. Ezek 36:11-32.

that they broke, though I was their husband, says the LORD. But this is the covenant that I will make with the house of Israel after those days, says the LORD: I will put my law within them, and I will write it on their hearts; and I will be their God, and they shall be my people. No longer shall they teach one another, or say to each other, "Know the LORD," for they shall all know me, from the least of them to the greatest, says the LORD; for I will forgive their iniquity, and remember their sin no more.

A new heart and spirit and a new covenant go hand in hand, and the law that will be written on the people's hearts will be none other than the one proclaimed in Deut 6:4, a law elucidated further in Deut 10:12. A similar vision was told to the prophet Micah, which he proclaimed to his community (Mic 6:6-8), which Third Isaiah later fleshed out (Isa 58:6-14), and which Jesus in the New Testament clarified (Matt 22:34-40). With the arrival of Jesus the promise and vision come to deeper fulfillment. Both the life and work of Jesus mirrored the heart of God—a heart of loving, nonviolent justice. Jesus' final word to his oppressors and the fickle crowd gathered around him at the time of his death was compassion: "Forgive them . . ." (Luke 23:34). What the prophets herald, Jesus lived. Jesus was the heart of God's heart and God's prophet *par excellence*.

Thus where Amos, Hosea, Micah, Ezekiel, Jeremiah, Zephaniah, Malachi, and others left off, John the Baptist and Jesus continue (see Matt 3:2; 4:17, respectively), and where John and Jesus left off, the apostles continue (see Acts 2:38) down through the ages and into present times. What the Latter Prophets have given to readers today is a picture of God's fidelity in the midst of the human condition, revealing to communities of believers the reality that in the midst of depravity, hope for salvation and redemption remains alive as a call and a promise that can be hastened through a people's repentance but is not necessarily contingent upon their repentance, for indeed, God's fidelity to covenant relationship is completely steadfast, and God's sustaining compassion is a gift free of human initiative or endeavors.

God's people have already received the gift of the new covenant. The question becomes: how deeply do God's people wish to enter into this new covenant? To what extent are God's people willing to experience an exchange of hearts and thus a change of heart? In light of the texts of the Latter Prophets, what remains to be done now is for people to repent of the myriad injustices that tear negatively at the web of life today. And when they cannot repent or refuse to repent, the good news is that there will always be prophets like those of Old and New Testament times who, with transformed hearts, become the word of God—word made flesh—as a sign of God's fidelity to the human condition that is already being transformed by and through God's enduring and grace-filled unconditional love.

## 2. Implications

The texts of the Latter Prophets offer us three key implications for a Christian theology of penitence today. First, repentance is an invitation to grace and to a renewal and deepening of covenant relationship so the "the good life" and the full flourishing of justice and peace can be enjoyed by all creation (cf. Lev 26:8-55). Second, for the one guilty of sin and injustice, external acts of penitence, i.e., fasting, weeping, recitation of prayers, are signs of contrition and sorrow, but they may have little to do with "repentance" that calls for a change of heart made manifest by a change in one's behavior and attitudes. Such a change can be recognized by a deepening of relationship with God, self, neighbor, and all creation, and by acts of justice, righteousness, and loving kindness toward God, self, neighbor, and all creation. Finally, the prophetic call to authentic repentance remains central not only to the prophetic vocation today but also to the prophetic mission activity of today's believing communities, who are called to be God's transformative presence in our world so that the eschatological reign of God can become more fully realized as the vision of the promised new heavens and a new earth continues to unfold in our midst.

## 3. Further Reading

Boda, Mark J. "From Complaint to Contrition: Peering through the Liturgical Window of Jer 14,1–15,4," *ZAW* 113/2 (2001) 186–97.

Ego, Beate. "The Repentance of Nineveh in the Story of Jonah and Nahum's Prophecy of the City's Destruction—A Coherent Reading of the Book of the Twelve as Reflected in the Aggada." In Paul L. Redditt and Aaron Schart, eds., *Thematic Threads in the Book of the Twelve*. New York: de Gruyter, 2003, 155–64.

Eldridge, Victor J. "Jeremiah, Prophet of Judgment," *RevExp* 78 (1981) 319–30.

Fretheim, Terence E. "The Repentance of God: A Study of Jeremiah 18:7-10," *HAR* 11 (1987) 81–92.

Goodhart, Sandor. "Prophecy, Sacrifice and Repentance in the Story of Jonah," *Semeia* 33 (1985) 43–63.

Lind, Millard C. "Hosea 5:8–6:6," *Int* 38 (1984) 398–403.

Ossom-Batsa, George. "The Theological Significance of the Root *SWB* in Jeremiah," *AUSS* 39/2 (2001) 223–32.

Paterson, Robert M. "Repentance or Judgment: The Construction and Purpose of Jeremiah 2–6," *ExpTim* 96 (1985) 199–203.

Smothers, Thomas G. "Preaching and Praying Repentance in Hosea," *RevExp* 90 (1993) 239–46.

Unterman, Jeremiah. "Repentance and Redemption in Hosea," *SBLSP* 21 (1982) 541–50.

Willis, John T. "The 'Repentance' of God in the Books of Samuel, Jeremiah, and Jonah," *HBT* 16 (1994) 156–75.

# 4. Hermeneutical Reflection

The texts of the Latter Prophets present us with some notion of and need for repentance, and being prophetic, these texts continue to call communities of believers today to repentance. With all of our advancement in technology, medicine, science, education, global politics, and acceptance of religious, cultural, and social pluralism and diversity, we have yet to understand fully the timeless message of Micah:

> He has told you, O mortal, what is good;
>> and what does the LORD require of you
> but to do justice, and to love kindness,
>> and to walk humbly with your God. (Mic 6:8)

If all people understood this simple poem, then we as communities of believers would be living differently in the midst of human and non-human biodiverse communities on a planet where sustainability and survival hang in the balance. Perhaps the most important phrase in Micah's poem is the last line that calls for a humble walk with God. This walk can lead to knowledge of God's heart wherein lies steadfast, compassionate, redemptive, and transformative love (Jer 31:3). This divine love, whether recognized or not, is what enables one to act justly and love tenderly not only toward other human beings but also toward all creation, for creation is an expression of God's holiness, goodness, beauty, mystery, and diversity. Creation—with humankind as part of the bigger picture—is the dwelling place of God, as Terence Fretheim has expressed so eloquently:

> [God's] place is in the world, and we might add, only in the world. Where there is world there is God; where there is God there is world. There is no God "left over" in some sphere which is other than world. God, who is other than world, has wholly immersed [God's self] in the world (cf. Jer. 23:24). Thus, whatever may have been the case before the creation of the heavens and the earth, since the creation God has taken up residence within that creation, and thus works from within the world, and not on the world from without.[17]

With great wisdom, Jesus Ben Sirach long ago proclaimed:

> The compassion of human beings is for their neighbors,
>> but the compassion of the Lord is for every living thing.
>> (Sir 18:13)

This view of creation as God's self-expression, reflection, and dwelling place is known as "sacramentality." God has entered into covenant with humankind—and with all creation (Gen 9:1-17; cf. Hos 2:16-23; Jer 31:31-34). This relationship continues to exist between God, humanity, and all creation today, and humanity is called to be faithful to it.

Throughout all of the writings of the Latter Prophets we have seen that when the people gave their hearts to other gods they became estranged from their God (Ezek 14:4-5) and encountered all sorts of painful repercussions and consequences, i.e., invasions, famines, droughts, that were, according to the Old Testament writers' understanding of God, delivered upon them by the hand of a jealous God (Deut 5:9; Ezek 5:13) whom the people had forsaken (Jer 19:4), along with the covenant relationship. The people's actions had caused them to be alienated from God and God's ways, and consequently from one another and the land. Forsaken and abandoned by a people loved so deeply, God also experienced pain that caused God to hide God's face (Mic 3:4). Seeing their painful, pitiful state, God's grace-filled plea to "return" and "repent" goes forth from the mouths of the prophets to a faithless people (Jer 3:12; Joel 2:12-13). Not until the people experience total loss and devastation do they weep and cry out in pain to their God. True repentance has yet to take place.

---

[17] Terence Fretheim, *The Suffering of God*, OBT (Philadelphia: Fortress Press, 1984) 35.

In her book *Sacred Longings: The Ecological Spirit and Global Culture*,[18] Mary C. Grey focuses on the heart and calls people today to have a "recovery of heart." In the context of the Latter Prophets, I would suggest that before we can return to God with our hearts we need to recover our own hearts that have been numbed, often deeply wounded, and hardened by a world of ever-increasing violence that far exceeds the violence of ages past that was uncovered by the prophets. Once that heart is recovered, it needs to be given to God who promises and who will, in turn, give us a new heart and a new spirit (Ezek 11:19-20), capable of covenant relationship with God and with all creation. Anthropocentric in nature, the biblical text reveals violence done to human beings by other human beings. Today violence has become cosmological. All the earth and its communities of life are suffering, in large degree because of varying forms of injustice on the part of some within the human community. New forms of idolatry and apostasy have sprung up and have taken root in some hearts, alienating humanity from itself, from the rest of creation, and from God. The cry of the Latter Prophets, "Turn back, O people," remains as prophetic today as it was in ancient days. Perhaps the way back to and recovery of our heart as a human community will happen only through and after much personal, communal, and global suffering, an experience that can be the greatest teacher of compassion and can lead us into the way of repentance.

I close with this prayer taken from the UN Environmental Program:

> We have forgotten who we are
>
> We have alienated ourselves from the unfolding cosmos
>
> We have become estranged from the movements of the earth
>
> We have turned our backs on the cycles of life.
>
> We have forgotten who we are.
>
> We have sought our own security
>
> We have exploited simply for our own ends
>
> We have distorted our knowledge
>
> We have abused our power.
>
> We have forgotten who we are.
>
> Now the land is barren

---

[18] Mary C. Grey, *Sacred Longings: The Ecological Spirit and Global Culture* (Minneapolis: Fortress Press, 2004).

And the waters are poisoned and the air is polluted.

We have forgotten who we are.

Now the forests are dying

And the creatures are disappearing

And humans are despairing.

We have forgotten who we are.

We ask forgiveness

We ask for the gift of remembering

We ask for the strength to change.

We have forgotten who we are.[19]

Would that we remember. Would that we repent.

---

[19] See Elizabeth Roberts and Elias Amidon, eds., *Earth Prayers* (San Francisco: HarperSanFrancisco, 1991) 70–71.

Four

# "May Your Eyes Be Open and Your Ears Attentive": A Study of Penance and Penitence in the Writings

*Richard J. Bautch*

## 1. Text

The *kĕtûbîm* (or "Writings") comprise a diverse collection of thirteen biblical books that are largely, although not exclusively, postexilic.[1] The late date of these texts relative to the rest of the canon coincides with the emergence of penitential piety within Second Temple Judaism, and not surprisingly portions of the books in question evince striking elements of penance and penitence. In fact, it is largely on the basis of these books

[1] More generally, the collection has been likened to "the wisdom of the ancients" (Eccl 39:1) as it comprises three lengthy wisdom books (Psalms, Proverbs, and Job), five books grouped in the order of the holidays when they are read aloud in the synagogue (Song of Songs, Ruth, Ecclesiastes, Lamentations, and Esther), and five books that are historical in nature (Daniel, Ezra, Nehemiah, 1 and 2 Chronicles). The order of this group of thirteen books was not fixed in antiquity due to the contested canonicity of Song of Songs, Ruth, Ecclesiastes, Lamentations, and Esther in rabbinic circles. In the Christian canon the Writings do not exist as a distinct collection and are found variously in the Old Testament.

that a significant body of scholarship on exilic and postexilic penitential prayers has appeared over the last decade.[2] One fruit of this scholarship is the following definition of penitential prayer:

> Penitential prayer is a direct address to God in which an individual, group, or an individual on behalf of a group confesses sins and petitions for forgiveness as an act of repentance.[3]

For the purposes of this essay the foregoing definition of prayer will serve as a heuristic device for exploring the multiple facets of penance and penitence in the Writings. By parsing the definition we find four points for consideration: (1) direct address to God from a penitential stance; (2) confession of sin by a party exercising penitence; (3) the movements of divine forgiveness; (4) theological reflection on the experience of repentance. These four points will now be developed in reference to penitential texts from the Writings. While many of these texts are prayers proper, other genres such as speeches and wisdom texts are represented as well. Discussions of the biblical texts are enhanced with literary-critical and historical-critical observations as well as references to the theological stances found in the Writings.

## a. Direct Address to God from a Penitential Stance

Because the penitential texts in question are inherently theological, they tend to provide an immediate focus on God, especially in the case

---

[2] See Richard J. Bautch, *Developments in Genre Between Postexilic Penitential Prayers and the Psalms of Communal Lament*, SBLAB 7 (Atlanta: Society of Biblical Literature, 2003); Mark J. Boda, *Praying the Tradition: The Origin and Use of Tradition in Nehemiah 9*, BZAW 277 (Berlin and New York: Walter de Gruyter, 1999); Judith H. Newman, *Praying By the Book: The Scripturalization of Prayer in Second Temple Judaism*, SBLEJL 14 (Atlanta: Scholars, 1999); Rodney A. Werline, *Penitential Prayer in Second Temple Judaism: The Development of a Religious Institution*, SBLEJL 13 (Atlanta: Scholars, 1998). These books treat penitential texts in the Writings and as well in the Apocrypha (see especially Newman and Werline) and in the library at Qumran (on the Qumran texts see Daniel K. Falk, *Daily, Sabbath and Festival Prayers in the Dead Sea Scrolls*, STDJ 27 [Leiden, Boston, and Cologne: Brill, 1997]).

[3] An initial definition from Werline is found in his *Penitential Prayer*, 2. He subsequently added the phrase "as an act of repentance" in his "Defining Penitential Prayer" (paper presented at the Annual Meeting of the SBL, Atlanta, 22 November 2003).

of the prayer texts that begin with an address. While some addresses are brief ("O my God," Ezra 9:6), in cases such as Daniel 9:4b the address constitutes a theologoumenon: "O Lord, great and awesome God." The address sketches an omnipotent God who is master of all things, including redemption as it is requested later in the prayer (9:15-19). Curiously, the address in Daniel appears elsewhere in the Old Testament with slight variations (Deut 7:21; Neh 9:32a). In the prayer of Nehemiah 9 the phrasing is different: "Our God—the great and mighty and awesome God." Nehemiah nonetheless underscores divine omnipotence as a prelude to beseeching God's help in hardship (9:32b). It is noteworthy that the authors responsible for these two books in the Writings adopted a conventional address to God and adapted it to their own penitential context. Their adaptations suggest a theology focused on God's exaltation.

The addresses to the Divinity in both Dan 9:4b and Neh 9:32a are linked to God's role in covenant, or God's role in the divine-human relationship. Somewhat paradoxically, the awesome God is complemented by the relational God, who is personified as someone attuned to the chords of penitence. This stance is epitomized in the petition, "May your eyes be open and your ears attentive." This, the title of our essay, quotes not only 2 Chr 6:40 but also the earlier, preexilic prayer in 1 Kings 8 (1 Kgs 8:52) associated with the dedication of the Temple. When the preexilic petition is reiterated in yet another postexilic prayer, Neh 1:6, it is clear that again the authors of the Writings have adopted conventional language and adapted it to their own context of penance and penitence. They have appropriated both divine omnipotence and divine associability. The result is a complex theology whose roots lie in the received (i.e., preexilic) Scriptures of the day. We will elaborate more of this theology in the essay's conclusion.

### b. Confession of Sin by a Penitent

#### (1) Toward a Mature Practice of Penitential Confession

While penance and penitence are conspicuous themes in the prayers of Daniel and Nehemiah, earlier writers are more circumspect in their treatment of such matters. They sketch in outline what Daniel and Nehemiah present in greater detail and punctuate with the confession of sin. Sin, in the precursor texts that are found in the Writings, is one element in a scenario of suffering, but it is rarely identified as the occasion for confession, a development that comes only later in the Writings. For example, Psalm 39 is spoken by someone who, upon becoming gravely ill (39:11) and contemplating death (39:5), offers to God a prayer that is petitionary and penitential inasmuch as it seeks deliverance from sins (39:9). The suffering in question is the result of God's punishing the psalmist's transgressions (39:10). Acknowledging the punishment, the psalmist asks to be heard and helped. Importantly, the psalmist never issues an explicit confession of sin and appears to be more focused on the fleeting nature of human existence (39:5-6). The existential concern is central to the psalm, with the matters of sin and repentance being secondary.

Psalm 79 is also a lament, but it is communal in nature. Invaders have devastated this community, which may be a cipher for Jerusalem after it fell to the Babylonians in 587 B.C.E. (79:1-4, 7, 11). In the invaders' wake the people plead with God and mention their iniquities and sins (79:8-9), although they make no causal connection between their sins and their misfortune. There is no confession of sin proper, and the mention of sin appears designed to elicit God's compassion and pardon. Psalm 79, like Psalm 39 and most of the lament psalms in the Psalter, contains relatively little penitential language and lacks a penitential intent.

An exception is Psalm 51, which is decidedly penitential. Through verbal expression and ritual action the speaker of Psalm 51 is seeking help, specifically cleansing and purification from his transgressions, iniquities, and sins (51:3-4). The misdeeds are mentioned in the context of a confession that appeals to God's mercy (51:3) and acknowledges God's justice (51:6). The confession seeks not only forgiveness, but restoration as well, with the psalmist asking God to create in him a new heart (51:10). The psalm is a classic example of penitential prayer that may well have ushered in the exilic and postexilic emphasis on penance and penitence, if the psalm is dated to the time of Jeremiah and Ezekiel based on common references to a "new heart" (see Jer 31:31-34 and Ezek 36:25-27).

Like Psalm 51, Lamentations 3 is another text in the Writings that serves as an immediate precursor to those espousing a theology of penitence proper. Lamentations 3:40-66 in particular evinces several dynamics of penitence. The speaker, after recounting his suffering (3:1-16) in a startling manner (God has "led and guided" him into pain and loss), affirms hope in God and vows to be patient (3:24-25). In connection with this patient hope, the speaker confesses rebellion and disobedience (3:42) as a justification for the punishment to which he has been subject. Penitence in the poem, however, is not extensive, as the speaker develops a trust in God that leads in turn to his calling forth God's wrath upon his persecutors (3:64-66). Although such a plea for revenge appears routinely in preexilic psalms (58:7-9; 69:23-29) and somewhat less frequently in exilic psalms (79:10), it is virtually unattested in the postexilic period, when the centrality and depth of penitential sorrow in a text preclude talk of vengeance.

### (2) More Highly Developed Confessions of Sin

The confession of sin, a minor convention in the preexilic texts included in the Writings (recall Ps 79:8-9), is greatly expanded and so recast in the postexilic texts. In these prayers the confession of sin is no token expression of emotional distress, as it had been previously. There is, rather, frank reference to human rebellion through the frequent mention of sins, iniquities, and transgressions (using the roots *ḥṭʾ*, *ʿwn*, *pšʿ*, as in Ezra 9:6, 7, 13; Neh 1:6; 9:2, 29, 33, 37; Dan 9:5, 8, 11, 13, 15, 16, 20). In addition to expressing sorrow, the newly elaborated confession of sin provides an explanation for why God seems to take leave of human history. The apparent loss of God is an effect of human sin. As the exile gave impetus to theology generally, so these prayers made sin and grace the defining dimensions of human history; any event may be explained in terms of what sin has wrought.

There are numerous examples of this thoroughgoing confession of sin. Nehemiah 1:5-11 is a brief prayer in which Nehemiah beseeches God for help as he prepares to approach the Persian king, Artaxerxes, on behalf of the postexilic community of Jews in Jerusalem. After invoking God, Nehemiah confesses the sins against God that "we, the people of Israel" have committed (1:6); he adds that "we" have greatly wronged God in not following the "commandments, statutes, and ordinances" given to Moses (1:7). Nehemiah implies that the people are now penitent (1:8) and ready to receive God's vouchsafed assistance in restoring Jerusalem (1:9). The confession of sin and the implication of penitence combine to imbue the prayer with a profound sense of sin and its deleterious consequences.

Later in Nehemiah the author issues a penitential treatise in the form of a prayer. Nehemiah 9:6-37 has two parts, a historical recital (9:6-31) and a prayer proper (9:32-37). The historical recital's primary function is to acknowledge Israelite sin so as to motivate God to act on the Judeans' petition. The prayer proper specifies the petition (9:32a) that God not make light of the Judeans' present travail. The petition is conjoined with a confession of sin and together these form the nucleus of the prayer proper. The confession of sin, 9:33-35, is highly complex as it is built on a reversal of subjects that in turn redefines the binary opposition of wicked and righteous, *rāšāᶜ* and *ṣadîq*, as it is normatively expressed in the Hebrew Scriptures. Specifically, the tone of lament psalms such as Psalms 44 and 74 implies that the people are *righteous* and have not failed God's covenant (44:17-18). In Neh 9:33, however, subjects and predicates have shifted so that the people penitently assert their own wickedness while imputing all justice to God.

The prayer in Ezra 9 also revolves around the confession of sin. When the prayer begins, the speaker is Ezra, but after one verse there is a change from first-person singular to plural. The change in Ezra 9:7 is intended to show that a solidarity of guilt binds together the speaker and all of his contemporaries while it reaches back to their ancestors. The language of sin is highlighted at the prayer's beginning and end (9:6-7, 15) and is in fact distributed copiously throughout the prayer. Ezra 9:6a is an individual confession of sins, followed by 9:6b-7 as a communal confession. In both cases Ezra confesses iniquities and guilt. Ezra 9:10-12 is a specific confession of sins with reference to intermarriage by which the people have forsaken God's commandments. In 9:13 they refer to their evil deeds and great guilt. Ezra 9:15 provides a concluding admission of guilt. Indeed, the confession of sin is a hallmark of this text.

### (3) Confession of Sin with a Cultic Tone

The penitential content of the prayers in Nehemiah 9 and Ezra 9 is amplified by a ritual context. The speaker in Nehemiah 9 fasts, wears sackcloth, and covers his head with dust (Neh 9:1). In Ezra 9, Ezra tears his cloak and mantle, plucks hair from his head and beard, kneels and extends his arms to God (Ezra 9:3, 5). Moreover, some of Ezra's gestures are coordinated with the time of the evening sacrifice. The fact that the biblical authors chose to report these details indicates their importance, and they should not be relegated to a secondary status. They appear to be intrinsic dimensions of the prayer itself, embodied expressions of the penitent's sorrow. This ritual or cultic dimension is especially prominent in the prayer in Daniel 9.

The prayer in Dan 9:4-19 evinces a clear structure that begins with an address. We have noted that Dan 9:4 addresses God as great and awesome, a formula whose fuller form is available in Neh 9:32. There follows a historical recital in Dan 9:5-14, filled with unrelenting self-accusation of the people, who have sinned and transgressed the law given by Moses and the prophets. One verse, 9:11b, is noteworthy: "And the curse and the oath written in the law of Moses, the servant of God, were poured out upon us, because we sinned against him." The expression "the curse and the oath" is comparable to cultic language in Num 5:21, and the admission of the people's sin *(kî ḥāṭānû lô)* is evocative of the rubrics for the sin offering or *ḥaṭṭāʾt* that was offered for unintentional sins (see Lev 4:1–5:13).

In 9:15 a petition begins with the formula "and now" *(wĕʿattāh)*, also found in Ezra 9:10. In what follows the text distinguishes its historical circumstances. There are repeated requests for God to restore the Jerusalem sanctuary, which has been left desolate *(haššāmēm;* 9:17-18). Thus the prayer arises out of a desecration of the Temple, which was in turn part of a larger conquest. One may identify this event both with the Babylonian sacking of Jerusalem in 587 B.C.E. and with the Temple's profanation by Antiochus IV in 168 B.C.E., when he erected in the Temple a statue of a foreign god.[4]

### c. The Movements of Divine Forgiveness

#### (1) A Pattern of Punishment and Mercy?

The biblical authors often correlate the confession of sin to a divine response of forgiveness. Although the Writings provide ample witness to the forgiveness God extends after humans have confessed their sin, for commentators it is nonetheless daunting to speak analytically about divine forgiveness in either quantitative or qualitative terms. As in the previous section, we do well to begin with a precursor text from the Psalter. Psalm 78 contains discrete elements of penitential prayer and communal lament (like the communal laments in the Psalter, Psalm 78 is likely preexilic). This psalm, for example, relates the people's distress when they are separated from God, an alienation understood to be caused by sin (78:17, 32, 40, 56-58). The people do not, however, acknowledge their own sin as it may have helped to cause the alienation. The people in the psalm never actually repent, and it is in this sense that Psalm 78 is a precursor text. Regardless, the human acknowledgment of sin is followed by a divine response. Specifically, there are two recitals of human sinfulness (78:12-37, 40-64), and each is followed by a

---

[4] John J. Collins holds that there is a "typological correspondence" between the Babylonian destruction and that of Antiochus Epiphanes. See his *Daniel: A Commentary on the Book of Daniel,* Hermeneia (Minneapolis: Fortress Press, 1993) 351.

merciful response from God (78:38-39, 65-72). Commentators see in the text a pattern of confession and forgiveness that proceeds as if in poetic stanzas.[5] But what exactly is the nature of this pattern?

Scholars commonly equate the pattern with the Deuteronomistic (Dtr) *topos* of retribution as it has been superimposed on Israelite history. After rebellion, punishment is inevitable, according to this *topos*. Thus the *topos* reports a cycle of sin-punishment-complaint-mercy. The cycle is evident in Psalm 78 and most strikingly in Judg 2:11-23, a Dtr passage that specifies sin as idol worship, punishment as subjugation to the enemy, complaint as groaning about suffering, and mercy as the raising up of a judge as deliverer.[6]

This Deuteronomistic *topos* appears to be operative in several of the penitential texts in the Writings. Its pattern is often observed in Neh 9:6-31, a historiographical passage that presents retribution as a key factor in Israel's mishaps over the centuries. Similarly, the theology found in Judg 2:11-23 is thought to have influenced the historical account in Ezra's penitential prayer (Ezra 9:6-15). Most survivors of the exile at the time of Ezra's mission interpreted history thus: The disasters that have beset Israel are divine punishment for faithlessness to God since "the days of our fathers" (Ezra 9:7). Ezra thus portrays history as a pattern of rebellion and forgiveness, as in Judg 2:11-23, with the Deuteronomic law standing as the fundamental test of Israel's obedience and at the same time a sign of divine promise and instruction.[7]

The author of Chronicles, whose views loom large in the Writings, has long been associated with retributional theology. The consensus view has been that recompense or retribution in Chronicles is subject to an economy whereby God deals with any given party exactly as its

---

[5] "The psalm is poetry designed to be recited or chanted as part of the liturgical agenda of a religious assembly." (James L. Mays, *Psalms,* IBC [Louisville: John Knox, 1994] 255).

[6] That a cyclical view of history typifies the time of the judges was observed by Yehezkel Kaufmann, *History of the Religion of Israel* (New York: Schocken, 1960) 2:363–65. Joseph Blenkinsopp has noted that the Dtr formulation of Judg 2:11-23 is easily distinguished from, for example, the Priestly compendium of misdeeds in Lev 26:3-45. *Ezra-Nehemiah: A Commentary,* OTL (Philadelphia: Westminster, 1988) 306.

[7] Peter R. Ackroyd, *Exile and Restoration: A Study of Hebrew Thought of the Sixth Century B.C.* (Philadelphia: Westminster, 1968) 75–76.

deeds dictate, for weal or for woe.[8] For example, scholars focus on the historical allusions in 2 Chr 6:24, 25, which form a part of Solomon's dedicatory prayer asking God "to forgive the sin of your people Israel." Second Chronicles 6:24-27, it is claimed, documents how national catastrophes such as defeat in war or drought are in fact punishment for sin, and the people's crying out in distress constitutes a repentance to which God may respond. The use of allusions to national catastrophes in order to solicit divine forgiveness, according to Sara Japhet, effectively illustrates the theological cycle of sin-punishment-repentance-forgiveness that derives from Dtr.[9] Like Solomon's prayer in 2 Chronicles 6, the treatment of King Manasseh in 2 Chr 33:11-20 is cited as evidence of the Chronicler's interest in the cyclical nature of divine forgiveness. In Chronicles, Manasseh repents, and does so not ad hoc but as part of a pattern of sin-punishment-repentance-forgiveness (2 Chr 33:12-13). The Chronicler has been characterized as a theologian of retribution par excellence, although that judgment has recently been questioned by scholars who argue that mercy is most central to divine forgiveness as it is presented in Chronicles and other books of the Writings.

### (2) Mercy as the Center of Forgiveness

In the theological reassessment of divine forgiveness in Chronicles, a key text is 2 Chr 7:12-16, God's response to Solomon's prayer and to the dedication of the Temple. The text is a ringing acceptance and endorsement of the penitential rituals described by Solomon. Specifically, God pledges forgiveness in response to prayers of humble submission and repentance made by persons who seek out God (2 Chr 7:14). With a subsequent reference to the prayer "of this place" (2 Chr 7:15) the Chronicler lays emphasis on one's personal involvement in the Temple cult, but not at the expense of the restored Temple's value as a symbol of God's will to forgive the repentant sinner in virtually all places and times. The text

---

[8] For a systematic description of how the Chronicler portrays historical events to establish causal connections between transgression and retribution as well as righteousness and reward, see Sara Japhet, *The Ideology of the Book of Chronicles and Its Place in Biblical Thought* (Frankfurt: Peter Lang, 1989) 166–67. See also Raymond B. Dillard, "Reward and Punishment in Chronicles: The Theology of Immediate Retribution," *WTJ* 46 (1984) 164–72.

[9] Sara Japhet, *I & II Chronicles: A Commentary,* OTL (Louisville: Westminster John Knox, 1993) 595.

takes the view that divine forgiveness expresses God's limitless desire to restore the people who have sinned and attempted to repent.

Brian Kelly has examined the whole of the Chronicler's "retributional" vocabulary and has argued that the expressions at issue are concerned principally with repentance and restoration. Focusing on passages such as 2 Chr 7:12-22, Kelly argues that the language of the Chronicler indicates a primary concern for repentance and restoration "rather than strict retribution as such."[10] He maintains that in the Chronicler's system of divine justice the decisive factors are typically repentance and mercy, not merit.[11] The system is thus covenantal in nature, Kelly argues, and not mechanistically historical. In challenging the *quid pro quo* depiction of divine mercy, Kelly represents a new trend.[12] Increasingly scholars are attempting to articulate the Chronicler's theology in a manner that avoids an overly narrow focus on retribution, caricatured as payback from God, immediate and individualized. Rather, they emphasize the Chronicler's references to divine mercy and compassion in his accounts of God's redressing human sin.

---

[10] Brian E. Kelly, *Retribution and Eschatology in Chronicles*, JSOTSup 211 (Sheffield: Sheffield Academic Press, 1996) 62. Kelly has refined his position and placed added emphasis on covenant as the matrix within which divine mercy is operative; see his "'Retribution' Revisited: Covenant, Grace and Restoration," in M. Patrick Graham, Steven McKenzie, and Gary N. Knoppers, eds., *The Chronicler as Theologian: Essays in Honor of Ralph W. Klein*, JSOTSup 371 (Sheffield: Sheffield Academic Press, 2003) 206–27.

[11] Kelly, *Retribution and Eschatology*, 108.

[12] Like Kelly, scholars have begun drawing attention to Chronistic themes beyond that of retribution. Donald F. Murray has revisited key statements by the Chronicler's David, including the admonition to Solomon in 1 Chr 28:9. Alongside the retribution motif expressed therein Murray discerns a revival motif. See his "Retribution and Revival: Theological Theory, Religious Praxis, and the Future in Chronicles," *JSOT* 88 (2000) 77–99. Harm W. M. van Grol has offered fresh analysis of 2 Chr 12:1-12, the episode about Shishak's invasion of Israel. Many analyses attribute the Egyptian Shishak's successful campaign against Jerusalem to the fact that King Rehoboam abandoned God's law. Van Grol has observed that although the king's sin is punished, "punishment can be averted by repentance, and repentance is rewarded with mercy." He concludes that the Shishak story is "inconsistent with chronistic ideology" as it is often defined by biblical scholars. See his "'Indeed, Servants We Are': Ezra 9, Nehemiah 9 and 2 Chronicles 12 Compared," in Bob Becking and Marjo C. A. Korpel, eds., *The Crisis in Israelite Religion*, OtSt 42 (Leiden: Brill, 1999) 209–27, at 223.

One scholar has attempted to conceptualize such dynamics of divine mercy in terms of models. Working largely in the Writings, Mark Boda identifies in the biblical texts an alternative to the Dtr model of retribution as it is based on the principle that "human response [to sin] stands side-by-side in partnership with divine action."[13] In the alternative "patience model" that Boda indicates, "punishment is not guaranteed after rebellion and consistently mercy breaks through to turn away divine anger."[14] Boda finds the patience model to be operative in Psalms 78 and 106, and in Nehemiah 9. [15] In Psalm 78 the response from God in 78:38-39 is said to reflect the patience model because it comes forth despite the fact that the people's repentance was not sincere (78:34-37). The patience model is also operative in Ps 106:6-12, a passage about the Exodus as an act of redemption, and in Neh 9:12-21, a section on the wilderness wandering. Occasionally, Boda adds, the biblical author blends the patience model and its Dtr correlative as in, for example, the retributional passage Neh 9:26-31, which contains select expressions of gratuitous mercy, namely Neh 9:31: "In your great mercies, you did not make a full end of them." Boda and Kelly draw attention to a theological calculus of human repentance and divine mercy in the Writings; mercy often overreaches repentance so that God's people might attain their place in history, although mercy never eclipses human freedom and responsibility as these are integral to covenant defined as the relationship between the human and divine parties.

As a postscript to the critique of retributory theology we note that the book of Job is often cited as an early point in this trajectory. That is, the lamentation that occurs sporadically in the dialogues between Job and his interlocuters (Job 3–27; 29–31) is said to challenge the doctrine of divine retribution within the larger wisdom tradition current in the postexilic period. The challenge is a complex one whereby Job calls into question one-dimensional thinking, as the work of Carol Newsom makes clear: "The dialogic and polyphonic commitment of the book of Job as a whole . . . ensures that monological perspectives will not be allowed to speak unchallenged."[16] Newsom and others conclude that Job, in asserting the penitential perspectives of both human lament and

---

[13] Boda, *Praying the Tradition*, 83.

[14] Ibid.

[15] Ibid., 84–85.

[16] Carol A. Newsom, *The Book of Job: A Contest of Moral Imaginations* (Oxford and New York: Oxford University Press, 2003) 198.

divine retribution, foments a tension that remains unresolved for the sake of exploring assumptions embedded within the two theological viewpoints at issue.

### d. Theological Reflection on the Experience of Repentance

As theology arises from reflection on experience, it is not surprising that the Writings include evaluative accounts that commend the wisdom of confessing sin. Not itself a penitential prayer, Psalm 32 is a wisdom psalm that teaches the value of confessing sin. The psalm begins with a double beatitude (32:1-2) that twice identifies blessedness with the forgiven sinner whose fault and guilt have been removed by God. There follows the psalmist's account of events. The psalmist suffered distress and grief (32:3-4) until he confessed to God, who then removed the sin and as well all guilt and distress (32:5). The account effectively illustrates the role of repentance in wisdom as well as blessedness or beatitude. A similar text is Proverbs 28, an extended contrast of the prototypical wicked and righteous persons. Proverbs 28:13 states that whoever conceals transgressions will not prosper, but whoever confesses transgressions and forsakes them will obtain mercy. Again, repentance is tantamount to blessedness and prosperity.

### e. The Context of Penance and Penitence

The preceding section took as its premise that there is an intrinsic link between theology and experience. What experience stands behind the penitential texts in the Writings? The issue is that of identifying the historical context or *Sitz im Leben* of the texts in question. The candidates are several. The so-called liturgy of repentance is one logical setting for prayers that seek to console the unfortunate by allowing them to confess their sin. Begun at the time of the exile, the liturgy of repentance accentuated the twin themes of penitence for one's failings and resolve to amend one's ways. The liturgy also allowed penitents to avow their loyalty to the past and their singular dependence on divine grace.[17] Details of this liturgy are not extant, although it probably entailed fasting (Zech 7:3, 5; 8:19), public mourning (Lam 2:10-11), and perhaps even self-laceration (Jer 41:5). The sources for the exilic penitential liturgy include Jer 14:1–15:4 and Lamentations 3. Regrettably, neither the exilic

---

[17] See Ackroyd, *Exile and Restoration*, 47.

nor the postexilic sources disclose as much as we would like about the penitential liturgy, and because the available sources say so little about the penitential liturgy, it is exceedingly difficult to argue that it is the *Sitz im Leben* of the prayers in question.

The synagogue would be another candidate for the *Sitz im Leben* of the penitential texts in the Writings. In his classic work on ancient Jewish prayer, Joseph Heinemann posits synagogal origins for much of the prayer of the Second-Temple period, including that based *in the Temple*.[18] From the same generation of scholars comes the view of Leon Liebreich. The language of the prayer in Nehemiah 9 may have influenced the synagogal prayers for Yom Kippur, according to Liebreich. He has suggested that the standing prayers for the Day of Atonement incorporate Neh 9:17b, the first three words of 9:19, and 9:33.[19] Liebreich also claims that 9:17b's mention of God's mercy, *sĕlîḥôt*, inspired the liturgical practice of reciting Exod 34:6-7 in the course of the prayers for forgiveness.[20]

In the most recent analysis, however, it would appear that many of the penitential prayers predate the synagogue, especially if one takes Lee Levine's view that the "dramatic initiative" of introducing obligatory, public communal prayer takes place in the post-70 Palestinian synagogue.[21] In light of current scholarship the work of Heinemann and Liebreich ultimately is not helpful in determining *Sitz im Leben*. There remains one candidate for the *Sitz im Leben* of the penitential prayers,

---

[18] Heinemann nuances his position thus: "Although we are inclined to regard most of the prayers which were recited in the temple as outgrowths of the popular creations which developed around the institution of the synagogue, we cannot deny that these temple prayers possess a distinctive nature of their own." *Prayer in the Period of the Tanna'im and the Amora'im: Its Nature and Its Patterns* (Jerusalem: Magnes, 1966) 133.

[19] Leon Liebreich, "The Impact of Neh 9:5-37 on the Liturgy of the Synagogue," *HUCA* 32 (1961) 236.

[20] Ibid.

[21] Levine writes: "There can be little doubt that obligatory daily prayer—both personal and communal—was conceived in the post-70 period under the auspices of Rabban Gamaliel. On the other hand, as noted, these prayers were not created *ex nihilo*. There were many precedents, and the Yavnean *tannaim* incorporated earlier materials, reworking, reformulating, and restricting them so as to fashion a prayer which they sought to make obligatory for Jews everywhere, as a community and as individuals." *The Ancient Synagogue: The First Thousand Years* (New Haven and London: Yale University Press, 2000) 503, 518.

the Temple itself. The prima facie evidence supports the existence of such a relationship.

Communal in character, the speeches and prayers of repentance may well have derived from the milieu of the Temple liturgy, although this influence is not necessarily univocal. From the Temple, the prayers incorporate significant cultic *realia* such as specific prayer times. In some cases the prayer times in question appear to have been festal dates on the calendar.[22] In other cases they were the hours of prayer in the Temple on an ordinary day. The prayers in Ezra 9:6-15 and Dan 9:4-19, we have noted, are both aligned with the daily sacrifice or *hattāmîd* (Ezra 9:5, Dan 9:21).[23] These explicit references indicate some level of relationship between the Temple cult and penitential prayers such as those found in the Writings.

There are essentially two schools of thought on the matter of Temple cult and penitential prayer. Some scholars resolve the matter by adopting Israel Knohl's reconstruction of Temple space and Temple worship.[24] Knohl designates a priestly realm as an inner circle and posits two concentric circles that form a periphery. He indicates tension among the circles, and also a countering force of complementarity. Knohl offers a model that

---

[22] In the fifth century B.C.E., even after the completion of the Second Temple and the restoration of national rites, penitential practices remained vital to the local liturgy. The gathering of Judeans described in Nehemiah 8 is explicitly liturgical (8:6-7), and it is significant that the people are disposed to mourn and weep (8:9, *bākāh* and *ʾābal*) and to grieve (8:11, *ʿāṣab*). The gathering in Nehemiah 8 may represent a penitential service initially associated with Sukkoth (Neh 8:18; 9:1), and the penitential prayer that follows in Neh 9:6-37 indicates a penitential service taking place on the twenty-fourth day of the seventh month, two days after the conclusion of the weeklong feast of Sukkoth. It is possible that the prayer has come from a rite of Sukkoth or some other special occasion in the festal year, including Yom Kippur (see Bautch, *Developments in Genre*, 121–22). Such associations link penitential prayer to the rites of national observance and to those of the Temple cult.

[23] In fact the daily sacrifice was offered twice daily; according to Shemuel Safrai, "The morning and afternoon whole-offerings constituted the essence of the divine service and the main function of the altar. Extreme importance was attributed to the daily whole offering." "The Temple," in Shemuel Safrai and M. Stern, eds., *The Jewish People in the First Century: Historical Geography, Political History, Social, Cultural and Religious Life and Institutions*, CRINT (Philadelphia: Fortress Press, 1976) 865–907, at 890.

[24] The following reconstruction is available in Israel Knohl, "Between Voice and Silence: The Relationship Between Prayer and Temple Cult," *JBL* 115 (1996) 23.

demonstrates the close proximity of popular prayer to the priestly cult of the Second Temple. Prayer is distinct from the inner circle, but it is not autonomous. Esther Chazon has adopted Knohl's terminology and his model of Temple space.[25] She groups together texts such as Dan 9:4-19, Ezra 9:6-15, and other penitential prayers that refer to the daily afternoon sacrifice. The common reference to sacrifice, she argues, "indicates that prayers said at the Temple remained on its *periphery* both geographically and cultically."[26] Most significantly, Chazon and those who take her position maintain that the penitential texts were actually prayed at the Temple.

The other school of thought comes to a different conclusion regarding Temple cult and penitential prayer. Observing a "shift in emphasis away from sacrifice and toward prayer," one scholar has suggested that prayer grew in popularity as sacrifice waned in the Persian, Hellenistic, and Roman periods.[27] According to this view, prayer in the time of the Second Temple evolved into a form of religious activity that was increasingly autonomous from the cult. Penitential prayer and the larger penitential discourse of the time was no exception. While penitential prayers such as those found in the Writings were often associated with a ceremonial context, the context was not reducible to the Temple cult and its sacrificial system. In fact, some claim that the penitence documented in the Writings reflects controversy surrounding the cultic activity carried out in the Temple. It has been argued that Nehemiah 8, with chapters 9–10, sets forth the confession of "the sins of the fathers" within the newly-built walls of Jerusalem as a substitute for the Temple and sacrifices performed by a high priesthood that had allied itself to the enemies of the restoration.[28] According to this vein of scholarship the penitential texts may have a discernible *Sitz im Leben*, but it is not the Temple per se.

[25] Esther Chazon, "When Did They Pray? Times for Prayer in the Dead Sea Scrolls and Associated Literature," in Randall A. Argall, Beverly A. Bow, and Rodney A. Werline, eds., *For a Later Generation: The Transformation of Tradition in Israel, Early Judaism and Early Christianity* (Harrisburg: Trinity Press International, 2000) 42–51, at 48 n26.

[26] Ibid. 48, emphasis added.

[27] This point is made by Joseph Blenkinsopp in "The Second Temple as House of Prayer," 109–22 in J. C. Petit, ed., *"Où demeures-tu?" La Maison depuis le monde biblique* (Quebec: Éditions Fides, 1994) 110.

[28] Jacob L. Wright, *Rebuilding Identity: The Nehemiah-Memior and its Earliest Readers,* BZAW 348 (Berlin and New York: Walter de Gruyter, 2004) 335.

## f. Conclusion

In an earlier part of this essay we noted that the biblical authors responsible for the Writings considered both divine omnipotence and divine associability as they worked toward an understanding of penance and penitence. Adopting and adapting the received (i.e., preexilic) Scriptures of the day, these authors developed an image of God as all-powerful and eminently relational. While these divine attributes are not absolutely opposed, neither are they synonymous in standard theological discourse. In the Writings, however, they are developed in light of each other and come to stand in a tensive relationship. This theological approach is apparent throughout the Writings, and a few examples must suffice. Recall that Psalm 51 appeals to God's mercy (51:3) as it acknowledges God's justice (51:6), with both attributes linked to the God who creates in the psalmist a new heart (51:10). Similarly, scholars have identified in the God of the Chronicler both the reflex of requital and, more recently, the predilection for mercy and forgiveness. Also relevant is the scholarly divide between those who maintain that the penitential texts were actually prayed at the Temple and those positing a shift whereby penance and penitence replaced Temple rites such as sacrifice. The data of the Writings allows no superficial consensus on this and any number of points, with Job the parade example. In what they report, these biblical books often transcend the categories of theology to suggest that the people's experience of the Divinity is being cut from a new cloth. These books recall that the quidditative knowledge of God is always incomplete, and that the sum total of the divine attributes falls far short of the infinite being that is God.

# 2. Implications

In the Writings penance and penitence are more often than not *communal* exercises (Neh 1:6-7; Ezra 9:7; Ps 79:8-9). When and why did the norm of communal repentance yield to the individualized practices of penance and penitence that predominate today, and what was lost in this shift? Are there situations today that require communal penitential prayer in order for healing and forgiveness to take place? These are vital questions for the church and the world.

The Writings often reflect practices of prayer and penitence that are embodied (Ezra 9:3, 5; Neh 9:1; Dan 9:3). We are thus reminded that the physical postures of prayer in the ancient Near East carried much significance, and that gesture was a key part of the overall expression. An adequate understanding of penance and penitence, in the period of the Second Temple and subsequently, requires attention to the words and the body of the one who prays. The object of study must be the overall expression of repentance.

Increasingly scholars report that the Writings emphasize divine mercy as a response to human penance and penitence. In doing so they challenge an earlier interpretive approach that hailed divine retribution. Early in 2005 criminal justice reform advocates in Texas called for the state to reevaluate its handling of clemency requests from inmates who in effect ask the state to reduce or forgive a punishment handed down by the courts. The current process, it was charged, is so veiled in secrecy that inmates' requests may not receive fair consideration. Contemporary scholarship on the Writings leads us to conclude that if a justice system is biased against clemency it is at odds with the biblical norm of divine mercy as a response to wrongdoing.

## 3. Further Reading

Balentine, Samuel E. *Prayer in the Hebrew Bible: The Drama of Divine-Human Dialogue.* OBT. Minneapolis: Augsburg Fortress, 1993.

Blenkinsopp, Joseph. "The Second Temple as House of Prayer." In J. C. Petit, ed., *"Où demeures-tu?" La Maison depuis le monde biblique.* Quebec: Éditions Fides, 1994, 109–22.

Boda, Mark J. *Praying the Tradition: The Origin and Use of Tradition in Nehemiah 9.* Berlin and NewYork: Walter de Gruyter, 1999.

Clifford, Richard J. "In Zion and David a New Beginning: An Interpretation of Psalm 78." In Baruch Halpern and Jon D. Levenson, eds., *Traditions in Transformation: Turning Points in Biblical Faith.* Winona Lake, IN: Eisenbrauns, 1981, 121–41.

Kelly, Brian E. *Retribution and Eschatology in Chronicles.* Sheffield: Sheffield Academic Press, 1996.

Lacocque, André. "The Liturgical Prayer in Daniel 9," *HUCA* 47 (1976) 119–42.

Newman, Judith H. *Praying By the Book: The Scripturalization of Prayer in Second Temple Judaism.* Atlanta: Scholars Press, 1999.

Plöger, Otto. "Speech and Prayer in the Deuteronomistic and the Chronicler's Histories." In Gary N. Knoppers and J. Gordon McConville, eds., *Reconsidering Israel and Judah: Recent Studies on the Deuteronomistic History.* Winona Lake, IN: Eisenbrauns, 2000, 31–46.

Smith-Christopher, Daniel L. *A Biblical Theology of Exile.* Minneapolis: Fortress Press, 2002, especially 105–23.

Werline, Rodney A. *Penitential Prayer in Second Temple Judaism: The Development of a Religious Institution.* Atlanta: Scholars Press, 1998.

## 4. Hermeneutical Reflection

A striking aspect of the Writings is the fact that penance and penitence are often communal experiences. Because I have worked closely with these biblical texts for several years, I take for granted the normativity of communal reconciliation. Discussions with other contributors to this volume, however, reminded me that this perspective is not widely shared in Christian churches today. Many of my colleagues observe a priority on individual confession, while the experience of communal confession and forgiveness remains a desideratum.

Nonetheless, it is important to recognize those ways in which Christians today are engaging penance and penitence communally. In the Catholic Church the seasons of Advent and Lent have proven opportune times to celebrate the Rite of Reconciliation of Several Penitents with Individual Confession and Absolution. The rite involves the community in singing hymns, hearing God's word, examining their consciences, making a general confession of sins, and confessing individually to a priest who gives absolution to the penitent. A crucial part of the liturgy is the homily, which is to be based on the biblical readings and is to lead the penitents to examine their consciences and renew their lives; forthright yet sound penitential preaching is a lost art, but this liturgy calls it forth. Another example is the Thomas Mass, a Lutheran worship service that is celebrated every Sunday in Helsinki. Named after the apostle Thomas, this service has for seventeen years attracted people who are spiritual searchers, and it caters to those who consider themselves sinners or persons of weak faith. The service is especially popular among young adults, and I am grateful to my fellow contributors for bringing it to my attention.

Communal repentance, the preceding examples suggest, has a place in Christian life today. Moreover, it may serve a vital need in terms of situations that require a collective reckoning and repentance in order for healing and forgiveness to follow. Internally a church may experience scandals or worse that resist closure until a sense of corporate sorrow has been credibly voiced through sacred ritual. The corporate model may, in turn, be of service to the world when it suffers evils such as discrimination, wholesale fraud, civil war and, increasingly, genocide. These wounds remain open and fester absent a plan for forgiveness and healing that includes all parties, especially those at the highest levels. Hope for repentance on an international scale is a gift that communities of Christians can give to the world simply by confessing their sins together and as one.

Communal repentance, it should be noted, does not lose track of the individual. In the words of Andrew Purves, "My sins are always particular." It is most unlikely that liturgies of communal repentance would leave people focused exclusively on social sin and inured to any personal sin of which they might be guilty. Rather, a habit of praying together as a response to sin will sensitize consciences more completely and make for a world that is more sanctified, one soul at a time.

Five

# "Repent, for the Kingdom of God Is at Hand": Repentance in the Synoptic Gospels and Acts

*Guy Dale Nave, Jr.*

## 1. Text

Over half a century ago William Chamberlain wrote:

> This formula, "Repent ye; for the kingdom of heaven is at hand," is not only a trumpet blast, but also the keynote of the New Testament message. Not only does it break the stillness of the Judean wilderness, but its reverberations are heard throughout the New Testament, reaching their climax in the thunders of the Apocalypse.[1]

If these words do constitute the keynote, we must understand them before we understand the New Testament.

Had the canon founders decided to give primacy to the oldest writings in the New Testament—the letters of Paul—it might have been difficult for Chamberlain to identify repentance as the key to unlock the New Testament. This is not because the concept of repentance is unimportant in

[1] *The Meaning of Repentance* (Philadelphia: Westminster, 1943) 17.

Paul's letters, but rather because they contain no specific demand to repent. Outside the Synoptic Gospels and Acts, an explicit demand to repent is found only in Revelation.[2] Beyond that the Greek verb *metanoeō*, commonly translated "repent," occurs only once.[3] Similarly, outside the Synoptics and Acts the noun *metanoia*, usually translated "repentance," occurs only eight times.[4] The principal Greek words for "repent" and "repentance" occur thirty-five times, however, in the Synoptics and Acts, accounting for nearly sixty-three percent of all the occurrences in the New Testament.

Most scholarly examinations of repentance begin by acknowledging that the New Testament writers used *metanoeō* and *metanoia* to convey the concept of repentance.[5] There have, however, been two assumptions that have flawed much of the scholarly research. First, many scholars have made the mistake of assuming that the early Christian "concept of repentance" is so special that there is nothing like it in pre-Christian Greek usage. On no other basis than theological convictions about the uniqueness of Christianity, many scholars assert that there is little or no affinity between the usage of *metanoeō* and *metanoia* in non-Christian Greek literature and its use in Christian literature. Second, most scholars who assert the uniqueness of the Christian concept of repentance assume that *metanoeō* and *metanoia*, when used in Christian literature, inherited their meanings exclusively from the "concept of repentance/conversion" found in the Hebrew Bible rather than from the commonly accepted meanings the words had among Greek-speaking people—including Greek-speaking Jews—at the time the New Testament documents were written. These two assumptions undermine any attempt at arriving at an understanding of repentance in the New Testament that is faithful to the social-cultural milieu in which these documents were written and read.[6]

---

[2] Rev 2:5, 16; 3:3, 19.

[3] 2 Cor 12:21.

[4] Rom 2:4; 2 Cor 7:9, 10; 2 Tim 2:25; Heb 6:1, 6; 12:17; 2 Pet 3:9.

[5] While the concept of repentance cannot be limited to occurrences of *metanoeō* and *metanoia*, in order to understand the New Testament concept of repentance we must begin with the Greek words that are traditionally translated "repent" and "repentance." Once we determine the meaning of *metanoeō* and *metanoia* within the historical context of the New Testament we can talk about ways in which the "concept of repentance" is manifested outside the use of *metanoeō* and *metanoia*.

[6] See Guy Nave, *The Role and Function of Repentance in Luke-Acts* (Atlanta: Society of Biblical Literature, 2002) 39–118 for a detailed assessment and critique of these two assumptions.

Immediately before, during, and after the time of Jesus *metanoeō* and *metanoia* literally meant "change of mind." The terms were consistently used in the literature of that time to express a fundamental change in thinking that leads to a fundamental change in behavior and/or way of living.[7] Often this change was prompted by a sense of remorse regarding previous thoughts and/or actions. This probably explains why Jews who translated the Hebrew Bible into Greek chose *metanoeō* to translate the verb *niḥâm*, "be sorry, be moved to pity, have regret," rather than the verb *šûb*, "turn."[8]

In the Synoptic Gospels, John the Baptist bursts onto the scene "preaching a baptism of repentance for the forgiveness of sins." While repentance was understood as the appropriate response to sin, the Synoptics suggest that sinners are not compelled to repent simply because sin demands repentance; instead, sinners are compelled to repent because a new period in history has begun. In Mark, Jesus declares, "The time is fulfilled, and the kingdom of God is at hand; repent, and believe in the good news" (1:15; cf. Matt 4:17). "The kingdom of God" refers to the establishment of God's reign over all creation.[9] Because of the inauguration of God's reign, people are compelled to repent. Repentance is the required human response. God's reign has created a situation that demands a fundamental change in the way people think and live.[10]

Neither Mark nor Matthew elaborates on the meaning of repentance or on what repentance entails. The demands for repentance and passing comments about repentance suggest that the authors assumed their audience knew what it meant. N. T. Wright argues that in Jesus' context "repentance" would have carried the connotation of what Israel

---

[7] Ibid. 40–70.

[8] Centuries of scholarship have perpetuated the myth that *šûb* is the term that best conveys the early Christian understanding of *metanoeō* and *metanoia*, even though neither word was used to translate an occurrence of the root *šûb* (cf. ibid. 111–18).

[9] See Aloysius M. Ambrozic, *The Hidden Kingdom: A Redaction-Critical Study of the References to the Kingdom of God in Mark's Gospel*, CBQMS 2 (Washington, DC: Catholic Biblical Association of America, 1975).

[10] Under the reign of God the poor and oppressed are delivered and exalted while the high and mighty are abased (Mark 10:23-25//Matt 19:23-24//Luke 18:24-25; Matt 5:3-10//Luke 6:20-25; Matt 10:7-8//Luke 6:8-11; Matt 12:28; 20:1-16; Luke 14:15-24).

must do if God is to restore Israel. He asserts that for Jesus "repentance" meant returning to God and renouncing nationalistic violence.[11] While I concur with Wright that repentance is closely linked with restoration, Wright robs the New Testament demand for repentance of its fuller significance by limiting it to "returning to God" and "renouncing nationalistic violence." A thorough examination of Hellenistic Jewish writings clearly demonstrates that for Jews living at the time of Jesus the demand for repentance was a demand to engage in a fundamental change in thinking and living.[12] That demand could have included renouncing nationalistic violence, but it was in no way limited to that. Since neither Mark nor Matthew elaborates on the meaning of *metanoeō* and *metanoia*, and since there are no explicit or implicit indicators that the authors were advocating a renouncing of nationalistic violence, it should be concluded that the gospel authors understood repentance as a demand for a fundamental change in thinking and/or living. We have to turn to the gospels themselves to see what that change might have entailed.

Although there are only three occurrences of *metanoeō* and *metanoia* in Mark, it is significant that all three are found in summary statements regarding the ministries of John the Baptist (1:4), Jesus (1:15), and the Twelve (6:12). The ministries of all three are summarized as the preaching of repentance. While this is the extent of the occurrences of *metanoeō* and *metanoia* in Mark, the notion of a fundamental change in thinking and living is central to the message of that gospel. A common theme in Mark is the failure to understand who Jesus is (Mark 6:14-16; 8:27-28). Those close to Jesus have the hardest time understanding him or recognizing who he is (Mark 3:21; 8:14-21). At times this confusion is exhibited as amazement at the power and authority he possessed (Mark 1:27; 4:41; 6:2-3, 49-51). Jesus is presented as the powerful one (Mark

---

[11] *Jesus and the Victory of God* (Minneapolis: Fortress Press, 1996) 246–58.

[12] Wright concludes, on the basis of a limited number of references to *metanoeō* and *metanoia* in the writings of Josephus, that repentance in the context of Jesus' preaching entailed renouncing nationalistic violence (*Jesus and the Victory of God*, 250). He fails, however, to carefully consider the more than seventy-seven references to *metanoeō* and *metanoia* in Josephus's writings. What is common to all of the references in the writings of Josephus—as well as in the writings of other Hellenistic Jewish authors of the time—is that they all refer to a fundamental change in thinking that is often accompanied by a fundamental change in living (Nave, *Role and Function of Repentance*, 70–118).

1:7-8). From the outset he casts out demons, heals the sick, controls the forces of nature, and even raises the dead (Mark 1:21-28, 29-34, 40-45; 3:7-12; 5:21-43). Jesus' exploits prove that the reign of God has arrived because oppressive powers are being destroyed (Mark 3:22-27//Matt 12:25-29//Luke 11:17-22). Even Roman occupation is being brought to an end (Mark 5:1-21).[13] Mark's Jesus, however, often attempts to keep his works and identity a secret (Mark 1:34, 43-44; 3:11-12; 5:43; 7:36; 8:30; 9:9, 30). The issue is not one of not identifying Jesus: the narrator identifies Jesus as the Messiah (i.e., "Christ") in the first sentence of the gospel. The issue is about not recognizing what Messiah means. While there is much scholarly debate over what first-century messianic expectations entailed, it is clear that the expectations were not that the Messiah would suffer and die (Mark 15:32).[14]

Peter is the first character in Mark to identify Jesus as the Messiah (Mark 8:29). In the literary world of Mark, Peter comes to this conclusion based on the acts of power manifested by Jesus. Peter does not understand that being the Messiah also entails suffering. When Jesus begins talking about the suffering and persecution he will experience, Peter rebukes him. Three times Jesus foretells the suffering he will experience, and each time his disciples fail to understand. Each time they associate Messiah with power, and they associate being a disciple of the Messiah with power and privilege. Jesus repeatedly informs them, however, that being his disciple means being a servant of others. The author challenges his readers' thinking about messiahship and discipleship. Like John the Baptist, Jesus, and the Twelve, the author's ministry is one of demanding a fundamental change in thinking and living. Being a disciple of the Messiah is not what many may have thought.

In Mark, Jesus calls his disciples to lose their life for his sake and the sake of the "good news" (Mark 8:31-38; 9:33-35; 10:35-45). The "good news" in Mark is that the reign of God has begun (Mark 1:14-15), which means the reign of oppressors is being brought to an end. According to Mark those willing to *lose* their lives for the sake of Jesus and the good news are those who are willing to *live* their lives under the reign of God, which means resisting, opposing, and even defeating oppressive,

---

[13] "Legion" was the name given to a Roman regiment of approximately six thousand soldiers.

[14] Cf. Jacob Neusner, William Scott Green, and Ernest S. Frerichs, eds., *Judaisms and Their Messiahs at the Turn of the Christian Era* (Cambridge: Cambridge University Press, 1987).

demonic, and imperialistic powers. It means living a life for the deliverance of others. While such a life is powerful, its focus is not personal power and privilege, but the liberation and empowerment of others. While such a life is powerful, it leads to rejection, persecution, suffering, and even death (Mark 11:15-18). According to Mark this is the life Jesus lived, and this is the life to which followers of Jesus have been called.

Matthew also summarizes the ministry of John the Baptist and Jesus as one of preaching repentance (Matt 3:1-11; 4:17).[15] As in Mark, occurrences of *metanoeō* and *metanoia* are rare in Matthew. The demand for change, however, is central to Matthew's message. Jesus is depicted primarily as a teacher in Matthew, and his teachings demand a change in thinking and living. Only in Matthew does Jesus talk about "righteousness." Many of the references to righteousness are found in Jesus' Sermon on the Mount, where Jesus concludes his declaration that he has come to fulfill the Law by saying, "Unless your righteousness exceeds that of the scribes and Pharisees, you can never enter the kingdom of heaven" (Matt 5:17-20). Within the immediate literary context Jesus had just proclaimed, "Repent, for the kingdom of heaven is at hand." The demand for repentance is a demand for righteousness. Righteousness in Matthew is about how one lives in relationship to God in terms of God's will for what is right. For Jewish people at that time the truest purveyor of God's will for what is right was the Law.

The author seems to have been responding to a conflict between his community of Jesus followers and the dominant Jewish leadership at his time: the Pharisees.[16] Throughout Matthew the author not only portrays Jesus as the anticipated Jewish Messiah, he also depicts traditional religious leaders—especially the Pharisees—as incapable of leading. The Pharisees have failed as leaders because they are nothing more than hypocrites who are concerned only about themselves (see Matt 23:1-36). In Matthew, Jesus demands a fundamental change in thinking regarding what it means to live righteously. He does this by challenging the Pharisees' interpretation of the Law. After declaring that he has come to fulfill the Law and demanding that his listeners' righteousness exceed that of the scribes and Pharisees, Jesus presents a series of antitheses contrasting the Pharisees' interpretation of the Law with his own interpretation of

---

[15] The author omits any reference to the disciples preaching repentance.

[16] See Anthony J. Saldarini, *Matthew's Christian-Jewish Community* (Chicago: University of Chicago Press, 1994).

the Law.[17] Matthew sets Jesus' authority against that of the scribes and Pharisees, and in so doing reminds the audience what it means to fulfill the Law. For Matthew, fulfilling the Law is about being concerned for others. On two occasions Matthew's Jesus provides a summary of the Law. The first is found within this sermon when Jesus tells the crowd, "In everything do to others as you would have them do to you; for this is the law and the prophets" (Matt 7:12).[18] The second summary comes in response to a question from a Pharisee regarding which commandment in the Law is the greatest. Jesus responds that all the Law is based on two commandments: the first and the greatest is to love God and the second is to love one's neighbor as oneself (Matt 22:34-40//Mark 12:28-31//Luke 10:25-28).[19] In proclaiming what it means to fulfill the Law, Matthew's Jesus exposes the Pharisees' failure to do so and demands the audience change its thinking regarding who is best suited to lead the people of God in fulfilling God's righteousness.[20] The author illustrates this point beautifully in a parable about two sons. Addressing the religious leaders, Jesus says,

> "What do you think? A man had two sons; he went to the first and said, 'Son, go and work in the vineyard today.' He answered, 'I will not'; but later he changed his mind and went. The father went to the second and said the same; and he answered, 'I go, sir'; but he did not go. Which of the two did the will of the father?" They said, "The first." Jesus said to them, "Truly I tell you, the tax collectors and the prostitutes are going into the kingdom of God ahead of you. For John came to you in the way of righteousness and you did not believe him, but the tax collectors and the prostitutes believed him; and even after you saw it, you did not change your minds and believe him." (Matt 21:28-32)

---

[17] Since this immediately follows the criticism of the righteousness of the scribes and Pharisees, and since Jesus says, "You have *heard* that it was said . . . but *I* say to you . . . ," Jesus seems to contrast his interpretation of the Law with that of the scribes and Pharisees.

[18] When Luke cites this command he makes no mention of the Law (Luke 6:31).

[19] In Matthew this summary immediately precedes Jesus' denouncing of the Pharisees and scribes as hypocrites.

[20] The Pharisees are "blind guides" whose instructions lead people to hell (23:15, 24).

The one who did the will of the father is the one who "changed his mind and went." Being a part of the kingdom of God requires a change in thinking and living. However, even when John the Baptist came in the way of righteousness, the religious leaders refused to change their minds. According to Matthew the religious leaders—especially the Pharisees— have failed to observe God's will for what is right, and have distorted the Law for their own sake (Matt 15:1-9). They are concerned only about themselves, not about others. Because of this God has taken authority away from them and given it to Jesus and his community of followers (Matt 21:33-46; 16:13-19 [cf. 18:15-20]; 28:18-20).

Not only did the religious leaders fail to repent after seeing the response of the tax collectors and prostitutes to John the Baptist, according to Matthew they are incapable of repentance. While the demand of John the Baptist to "Bear fruits worthy of repentance" is delivered to the crowds in Luke, in Matthew it is delivered specifically to the Pharisees and Sadducees (Matt 3:7-10//Luke 3:7-9). According to the preaching of John the Baptist, as preserved in the source material used by Matthew and Luke, repentance is a change in thinking that must be accompanied by a change in behavior. The tradition clearly indicates that repentance requires fruit, and it stresses the urgency of bearing such fruit through the use of apocalyptic imagery such as, "the ax is lying at the root of the trees; every tree therefore that does not bear good fruit is cut down and thrown into the fire."[21] In Luke the crowd responds to this sense of urgency by asking what they must do. The Pharisees and Sadducees in Matthew, however, do not ask because there is nothing they can do. They are incapable of bearing fruit worthy of repentance, and therefore are unable to escape the impending destruction.[22]

---

[21] While much of Q scholarship asserts that Q focuses on eschatological warning and imminent judgment rather than on the "fruits of repentance," Melanie Johnson-DeBaufre persuasively demonstrates how Q emphasizes the ethical fruits of repentance (*Jesus Among Her Children: Q, Eschatology, and the Construction of Christian Origins* [Cambridge, MA: Harvard University Press, 2005] ch. 3).

[22] Matthew gives an extremely negative portrayal of the Pharisees, Sadducees, and other religious leaders. They are commonly portrayed as "blind." They are incapable of seeing the truth (15:14; 23:16, 17, 19, 24, 26), and incapable of receiving revelation from God (2:1-12; 9:6-8; 11:25-27; 28:11-15). They are incapable, therefore, of repenting of their sins and receiving forgiveness (12:22-42). Not only are they blind, they are also "evil" (9:4; 12:34, 39, 45; 16:4; 22:18). The concept of evil (*ponēros*) plays a prominent role in the narrative world of Matthew. To be evil implies a

Unlike Mark and Matthew, Luke elaborates at great length on what repentance entails because the concept has a prominent literary function in Luke-Acts.[23] Here repentance is not merely a change in thinking that leads to a change in behavior; instead it is *the necessary* change in thinking and behavior required in order to help fulfill God's plan of universal salvation and establish a community that embraces all people.[24] In Mark the passage about John the Baptist "proclaiming a baptism of repentance for the remission of sins" follows the Isaian prophecy; in Luke, however, the passage has been moved immediately before the Isaian prophecy. The result is that the "baptism of repentance for the remission of sins" becomes the object of the prophecy rather than John the Baptist being the object.[25] It is John's baptism and, more importantly, his preaching of repentance that fulfills Isaiah's prophecy.[26] Furthermore, the extension of the Isaian prophecy to include "and all flesh shall see the salvation of God" has the effect of linking repentance with the Lukan theme of universal salvation.

---

relentless opposition to God and a fundamental association with the devil, who in Matthew is known as "the evil one" (13:19, 38). Throughout Matthew, judgment has already been pronounced on the religious leaders. On three occasions they are described with the epithet "brood of vipers" (3:7; 12:34; 23:32). They are also identified as "[children] of hell" (23:15). Matthew even suggests that because of their unrighteousness they will never enter the kingdom of heaven (5:20).

[23] Of the thirty-five occurrences of *metanoeō* and *metanoia* in the Synoptics and Acts, twenty-five are found in Luke-Acts.

[24] Nave, *Role and Function of Repentance*, 7–38, 145–224.

[25] Luke 3:1-6//Mark 1:1-6//Matt 3:1-6. Although the reference has been moved before Isaiah's prophecy in Matthew, the passage has been significantly redacted and is followed by the Matthean summary statement, "This is the one of whom the prophet Isaiah spoke." So in Matthew the focus is not on the "baptism of repentance" (which is not even mentioned), but on John the Baptist.

[26] Joseph A. Fitzmyer states that "The introductory conj. *hōs*, 'as,' shows that Luke regards John's baptism and preaching as a fulfillment of Isaiah's prophetic message." *The Gospel According to Luke,* AB 3, 3A (Garden City, NY: Doubleday, 1981–1985) 1:460. Robert Tannehill not only makes reference to the prefacing of the Isaian quote by the phrase "a baptism of repentance for the remission of sin," but also points out that "following the quotation, we are given a sample of John's call to repentance. Thus the quotation is framed by John's preaching of repentance and is partly interpreted by this context. Preparing the Lord's way means preparing the people through repentance, as 1:17 indicated" (*The Narrative Unity of Luke-Acts. A Literary Interpretation.* 2 vols. [Philadelphia: Fortress Press, 1986–1990] 48).

In Luke people respond to John's demand for repentance by asking, "What then shall we do?" The question is in direct response to the command, "Bear fruits worthy of repentance," as well as to the warning for the people not to trust in their ancestral connection to Abraham as a way of escaping the impending wrath of God.[27] Unidentified members of the crowd are the first to ask what they must do. John tells everyone who has food and clothing in excess of what is needed for survival to share their excess with those who have nothing. John then addresses tax collectors and soldiers. He instructs the tax collectors to collect no more than the amount prescribed, and he tells the soldiers not to extort money by threats and false accusations. For both tax collectors and soldiers, obedience to John's instructions would have entailed a total rejection of their occupation because the instructions struck at the root of the systemic violence and economic injustice associated with their occupations.[28] Furthermore, unlike Matthew, which depicts the religious leaders as unable to repent, Luke demonstrates that everyone is capable of repenting.[29] This notion may have required a fundamental change in thinking on the part of some in the Lukan community. Those who had treated tax collectors and soldiers (as well as other socially unacceptable people) with contempt were being forced to change their way of thinking.[30] In a small but significant redaction Luke portrays Jesus informing the Pharisees and scribes that he has "not come to call the righteous, but sinners *to repentance*" (Luke 5:32). Because of the Lukan development of the ethical preaching of John the Baptist, the reader understands repentance to be associated with bearing fruits of economic and social justice.

---

[27] A rich man later discovers that it is repentance, not Abrahamic descent, that protects one from God's wrath (16:24, 27, 30).

[28] For a detailed examination of the implications of the instructions see Nave, *Role and Function of Repentance*, 155–58.

[29] Although it was commonly believed by many Jews during the first century that it was virtually impossible for tax collectors to repent (John R. Donahue, "Tax Collectors and Sinners: An Attempt at Identification," *CBQ* 33 [1971] 41; Joachim Jeremias, *Jerusalem in the Time of Jesus*, trans. F. H. and C. H. Cave [London: SCM, 1969] 310–11), tax collectors in Luke are often characterized by repentance and faith (cf. 5:27-32; 7:29; 15:1; 18:13; 19:1-10).

[30] In the account of the repentance of Zacchaeus, the chief tax collector, not only does Zacchaeus repent, but those who despise Zacchaeus must also repent by changing their opinion of him and accepting him as a "son of Abraham" (Luke 19:1-10).

The reader assumes, therefore, that Jesus is calling his followers to a life of economic and social justice.[31]

Luke 13:1-9 again emphasizes the importance of repentance and bearing fruit that attests to repentance. People in a crowd ask Jesus a question that suggests divine punishment is a response to sin. Many of the scenes in Luke 9:21–12:59 demonstrate that sin is part of the human condition. Chorazin, Bethsaida, and many who have heard Jesus, however, are not condemned because of their sin, but because of their failure to repent.[32] In his rebuke of those who asked the question regarding some Galileans, Jesus stressed that it is not sin but rather the lack of repentance that leads to destruction.[33] Jesus' remarks imply that neither the Galileans nor those in Siloam were destroyed because of their sin; instead, they were destroyed because of their failure to repent. Jesus informs those questioning him that they likewise will perish if they do not repent.[34]

Luke ends just as it began—by presenting the preaching of repentance as the fulfillment of Scripture. The resurrected Jesus declares to his disciples, "Thus it is written, that the Messiah is to suffer and to rise from the dead on the third day, and that repentance and forgiveness of sins is to be proclaimed in his name to all nations" (Luke 24:46-47). The preaching of repentance by the disciples is in fulfillment of God's plan. The opening speech in Acts portrays Peter condemning the crowd for crucifying the Messiah. The crowd responds with the same question that was asked of John the Baptist—"What shall we do?" Peter answers,

---

[31] This impression is strengthened by Jesus' earlier preaching in the synagogue at Nazareth, where he declared he had been anointed by the Spirit of the Lord to bring deliverance to the poor and oppressed (Luke 4:16-21). It is also strengthened by the account of the interaction between Jesus and Zacchaeus, where Zacchaeus' response to Jesus includes financial restitution.

[32] Luke 10:13-14//Matt 11:20-21; Luke 11:32//Matt 12:41.

[33] As conveyed throughout Luke-Acts, repentance provides forgiveness of sins and deliverance from destruction (Luke 3:3, 7-14; 10:13-14; 11:32; 16:27-30; 17:3-4; 24:47; Acts 2:38; 3:17-23; 5:31; 8:20-24; 17:30-31; 26:16-20).

[34] Jesus illustrates this point with the parable of the barren fig tree at the end of this unit (vv. 6-9). The Parable of the Prodigal Son (15:11-32) illustrates that repentance leads to forgiveness, deliverance, and acceptance. The Parable of the Rich Man and Lazarus (16:19-31), however, illustrates that a failure to repent leads to destruction. The rich man did not end up in Hades because he was rich or because of his treatment of Lazarus. He ended up in Hades because he failed to repent. Even though his brothers also failed to care for Lazarus, they can avoid Hades if they repent.

"Repent, and be baptized every one of you in the name of Jesus Christ for the forgiveness of your sins" (Acts 2:22-38). As in the gospel, *metanoeō* and *metanoia* again represent a change in thinking that leads to a change in behavior and/or way of life. In Acts this change in thinking often has to do with a change in thinking regarding Jesus' identity. This change in thinking about Jesus, however, also results in a change in the way people think about and live in relationship with others.

In the synagogue at Nazareth, Jesus made it clear that God sent him for others, not simply for those listening (Luke 4:18-30). Because of this emphasis on others, the audience became hostile and rejected Jesus. By rejecting him they were rejecting the notion of God's acceptance of all people. In Acts, repentance for the Jews involves a change in thinking regarding Jesus; however, if they are going to change their thinking regarding Jesus they are also going to have to change their thinking regarding Jesus' teachings concerning the acceptance of all people. This change in thinking regarding the acceptance of all people is climactically depicted in the encounter between Peter and Cornelius (Acts 10).

The stage is set for this encounter by a series of visions and revelations. While Cornelius understands his vision, Peter does not initially understand his. It is not until Cornelius informs Peter about his own visionary experience that Peter understands his vision and declares what is clearly one of the defining programmatic statements of Luke-Acts: "Truly I perceive that God is not one who shows partiality, but in every nation anyone who fears him and does what is right is acceptable to him" (Acts 10:34-54). When Peter returns to Jerusalem he is greeted with criticism for going to the Gentiles and eating with them. Peter responds by recounting the entire interaction. The substance of Peter's argument is that if the Lord had demonstrated that there is no distinction between Jews and Gentiles, how could he oppose God by trying to maintain such a distinction? When the leaders hear Peter's account, they praise God and declare, "Then even to the Gentiles God has given the repentance that leads to life" (Acts 11:4-18).

While Cornelius and the other Gentiles are the ones depicted as repenting, as was the case with the tax collectors and soldiers in the preaching of John the Baptist, the acceptance of the Gentiles into the community of God's people required a fundamental change in thinking on the part of those who considered themselves God's chosen ones. The repentance of tax collectors, soldiers, Gentiles, and other so-called sinners gains them forgiveness and helps fulfill God's plan of universal salvation; however, it is the repentance of those who consider themselves the only ones worthy of membership in the community of God's people that leads to the establishment of a community that embraces all people.[35]

A similar theme appears in Paul's speech in Athens.[36] Here Paul acknowledges that the Athenians' idols, altars, and inscriptions testify to the fact that they are more religious than most. Paul seeks to persuade them, however, to change their thinking. Paul proclaims a God who is lord of all things and all people and who has caused all the nations of the world to spring forth from one common ancestor so that everyone together might seek after and serve the same God. According to Paul the Jews had acted out of ignorance with regard to Jesus, and the Gentiles had acted out of ignorance with regard to God. However, since God has revealed God's nature through Jesus, ignorance is no longer an excuse. God now commands everyone everywhere to repent. This speech requires more than Gentiles changing the way they think about God; it also requires people to change the way they think about their relationship to others. Paul's speech testifies to the sovereignty of God and the oneness of humanity. The author combines in this one speech the two aspects of repentance that are central to the overall purpose of Luke-Acts: (1) to promote a change in thinking about God/Jesus that enables everyone to receive the salvation of God, and (2) to promote a change in thinking about others that enables all people to live together as a community of God's people.

## 2. Implications

Several implications can be drawn from the depiction of repentance found in the Synoptics and Acts.

---

[35] Although utilizing the language of "conversion" rather than "repentance," Chan-Hie Kim makes the same point by declaring, "The narrative is traditionally known as the story about the first gentile convert, but a closer look at it indicates that it is about the 'conversion' of Peter instead of Cornelius' conversion to Christianity" ("Reading the Cornelius Story from an Asian Immigrant Perspective," in Mary Ann Tolbert and Fernando Segovia, eds., *Reading from this Place*, Vol.1 [Minneapolis: Fortress Press, 1995] 170; see also Beverly Roberts Gaventa, *From Darkness to Light: Aspects of Conversion in the New Testament* [Philadelphia: Fortress Press, 1986] 109).

[36] Acts 17:22-31. According to Acts, Paul was called by God to demand that people repent and perform deeds worthy of repentance (26:19-20).

a. Repentance is not an option; it is a requirement for all those who intend to live as disciples of Jesus.

b. Repentance is not merely change for the sake of change, but rather change in response to the inbreaking of the kingdom of God.

c. Repentance is public, not private. Since it is in response to the kingdom of God, it addresses communal issues and concerns rather than merely individual issues and concerns. It is not simply about personal improvement and individual contrition and/or remorse over personal failings. It is about changes in thinking and living that address the needs of all those for whom God is concerned.

d. Because repentance is in response to the kingdom of God, it addresses issues of power. It speaks to power dynamics and relations. It requires all Christians to engage in an ongoing examination of their ways of thinking and living. The demand for repentance causes us to examine to whom and to what manifestations of power we have given our allegiance. The status quo, which serves the interest of the powerful at the expense of the powerless, is no longer acceptable.

e. Confronting systems of power on behalf of oppressed people often results in opposition. Since those in power never surrender power without a fight, the demand for repentance is a demand to lose one's life for the sake of Jesus and the good news.

## 3. Further Reading

Blount, Brian. *Go Preach! Mark's Kingdom Message and the Black Church Today.* New York: Orbis, 1998.

Johnson-DeBaufre, Melanie. *Jesus Among Her Children: Q, Eschatology, and the Construction of Christian Origins.* Cambridge, MA: Harvard University Press, 2005.

Mitchell, Joan. *Beyond Fear and Silence: A Feminist-Literary Approach to the Gospel of Mark.* New York: Continuum, 2001.

Nave, Guy. *The Role and Function of Repentance in Luke-Acts.* Atlanta: Society of Biblical Literature, 2002.

Rhoads, David. "The Gospel of Matthew: The Two Ways: Hypocrisy or Righteousness," *CTM* 19 (1992) 453–61.

Sanders, E. P. *The Historical Figure of Jesus*. London: Penguin, 1993.

Schnackenburg, Rudolf. "The Demand for Repentance." In idem, *The Moral Teaching of the New Testament*. Trans. J. H. Smith and J. W. J. O'Hara. New York: Herder and Herder, 1962, 25–33.

Song, Choan Seng. *Jesus and the Reign of God*. Minneapolis: Fortress Press, 1993.

Theissen, Gerd, and Annette Merz. *The Historical Jesus: A Comprehensive Guide*. Minneapolis: Fortress Press, 1998.

Willis, Wendell, ed. *The Kingdom of God in 20ᵗʰ Century Interpretation*. Peabody, MA: Hendrickson, 1987.

# 4. Hermeneutical Reflection

"What about God? Surely repentance entails sinners returning to God?" Fellow participants in this project often asked me this question. My response was that at no time before, during, or immediately after the writing of the New Testament documents were *metanoeō* or *metanoia* ever used to convey a returning to God. Furthermore, nowhere in the Synoptics or Acts does *metanoeō* or *metanoia* explicitly or implicitly suggest a returning to God. While this is true, the response does not address the experiential variables that have contributed to my own discomfort with how repentance has been traditionally presented within Christian theology.

We all began this project with our own understanding of repentance. Many of us talked about "*the* Christian concept of repentance," as if there was one definition that governed how we all understood repentance. It was obvious, however, that while we all talked about "repentance" we were not all talking about the same thing. When I work with biblical texts I try to be as faithful to the text as I can. This is often difficult because I, like others, am a person situated within a matrix of social experiences that affect and influence the way I understand and interpret the Bible. My experience with those who talk about repentance as "returning to God" is that they privatize repentance as something simply between God and the individual. They do not want to discuss social implications. They do not want demands being made of them to change their way of thinking and living. By reducing repentance to a private matter between an individual and God, they can avoid a critique of their responsibility to society. Repentance in the Synoptics and Acts, however, is not a private matter; it is very public. It requires fruit, and that fruit is manifested within society.

In 2003 and 2005 I took a group of U.S. college students to South Africa to study the results of the Truth and Reconciliation Commission

(TRC). In order to help facilitate the transition from apartheid to democracy, the South African government decided to deal with the atrocities of its past via a truth commission. The government asserted that reconciliation was the ultimate goal of its truth commission. Apartheid had systematically divided South Africa along racial lines. Many white South Africans, however, denied that racially motivated atrocities ever occurred under apartheid. The government believed the only way to reconcile the nation was to make the truth public. In order to facilitate the revealing of the truth, the government promised amnesty to all who came forward to tell the truth about atrocities they had committed.

While repentance was not a requirement of the TRC, some South Africans equated telling the truth with repentance. During our time in South Africa, many white South African Christians made comments like, "What do Blacks want? White South Africans have admitted to the atrocities. We've repented. They have a Black government now. What more do they want?" One white South African who was granted amnesty said to me, "I have repented and God has forgiven me, that's all that matters to me."

South Africa celebrated ten years of democracy in 2004, but many South Africans are saying that in order for there to be reconciliation there has to be a fundamental change in thinking and living that seeks to correct the injustices done under apartheid. Many white South Africans, however, do not want to change their ways of thinking and living. They have "made things right with God" and don't understand why people can't move on. They point to the presence of a Black middle class as proof of change. While the presence of Blacks in government has given rise to a black middle class, the majority of black South Africans still live in abject poverty, and most of the wealth and privileges remain in the hands of white South Africans. Many white South Africans see nothing wrong with this and do not want to talk about their responsibility for ensuring wealth and privileges are distributed equitably. Repentance, however, demands a change in thinking and living that requires white South Africans to love nonwhite South Africans as they love themselves and to live as passionately for others as they live for themselves.

Although my experiences have shaped the way I think about repentance, engaging in this project has forced me to give more attention to the place of God within a Christian understanding of repentance. Repentance in the Synoptics and Acts is in response to the kingdom of God; therefore a (re)turning to God is inevitable. Living under the reign of God means being passionate about the things God is passionate about.

This is why Peter and Paul say, "Repent therefore, and *turn to God"* (Acts 2:19; 26:19-20). Repentance is not synonymous with turning to God, but it is associated with turning to God.

It may be possible, therefore, to talk about *"the* Christian concept of repentance." In the Synoptics and Acts the demand for repentance is a demand to live life based on the teachings and lifestyle of Jesus. Jesus was killed because in response to the kingdom of God he lived a life challenging systems of power—both religious and political—on behalf of those oppressed by systems of power. Jesus proclaimed this mission by declaring:

> The Spirit of the Lord is upon me, because he has anointed me to bring good news to the poor. He has sent me to proclaim release to the captives and recovery of sight to the blind, to let the oppressed go free, to proclaim the year of the Lord's favor. (Luke 4:18-19)

The message of the Synoptics and Acts is that in response to the kingdom of God we are called to live our lives on behalf of those oppressed by systems of power. While such living will often lead to opposition, resistance, and even persecution, the demand for repentance is a demand to live for others as passionately as we live for ourselves.

Six

# "And I Shall Heal Them":
# Repentance, Turning, and Penitence in the Johannine Writings

*Edith M. Humphrey*

## 1. Text

"He has blinded their eyes and hardened their heart, lest they should see with their eyes and perceive with their heart, and *be turned*—and I shall heal them" (John 12:40).[1]

Here is an unpromising start for a consideration of repentance in the Johannine writings! The Fourth Gospel, at the sole point where "turning" is detailed, employs the term within a pessimistic prophetic indictment. Such is also the perspective of Revelation, where no less than five times the reader hears of those who do not repent, and where a closing exhortation hardly bodes well for the penitent: "Let the evildoer still do evil, and the filthy still be filthy, and the righteous still do right, and the holy still be holy" (Rev 22:11). Though more pastoral, the Johannine

---

[1] This is my own translation, which I prefer to both the *RSV* and the *NRSV* for reasons that will become apparent.

epistles, too, speak soberly about the "sin unto death" for which there is no repentance.

Though few consider these books to be from the same hand, and though they differ in genre, the Fourth Gospel, the Johannine epistles, and Revelation (the Apocalypse of Jesus to John) share one common remarkable trait: that overarching theme of light over against darkness. What has happened to the dominical call, "Repent, for the kingdom of heaven is at hand"? Has repentance been banished from the Johannine writings, replaced by a stark dualism between the children of light and the children of darkness? So thought C. G. Montefiore, who declared "[t]he doctrine of repentance . . . is wholly absent from the Fourth Gospel."[2] But is this actually the case? Is the dualism so absolute? Does it evoke a world in which, for some, the moment for repentance has been missed, forever elusive?

*Mē genoito!* Though the Fourth Gospel never uses any cognate of the usual term for "repentance" (*metanoia*) and only once appeals to the theological motif of "turning," its unfolding narrative offers readers a series of penitential characters, both of major importance and of the type that R. Alan Culpepper calls "ficelles."[3] While the Johannine epistles firmly separate believers from "those who are not of us," they also issue a tender call to confession. Finally, in Revelation the call to repentance is unrelenting and urgent. Though the rhetorical approaches of evangelist, elder, and seer differ, nowhere in these writings is the call to repentance muted, and nowhere has the penitent cause to be disheartened.

### a. The Fourth Gospel: A Drama of Turning

Scholars puzzle over the absence of the term *metanoia* in this gospel, especially since the Synoptics uniformly begin with the call of both the Baptizer and Jesus to repentance. Some have explained this by positing a different approach on the part of the evangelist, for example, "mystical union" over against pardon as a key to soteriology.[4] Others consider that the term "repentance" has been swallowed up by a larger

---

[2] C. G. Montefiore, *Rabbinic Literature and Gospel Teachings* (London: MacMillan, 1930) 390.

[3] A "ficelle" is a minor character used by the evangelist to a particular end. R. Alan Culpepper, *Anatomy of the Fourth Gospel* (Minneapolis: Fortress Press, 1994).

[4] For example, Mary Edith Andrews, "Paul and Repentance," *JBL* 54 (1935) 125.

concept, such as "faith."[5] Such observations do not fully explain why a gospel that begins with the preaching of the one destined to "turn" hearts (the Baptizer, i.e., Elijah "returned"), and ending with Peter's restoration, should omit an explicit treatment of repentance. Perhaps we must consider the way in which the gospel works: it is typical of the Fourth Gospel to use an indirect approach toward crucial matters. This gospel elides the baptism of Jesus, though water imagery and Jesus' messianic identity are everywhere present. Similarly, there is no Transfiguration account, though glory shines from every page. Again, the Lord's Supper is never instituted, despite powerful meditation on Christ's body and blood. There is no Ascension, yet everywhere there is talk of the return to the Father.

So it is with repentance. The gospel does not issue an explicit call. Nonetheless, the reader is brought, ineluctably, to repentance, both as an initial turn and as an ongoing way of being in Christ. Indeed, the reader is, through the narrative, *rendered* a penitent: "these things are written that you might believe that Jesus is the Christ . . . and that through believing[6] you may have life in his name" (20:31).

The gospel proceeds through a series of reorientations: John's disciples turn and follow the Lamb; Nathaniel's mind is changed; Nicodemus begins in ironic confrontation with the master (3:2-15) but converts offstage (19:39-42); Jesus transforms the Samaritan woman from cynic to evangelist; the paralytic's entire life is straightened by the Master (5:11); those offended by Jesus' "hard saying" come to a point of recommitment (6:60-69); the adulterous woman is released with an instruction not to sin again (8:1-11);[7] the blind man is illumined (ch. 9); Lazarus's sisters (ch. 11) are moved beyond a conventional belief in resurrection to trust in the One who is the Lord of life; Thomas is changed, no longer requiring to touch Jesus' wounds; the grieving Mary is surprised by joy; Peter is restored and redirected toward his designed paths in God's service. By entering into all these stories the reader is initiated into the miracle of

[5] For example, Gross Alexander, "Repentance," in James Hastings, ed., *A Dictionary of Christ and the Gospels* (New York: Scribner, 1908) 2:499; also John Cecil Anderson, "Repentance in the Greek New Testament" (Ph.D. diss., Dallas Theological Seminary, 1959) 370.

[6] Here, surveying the variants, I read a present participle, πιστεύοντες.

[7] I consider the gospel in its canonical shape, without reference to the debate concerning the origin of this passage.

repentance and the new disposition of penitence that is the province of God's children.

Debates about this gospel frequently have as their backdrop the Protestant-Catholic argument concerning repentance and penitence. Some co-opt John's writings to bolster a Romaphobic eschewal of ongoing penitence, distinguishing between "Jewish" (or Pharisaic) *teshuba* ("turning," "repentance") and an "authentic" *metanoia* consonant with *sola fides*.[8] Pharisaism or "late Judaism" becomes a cipher for Roman dogmatic error, while *metanoia* is rendered literally as "a change of mind," and not subdivided into contrition, decision of the will, and satisfaction. Others counter that Jewish tradition provided a *godly* trajectory toward the Roman teaching concerning repentance, from middle Judaism, to the New Testament, to the sub-apostolic fathers[9]: "Metanoia . . . is *the* determining factor in . . . the relationship between God and man,"[10] "a condition for participation in Messianic Blessings."[11]

However, we can neither trace a straight line from the Jewish concept of *teshuba* to the Apostolic Fathers nor posit complete discontinuity between Hebrew piety and the surprise of the gospel. A richer understanding of the complexities of Judaism in the first century means that we will not caricature the Pharisees or assume that their views were the only ones available to middle Judaism. Instead, the Fourth Gospel helps us to see that in the New Testament there are two tributaries to follow in understanding repentance. The New Testament, including the Fourth Gospel, pictures the "righteous" in Israel, who sought the impending rule of God, in such figures as Nicodemus and the sisters of Lazarus. Then

[8] Some Protestant commentaries retain the perspective of William Tyndale, *Doctrinal Treatises and Introductions to Different Portions of the Holy Scriptures* (Cambridge: Cambridge University Press, 1848), who complained that Catholic theologians had distorted repentance, rendering it "penance, to blind the people," 260.

[9] E.g., Aloys H. Dirksen, *The New Testament Concept of Metanoia* (Washington: Catholic University of America, 1932).

[10] Ibid. 2, my italics.

[11] Ibid. 1. This is not the place to rehearse either his tendentious argument (in which Clement's hope that his congregation "might be disciplined unto repentance" [*1 Clem* 7–8] is seen as a reference to specific penances and rituals) or to lament the opposite error of those "Romaphobes" who are happy to ignore the presence of believer's penitence in the Fourth Gospel, or indeed in the New Testament as a whole.

there are those, embodied in the Samaritan woman, who were wholly overtaken by surprise. Both the "righteous remnant" and the wayward are called to "be turned," with the emphasis falling upon God's action.

Indeed, the Fourth Gospel accentuates the divine initiative by its elision of the term "repentance" and its single reference to "turning" (John 12:40, *strephō*). Alfred Edersheim observes, "Christ first welcomes 'the sinner' to God and so makes him a penitent."[12] Not to emphasize the human action of "changing the mind" *(metanoeien)* places the accent on God. One shines in the darkness: we watch for the response of those on whom this light shines. Which way will they "turn?" And what will God do in the lives of those who "are turned" to their orientation?

Though in the New Testament the technical term for conversion is *metanoeō,* both the LXX and the New Testament use *strephō* (and, more regularly, *epistrephō*) cognates to translate the Hebrew *šûb* (noun *teshuba,* Greek *epistrophē*). Moreover, the verb "turn" and "turn to" can be used in a physical sense, as well as to suggest a *mistaken* turning.[13] The allusive Fourth Gospel sometimes employs *strephō* for a physical action, but with a spiritual *double entendre,* inviting us to see the physical actions of the main characters as a "turning to" the Christ. Typically the Fourth Gospel neither psychologizes nor dwells upon the emotions of its characters—everything is in the doing, the words, and the theological commentary. Thus there is no reference to the affective dimension of "sorrow" or "regret" *(metamelesthai).* The gospel is designed not to elicit empathy, but to bring the reader into the divine drama!

How, then, does the Fourth Gospel use the motif of "turning" in order to point the way to repentance? Light comes into the world, and shines; we expect certain reactions to this light, and will not be disappointed. Before our eyes the world is divided into those who face the light and follow, and those who turn away. Networks of metaphors spin the story, depicting those who stand, follow, come and see (1:35), who "believe" (2:23-24) and "come to the light" (3:20-21), who "believe and obey" (3:36), who "hear and believe" and so pass from death to life

[12] Alfred Edersheim, *The Life and Times of Jesus the Messiah* (New York: Longmans, Green, 1896) 2:253.

[13] In the Acts of the Apostles (Acts 3:19 and 26:20) *metanoeō* and *epistrephō* are coupled, with the first word describing the negative turn away from wickedness and the second indicating the turn to God. See J. Goetzmann, μετάνοια, in Colin Brown, gen. ed., *New International Dictionary of New Testament Theology.* 4 vols. (Grand Rapids: Zondervan, 1975–1986) 1:359.

(5:22-24), who turn from food that perishes to food that endures (6:27), who come and drink (7:37), who are divided one from the other (7:40-44), who are healed and told to sin no more (8:11), who follow and walk in the light (8:12), who hear the shepherd's voice and follow (10:1-4), who have bathed but must continue to wash (13:10), and who must as branches be "pruned" (15:2).

As the plot moves toward Christ's Passion we might expect more internal *angst*. Surprisingly, even at the point of Peter's denial the story is sparse, offering no comment regarding Peter's sorrow—though this *is* found in Mark's parallel account. Despite this omission of Peter's internal state, the Fourth Gospel does include Peter's rehabilitation, when Jesus questions him regarding love and commissions him as apostle. There Peter is distracted, and "turns" *(epistrephō)* toward "the other disciple" only to be pulled up short by the Lord: "What is that to you? Follow me!" (21:22). Peter's mis-turn to his colleague is to be contrasted with the double "turning" of the mourning Mary *(strephō,* 20:14, 16) who, in orienting herself toward the risen Lord, is commissioned as apostle to the apostles. "Casting away the ancestral curse,"[14] the division between male and female and the breach between death and life, she "elatedly announces to the disciples" Jesus' good news of the resurrection, the ascension, and our adoption as children of light. The Son both redirects the distracted and illumines the eyes that are blinded by grief, transforming them into "seers of the Lord" (20:31) and bearers of his word. Their turning and returning ends in the glory of God (21:19) and in the encouragement of God's people.

Now that we have seen that this text is "thick" with references to "turning," we may look more closely at John 12:31-43. This citation from Isa 6:10, found in other parts of the New Testament, was obviously a key teaching passage in the early church—one that explained God's economy, the miracle of repentance, and the mysterious denial of God's Son. The immediate context in the Fourth Gospel is that of the triumphal entry, and Jesus' introduction to the only Gentiles mentioned in this gospel. All of Jesus' signs, save for the resurrection, have been performed; the evidence is before the leaders and the people. The die is cast—Jesus will be rejected even by those who have on one level "believed"—yet we have heard the promise that there will be "much fruit" (12:24) of believ-

---

[14] The phrases come from the thrice-sung Orthodox *troparion* (the fourth tone in a cycle of resurrectional *troparia* in the Great Vespers).

ers, even beyond the immediate people of God. Jesus speaks about his coming death and encourages those who hear him to "walk in the light." Once the signs have been given, he departs from them (12:36b).

Here the narrator fuses two quotations from Isaiah (Isa 53:1; Isa 6:10), commenting that many had seen the signs but this had not issued in (true) belief. Though the evidence, the glory, is before these witnesses, "they loved human glory more than the glory that comes from God" and feared the reaction of others (12:42-43). This should be no surprise, implies the evangelist, because Isaiah himself had exclaimed that God's message would not be heeded.

The recasting of the second Isaiah quotation is significant. In the Masoretic text of Isa 6:10 the LORD commands the prophet, by means of his unrequited proclamation, to "make" the mind, ears, and eyes of the people dull, deaf, and blind, lest they turn and be healed. The LXX of the same verse, which is reproduced almost exactly in Matt 13:14-15 and Acts 28:26-7, instead describes a state: "The heart of this people *has grown dull . . . ."* As with the Masoretic text, there is in LXX/Matthew/Acts a triadic chiasmus of affected organs (ABCC'B'A'—heart, ears, eyes; eyes, ears, hearts):

A ἐπαχύνθη γὰρ ἡ καρδία τοῦ λαοῦ τούτου,

B καὶ τοῖς ὠσὶν [αὐτῶν, LXX] βαρέως ἤκουσαν

C καὶ τοὺς ὀφθαλμοὺς αὐτῶν ἐκάμμυσαν,

C' μήποτε ἴδωσιν τοῖς ὀφθαλμοῖς

B' καὶ τοῖς ὠσὶν ἀκούσωσιν

A' καὶ τῇ καρδίᾳ συνῶσιν καὶ ἐπιστρέψωσιν καὶ ἰάσομαι αὐτούς.

These organs are described as impaired, so that the people do not turn— but if they turn, says the prophetic LXX voice, "I (i.e., the LORD) will heal them (καὶ ἰάσομαι αὐτούς)." Though John has followed the Masoretic text in some particulars, here he agrees with the other New Testament writers[15] and the LXX, where God is clearly the subject of the healing action. This version, over against the indeterminate Masoretic construction, "and someone heals him" *(wĕrāpā' lô),*[16] is consonant with the purpose of all the evangelists, emphasizing God's initiative. Moreover, despite

[15] Except for Mark 4:12, which ends with a pessimistic subjunctive.

[16] Note however, that one variant of the Masoretic text (𝔊, "and I heal them") is more consonant with the LXX, "and I will heal them."

the subjunctive mood of the first two clauses ("lest they turn . . . lest they perceive"), the citation closes in the future tense: "and I will heal them." Both the Greek and the English are torturous: it is unfortunate that English translators have smoothed out the phrase, rendering it in the subjunctive (*NRSV:* "and I would heal them") or as a purpose clause (*RSV:* "for me to heal them").[17] Rather, the reworked quotation seems designed to move from an unlikely prospect to a positive statement of God's intent: the pessimism is not complete.

However, the Fourth Gospel reverts (unlike Matthew and Acts) to the troublesome prophetic voice of the Masoretic version at the point where it assigns the dulling of receptive faculties to God's action (Τετύφλωκεν . . . καὶ ἐπώρωσεν). The mystery of human rejection is connected with divine agency.[18] Light has come into darkness, and is doing its separating work. As we have heard three times, there is a *schisma* among them because of him (7:43; 9:6; 10:19). This is the *krisis:* Jesus' presence either draws or repulses, either opens or closes, either blinds or makes to see.

In line with the gospel's artistic and theological purposes, the evangelist further adapts, substituting a parallel structure for the original triad. The parallel moves two times from eyes to heart, suggesting the

[17] Preliminary research on various passages that use strings of subjunctives after a negative (μήποτε or ἵνα μη) has not yielded many parallels: there are few passages that move from subjunctive to a future indicative. Matthew 27:64 has a similar series of subjunctives, as does LXX Exod 34:15ff., but there is no true parallel here. Matthew 7:6 moves from a subjunctive to a future, "lest they trample them and turning, they will attack you!" as does Matt 21:34; both examples, by use of the future, give a vivid aspect to the final action, as perhaps also does our text. All in all, however, the LXX Isa 6:10 is a rare grammatical construction. Despite its rarity the move is replicated, in the citation of Isaiah's verse, by three evangelists—Matthew, Luke, and John, even where John alters other points of the citation. This seems significant. Could it be that this particular rendering of the prophetic word was particularly important to the teaching of the early church, as they struggled with the anomaly of resistance to God's will, first in the case of the Jewish community and then (as is likely the case in John) in the case of "secessionists" (the term is from Raymond Brown; see the discussion of the epistles below, where the history of the Johannine community is considered).

[18] It may be that the divine agency is also stressed in John's use of the passive for turning (καὶ στραφῶσιν, "and they be turned") though this may simply be the use of passive with a reflexive meaning; cf. Matt 18:3.

desired but frustrated progression of outer knowledge (seen by eyes) to inner understanding (in the heart):

Τετύφλωκεν αὐτῶν τοὺς ὀφθαλμοὺς

κα ἐπώρωσεν αὐτῶν τὴν καρδίαν,

ἵνα μὴ ἴδωσιν τοῖς ὀφθαλμοῖς

καὶ νοήσωσιν τῇ καρδίᾳ καὶ στραφῶσιν,

καὶ ἰάσομαι αὐτούς. (John 12:40)

This modification highlights the dynamic of divine signs and incomplete human response that John has set up. Seven times people have been confronted with Jesus' identity and mission—water transformed, a child healed, a lame man cured, food and chaotic storm mastered, the man born blind illumined, and Lazarus raised from the dead. So the evangelist speaks of those who "believe" what they see, but do not really "believe" (12:42) with the heart. All has been done, yet the plaintive cry of the prophet remains: "Who has believed our report, and to whom has the arm of the Lord been revealed?" "Turning" means that the reception of revelation moves from the outside to the inside[19]—and only then will God fully heal. The rest of the gospel traces how those with a superficial faith will be brought from "the night" (13:30) to resurrection morning. The definitive "turn" takes place first in Jesus, then in his followers. With Mary the reader is invited to turn, and turn again, to see the Lord. With Peter the reader is restored, recalled from turning to other concerns, and redirected: "Follow me!"

### b. The Epistles: Pastoral Guide for Penitents

Thus the gospel, though it makes no outright references to *metanoia*, places *strophē* at climactic points, tracing the "turn" for readers as they are welcomed into its narrative. The pastoral epistles of John deal specifically with the components of repentance although, like the gospel, they do not name this action. As with the gospel, contrasts abound. The epistles struggle with the disparity between what is normative for Christians—to walk in the light—and the fact of sin. Absolute language

[19] Rod Whitacre, *John* (Downers Grove and Leicester: InterVarsity Press, 1999) comments "In this way [John] focuses on the signs of Jesus (cf. v. 37) and moves from the outer to the inner, as he has done before," 321.

conveys the seriousness of the elder's message: "Everyone who commits sin is a child of the devil . . . . Those who have been born of God do not sin" (1 John 3:6, 9); "Everyone who does not abide in the teaching of Christ, but goes beyond it, does not have God" (2 John 8b); "Whoever does good is from God; whoever does evil has not seen God" (3 John 11b). Coupled with a seeming dualism, however, is a tenderness toward those caught in trespass ("But if anyone does sin . . ." 1 John 2:1b) and a confidence that the *dikaios* Jesus is the *hilasmos* (atoning sacrifice) not simply "for us" but for the entire *kosmos* (1 John 2:2). The imagery is black and white, constructed with boundaries; the explicit teaching is that these boundaries are "soft" and admit turning, or travel from one side to the other.

Some have understood this dualism in the context of an ecclesial story glimpsed between the lines of the text. The late Raymond E. Brown, along with others, traces the elusive history of the "community of the beloved Disciple"[20] using the elder's oppositions as clues to the character of the community's opponents. Some of the speculations do not involve a vicious degree of "mirror reading"—for example, it is sensible to presume that there were some who "denied that Jesus had come in the flesh" and some who "went beyond" the teaching of Christ to adopt novelties.

With regard to our specific theme Brown suggests that the schismatic error claimed to be "without sin"—hence the admonitions about admitting sin at 1 John 1:8-10.[21] This construction fits well with some of the perfectionist groups that arose in the second century; however, on the basis of the text alone they are not incontrovertible. Perhaps, rather than indicting the schismatics these verses are directed toward the elder's own flock, which, like him, struggles with the anomaly of sin in the community of light. Both Pheme Perkins[22] and Judith Lieu[23] plead that the epistles ought not to be read as polemical texts, but as letters of edification in a strong rhetorical style, to teach the community how to walk in the light.

[20] See the monograph by Raymond E. Brown, *The Community of the Beloved Disciple* (New York: Paulist, 1979), who also details alternate scenarios for the development of the "Johannine community/ies" offered by J. Louis Martyn, Georg Richter, Oscar Cullman, Marie-Emile Boismard, and Wolfgang Langbrandtner.

[21] Brown remarks: "The secessionists may have claimed that by becoming children of God, they became sinless," *Community*, 126.

[22] Pheme Perkins, "Koinonia in 1 John 1:3-7," *CBQ* 45 (1983) 631–41.

[23] Judith Lieu, "What was from the Beginning," *NTS* 39 (1993) 458–77.

This "walking" includes the discipline of turning from sin—sin that ought not to exist[24] but that still plagues the life of his "little children." The prescription for dealing with the deeds of darkness is this: recognition that there is sin (1 John 1:8), confession of sin (1 John 1:9), reception of forgiveness, and cleansing from sin and "unrighteousness" *(adikia).* The epistle also offers some litmus tests to make sure that this watching and walking are effective. Do we love the children of God (2:7 *et passim*)? Do we love God, or the things of this passing age (2:15-17)? Do we place our confidence in those teachers who confess that Jesus is the Messiah (2:22; 4:2), and that he has come in the flesh? Do we give active help to those in trouble (3:17)? Do we recognize the gift of the Holy Spirit in our midst (4:13)?

Where the answer is given in the negative, the elder warns his readers to confess sin and so begin the walk once again. Moreover, repentance is not a solitary endeavor, but something that takes place within the community. Thus Christian siblings are instructed to pray for a member of the family who is "missing the mark" by sinning. Here we detect the sober note that this epistle shares with Hebrews and the gospels: there is a dread sin that is *unto death,* for which prayer is useless. Except for this sin (unexplained by the elder) God will grant life when a Christian prays for the wrongdoings of another.

We are aware of the difficulty such verses caused for the sub-apostolic church, which wrestled with the phenomenon of post-baptismal sin (cf. *The Shepherd of Hermas*). Within the context of the Scriptures as a whole, however, this sin *unto death* is less enigmatic. Jesus speaks frankly regarding the "sin against the Holy Spirit" (Mark 3:29 and parallels)—which involves, it would seem, hardening the heart and mind to what the Spirit is saying, including the Spirit's pointed witness regarding sin and conviction. According to Raymond Brown, who understands much of the epistles in terms of community conflict, the "sin unto death" is the sin of those who have left the community and so abandoned the truth.[25] Apostasy may well be included in the elder's closing words. Yet it would seem that this explanation is not nuanced enough to explain the meaning of 5:16, since the instructions

---

[24] St. Symeon the New Theologian remarks that the elder intends to bring his community to sensitivity concerning the anomaly of sin in the Christian life. See his reference to 1 John 1:9 as recorded by John Chryssavgis, *Repentance and Confession in the Orthodox Church* (Brookline: Holy Cross Orthodox Press, 1988) 81.

[25] Brown, *Community*, 133.

speak about praying "for a brother."[26] Later generations were to fall into a rigorist interpretation, as with Tertullian, who insisted that Christ would not advocate for mortal offenses, during the Donatist controversies, when forgiveness was denied to the *traditores* who had foresworn Christ under duress. However, given the seer's initial affirmation that Jesus' death is "for the whole world," who can maintain with assurance that the one who has "turned away" might not turn back? Many wise pastors read this warning in terms of the *refusal* to repent, that is, an unchanged and unchangeable denial of our sinful state and Christ's mercy. In this vein Mark the Ascetic warns: "There is a sin which is always 'unto death' [1 John 5.16]: the sin for which we do not repent. For this sin even a saint's prayers will not be heard."[27] The reference to this unhealed (and incurable) sin brings us back to the enigma of Isaiah 6: if there is no turning, there can be no healing. Otherwise, God whispers, "I shall heal them."

Despite this dark shadow, God's tenderness is held out as a pattern for those who are in his fellowship. The love of God creates love between brothers, including the fervent desire that the ones we love turn and are healed. Reconciliation, enacted by Jesus, becomes the action of his church. Repentance takes on a corporate as well as a personal character. All this happens, though, without a whiff of the sentimental. The elder knows that there are some times when prayer is wasted (cf. Jesus' pearl before swine, Matt 7:6) and comforts his children by saying that those who have left them really never belonged.

The epistle, then, treats repentance pastorally, prescribing it as necessary and breaking it down into manageable parts, while understanding it within the larger context of the church's *koinōnia*. Hopeful instruction characterizes the letter, even while the elder allows for the tragedy that some will not subscribe to discipline or follow in the path of Light. And so, concludes the elder, "Little children, keep yourselves from idols" (1 John 5:21).

---

[26] See John Painter, *1, 2, and 3 John*, SP 18 (Collegeville: Liturgical Press, 2002) 319. He argues convincingly that this statement is certainly about the possibility of a "sin unto death" among the brothers. Painter believes the sin "probably has to do with rejection of the confession of faith" though he visits other possibilities. On the overall debate see also the detailed discussion by Ruth B. Edwards, "Sin, Forgiveness, Judgment and Eschatology," in Barnabas Lindars, Ruth B. Edwards, and John M. Court, *The Johannine Literature* (Sheffield: Sheffield Academic Press, 2000) 184–94.

[27] Cited in Chryssavgis, *Repentance and Confession*, 28.

## c. Revelation: Trumpet of Repentance

Unlike the Fourth Gospel and the epistles, Revelation explicitly urges repentance of anyone with ears to hear. References to *metanoia* and to *strophē* abound, addressing both the Christian community and the world. Indeed, John's initial vision of the Son of Man commences with a "turning"—"I turned and saw the Son of Man" (1:12). This is not clearly a reference to repentance, but it sets the tone for a book that is unremittingly perspectival. In the fashion typical of an apocalypse, the book encourages readers to change perspectives and see reality from a standpoint that is at once more remote and more near to those things that disturb us. With the seer we are whisked up and away—to the heavenlies (4:1), to the heavenly city (11:1), to the wilderness (17:3), to a mountain (21:10)—and see what reality (space, time, and identity) looks like from God's perspective. Along with John we are invited to "come up here" and behold the larger drama of which our world partakes, rejoicing in God's presence, peering into the abyss, and beholding the solemn judgment of God (20:1-2, 11-15). Through John's eyes we move through ages, to the moment of Jesus' incarnation, death, and resurrection (12:5-6), and to the protological heavenly battle in which our Advocate fought for us (12:7-9), perceiving that these times are one. By means of John's images we picture ourselves as other—as the woman and her children pursued by the dragon (ch. 12), as the 144,000 with the great multitude, as the Bride adorned for her husband. So we change vantage points in space, time, and identity, and trace our own transformation.[28]

These visions lead the faithful to a startling conclusion. Human activity, when performed in Christ, the firstborn witness, is utterly significant. The suffering of those in Christ is caught up into His suffering and is used to fight the battle: we have a *koinōnia* of tribulation and faithful endurance as we come to reign with Christ (1:9). The woman of chapter 12, exiled in God's Lenten wilderness, thus prepares herself and emerges as the City-Bride of God. Faithful suffering finds its prototype in the arch-martyr, Jesus. Those who turn from Babylon's ease and join in the witness of Jesus and his followers participate in that particular moment when the human and divine world are joined. That is, evil-resistant suffering and godly sorrow become human echoes of God's incarnation,

---

[28] For more on John's use of perspective, typical of apocalypses, to indicate the transformation of God's people, see Edith M. Humphrey, *The Ladies and the Cities* (Sheffield: Sheffield Academic Press, 1995).

the places where God meets with us: "They have conquered him by the blood of the Lamb and by the word of their testimony/martyrdom" (12:11). The "testimony" of those who are in Christ entails confession of sin, admission of our needy status before a holy God, and a repentant turn to God's service (2:5). Jesus, the slaughtered Lamb, recognizes the sacrifices of a broken and contrite heart and invites his own to "hear what the Spirit says" and "repent."

The central position of the "slaughtered Lamb" in the heavenlies (5:6) and the inability of anyone but that One to open the scroll tells the Christian community that repentance is a necessary part of our witness; the triumph of the "standing" Lamb declares God's victory over our dark shadows. Though the tribes of the world will see his glory and "wail," the faithful are called to a deeper action than this emotive (cf. *metameles-thai*) regret. As Kallistos Ware puts it, "Repentance is not a paroxysm of remorse and self-pity, but conversion, the re-centering of our life upon the Holy Trinity."[29] John has been caught up to the center of this holiness, and like Isaiah he has wept for the human plight; in response he offers us the standing slaughtered Lamb, who is worthy to open the seal of historical inscrutability, of human hardness, of disjointed events. While there remains the dark possibility of some outside God's gate, John Court is correct: "Potentially anyone who responds to the prophetic warning, and then repents, can be rescued . . . . The Spirit's words to the churches are not only addressed to the elect; potentially the prophetic warning and exhortation can be heard by anyone."[30] Though judgment is imminent, John sees that "from every tribe and tongue and people and nation" there shall be made "a kingdom and priests to our God" (5:10).

The overall shape of the book, then, involves "turning": we change as we are startled by the visions of the Son of Man. From the beginning to the end we hear the call to repentance, beginning with Christ's imperial decrees (2:5, 16, 21, 22; 3:2-3, 19) and followed by warnings regarding those who will not repent (9:20-21; 16:9, 10-11).

Those who are hard-hearted have grown like the gods they worship—unable to see, hear, or walk in the way of life. Giving up the proper God has meant that they have also given up their proper providence as human beings, so they can neither give thanks, nor repent, nor give God glory.

---

[29] Kallistos Ware, "The Orthodox Experience of Repentance," *Epiphany Journal* (Summer 1986) 12.

[30] John M. Court, "The Abiding Theological Values and Doctrines of Revelation," in Lindars, Edwards, and Court, *Johannine Literature*, 304.

This contrast between the intransigent and the hopeful call issued to the churches poses the same problem as that found in the gospel and the epistles. Some have seen Revelation as irredeemably dualistic, especially those older commentators for whom the overall tenor of apocalyptic language was distasteful.[31] The seer John's rigor has been excused by appealing to the book's supposed venue (marginalized or suffering Christians for whom vengeance and boundary-erection were safety devices). Though uncomfortable to the politically correct contemporary Western world, the vision of souls calling out under the altar for vindication is understandable in that context, say some.

Yet sociological excuses emasculate the prophecy, and condescend. Leonard Thompson remarks with insight that the "boundaries" in Revelation are "soft." [32] It might be better to say "soft" *while they are also hard.* The seer knows well that repentance and forgiveness are such as to startle us. He shows, in visionary contrasts, the same truth articulated solemnly by our Lord: "It is harder to enter the Kingdom of Heaven than for a camel to pass through the eye of a needle" (Mark 10:25). The natural course of action for those who are earthbound, blind, and hardened is to flee away before the sight of the Almighty. But God thinks better for us. So, then, Jezebel and her children will be "thrown into great distress, *unless they repent*" (2:22). Again, at the point of judgment, where the suspended woes of God will be finally leveled against the rebellious, God yearns for his compromised children: "Come out of her [i.e., Babylon] my people, that you do not take part in her sins, and so that you do not share in her plagues" (18:4).

Finally, then, Anne-Marit Enroth is correct when she says: "there is no connection with hardening and divisions of the hearers into two groups: those who do not hear and those who do."[33] Like the prophets of old, John the seer prophesies against unrighteousness, going through the world like Jonah through Nineveh, with an absolute message of judgment devoid of any "escape clause." Side by side with the indictment,

---

[31] As Klaus Koch declared, scholars have long been *ratlos vor* ["perplexed concerning"] *der Apokalyptik*. Koch's translated work, *The Rediscovery of Apocalyptic: A Polemical Work on a Neglected Area of Biblical Studies and its Damaging Effects on Theology and Philosophy,* trans. Margaret Kohl (London: SCM Press, 1972) offers a less picturesque title than the 1971 German original, *Ratlos.*

[32] Leonard L. Thompson, *The Book of Revelation—Apocalypse and Empire* (New York: Oxford University Press, 1990) 87.

[33] Anne-Marit Enroth, "The Hearing Formula in the Book of Revelation," *NTS* 36/4 (1990) 603.

however, sounds the call for repentance. Here is the paradox: that deaf ears, blind eyes, and hard hearts should be healed. So the veil is lifted, that ears should hear the Spirit, eyes should be dazzled by the One upon the throne, and hearts should be stirred by the sight of the Lamb. To this One by whose will all exist and were created, and to this One who is both in the midst of his creation and in the midst of the throne (5:6), and through the rejoicing voice of the Spirit, unceasing worship sounds in that City whose gates remain confidently open. Despite the specter of judgment, in the final vision there is no slamming of the holy gates. Instead, we hear the persistent invitation of the Spirit: "Come."

### d. Conclusion

Gospel, epistles, and Revelation together provide a triptych in which we see how to turn, turn, and turn again. Here, in gospel narrative, we are welcomed into a narrative studded with stories of repentance. Then, by instructive letters that reach across twenty centuries, penitents receive pastoral guidance and so walk in the light. Finally, to our debauched Western ears comes the clarion call upon the Wind of God: "Repent! Do the works that you did at first." Across every register, in three different modes, the divine Composer woos us, offering good news to address our imaginations, letters to instruct our minds, and an apocalypse to stir our hearts. For he will heal us.

## 2. Implications

The Johannine writings are a *locus classicus* for spiritual advisors. Symeon the New Theologian notes the urgent call: "By repentance run in the way of His commandments . . . . Run, run, while . . . He shines on you, before the night of death overtakes you [cf. John 9.4] . . . . He who does not repent commits sin, because he is not penitent . . . . He 'hates the light and does not come to the light, lest his deeds should be exposed'" [John 3:20].[34]

Symeon's words may not easily find their mark in an age allergic to dogmatic and ethical pronouncements. Yet the Johannine writings invite repentance by placing it within a drama rather than prescribing it as duty. The evangelist, who applies repentance to the "profligate" *and* the "faith-

---

[34] Cited in John Chryssavgis, *Repentance and Confession in the Orthodox Church* (Brookline: Holy Cross Orthodox Press, 1988) 62–63.

ful," may still be winsome to egalitarian ears. As it moves from indictment to hope (John 12:40), as it places Magdalene at the surprising climax, as it rehabilitates Peter, the Fourth Gospel compels. Similarly, the epistle disarms by combining realism with tenderness, while Revelation offers a perspective by which readers may grasp the cosmic significance of repentance. These differences in rhetorical method indicate that there is more than one way to commend change. The imagination, once kindled by the gospel's vignettes, may well go on to heed the crisp realism of the elder and finally embrace the larger implications shown by the seer. Though in our texts regret and remorse are never explicitly treated, the affections are quickened by the narrative, the paraenesis, and the vision. This affective dimension, accompanied by comprehension, represents our contribution to the world that God opens to us through the window of the text.

## 3. Further Reading

Alexander, Gross. "Repentance." In James Hastings, ed., *A Dictionary of Christ and the Gospels.* New York: Scribner, 1908, 2:499ff.

Anderson, John Cecil. "Repentance in the Greek New Testament," Ph.D. diss., Dallas Theological Seminary, 1959.

Andrews, Mary Edith. "Paul and Repentance," *JBL* 54 (1935) 125.

Behm, Johannes, and Ernst Würthwein, μετανοέω, μετάνοια. In Gerhard Kittel and Gerhard Friedrich, eds., Geoffrey W. Bromiley, trans., *Theological Dictionary of the New Testament.* Grand Rapids: Eerdmans, 1964–1976, 4: 975–1008.

Bertram, Georg. "ἐπιστρέφω, ἐπιστροφή." In Gerhard Kittel and Gerhard Friedrich, eds., Geoffrey W. Bromiley, trans., *Theological Dictionary of the New Testament.* Grand Rapids: Eerdmans, 1964–1976, 7: 722–29.

Brown, Raymond E. *The Community of the Beloved Disciple.* New York: Paulist, 1979.

Chryssavgis, John. *Repentance and Confession in the Orthodox Church.* Brookline: Holy Cross Orthodox Press, 1988.

Dirksen, Aloys H. *The New Testament Concept of Metanoia.* Washington, DC: Catholic University of America, 1932.

Edersheim, Alfred. *The Life and Times of Jesus the Messiah,* Vol. 1. New York: Longmans, Green, 1896.

Enroth, Anne Marit. "The Hearing Formula in the Book of Revelation," *NTS* 36/4 (1990) 598–608.

Gibbs, Lee W. "Richard Hooker's *Via Media* Doctrine of Repentance," *HTR* 84/1 (1991) 59–74.

Goetzmann, J. μετάνοια. In Colin Brown, gen. ed., *New International Dictionary of New Testament Theology.* 4 vols. (Grand Rapids: Zondervan, 1975–1986)

1:357–59. Translated with additions and revisions from Lothar Coenen, Erich Beyreuther, and Hans Bietenhard, eds., *Theologisches Begriffslexikon zum Neuen Testament*. 2 vols. in 3 (Wuppertal: Brockhaus, 1965–1971).

Humphrey, Edith M. *The Ladies and the Cities: Transformation and Apocalyptic Identity in Joseph and Aseneth, 4 Ezra, the Apocalypse and the Shepherd of Hermas.* Sheffield: Sheffield Academic Press, 1995.

Koch, Klaus. *The Rediscovery of Apocalyptic: A Polemical Work on a Neglected Area of Biblical Studies and its Damaging Effects on Theology and Philosophy.* Trans. by M. Kohl from the 1971 German original, *Ratlos vor der Apokalytik.* London: SCM Press, 1972.

Lindars, Barnabas, Ruth B. Edwards, and John M. Court. *The Johannine Literature.* Sheffield: Sheffield Academic Press, 1990.

Montefiore, C. G. *Rabbinic Literature and Gospel Teachings.* London: MacMillan, 1930.

Painter, John. *1, 2, and 3 John.* SP 18. Collegeville: Liturgical Press, 2002.

Thompson, Leonard L. *The Book of Revelation—Apocalypse and Empire.* New York: Oxford University Press, 1990.

Ware, Kallistos. "The Orthodox Experience of Repentance," *Epiphany Journal* (Summer 1986) 11–19.

Werline, Rodney Alan. *Penitential Prayer in Second Temple Judaism: The Development of a Religious Institution.* Atlanta: Scholars Press, 1998.

Whitacre, Rodney A. *John.* Downers Grove and Leicester: InterVarsity Press, 1999.

# 4. Hermeneutical Reflection

The reading of three texts side by side has been instructive. The diversity of my raw material has built into my task an internal dimension of diversity alongside the external dimension of our group's varied constituencies and approaches. As a person who considers that communication, even between cultures, is possible (cf. Terence's *humani nihil a me alienum puto*, "I consider nothing human to be alien to me"), and as an exegete who still believes in theology (!) I approach the interpretation of the Scriptures with a hermeneutic of reception. This springs from a conviction that the text, with its divine and human authors, has something, and indeed someone to communicate ("You search the Scriptures, because you think that in them you have eternal life; and it is they that bear witness to me," John 5:39). To acknowledge that the text can indeed speak and show (or, if one prefers, that authors can indicate through their texts) does not in itself allow for a complexity of communicative moves or the diverse modes by which communion occurs. However, sympathy for what we are reading will allow the reader more easily to apprehend the probable meanings of any given text as well as its possible "openings." Frank orientation toward the text and its world at the same time prevents the exegete from flights of fancy in which the text becomes a pretext. The line between possibilities and pretexts may be sometimes hard to trace. This is where the check of other readers comes into play: we read together as a community, and in consciousness of those who have read and understood before us.

Because the Johannine writings are interconnected both with the canon and the ongoing Christian family, both the correction and the enrichment offered by my colleagues (who deal with other writings, and from varied Christian traditions) are pertinent. In particular, because of my own predilection, but also because of the nature of the Johannine writings, the interface with Eastern Orthodoxy has been particularly apposite. Fr. John Chryssavgis alerts us to repentance in the context of our life's "passover from death to life"—an Orthodox motif that beautifully encapsulates the dynamic of both the Fourth Gospel and the Apocalypse. Again, his emphasis on *synchōresis* ("forgiveness," "dwelling in the same space") as a communal mode of being is a natural extension of the realism and generosity of the Johannine epistles. In a similar vein Ralph Del Colle, representing the Catholic tradition, reminds us that "penance is an ecclesial act, inherently social." Lest some might imagine that this is simply an agreement of the high-church constituency, we also hear from Michael Battle that African and African-American spirituality incorporates a penitence "more communal . . . than . . . other cultural worldviews." Again Andrew Purves (via John McLeod Campbell) highlights the role of Jesus as "our representative penitent"—even though the Reformed delimiting mind recoils from classing repentance as "sacramental." Repentance, then, is no private matter. Evangelist, elder, and seer would agree: this concord offers a strong word for our incorrigibly individualistic age, when even among Christians we consider repentance to be a matter between one person only and God.

In my own paper I sketched the mysterious nature of our subject, signaled in the surprise when characters of the Fourth Gospel "turn," disturbing to the elder in the continuing sin of believers, and disorienting in the seer's erection of (permeable) barriers between Babylon and the New Jerusalem. That repentance and the passover into life are mysterious is not, however, an excuse for lack of clarity. During our second discussion (November 2004), Walter Brueggemann challenged the group regarding our lack of a clear definition for penance. This lack of clarity, he argued, might well bolster an elitist imposition of penance on the over-scrupulous—a move he would uncover by an appropriate "hermeneutics of suspicion." He challenged us to consider whether penance ought to be individual or corporate, whether it is a rite (or an attitude, policy, mode of conduct), and whether it is a human factor or divine grace. More troubling still are his questions: "who defines the sins to be confessed?" and "who has the power to forgive?"

The challenge of his hermeneutics of suspicion to my own open approach is apparent, and not to be lightly dismissed. Certainly the whole area of repentance/penitence/penance has been, in past eras, a fertile field for abuse in the churches; however, so far as twenty-first-century Western culture is concerned, scrupulosity and overbearing clericalism seem not nearly as threatening to the health of the church as presumption, rank ipseity, and carelessness. In reading biblical passages concerned with repentance, and in considering how these have been both used and abused in the history of Christianity, we may do well to pay heed to Jesus' words concerning the ideal character of his followers—we must discern when to be serpents among wolves, and when to be innocent.

The very gathering together of scholars who share a common foundation, but who express this differently in terms of disciplines and in terms of ecclesial home, encourages such discernment. One of the things that became apparent in our discussion is how hard it remains, even in an "ecumenical age," to move outside our own communities of understanding. The sensitivity of Michael Battle to a "sad joyfulness" among Christians consonant with the wonder of repentance is welcome to those of us who struggle with repentance as a natural and ongoing part of the Christian walk. Similarly, Stanley Porter's broad consideration of the whole panoply of New Testament terms reminds us that the New Testament epistle writers indicate repentance for not only the initial "turn" but also for subsequent reorientations. This observation issues a challenge to those who limit "repentance" as exclusively linked to conversion, although some readers will, with Porter, continue to draw a conceptual line between initial repentance and subsequent acts of penitence/remorse/contrition. The tension Porter sees between the book of Hebrews (often read as denying post-baptismal repentance) and 2 Cor 7:9-11 (which speaks of the first turn and subsequent turns in one breath) is an important one for Christians of all traditions to note, and one with which we must struggle. Our sense of superiority over the early Christians who despaired of second repentance, thus delaying baptism, may be misplaced—perhaps the *volte face* Christians have made concerning this issue is due more to careless tolerance than to a eucharistic apprehension of the great mercy of God!

I am also thankful for the careful work of Mark Boda, who helpfully notes the distinction in appeals for repentance between the Torah and the prophets. Repentance may be evoked prophylactically to avoid God's judgment (the prophets), or as a response to reverse that doom (the Torah): so we see how the Bible comprehends a striking diversity of rhetorical and/or theological emphases. These observations, coupled with my own appeal to the particular effects of different genres, remind us that repentance remains the constant, though approaches to it may vary.

In the end, certainly we have as much to learn about the rich concept of repentance as we do about the practice of it. Ever a hard issue, it provides growing edges, across the Christian traditions, and across the canon, as we grapple with those facets and those passages that prove difficult for us in our particular contexts. My suspicion, as I analyzed my prescribed texts, was that my Christian contemporaries would find most troublesome the crisp realism of the Johannine epistles, and the seeming harshness of the Apocalypse. We are, I assumed, a soft age in which a no-nonsense approach seems inhumane. Yet, behind many balking reservations that we harbor may be truths that we would prefer not to face. There are times when plain speaking is liberating—even necessary for the health of the Church. In 1934, the Confessional Synod of the German Evangelical Church published the Barmen Declaration, crafted by theologian Karl Barth, as a call to resistance against Hitler's idolatrous ideology and the complicity of the national church; in 1982 the World Alliance of Reformed Churches suspended from its membership the Dutch Reformed Church of South Africa for its apartheid mentality and practices. Both acts, though controversial and costly at the time, have in retrospect been recognized as faithful.

Many believe that a similar watershed has occurred in the Anglican Church, which has been in crisis over moves by some of its members to modify traditional Christian teaching and practices in the area of human sexuality. This crisis has included but has not been limited to the ratification of clergy actively engaged in homoerotic relationships, the possibility of a "local option" for churches or dioceses to perform liturgical rites that solemnize homosexual unions, and explicit teaching concerning marriage that departs from the church's historic and catholic understanding of that mystery. Since these actions are interconnected with deeper theological and ethical confusions, it is not surprising that repeated calls to repentance have been issued by leaders of the worldwide Anglican Communion, supported by ecumenical Catholic and the Eastern Orthodox partners. During the past few years, Anglicans and

Episcopalians concerned for creedal orthodoxy have continued to meet together, engaging in their own introspection and repentance, as they come to terms with what has happened in their institutional church. Here also clarity of purpose has emerged. There has been a palpable change in direction, as it becomes clear that revisionists will not repent but are continuing to advocate novel ideology, liturgies, and practices. Those concerned for "the Great Tradition," who once joined in a concerted effort to reform and renew national church structures, are now expressing one form or another of disassociation—verbal, provisional, or even formal and permanent—from those bodies that affirm these changes.

While the situation is especially acute among Anglicans, there is every reason to believe that analogous decisions may be soon replicated in other major denominations. God's children who, in grief, are compelled to sound a word of judgment, may be helped by remembering the closing tag of the Barmen Declaration, *Verbum Dei manet in aeternum* ("The word of God endures forever"). This assurance remains true even when the "word" that must be declared is hard to hear and harder still to speak. In the story of the prophet, Jonah declared an unmitigated sentence of judgment which contained no conditions or escape clause (Jonah 3:4b)—and yet Ninevah repented and was saved. Who knows whether God might not redeem today, through an equally clear word?

Seven

# Penitence and Repentance in the Epistles

*Stanley E. Porter*

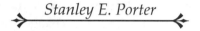

## 1. Text

The terminology regarding penitence and repentance in the epistles of
the New Testament is not used widely, and hence does not appear—at
least at first glance—to imply a strongly developed notion of penitence
or repentance in this corpus of material.[1] Furthermore, at least one of the
passages I will discuss below, Hebrews 6, is often seen as highly unusual
within the New Testament itself and has caused considerable controversy
among interpreters. However, there is probably more to the notion of
penitence and repentance in the epistles than first meets the interpretive

---

[1] I should define the corpus with which I am dealing. I am considering all
thirteen of the Pauline letters, Hebrews, James, the Petrines, and Jude. I exclude
the Johannine epistles since they fall within the purview of the Johannine writings
(treated elsewhere). It might be interesting to trace a trajectory of development
of the notion of penitence/repentance in the deutero-Pauline epistles, but since
I believe that all of them are authentic such a trajectory would need to be com-
pressed considerably—in any case, the instances from these letters are few. For
comments on authenticity see Lee Martin McDonald and Stanley E. Porter, *Early
Christianity and its Sacred Literature* (Peabody, MA: Hendrickson, 2000) *passim*.

127

eye—even though New Testament scholars on the whole do not devote much space to discussing it in this body of writings.[2]

One of the major first steps in examining this corpus of material, where penitence and repentance references are not apparently prominent, is to delimit the significant passages one must scrutinize. One does not wish to fall victim to either extreme of focusing too much on single word occurrences or attempting to establish a broad concept without any linguistic substance with which to support one's case.[3] In order to try to avoid either extreme situation I have focused on words used in the wider semantic field of changing one's behavior toward God (according to the Louw–Nida lexicon of semantic domains),[4] and especially passages where such words are used in a confluence rather than simply in isolation. Within the semantic field of words for "changing behavior" (domain 41), five words are used in the New Testament: στρέφομαι, "change one's manner of life, with the implication of turning toward God," ἐπιστρέφω and ἐπιστροφή, "change one's manner of life in a particular direction, with the implication of turning back to God," μετανοέω and μετάνοια, "change one's way of life as the

---

[2] A survey of a number of New Testament theologies, and specialized theologies of, for example, Paul, confirms that there is little extended discussion of the notion of penitence or repentance in the epistles. The most noteworthy discussions are found in Alan Richardson, *An Introduction to the Theology of the New Testament* (London: SCM Press, 1958) 33, and Donald Guthrie, *New Testament Theology* (Leicester, England, and Downers Grove, IL: InterVarsity Press, 1981) 589–91; the latter links repentance to justification, that is, there is a basic assumption that a justified person "cannot be unrepentant" (p. 590). More typical is I. Howard Marshall, *New Testament Theology: Many Witnesses, One Gospel* (Downers Grove, IL: InterVarsity Press, 2004) 478, who says that repentance "is generally not part of the vocabulary of conversion in Paul (though see Rom 2:4; 2 Tim 2:25); occasionally he mentions it in relation to backsliding believers (2 Cor 7:9-10; 12:21)."

[3] Thus one wishes to avoid the kind of word-concept confusion that has led to much "illegitimate totality transfer" (to use James Barr's phrase) and the kind of biblical theologizing that is only tangentially related to the biblical text itself. See James Barr, *The Semantics of Biblical Language* (Oxford: Oxford University Press, 1961), who in effect addresses both problems. An example of the latter is found in W. Morgan, "Repent, Repentance," in James Hastings, ed., *A Dictionary of the Bible*, 4 vols. (Edinburgh: T & T Clark, 1902) 4:225–26, especially 226.

[4] See Johannes P. Louw and Eugene A. Nida, *Greek–English Lexicon of the New Testament Based on Semantic Domains*, 2 vols. (New York: United Bible Societies, 1988). See also Eugene A. Nida and Johannes P. Louw, *Lexical Semantics of the Greek New Testament* (Atlanta: Scholars Press, 1992).

result of a complete change of thought and attitude with regard to sin and righteousness,"[5] γεννάω ἄνωθεν and παλιγγενεσία, "experience a complete change in one's way of life to what it should be, with the implication of return to a former state or relation," and ἀμετανόητος, "pertaining to not being repentant."[6] Not all of these words within the semantic domain of "changing behavior" are used within the New Testament epistles, however. For example, στρέφομαι and γεννάω ἄνωθεν are not used. The verb ἐπιστρέφω (but not the noun form) is found in 2 Cor 3:16; Gal 4:9; 1 Thess 1:9; Jas 5:19, 20; 1 Pet 2:25; and 2 Pet 2:22. Μετανοέω is found only in 2 Cor 12:21, but μετάνοια appears in Rom 2:4; 2 Cor 7:9, 10; 2 Tim 2:25; Heb 6:1, 6 (not v. 4 as most translations); 12:17; and 2 Pet 3:9. Παλιγγενεσία is found in Titus 3:5, and ἀμετανόητος in Rom 2:5.[7] This mix of references would seem to indicate that there are a number of places where repentance is discussed in the epistles. There are indeed places where a word translated with repentance or the like is used. However, the advantage of using semantic fields as a means of approaching word and concept studies is that one can see where there are concentrated uses of words within the same domain. The reasoning is that when more significant or extensive discussion of a concept occurs it is more likely that a number of different conceptually related words are utilized by the author. When this analysis of the above usage is done, there are four major passages in the epistles to consider, supported by several lesser passages. Two of these major passages are Pauline ones—Romans 2 and 2 Corinthians 7, along with use in 2 Corinthians 3 and 12 as well—and one each in Hebrews (ch. 6) and James (ch. 5). The other supporting passages of interest will be referred to in the course of treating these four major passages.

### a. Passages on Repentance in the Epistles

One of the features of epistolary interpretation that I have come to appreciate in recent years is the importance of considering where a given

---

[5] The best, recent treatment of this word—but only of this word, unfortunately—is Guy D. Nave, Jr., *The Role and Function of Repentance in Luke-Acts* (Atlanta: Society of Biblical Literature, 2002).

[6] Among words for "changing an opinion concerning truth" (domain 31) there is one further word that might be considered, μεταμέλομαι, "change one's mind about something, with the probable implication of regret."

[7] The verb μεταμέλομαι is found in 2 Cor 7:8 and Heb 7:21, but these two uses do not fit the notion of repentance or penitence we are discussing here.

passage falls within the unfolding argument of a letter.[8] Letters in the ancient world were written according to a set of conventions. Most of the New Testament letter writers followed these conventions fairly closely. Their major departures, where these are found, seem to be in terms of expanding upon or developing a standard feature of the letter in order to support the author's theological purposes. This approach to repentance and penitence passages in the New Testament helps us to understand the sense in which the authors discuss this concept. To anticipate my conclusion, there appear to be two major uses of words regarding "changing one's behavior" in the New Testament epistles, one involving initial change of behavior, what I will call initial repentance, and secondary repentance, what is often called penitence, remorse, or contrition.[9]

### (1) Pauline Passages

The language of repentance appears in only two major contexts in the Pauline epistles, Romans 2 and 2 Corinthians 3, 7, and 12. However, the language is also found in three other more restricted contexts, 1 Thess 1:9, 2 Tim 2:25, and Gal 4:18-19, that further elucidate the notion.

*(a) Romans 2.* The first major passage to be discussed is Rom 2:4-5. These verses read: "Or do you think lightly of the riches of his kindness and forbearance and patience, not knowing that the kindness of God leads you to repentance (μετάνοιαν)? But because of your stubbornness and

---

[8] See McDonald and Porter, *Early Christianity*, 377–88, where the Pauline letter form is discussed. Comments on other letter forms are made where appropriate below.

[9] There is a tendency by some to equate initial repentance with the notion of conversion. I consider the idea of repentance to be a more tightly defined concept under the idea of conversion, specially addressed to behavior. Thus the entry by J. Goetzmann, "Conversion, Penitence, Repentance, Proselyte," in *NIDNTT* 1:353–62, is probably too broad, but it is certainly more useful than *TDNT*, where each word is treated (and theologized!) separately but arranged according to root (e.g., Johannes Behm and Ernst Würthwein, "νοέω, κτλ," *TDNT* 4:948–1022, including μετανοέω, μετάνοια, and ἀμετανόητος; cf. Ceslas Spicq, *Theological Dictionary of the New Testament*, trans. and ed. J. D. Ernest, 3 vols. [Peabody, MA: Hendrickson, 1994] 2:471–77, who does not even cite the entire entry in Behm and Würthwein; Georg Bertram, "στρέφω, κτλ," *TDNT* 7:714–29). As Goetzmann says regarding the lack of instances of μετανοέω in Paul, this "does not mean that the idea of conversion is not present there but only that in the meantime a more specialized terminology had developed" ("Conversion," 1:359).

unrepentant (ἀμετανόητον) heart you are storing up wrath for yourself in the day of wrath and revelation of the righteous judgment of God" *(NASB)*. These two verses provide a typically Pauline set of contrasts.[10] Paul lays out the positive features exemplified by God in terms of his kindness, forbearance, and patience, in contrast to the stubbornness and unrepentant heart of humanity.[11] It is these features of God that, Paul says, lead a person to repentance.

These two verses are found within the major first section of the body of Paul's letter to the Romans. The body of the letter is divided into six parts.[12] The first part is the theme statement of 1:16-17, in which Paul speaks of the gospel as the power of God for salvation to both Jew and Gentile who believe. The second part of the letter contains Paul's definition of the human condition, and his solution to the forensic guilt of humanity. Romans 1:18-32 offers an assessment in terms of the spiritual, passion-driven, and communal dimensions of the unrighteousness of humanity. Then, in 2:1-16, before turning to consider the case of the Jews (2:17–3:8), Paul examines the situation of a discerning person who believes that he or she is above such condemnation.[13] Paul's verdict on a person like this is that such a one is also without excuse before God, because the person who judges others is involved in doing the very same things. God, being the righteous judge, will not allow anyone to escape judgment, even the person who thinks he or she is superior to

---

[10] The dialogical question and answer style of Paul is typical of diatribe, a literary medium Paul uses throughout Romans.

[11] Rather than trying to distinguish each of the positive and negative terms, we can observe a probable piling on of synonyms to emphasize the strength of the positive and negative features. See, e.g., C. E. B. Cranfield, *A Critical and Exegetical Commentary on the Epistle to the Romans*, ICC, 2 vols. (Edinburgh: T & T Clark, 1975, 1979) 1:144; Matthew Black, *Romans*, NCB (Grand Rapids: Eerdmans, 1973) 54–55.

[12] On this outline see Stanley E. Porter, *Romans*, Readings (Sheffield: Sheffield Phoenix Press, forthcoming). Cf. Nave, *Role and Function*, 123–24, for a similar perspective on this passage.

[13] This is *contra* a number of commentators, who understand this section as addressed to Jews and interpret the language regarding repentance in terms particularly of Wisdom of Solomon 11–15, especially 11:23; 12:10, 19; 15:1-2. Some even speculate that Paul may be using Jewish material in this section, hence the unusual vocabulary, such as language of repentance. See John A. Ziesler, *Paul's Letter to the Romans*, TPI New Testament Commentaries (Philadelphia: Trinity Press International, 1989) 82.

such treatment. This leads to vv. 4 and 5. After clearly drawing the lines regarding human behavior, including that of the one who considers himself or herself more discerning, Paul reinforces his belief in the goodness of God. It is this goodness, Paul says, that leads "you," the person who judges others but is in just as much need of God's mercy as anyone else, to repentance. As Sanday and Headlam say, "its purpose or tendency is to induce you to repent."[14] In contrast is the hard and unrepentant heart, such as Paul sees evidenced in chapter 1 when he soundly condemns those who willfully disregard God's standards, and here in v. 4 when he singles out those who believe themselves above such discussion and who, in effect, despise God's mercy.[15] They too are accumulating for themselves the wrath of God (cf. 1:18, where Paul begins the section by proclaiming that the wrath of God is poured out against all humanity, in effect the theme statement for this entire subsection), which will come in a dreadful day when God's righteous judgment is revealed—even though it is being withheld to this point.[16]

In this context repentance seems to be a fundamental category in Paul's thought, what I am calling initial repentance.[17] Repentance is not the first step in remedying the relationship between God and humanity since that first step is taken by God, who is the author and provider of forbearance, patience, and kindness; however, it is the human response in terms of behavior. God's gracious and evident provision is what should motivate the sinful human to repentance, that is, to turn from hard-heartedness deserving of God's righteous anger. Willibald Beyschlag uses the felicitous wording that the "fundamental notion in all is, that

---

[14] William Sanday and Arthur C. Headlam, *A Critical and Exegetical Commentary on the Epistle to the Romans*, ICC (5th ed.; Edinburgh: T & T Clark, 1902) 56.

[15] C. K. Barrett, *A Commentary on the Epistle to the Romans*, BNTC (London: A & C Black, 1957) 45.

[16] On the withholding of divine judgment see Nave, *Role and Function*, 124 n405.

[17] On the one hand J. D. G. Dunn (*Romans*, WBC 38A, B [Waco, TX: Word Books, 1988] 1:82, who takes Paul's interlocutor as a Jew) wants to equate repentance with conversion, while on the other hand Douglas Moo (*The Epistle to the Romans*, NICNT [Grand Rapids: Eerdmans, 1996] 133–34) posits that the notion is not a significant one for Paul, probably because it is too reliant upon Old Testament imagery. The former conflates too many notions together in jumping to biblical theology, and the latter relies too heavily on counting words rather than looking at usage.

salvation is conditioned by repentance toward God (μετάνοια conversion) and faith in the gospel of Jesus."[18] Paul does not use words within the "changing behavior" field again in the book of Romans. However, that is not to say that he is not concerned with humans turning from their unrighteous ways and accepting God's grace, the image that seems to dominate use of this word here. It is worth noting that the singular set of references to repentance in Romans occurs at the outset and places repentance in the context of constituting a fundamental event in turning from wickedness to God and his righteousness.

*(b) 2 Corinthians 3, 7, and 12.* Second Corinthians has a number of references to repentance or penitence[19]—in fact, this is probably the only Pauline book that actually contains the notion of repentance by those who are already Christians, or what has often been called penitence, remorse, or contrition.[20] The first instance is found in a passage from Exod 34:34 quoted in 2 Cor 3:16. Referring to when Moses put a veil over his face so that the Israelites would not see him, and claiming that a veil still rests over their understanding, Paul says that whenever a person "turns to the Lord (ἐπιστρέψῃ), the veil is taken away" *(NASB).*[21] When one comes to faith, one understands. Then, in 2 Corinthians 7, Paul expresses his confidence in the Corinthian Christians now that their

---

[18] Willibald Beyschlag, *New Testament Theology,* trans. Neil Buchanan, 2 vols. (Edinburgh: T & T Clark, 1895) 2:486.

[19] One instance that does not qualify, though a word that I am examining is used, is 2 Cor 7:8, although there may be a play on words in this context (see discussion in the main text).

[20] See C. K. Barrett, *The Second Epistle to the Corinthians,* HNTC (New York: Harper & Row, 1973) 211, taking the suggestion from Rudolf Bultmann, *Exegetica,* ed. Erich Dinkler (Tübingen: Mohr Siebeck, 1967) 402; idem, *The Second Letter to the Corinthians,* trans. Roy A. Harrisville, ed. Erich Dinkler (Minneapolis: Augsburg, 1985) 55, 56 (remorse); Victor P. Furnish, *II Corinthians,* AB 32A (Garden City, NY: Doubleday, 1984) 387 (contrition). This is even maintained by the scholar Philip E. Hughes, *Paul's Second Epistle to the Corinthians,* NICNT (Grand Rapids: Eerdmans, 1962) 271–72, although he has to do some juggling with his theology.

[21] I take the subject of the verb as "anyone," but on the options see Margaret E. Thrall, *A Critical and Exegetical Commentary on the Second Epistle to the Corinthians,* ICC (Edinburgh: T & T Clark, 1994, 2000) 1:268–71.

relational situation is resolved (at least for the time being).[22] He says in v. 8 that he does not regret (μεταμέλομαι) that he caused them sorrow, because it turned out for the best. As he writes in vv. 9-10: "I now rejoice, not that you were made sorrowful, but that you were made sorrowful to the point of repentance (μετάνοιαν); for you were made sorrowful according to the will of God, in order that you might not suffer loss in anything through us. For the sorrow that is according to the will of God produces a repentance (μετάνοιαν) without regret (ἀμεταμέλητον), leading to salvation; but the sorrow of the world produces death" *(NASB)*. Then, at the end of the letter, Paul writes in 2 Cor 12:21: "I am afraid that when I come again my God may humiliate me before you, and I may mourn over many of those who have sinned in the past and not repented (μετανοησάντων) of the impurity, immorality, and sensuality which they have practiced" *(NASB)*.

Discussion of 2 Corinthians is complicated by various theories regarding how many of Paul's letters are to be found in the canonical text. Some might see use of repentance language in these passages as arguing for multiple letters, especially with the tone of Paul's concluding words in 2 Corinthians 7 that do not seem to finish, but go into subsequent chapters of the letter.[23] This source hypothesis may be true, but without substantial external evidence, such speculation remains merely that, speculative. There is perhaps another way to look at these passages within the unfolding argument of the letter.

Paul's references in 2 Cor 3:16 and 7:9, 10 are both in the major part of the body of the letter, where Paul is concerned to defend his apostolic ministry (2:14–7:16).[24] At the beginning of this section he speaks of the glory that accompanies a ministry of righteousness, which warrants his approach to his apostolic ministry. It is not like that of Moses, who needed to be veiled when he was before the people, a people who remain veiled to this day, Paul says. If a person does turn to the Lord—that is, turns away from her or his veiled position of being hardened and not

---

[22] The question of the resolution depends on whether one decides that there is only one letter in 2 Corinthians or many. See Barrett, *Second Epistle to the Corinthians*, 210.

[23] It has been proposed that 2 Corinthians 8 and 9 as well as 2 Corinthians 10–13 constitute individual letters written by Paul but assembled here into canonical 2 Corinthians. For discussion of various theories, see McDonald and Porter, *Early Christianity*, 441–46.

[24] See ibid. 449.

perceptive of the will of God—the veil that stands in the way of understanding is removed. This is repentance in the sense in which Paul uses it in Romans 2 (see above). Paul goes on to talk of the message of his apostolic ministry in chapter 4 before turning to the centrality of reconciliation and the work God has done in reconciling the world to himself through Christ. This reconciling action has created an atmosphere of grace that has empowered Paul in his ministry and results in his call to the Corinthians to distinguish themselves from their environment. This leads to his statements regarding repentance in chapter 7. He knows that he has written to them some very difficult things on previous occasions, but he does not regret it. He has offered his view of his apostolic ministry and how that ministry is focused on the work of God in reconciling the world to himself. His call is for the Corinthians to be fellow ministers of this gospel. They had strayed from this calling, to which they had originally answered positively, and this led Paul to call them to repent. Here the wording means showing penitence or contrition over sin, wrongdoing, or straying from the right path. He does not regret how hard he has been on them, because it resulted in their repentance. Their sorrow preceded their repentance, Paul says, because of his strong words that brought them to that sorrow. Sorrow of this sort, Paul says, that is according to the will of God, is to be welcomed because it produces a repentance that leads to salvation without regret. The notion of salvation here implies the fullness of Christian life.[25] The sorrow or grief that is not brought about by God, however, but is produced by the world, leads to death. This appears to be the death of the person who is unrepentant even though God has prodded him or her to repentance. These are the kinds of people Paul alludes to in 2 Cor 12:21 when he speaks of those who have sinned and not repented or had remorse and penitence over their wrongdoing.[26] They have continued to practice their impurity, immorality, and sensuality.

In 2 Corinthians 7, Paul places repentance within a different salvific framework than he did in Romans. Repentance there was spoken of in terms of an initial kind of repentance brought about by God's graciousness in response to human sin, and is also found in the reference in 2 Cor 3:16.[27] However, there is another use of the concept in 2 Cor 7:9,

---

[25] Furnish, *II Corinthians*, 388, not initial salvation.

[26] See Bultmann, *Second Letter to the Corinthians*, 55.

[27] Paul Barnett (*The Second Epistle to the Corinthians*, NICNT [Grand Rapids: Eerdmans, 1997] 375 n15) says that Paul prefers the "concept of 'faith'" to the

10.[28] The repentance spoken of here is not initial, but involves those who have already become followers of Christ yet are involved in wrongdoing or sin. In response to their rejecting Paul and rebuffing his attempts to instruct them, he wrote them a strong letter. Then Titus visited them and they repented of, or showed penitence regarding, their actions. Like initial repentance, subsequent repentance or penitence comes in response to other actions that convince of one's wrongdoing. In terms of the Corinthians, Paul sees their previous behavior as meriting his strong words to them. These words produced sorrow. Their sorrow over their previous behavior is what led them to repentance. Paul says that it was God who made them sorrowful over what they had done, so that their repentance would keep them from harmful consequences. There is a two-sidedness to the description Paul gives of repentance here. On the one hand repentance involves turning away from behavior with potentially harmful consequences, and on the other hand it involves turning toward and accomplishing fullness of life, or salvation. There are no regrets, Paul says, since these regrets bring about the repentance that restores them.[29]

*(c) 1 Thessalonians 1:9, 2 Timothy 2:25, and Galatians 4:18-19.* There are three further Pauline passages using language of repentance that also merit attention. The usage here is consistent with and reinforces what has been noted above in the two major Pauline passages on repentance and penitence.

*1 Thessalonians 1:9.* Paul's statement in 1 Thess 1:9 serves as an excellent encapsulation of what underlies his fuller expositions of initial repentance noted above. The fact that this verse appears in the thanksgiving part of a letter that is given to much thanksgiving perhaps accounts for why it is so bald in its statement. He says of the Thessalonians that others know of "how you turned (ἐπεστρέψατε) to God from idols to serve a living

---

use of the term μετάνοια. It is unclear to me how these are seen as so easily interchangeable, unless one is working solely at a theological level and lumping together all metaphors for Christian initiation.

[28] Nave (*Role and Function*, 121–23) seems to be ambivalent about the context of usage here. On the one hand he recognizes that Paul is writing to Christians in Corinth (p. 121), but his treatment of the notion of repentance seems to imply initial repentance.

[29] See Furnish, *II Corinthians*, 388.

and true God" *(NASB)*. This encapsulation—drawing on language found elsewhere to describe pagans turning to God (e.g., Acts 9:35; 14:15; 15:19; 26:18, 20)—clearly articulates what Paul sees as the fundamental change involved in initial repentance.[30] The choice is between serving idols and serving the living and true God. He commends the Thessalonians because they turned from these idols to the living God. The entire commendatory tone of the letter apparently does not support Paul's going into further detail about what precedes and leads to repentance or what follows from it. He is simply content to commend the Thessalonians that they have made the right initial choice, and that others are noticing this.

*2 Timothy 2:25.* In 2 Tim 2:25, Paul at the close of his ministry is offering instructions to his protegé Timothy regarding how to continue successfully in his own calling as a servant of the Lord. His instructions are geared toward Timothy, so he advises him regarding dealing with others and his own self-control. He notes that the Lord's servant must have a particular character, including correcting those in opposition, "if perhaps God may grant them repentance (μετάνοιαν) leading to the knowledge of the truth" *(NASB)*. Repentance is born out of a context of opposition to God. On the basis of what we have seen above, the usage here is consistent with the Pauline framework of initial repentance.[31] Timothy's opponents are described as those who are caught in the snare

---

[30] See Ernest Best, *A Commentary on the First and Second Epistles to the Thessalonians*, BNTC (London: A & C Black, 1972) 82; Frederick F. Bruce, *1 & 2 Thessalonians*, WBC 45 (Waco, TX: Word Books, 1982) 17; I. Howard Marshall, *1 and 2 Thessalonians*, NCB (Grand Rapids: Eerdmans, 1983) 57; Charles A. Wanamaker, *The Epistles to the Thessalonians*, NIGTC (Grand Rapids: Eerdmans, 1990) 85; Gene L. Green, *The Letters to the Thessalonians* (Grand Rapids: Eerdmans, 2002) 106–108—although many commentators wish to label this simply conversion (e.g., Marshall, Bruce). The notion of conversion can be much wider still. See Arthur Darby Nock, *Conversion* (Oxford: Clarendon, 1933), who notes various types of conversion, including three different kinds in Acts alone; and Beverly Roberts Gaventa, *From Darkness to Light: Aspects of Conversion in the New Testament* (Philadelphia: Fortress Press, 1986) 17–51, especially 41–43.

[31] On the opponents as not being members of the believing community, I. Howard Marshall, with Philip H. Towner, *A Critical and Exegetical Commentary on the Pastoral Epistles*, ICC (Edinburgh: T & T Clark, 1999) 766–67; William D. Mounce, *Pastoral Epistles*, WBC 46 (Nashville: Nelson, 2000) 536–37; cf. Gordon D. Fee, *1 and 2 Timothy, Titus* (Peabody, MA: Hendrickson, 1988) 264–66; George W. Knight, III, *The Pastoral Epistles*, NIGTC (Grand Rapids: Eerdmans, 1992) 11–12.

of the devil and are held captive by him, and hence are actively opposing
Timothy in his ministry. If they are granted the opportunity and impul-
sion by God to repent, then their repentance may lead to knowledge of
the truth, that is, truth that leads to salvation. Knowledge of the truth
is seen as the consequence of their turning from their doing the will of
Satan in opposing God's servant to acceptance of him.

*Galatians 4:8-9.* Galatians 4:8-9 begins by reminding the Galatians how
they had been slaves to other things before they had known God. Paul
asks how it is that, now that they know God or are known by him, they
could turn back (ἐπιστρέφετε) to the basic elements to which they had
been enslaved before. Rather than being a repentance passage strictly
speaking, this passage raises the question of whether the Galatians could
turn away from their repentance and back to the condition they were
in before that time. Many commentators do not take this as a serious
warning, labelling it rhetorical or even sarcastic.[32] However, in light
of Paul's strong words to the Galatians throughout the letter and his
descriptions of the behavior he hears they are involved in, this appears
to be a very real concern (see Hebrews 6 below). Paul fears that the
Galatians could un-repent, that is, apostasize back to the time when they
did not know God and were beholden to the basic elements.[33]

### (2) Hebrews 6 and 12

One of the most highly controverted passages in the New Testament—and one that stands out because it is so different from others—is
Hebrews 6. Those on all sides of a variety of theological issues have taken
up the challenge of offering a plausible explanation of this passage within
the framework of their particular theological tradition. The passage continues to thwart interpreters.[34] No doubt this is in part because the biblical

---

[32] Rhetorical: E. D. W. Burton, *A Critical and Exegetical Commentary on the Epistle
to the Galatians,* ICC (Edinburgh: T & T Clark, 1920) 230; Richard N. Longenecker,
*Galatians,* WBC 41 (Dallas: Word Books, 1990) 180; sarcastic: J. Louis Martyn,
*Galatians,* AB 33A (New York: Doubleday, 1997) 411.

[33] Ben Witherington III, *Grace in Galatia* (Grand Rapids: Eerdmans, 1998) 301.
Note that Paul says nothing about whether the Galatians could return to the
faith or not.

[34] For a recent treatment of the issues see Lusitone Salevao, *Legitimation in
the Letter to the Hebrews: The Construction and Maintenance of a Symbolic Universe,*
JSNTSup 219 (Sheffield: Sheffield Academic Press, 2002) 250–338.

text always seems to be larger than numerous theological traditions and constraints, and it keeps splitting the straitjacket of interpretation people try to put around it. One of the things that has struck me in examining this passage afresh is that it is ultimately disappointing to both of the major sides in this debate. It appears to represent not a hypothetical case that could never happen but a real case that can and does happen. However, the options that are offered to the person involved are few, not the openended set of repeated opportunities so often promoted by some interpreters.

Hebrews 6 has two major instances in which language of repentance is used. The first is in v. 1 where the author says: "therefore leaving the elementary teaching about the Christ, let us press on to maturity, not laying again a foundation of repentance (μετανοίας) from dead works and of faith toward God" *(NASB)*. He then speaks of some who have "tasted of the heavenly gift and have been made partakers of the Holy Spirit" (v. 4; *NASB*) and who "have fallen away," saying that "it is impossible to renew them again to repentance (μετάνοιαν), since they again crucify to themselves the Son of God, and put Him to open shame" (v. 6; *NASB*). There is a third instance as well in 12:17, which says of Esau that "even afterwards, when he desired to inherit the blessing, he was rejected, for he found no place for repentance (μετανοίας), though he sought for it with tears" *(NASB)*.

The book of Hebrews, in contrast to the Pauline epistles, is structured in an entirely different way,[35] unfolding its content in terms of three major blocks of material.[36] The first of the three is concerned with demonstrating the superiority of the Son to other beings (1:5–7:28). Within this section the author argues this with regard to angels (1:5–2:4), other humans (2:5-18), Moses and Joshua (3:1–4:13), the high priest (4:14–5:10), any elementary teaching (5:11–6:20), and Melchizedek and any other priest (7:1-28). It is within discussion of Christ's superiority to any elementary teaching that the author states that his audience should, by this time, be teachers, but instead they still have the need for someone to teach them the elementary principles of God's oracles. They are still spiritually immature (babes) when they should be mature (and eating solid food). This sounds like a very realistic and serious situation in the

---

[35] This may be because it is not a letter in a conventional sense. For discussion of what exactly it is see McDonald and Porter, *Early Christianity*, 524–26.

[36] See ibid. 526, 528.

author's eyes. Therefore, the author says, his audience needs to move beyond the elementary teaching and press toward maturity, rather than repeating the work of laying a foundation that includes repentance from dead works, faith, and being taught regarding baptism, the laying on of hands, resurrection from the dead and eternal judgment.[37] In other words, the audience at one time had repented from their dead works, put faith in God, and been instructed—all signs of the initial stage of their spiritual experience. At this stage in their lives they should be moving to more advanced teaching. By God's will, the author says, they can expect to do this. At this point the author abruptly introduces what he calls an impossibility. He describes people who have once been enlightened (by God), tasted the heavenly gift, become sharers in the Holy Spirit, and tasted the good word of God and the powers of the coming age.

Two factors are to be noted here. The first is that the author gives no indication that the persons he describes are any less real than the audience he has already depicted. Indeed, and this is the second factor, it follows from what he has been saying about the contrast between the spiritual immaturity of the audience and the desirable spiritual maturity they should be cultivating that such people as he now describes may well represent those within his audience or what might potentially happen to some of them—that the situation is potentially an all-too-real one. As Bruce says, "The warning of this passage was a real warning against a real danger, a danger which is still present so as 'an evil heart of unbelief' can result in 'deserting the living God' (3:12)."[38] The people he describes

---

[37] On the relation of the elements mentioned in 6:1-2 see Paul Ellingworth, *The Epistle to the Hebrews*, NIGTC (Grand Rapids: Eerdmans, 1993) 313–14. It is outside the boundaries of this paper, but nevertheless worth speculating upon, what the relation of the "baptism of repentance for the forgiveness of sins" of John the Baptist (Mark 1:4) has to do with this passage, or even the Pauline passages regarding repentance and baptism. See Leonhard Goppelt, *Theology of the New Testament*, trans. John E. Alsup, 2 vols. (Grand Rapids: Eerdmans, 1982) 2:7.

[38] See Frederick F. Bruce, *The Epistle to the Hebrews*, NICNT (Grand Rapids: Eerdmans, 1990) 147–48, who argues for a credible situation, but one that should not be exaggerated in either direction. For a discussion of proposals regarding this passage through the centuries see Philip E. Hughes, *A Commentary on the Epistle to the Hebrews* (Grand Rapids: Eerdmans, 1977) 212–22. The situation is not mitigated by assessing Hebrews simply in terms of patron-client relations (as in David A. deSilva, "Exchanging Favor for Wrath: Apostasy in Hebrews and Patron-Client Relations," *JBL* 115 [1996] 91–116).

are simply people who have at one time repented and turned to God and received the blessings that accompany these actions. But the author continues. This impossible situation, he says, is characterized further as involving people in falling away but then wanting to be renewed again to repentance (the verb has a preposition that indicates repetition, ἀνά, as well as the adverb πάλιν). The impossibility is not that there are such people, who are described in terms of falling away from the Christian community (the description of these people relies on a series of parallel participial constructions),[39] even though the act of falling away has "its most sinister sense,"[40] but that such people who might fall away cannot be renewed again through repentance (there is a shift from the participles to the infinitive).[41] The repentance referred to seems to be the one already mentioned in 6:1, that is, the laying of the foundation, in which the notion of the foundation remaining standing and not being re-layable is paramount.[42] The reason, the author says, is that (the participial construction is renewed) the people described as falling away, but who want to be renewed again to repentance, are crucifying again for themselves (the dative appears to be one of advantage) the Son of God and making him an example, the implication being that it is a negative example.[43] Here is where the example in Heb 12:17 is pertinent. In the only other place where language of repentance is used in the book of Hebrews, the author says that in the case of Esau here was a person for whom, even though he desired with tears to change the situation and receive the blessing, there was no opportunity for repentance.

The notion of repentance in Hebrews seems consonant with that in the Pauline writings. Repentance appears to imply a condition that merits reorientation, and when one repents, one can be oriented toward God and participate in this existence: enlightened, tasting of the heavenly

---

[39] See B. F. Westcott, *The Epistle to the Hebrews* (London: Macmillan, 1892) 147–50 on the not-quite-parallel parallel participles and their connecting words.

[40] James Moffatt, *A Critical and Exegetical Commentary on the Epistle to the Hebrews*, ICC (Edinburgh: T & T Clark, 1924) 79. The implication is a kind of complete apostasy, as in Heb 10:26-31. See Goppelt, *Theology*, 2:257.

[41] Cf. Hugh Montefiore, *The Epistle to the Hebrews*, HNTC (New York: Harper & Row 1964) 109, who raises the question of whether it is God or the preacher who cannot bring the sinner, or himself, back to repentance.

[42] William L. Lane, *Hebrews*, WBC 47A, B (Dallas: Word Books, 1991) 1:142.

[43] These two participles are unique to the New Testament. See Westcott, *Epistle to the Hebrews*, 150.

gift, partaker of the Holy Spirit, a taster of the good word of God and the powers of the coming age. However, the author of Hebrews adds something not found in any other place in the New Testament, and that is the notion that repentance is only to be had once. There is nothing inherent in the notion of repentance that says it cannot be repeated. It indicates a change of behavior. Nevertheless, the author—at this point consonant with Paul—focuses the notion of repentance on this fundamental transformation from dead works (for the author of Hebrews, but for Paul stubbornness and an unrepentant heart awaiting God's wrath) to faith in God. For the author of Hebrews this transformative action cannot be repeated (hence this passage goes further than Gal 4:8-9). It is possible, he seems to begrudgingly admit, that someone might fall away from this allegiance toward God, but it is impossible, as Esau experienced, to repent again in this way and to re-establish one's relationship with God.

### (3) James 5

The letter of James ends with two verses (5:19, 20) that have aroused discussion because they appear to be an abrupt way to end the letter. In and of themselves these verses are not as controversial in terms of repentance as the verses in Hebrews treated above, but they nevertheless merit discussion. The final verses of the letter end in this way: "My brothers and sisters, if any among you strays from the truth, and one turns them back (ἐπιστρέψῃ), let them know that the one who turns (ὁ ἐπιστρέψας) a sinner from the error of their way will save their soul from death, and will cover a multitude of sins" (trans. Porter, based on *NASB*).

The letter of James, though presented in the form of a letter, has been widely discussed regarding its literary type. One of the major theories has been that it is a series of paraenetic statements drawing on analogies from all kinds of situations in nature, society, and the like.[44] Regardless of whether this theory is correct, there is in any case a definite sense in which the letter of James focuses on how one, as a member of the group of twelve tribes of the dispersion (1:1), is to act. However, the section in which the passage on repentance occurs is the last part of the book,

---

[44] See Martin Dibelius, *James*, Hermeneia, ed. Heinrich Greeven (Philadelphia: Fortress Press, 1975) 3–11. Cf. Peter H. Davids, *The Epistle of James*, NIGTC (Grand Rapids: Eerdmans, 1982) 198, who seems to want to isolate the final two verses.

which is given to closing exhortations (5:7-20).[45] There are exhortations regarding patience (5:7-11), swearing (5:12), prayer for others (5:13-18), and finally repentance (5:19-20). The two verses themselves are in some tension grammatically and conceptually. Verse 19, within the larger context of the letter itself, is addressed to those within the community, ἀδελφοί. The author begins to speak of one of those straying from the truth and someone turning him or her back, but then changes constructions. On the basis of the use of the third person singular imperative, v. 20 is addressed not to one who strays (as might be expected) but to one who turns a sinning believer from the error of his or her way.[46] That person will save the other from death and will cover a multitude of sins, whether her or his own or the sinner's.[47] The grammatical oddities make it difficult to understand the flow of thought—whether the same person is being addressed in each verse, what the relationship is between the brethren and one who strays, and what the relationship of repentance is to both of these. Nevertheless, a fundamental conceptual commonality is found between the two statements regarding repentance. The context is one in which a member of the community has wandered from the truth, that is, departed from the behavior expected of a member of the community.[48] One who is able to turn such a one from their straying way (the phrase "error of his way" is another way of characterizing someone who has "wandered") will save his or her soul.[49] The saving of one's soul here does indicate eschatological consequences for unrepentant straying from the truth, but does not necessarily have to indicate initial salvation.[50]

---

[45] See McDonald and Porter, *Early Christianity,* 534.

[46] A number of commentators address the fact that there is a textual variant at this point, but few successfully handle the grammatical shift.

[47] See Joseph B. Mayor, *The Epistle of St James* (London: Macmillan, 1892) 184–187, who discusses the options that have been proposed.

[48] James B. Adamson, *The Epistle of James,* NICNT (Grand Rapids: Eerdmans, 1976) 203. Davids (*James,* 198) goes further and seems to imply that the person has fully apostatized. See below for discussion of how this fits with Hebrews 6.

[49] See C. Leslie Mitton, *The Epistle of James* (London: Marshall, Morgan & Scott; Grand Rapids: Eerdmans, 1966) 212: "If it were a non-Christian who is involved here, to turn him back from error may mean no more than a moral improvement in conduct. But James is here thinking of one who has been a believing Christian, and whose lapse in moral conduct coincides with abandoning his faith in God."

[50] See Kurt A. Richardson, *James,* NAC 36 (Nashville: Broadman, 1997) 245.

### (4) 2 Peter 3

The last passage I want to address is the repentance passage in 2 Pet 3:9. Like the Pauline passages treated briefly above, this verse, which stands on its own, mentions repentance almost inadvertently and does not develop the notion in any significant way. The passage says that the Lord is not slow concerning his promise, but is patient toward those of faith (cf. 1:1), "not wishing for any to perish but for all to come to repentance (μετάνοιαν)" *(NASB).* The dichotomy found in other passages is reflected here, in that the opposition is drawn between those perishing and those who repent. Repentance is seen as the preferred option, and people are seen as moving from the condition of perishing to repentance. In that sense this passage also endorses the notion that the human condition in need of repentance precedes repentance and then results in being relieved from that condition. Here this is described in terms of being rescued from perishing, especially at the time of the "day of the Lord" (v. 10).[51]

### b. Conclusion

Although language regarding repentance is not frequent within the epistles, there is enough said to let us recognize that the epistolary authors, namely Paul, the author of Hebrews, James, and Peter,[52] share a common conception of the initial stages of coming to faith within the Christian community. In all of the writings there is a common conception of the human predicament that makes repentance a necessity, of the nature of repentance as a turning from evil to God, of the role God and the Christian community and its "preachers" play in such a process, and of the rewards such repentance entails. It is fair to say, I believe, that the major passages that develop these ideas present a fairly full explication of such a theological notion, so that it is not hard to extrapolate that such a fundamental framework also underlies other incidental uses in which the necessity of repentance is assumed rather than argued.

---

[51] See Richard Bauckham, *Jude, 2 Peter,* WBC 50 (Waco, TX: Word Books, 1983) 312–13.

[52] Here is not the place to defend the notion of Jacobean or Petrine authorship, but I have come increasingly to accept these. Certainly the common emphasis does nothing to argue against this. On the issue of authorship see McDonald and Porter, *Early Christianity,* 528–31, 534–37, 539–42.

## 2. Implications

The amount of evidence in the New Testament epistles, though not large, illustrates several recurring patterns of usage of repentance language that provide useful insights for a theology of penitence and repentance. The two major uses of the language of repentance in the epistles are that of initial repentance and that of secondary repentance, or repentance understood as penitence, remorse, and contrition. In a number of ways the fundamental theological concepts involved are sufficiently different to warrant separate discussion. In terms of the purposes of this symposium, one might well argue that the only passages of direct relevance would be 2 Cor 7:19-20 and Jas 5:19-20, passages concerned with penitence, remorse, and contrition by those within the community of faith. However, there are sufficient similarities between the two notions, as illustrated above, for the two sets of uses to be placed together to form a more holistic notion of penitence and repentance, one that moves from initiation to experience, from outside to inside, and from fallen to restored. As Alan Richardson says, "Repentance is thus a *sine qua non* of the Christian life, not only in its beginning but at every stage; it involves a constant awareness of the fact that all our faith and all our virtue are God's gift and not our achievement. But it is inevitably specially associated with the beginning of the Christian life."[53] As Richardson points out, and as was seen above, the New Testament epistolary evidence tends to emphasize repentance language in terms of initial repentance and, at least so far as Hebrews is concerned, a one-time act of turning from sin to God. The context in which repentance occurs is one in which the human is found within fallenness. This fallenness is described with different words by the different authors—such as stubbornness and unrepentance, error, evil, or sin—but in any case assumes that the person who is unrepentant, or rather who is pre-repentant, is outside the community of faith. Repentance comes in response to becoming aware of the dire circumstances of the human condition, ultimately by the will of God but also in response to the proclamation of the need for repentance by a member of the already-repentant community of faith.[54] Repentance is seen as a necessary and essential, even a first, response to the human condition and necessary for making progress along the path that results

[53] Richardson, *Introduction*, 33.
[54] See Guthrie, *New Testament Theology*, 590, who equates conversion with justification, but with repentance assumed.

in becoming the mature Christian who has been enlightened, who has tasted the heavenly gift, become a partaker of the Holy Spirit, and tasted the good word of God and the powers of the coming age. So far virtually all the passages regarding repentance hold the same essential conceptual framework in common. Some are wont to call this conversion, although repentance in this sense is a more focused concept than the larger notion of conversion in the ancient or even Christian world. Nevertheless, even if it is not the most widespread usage, there is also language of secondary repentance, including penitence, remorse, or contrition for those within the community of believers. The situation assumes that the person has already experienced initial repentance but has strayed into wrongdoing. Those of the Christian community have an obligation to try to bring that person back to obedience. Even though the notions are not identical, repentance and penitence have in common that there is a situation of sinfulness that calls for the person to respond by turning away from wrongdoing and turning toward God, whether for the first time or in an act of restoration.

It is in the light of the use of language of penitence, remorse, and contrition in 2 Cor 7:19-20 and Jas 5:19-20 that the importance of Hebrews 6 emerges. The passages from 2 Cor 7:19-20 and Jas 5:19-20 suggest that there may be a place for one of the "faithful" who has strayed from the truth to repent again and return to the community of faith. Hebrews 6:6 categorically denies that someone who has entered the community and enjoys what it means to be a member of the community of faith can fall away and then return by means of repentance. The author of Hebrews, however, says that one who has built the initial foundation of repentance, and experienced the benefits of being a follower of Christ, cannot be restored if he or she falls away. Hebrews even goes further and states that, like Esau, one cannot do so because this represents an attempt to crucify Christ again and makes a mockery of his example. However, there is also the indication in 2 Cor 7:19-20 and Jas 5:19-20 that one can repent of wrongdoing and restore a relationship to God and within the Christian community. One is encouraged to do so. It is possible that these two perspectives will need to remain in tension. However, there is another explanation, as noted above. That explanation is that they are speaking of slightly different things. In the logical sense it is impossible for someone to do something again for the first time. If one is speaking about going back and beginning again with the Christian experience, then the author of Hebrews says that is impossible. One cannot go back and rebuild the foundation, as if Christ were to be crucified again. However, this is not to say that, with the foundation still intact, there cannot be those who come back from their wrongdoing and continue to build upon the still-standing foundation. In other words, short of complete apostasy there is still a place for contrition, remorse, and penitence within the Christian community, although one can only experience initial repentance once.

## 3. Further Reading

Beyschlag, Willibald. *New Testament Theology.* Trans. Neil Buchanan. 2 vols. Edinburgh: T & T Clark, 1895.

Goetzmann, J. "Conversion, Penitence, Repentance, Proselyte," in *NIDNTT* 1:353–62.

Goppelt, Leonhard. *Theology of the New Testament.* Trans. John E. Alsup. 2 vols. Grand Rapids: Eerdmans, 1982, especially vol. 2.

Guthrie, Donald. *New Testament Theology.* London: InterVarsity Press, 1981, 589–91.

Marshall, I. Howard. *New Testament Theology: Many Witnesses, One Gospel.* Downers Grove, IL: InterVarsity Press, 2004, 478.

Nave, Guy D., Jr. *The Role and Function of Repentance in Luke-Acts.* Atlanta: Society of Biblical Literature, 2002.

Richardson, Alan. *An Introduction to the Theology of the New Testament.* London: SCM Press, 1958, 33.

## 4. Hermeneutical Reflections

One of the major goals of this project, it would appear, has been to bring together biblical scholars, historians, theologians, and hermeneutics/homiletics specialists to reflect on a common topic. The presumption is that the compartmentalized nature of recent academic theological study can be overcome by sitting down and hearing each other.[55] The exercise has been beneficial, I believe, but it has also made me more cognizant than ever that there are reasons why individual disciplines have their own ways of doing and saying things. I found it instructive to hear from those who reflect theologically and historically on how the notion of repentance has developed within Christian thought—though I also found it frustrating since so much of it seemed to assume that the Bible presented a unified and important concept of repentance and penitence.

---

[55] There is probably the further assumption that such compartmentalization is regrettable, if not deleterious to theological study.

Some traditions have more greatly emphasized and have retained the notion of repentance in their contexts of worship and further theological reflection, while others have not placed great emphasis on this. All of this is for a variety of interesting historical and theological reasons.

This discussion, however, does not get to the heart of the issues involved, so far as I am concerned. Three major issues remain for me as a result of this ongoing discussion. The first is that we have not settled how one defines the very notion of penitence, and along with it repentance. Language can be both friend and foe of communication, and this may well be a good example of that fact. The language of penitence and repentance is bandied about relatively more freely by those in theological and historical circles than it is by those in the biblical disciplines. Once one tries to define these notions more precisely, especially with reference to particular biblical passages, one realizes that it is not so easy to overcome disciplinary boundaries simply by putting people from these different academic traditions in the same room. Theologians are much more ready to throw this language around than are biblical scholars—although biblical scholars are not without their volubility. There is a sense in which theologians know what this idea is, and regret that there is not more emphasis on it. I am not convinced that I see any more genuine repentance or penitence among those traditions that generally include more specific reference to it within their liturgies. In fact, at the end of the day I am not even sure that we really know what the notion is and entails.

The second issue is that of how one defines such terms within the biblical corpus. As I have tried to reflect in my own paper, one wants to avoid moving from one extreme to another. On the one extreme one confines oneself to a single word or set of cognate words as a means of determining the presence of the notion. This certainly runs the risk of either equating word with concept or of being overly restrictive and narrow in material one takes into consideration. The other extreme is to draw the boundaries so widely and loosely that not only are all corpora included within the body of evidence but the one notion subsumes most others. The result is a lack of controls on interpretation, and such large notions as conversion and repentance become facilely equated. I have chosen to try to focus on a set of related lexical items found in a number of key passages. I tried not to prejudge the centrality of the notion of repentance or penitence in my corpus of writings, but instead to let the concept emerge from the recognizable contexts. I find, as a result, that this notion is not as central to this portion of the New Testament as some others might think, or as central as it is in other portions of the Bible. Even with the variety of categories utilized in the biblical papers, however, one sees that there are major bodies of material that do not discuss or treat penitence or repentance as central, or even in some cases as important. The Johannine writings are a case in point, but so are the epistolary writings. Perhaps we need simply to recognize that some good theological and even biblical notions are not as important throughout the Bible as are others. In fact, it may even be the case that some notions are more testamentally focused than others.

The third issue is that my discussion has led me to differentiate two distinct notions that are often equated or not distinguished by the use of penitence and repentance language. My differentiation of initial and secondary repentance, I believe, captures the kind of language that is used in a number of places within the epistles. I was pleased to note that in further discussion there were those who had also arrived at such a distinction—although for the most part it was not developed sufficiently, I believe. There were also those who did not wish to make such a distinction. There were even some who wished to extend the notion in ways that are not apparently entailed by the biblical evidence. This complex set of debated definitions illustrates well the dilemma of such a project, because it raises the question of the driving force behind such a symposium. On the one hand, if it is examining the biblical evidence one cannot start with the presumption that all biblical sub-corpora will be equally concerned with the notion at hand or that they will handle the notion in the same way. This became evident in the discussion of material from both testaments. The pentateuchal and prophetic materials treat the notions in different ways, and the New Testament sees very little commonality when the gospels, Johannine material, and epistolary material are compared. Indeed, the New Testament has a relatively underdeveloped notion of repentance compared to the Old Testament, with only the gospels witnessing significant usage. This makes it very difficult for theological discussion to grab hold of the "biblical notion" to provide a foundational concept for theological development. If on the other hand the idea of a common theological notion is asserted, then it makes it difficult to find a way of including the intractable and varied biblical material or to focus discussion on significant biblical passages. It might even mean that certain biblical passages will need to be discounted from discussion because they do not conform to the posited governing notion.

My impression is that this project has made progress in the recognition that the notion of repentance is more variegated than one might first think—that it is concerned with far more than simply an attitude of contrition and regret that has in some way been lost in contemporary liturgy, and that it is concerned with far less than simply every regretful feeling for bad things that people have done or that have happened in the world. The concept of repentance is probably best discussed as a complex theological notion grounded in a number of crucial passages in Scripture, in which the human response is one of distinct change of behavior and attitude in relation to God—what sometimes is best called repentance or conversion—and that it requires a continual reassessment of one's actions and responses toward God, to ensure purity of heart and behavior—what is sometimes called penitence or contrition. This is not a notion that includes every other theological notion, nor is it one that is so limited that one cannot see that there is a need for its use within the contemporary church. It is unreasonable to expect that biblical scholars, theologians, historians, and homileticians will all be able to speak the same language about such a notion, but it is unwise to leave them only talking to themselves and not to each other about what such notions involve. Penitence and repentance are not necessarily the same thing, nor are they easily seen everywhere in the Bible, but they are clearly a notion, or some notions, that the church needs to come to terms with as an expression of its ongoing life in Christ and before God.

# Section Two

# Historical Perspectives

Eight

# Penitence in Early Christianity in Its Historical and Theological Setting: Trajectories from Eastern and Western Sources

*Cornelia B. Horn*

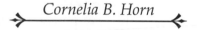

## 1. History

This chapter surveys Christian texts from Greek, Latin, and Syriac sources to discuss characteristics of penitence and repentance. It is necessary to limit the source material for this study due to the format of this article, which examines selected works from the period of the so-called "Apostolic" fathers (the *Shepherd of Hermas*), from other early Greek sources (Clement of Alexandria), from early Latin sources (Tertullian), from the earliest Christian Syriac writers (Aphrahat), as well as from the ascetic traditions of early Egypt and Palestine. The selected material reveals several trajectories of early Christian views concerning penitence. Penitence is connected with the experience of sin and a quest for change in order to restore a pristine state before the Fall. It emerges as "second repentance" from the realization that despite baptismal purification, sin continues to have power over the Christian. Early Christian sources from the West begin to emphasize penance as a requirement of justice in an attempt to appease God, thus revealing more of a legal mindset on the part of their authors. Sources from the East begin to see penitence in the light of specific christological conceptions and highlight the connections between penitence and healing, purification, knowledge, perfection, and asceticism more generally. Slowly but surely, both in the West and in the East, distinct bodily expressions of penitence and specific rituals of penance of the individual as well as of the community start to emerge, a point that could be developed more strongly than what this survey chose to emphasize.

### a. Responding to Crises: the *Shepherd of Hermas*

From among the noncanonical texts of the period of the Apostolic Fathers, the *Shepherd of Hermas* was the most popular in pre-Constantinian times.[1] It consists of five *visiones*,[2] twelve *mandata*, and ten *similitudines*. The text shares much in common with literature of the apocryphal genre and has been described as apocalyptic paraenesis.[3]

As apocalyptic literature tends to address crises that affect a given community,[4] the *Shepherd of Hermas* constitutes an attempt to deal with the experience of sin and the quest for change and restoration of the fallen individual as well as of the Christian community harmed by sin. The realization that the attacks of sin and the giving in to sin had not disappeared with baptism describes one of the major crises faced by the Christian church in the second century.

The *Shepherd of Hermas* is the most explicit and urgent admonishment to a life of penance one can find in the second century.[5] The main theme

---

[1] For further discussion see Carolyn Osiek, *Shepherd of Hermas: A Commentary*, Hermeneia (Minneapolis: Fortress Press, 1999) 1.

[2] For a detailed study of the structure of the *visiones* see David Hellholm, *Das Visionenbuch des Hermas als Apokalypse. Formgeschichtliche und texttheoretische Studien zu einer literarischen Gattung. Vol. I: Methodische Vorüberlegungen und makrostrukturelle Textanalyse*, ConBNT 13:1 (Lund: Gleerup, 1980).

[3] See Osiek, *Shepherd of Hermas*, 11.

[4] See Carolyn Osiek, "The Genre and Function of the *Shepherd of Hermas*," in Adela Yarbro Collins, ed., *Early Christian Apocalypticism: Genre and Social Setting*, Semeia 36 (Decatur, GA: Scholars Press, 1986) 113–21, at 116–17; see also Osiek, *Shepherd of Hermas*, 12.

[5] See the appendix on the question of penance in the *Shepherd of Hermas* in Norbert Brox, *Der Hirt des Hermas*, Kommentar zu den Apostolischen Vätern 7 (Göttingen: Vandenhoeck & Ruprecht, 1991) 476–85, at 476; see also Oscar D. Watkins, *A History of Penance, Vol. 1: The Whole Church to A.D. 450* (London:

of the work is the penitence of Christians for post-baptismal sins.[6] Cast in the style of a succession of revelations by two heavenly figures, one in the form of a woman representing the church[7] and one appearing in the shape of a shepherd, the Angel of Repentance,[8] the work conveys to its readers a message that the remission of sins committed after baptism is possible, in principle, yet only under certain conditions and with some limitations.

A key passage of Hermas's teachings on repentance is found at *Mandatum* 4.3.1-6. "Certain teachers" had told Hermas "that there [was] no other repentance possible than the one when we went down into the water and received remission of our former sins."[9] When asked what to think about this, the Angel of Repentance in response confirmed to Hermas that "the one who has received remission of sins ought never to sin again, but to live in purity."[10] This was to be the normal situation. Nevertheless, the Angel continued by saying that

".  .  . those who have already come to believe or are about to believe

---

Longmans, Green, 1920) 47. I wish to thank my research assistant Mrs. Inta Ivanovska for having brought Watkins's work to my attention.

[6] See also Karl Rahner, "Die Bußlehre im Hirten des Hermas," *ZKT* 77 (1955) 385–431; and idem, "The Penitential Teaching of the Shepherd of Hermas," in his *Theological Investigations 15. Penance in the Early Church* (New York: Crossroad, 1982) 125–51.

[7] For a recent discussion of this representation of the church as woman see also Athanasius Schneider, *"Propter Sanctam Ecclesiam Suam": Die Kirche als Geschöpf, Frau und Bau im Bußunterricht des Pastor Hermae,* SEAug 67 (Rome: Institutum Patristicum Augustinianum, 1999) 165–263. For a study of the church in connection with the concept of penitence see Lage Pernveden, *The Concept of the Church in the Shepherd of Hermas,* STL 27 (Lund: Gleerup, 1966) 223–76.

[8] For commentary on both of these figures see also Osiek, *Shepherd of Hermas,* 16. On the shepherd/angel more specifically see Halvor Moxnes, "God and his Angel in the *Shepherd of Hermas,*" *ST* 28/1 (1974) 49–56.

[9] *Shepherd of Hermas, Mand.* 4.3.1, in Molly Whittaker, ed., *Der Hirt des Hermas,* GCS Die Apostolischen Väter 1 (2d rev. ed. Berlin: Akademie Verlag, 1967) 27–28; trans. Johannes Quasten, *Patrology,* 3 vols. (Utrecht: Spectrum, 1950; Allen, TX: Christian Classics, eighth paperback reprint, 1995) 1:97, translation modified. See also Osiek, *Shepherd of Hermas,* 113, translation modified.

[10] *Shepherd of Hermas, Mand.* 4.3.2, in Whittaker, ed., *Hirt des Hermas,* 28; trans. Quasten, *Patrology* 1:97, translation modified; see also Osiek, *Shepherd of Hermas,* 113, translation modified.

have no repentance of sins, but have forgiveness of their former sins. For those who were called before these days, the Lord has appointed [the chance for] repentance, for the Lord knows the heart and has foreknowledge of everything. [Thus] he knew human weakness and the cunning craftiness of the devil, that he would do something evil to the servants of God and would deal wickedly with them. The Lord therefore being full of compassion had mercy on his creation and established this [chance for] repentance and to me was given authority over this repentance." [Then the Angel continued] "I tell you . . . after that great and solemn calling, if anyone should be tempted by the devil and sin, he or she has one repentance. But if such a person should sin repeatedly and repent, it is unprofitable for such a person, for hardly shall he or she live."[11]

Thus after baptism one more chance was given, even to grave sinners, to repent.[12] A comparison with texts from the earlier post-apostolic tradition shows that the teaching of a "second repentance" as defended in the *Shepherd of Hermas* was not an innovation produced by the author of this text. Rather, one may go along with Bernhard Poschmann and see the *Shepherd of Hermas* as a witness to the already established and practiced authority of the church to forgive sins.[13]

In the *Shepherd of Hermas* two elements seem to complement one another. While the text sees the grace of penance grounded in God's mercy, at the same time it exhorts sinners to be scrupulously conscious of their sins. Even the smallest sins have to be taken seriously, whether committed with the body or with the mind. At the very beginning of the text the lady had warned Hermas that even the intention of his heart had to be pure and undefiled. Otherwise it would be reckoned to him

---

[11] *Shepherd of Hermas, Mand.* 4.3.3-6, in Whittaker, ed., *Hirt des Hermas,* 28; trans. Quasten, *Patrology* 1:97–98, translation modified; see also Osiek, *Shepherd of Hermas,* 113, translation modified.

[12] For further commentary see Osiek, *Shepherd of Hermas,* 114–15.

[13] See Bernhard Poschmann, *Paenitentia Secunda. Die kirchliche Buße im ältesten Christentum bis Cyprian und Origenes. Eine dogmengeschichtliche Untersuchung* (Bonn: Peter Hanstein, 1940) 134–205, on the teachings regarding penitence in the *Shepherd of Hermas,* including a discussion of the role of the church. More recently see Bernhard Poschmann, *Buße und Letzte Ölung,* Handbuch der Dogmengeschichte 4, fasc. 3 (Freiburg: Herder, 1951) 14–16. Also note the discussion in Gustav Adolf Benrath, "Buße V. Historisch," in *TRE* 7 (1981) 452–73, at 452.

as evil.[14] For all sins one was called upon to exercise severe penance. Obtaining forgiveness, however, was not seen as something easy, since it required the exercise of humility and a willingness to bear sufferings. The Angel of Repentance instructs Hermas that even those who repent with all their heart do not immediately receive remission of their sins. Rather, "the one who has repented must torment his or her soul and be greatly humbled in every deed and be afflicted with many afflictions of different kinds."[15]

One of the five visions Hermas received is especially descriptive of the text's view of repentance and forgiveness within the church. In vision three the figure of the aged woman representing the church allows Hermas to see how six young men, possibly angels, aided by about ten thousand other men or angels, are building a tower.[16] The building of the tower "on water" could take place, as Hermas learned, "because [your] life [was] saved and shall be saved through water,"[17] a comment referring rather clearly to baptism. As the six young men or angels continue their work they select clerics, martyrs, those who are from among the just ones, and newly baptized Christians who have proven faultless in their new faith to be the stones for the building. Others, including people who only pretend to have faith or who have doubts, those who have gone astray, as well as those who are unrepentant and those who have apostatized, are thrown aside and end up lying around at the base of the tower or even being burned in the fire.[18] Yet that need not be their final destination. Even those sinners who initially had been rejected and cast aside are promised the hope of forgiveness. No sin is seen as too grave for forgiveness. Even adultery can be forgiven for the sinner who

---

[14] See *Shepherd of Hermas*, *Vis.* 1.1.8, in Whittaker, ed., *Hirt des Hermas* 2; trans. Osiek, *Shepherd of Hermas*, 41.

[15] *Shepherd of Hermas*, *Sim.* 7.4, in Whittaker, ed., *Hirt des Hermas*, 64; trans. Osiek, *Shepherd of Hermas*, 191, translation modified.

[16] See *Shepherd of Hermas*, *Vis.* 3.2.4-8, in Whittaker, ed., *Hirt des Hermas*, 9–10; trans. Osiek, *Shepherd of Hermas*, 61.

[17] *Shepherd of Hermas*, *Vis.* 3.3.5, in Whittaker, ed., *Hirt des Hermas*, 10–11; trans. Osiek, *Shepherd of Hermas*, 65.

[18] See *Shepherd of Hermas*, *Vis* 3.5.1–3.7.3, in Whittaker, ed., *Hirt des Hermas*, 11–14; trans. Osiek, *Shepherd of Hermas*, 66–67. For discussion see Osiek, *Shepherd of Hermas*, 72–75; Norbert Brox, "Die weggeworfenen Steine im Pastor Hermae, Vis. III,7,5," *ZNW* 80/1-2 (1989) 130–33; Watkins, *History of Penance*, 49–50; and Benrath, "Buße," 452–53.

repents of it.[19] If grave sinners take up active penance, a penance that is not afraid even of harsh sufferings as part of the punishment, even they can be fitted into the building of the church. Their place, however, is only on a lower level and not anywhere higher up in the tower.

The concessions the *Shepherd of Hermas* made with regard to the possibility of a "second penance" were not meant to lower the weight and the respect owed to baptism as the "first penance." Moreover, no third, fourth, or even further penance could follow the "second penance." If the baptized person, after his or her one and only chance of post-baptismal repentance, sinned again, all attempts to reach forgiveness would be "unprofitable" and the person would barely live.[20]

Nevertheless, the text spells out clearly that "turning from sin means life, [while] not turning [from sin] means death."[21] This emphasis certainly contributed to the more widely accepted practice of granting most sinners who had publicly confessed their sins a penance.[22]

### b. The Impact of Legal Education and Controversial Theology: Tertullian of Carthage

From the later second century onward the theological views and interpretations early Christians had developed with regard to repentance and penance took on different emphases in different regions of the Mediterranean world. Views in the West were shaped by the teachings of Tertullian, Cyprian, Augustine, and Ambrose. Space only permits a consideration of Tertullian's thought here.

From relatively early on, Western theology emphasized penance as a requirement of justice. The baptized Christian could attempt to live up to the call God had placed on his or her life only by being a repentant sinner. Penance *(paenitentia)* came to be seen as the only way to respond to and handle the punishment *(poena)* that was measured out for the Christian's transgressions. That the two words sounded similar to the

---

[19] *Shepherd of Hermas, Mand.* 4.1.8-11, in Whittaker, ed., *Hirt des Hermas,* 26–27; trans. Osiek, *Shepherd of Hermas,* 109.

[20] *Shepherd of Hermas, Mand.* 4.3.6, in Whittaker, ed., *Hirt des Hermas,* 28, translated above.

[21] *Shepherd of Hermas, Sim.* 8.6.6, in Whittaker, ed., *Hirt des Hermas,* 72: ἡ μετάνοια τῶν ἁμαρτωλῶν ζωήν ἔχει, τό δὲ μὴ μετασῆσαι θάνατον. See also Osiek, *Shepherd of Hermas,* 197.

[22] See also Benrath, "Buße," 453.

ear of the Latin speaker enhanced the urgency and appropriateness of this connection.[23]

The early phase of the development of the theology of penance in North Africa was shaped decisively by the work of Tertullian of Carthage (ca. 160–after 212 C.E.).[24] Tertullian developed his views on penance primarily in two works: *On Penance* and *On Modesty*.[25] The earlier of the two, *On Penance*, probably was delivered originally as a sermon, preached to his congregation in Carthage. Its approach is quite direct and is characterized by a personal and often admonitory tone. Thus, like the *Shepherd of Hermas*, this composition is to be grouped with what is known as paraenetic literature.[26] Tertullian's treatise *On Modesty* originated during the later years of his life when he showed great sympathies to the somewhat rigorist movement of Montanism. Thus *On Modesty* is significantly more argumentative in style and has been characterized as a "violent . . . party pamphlet."[27]

In his approach to penance Tertullian availed himself of the basic principles of the theory of recapitulation advanced by Irenaeus of Lyons, namely the idea that in Christ and in events in Christ's life, Old Testament events and people reemerged and were restored to their full meaning and potential, so that finally they could become perfected.[28] Consequently,

---

[23] See also Jürgen Werbick, "Busse. II. Historisch-theologisch," in *LThK* 2 (1993) 828–30, at 828.

[24] On Tertullian's view of penance see also Poschmann, *Paenitentia Secunda*, 283–348; Guy G. Stroumsa, "From Repentance to Penance in Early Christianity: Tertullian's *De Paenitentia* in Context" (see Selected Further Readings); Mark DeVine, "Two Treatises on Penance: an Inquiry into Tertullian's Exegesis and Montanism," *Churchman* 109/2 (1995) 143–53; and Benrath, "Buße," 453–54.

[25] For an English translation of these works see William P. Le Saint, trans., *Tertullian of Carthage. Treatises on Penance: On Penitence and On Purity*, ACW 28 (Westminster, MD: Newman Press, 1959).

[26] See Le Saint, *Tertullian of Carthage*, 9.

[27] See Le Saint, *Tertullian of Carthage*, 5.

[28] See, e.g., Irenaeus of Lyons, *Adversus haereses* 5.19.1, in Adelin Rousseau, Louis Doutreleau, and Charles Mercier, eds., *Irénée de Lyon. Contre les heresies. Livre V. Édition critique d'après les versions arménienne et latine. Tome II. Texte et Traduction*, SC 153 (Paris: Cerf, 1969) 248–50; trans. in Cyril R. Richardson, ed., *Early Christian Fathers*, Library of Christian Classics 1 (New York: Westminster; reprinted Touchstone, 1996) 389–90. For a study of this concept in Irenaeus see Emmeran Scharl, "Der Rekapitulationsbegriff des heiligen Irenaeus," *Orientalia Christiana Periodica* 6/3-4 (1940) 376–416. Tertullian wrote in Latin and Greek, but

Tertullian conceived of the death of Christ as a way of obtaining remission of the sins of Adam and of all subsequent human beings by means of compensation. In Tertullian's view the sinner owed satisfaction to God's justice. Repentance was to become the mechanism that achieved the effect of compensation. According to Tertullian, "the Lord has set [a price] on the purchase of pardon, [namely] he offers impunity *(impunitas)* to be bought in [compensating] exchange for penitence *(paenitentia).*"[29] If the sinner did not voluntarily accept penance, God had to lay it upon him or her. Thus, Tertullian told his audience, "To the extent that you have not spared yourself, believe me, in just this same measure [God] will spare you."[30] In such a framework pride of place belonged not so much to repentance as a state of mind as to penance as a human deed or work. Acting in a penitential way was seen as an activity endowed with the effective power of removing punishment for sin.[31]

As in regard to other questions, so also in his formulation of penitential theology Tertullian's training as a lawyer influenced him to develop his thought by having recourse to legal metaphors.[32] Thus he characterized penance as penitential compensation, or *satisfactio*,[33] owed to the Lord, over which he like

---

his compositions in Greek have generally not survived into modern times. Thus knowledge of Irenaeus's writings and ideas on Tertullian's part is possible.

[29] Tertullian, *De paenitentia* 6.4, in J. G. Ph. Borleffs, ed., "Q. S. Fl. Tertulliani *De Paenitentia*," in *Tertulliani Opera*, CCSL 1 (Turnhout: Brepols, 1954) 321–40, at 330; trans. Le Saint, *Tertullian, Treatises on Penance*, 24, translation modified.

[30] Tertullian, *De paenitentia* 9.6, in Borleffs, ed., "Tertulliani *De Paenitentia*," 336: *In quantum non peperceris tibi, in tantum tibi deus, crede, parcet*. See also Le Saint, *Tertullian, Treatises on Penance*, 32, translation modified.

[31] See also Benrath, "Buße," 453.

[32] Concepts and ideas the presentation of which in Tertullian is influenced by his legal background include baptism, merit, and reason. See the studies by J. Albert Harrill, "The influence of Roman contract law on early baptismal formulae (Tertullian, *Ad Martyras* 3)," *StPatr* 35 (2001) 275–82; Gösta Hallonsten, "Some aspects of the so-called *Verdienstbegriff* of Tertullian," *StPatr* 17.2 (1982) 799–802; and Gerald Bray, "The Legal Concept of *ratio* in Tertullian," *VC* 31.2 (1977) 94–116.

[33] Tertullian, *De paenitentia* 5.9, in Borleffs, ed., "Tertulliani *De Paenitentia*," 328–29; trans. Le Saint, *Tertullian, Treatises on Penance*, 23. See also Gösta Hallonsten, *Satisfactio bei Tertullian: Überprüfung einer Forschungstradition* (Malmö: Gleerup, 1984).

every judge *(iudex)* [who] settles a case on its merit . . . presides as judge *(iudex)* in order to exact and safeguard justice, something so precious in His sight, and since it is for this that he establishes every single precept of His moral law, can it be doubted that, just as in all of our actions, so, too, in the case of repentance justice must be rendered to God?[34]

The use of legal language permeates this treatise, e.g., when Tertullian speaks of repentance following upon *(inrogatur)* people's actions as a kind of sanction,[35] when he connects impunity to penitence by way of describing the former as compensation *(compensatio)* for the latter[36] *(compensatio* was a word regularly employed in Roman jurisprudence),[37] or when he speaks of eternal torments being cancelled *(expungat)*,[38] here using a term that in legal contexts was employed to speak of the cancellation of a debt.[39] This choice of legal language that depicts God as judge presiding in a court of law would supply the dominant model for Western penitential theology into medieval times.[40]

Tertullian also provided first indications for the development of specific steps individuals followed in the penitential process.[41] The first step toward penance was humility, which constituted the attitude a sinner needed to have in order to be willing to confess his or her transgressions publicly. The act of public confession *(exomologesis)* demanded that the sinner prepare

[34] Tertullian, *De paenitentia* 2.11-12, in Borleffs, ed., "Tertulliani *De Paenitentia*," 323; trans. Le Saint, *Tertullian, Treatises on Penance*, 17.

[35] See Tertullian, *De Paenitentia* 1.5, in Borleffs, ed., "Tertulliani *De Paenitentia*," 321; trans. Le Saint, *Tertullian, Treatises on Penance*, 14. According to Le Saint, *Tertullian, Treatises on Penance*, 139 n14, *inrogare* is used as a legal term to indicate "that something is set as a sanction or inflicted as a punishment."

[36] Tertullian, *De Paenitentia* 6.4, in Borleffs, ed., "Tertulliani *De Paenitentia*," 330; trans. Le Saint, *Tertullian, Treatises on Penance*, 24.

[37] See Le Saint, *Tertullian, Treatises on Penance*, 158–59 n88.

[38] Tertullian, *De Paenitentia* 9.5, in Borleffs, ed., "Tertulliani *De Paenitentia*," 336; trans. Le Saint, *Tertullian, Treatises on Penance*, 32.

[39] See Le Saint, *Tertullian, Treatises on Penance*, 175 n162, who also points to Tertullian, *Apologia* 2.15, as an instance where Tertullian employs this same word more strictly to elaborate a "Roman juridical procedure."

[40] See Benrath, "Buße," 453.

[41] See also Bernhard Poschmann, "Bußstufen," in *RAC* 2 (1954) 814–16, at 814; more fully developed with regard to Tertullian in Benrath, "Buße," 453. See also Josef Grotz, *Die Entwicklung des Bußstufenwesens in der vornicänischen Kirche* (Freiburg: Herder, 1955).

him- or herself with prayers and fasting, overcome his or her shame, and appear in sackcloth and ashes and with tears before the priests and the faithful. In his treatise on penance Tertullian described very colorfully how

> this way of life . . . even in the matter of food and clothing, appeals to pity. It bids [the sinner] to lie in sackcloth and ashes, to cover his [or her] body with filthy rags, to plunge his [or her] soul into sorrow, to exchange sin for suffering. Moreover, it demands that you know only such food and drink as is plain; this means it is taken for the sake of your soul, not your belly. It requires that you habitually nourish prayer by fasting, that you sigh and weep and groan day and night to the Lord your God, that you prostrate yourself at the feet of the priests and kneel before the beloved of God, making all the brethren commissioned ambassadors of your prayer for pardon.[42]

Tertullian saw the Christian congregation as representing Christ himself, for whose intercession the sinner asked, and which he or she received.[43] He was convinced that

> [w]here there are two together, there is the Church and the Church is Christ. When, therefore, you stretch forth your hands to the knees of the brethren, you are in touch with Christ and you win the favor of Christ by your supplications. In like manner, when they shed tears for you, it is Christ who suffers, Christ who supplicates the Father. And what the Son requests is always easily obtained.[44]

Confession in a way created penance and prepared the sinner for reparation *(satisfactio)*. Tertullian thought that "[c]onfession gives birth *(nascitur)* to penitence and by penitence God is appeased."[45] As calculat-

---

[42] Tertullian, *De paenitentia* 9.3-4, in Borleffs, ed., "Tertulliani *De Paenitentia*," 336; trans. Le Saint, *Tertullian, Treatises on Penance,* 31–32. See also Herman Josef Vogt, "Zu Tertullian *De paenitentia* 9.4," *VC* 38/3 (1984) 196–99.

[43] For a discussion of Tertullian's christology with regard to soteriological concerns see Alberto Viciano, *Cristo Salvador y Liberador del hombre: Estudio sobre la soteriologia de Tertulliano* (Pamplona: Ediciones Universidad de Navarra, 1986).

[44] Tertullian, *De paenitentia* 10.6, in Borleffs, ed., "Tertulliani *De Paenitentia*," 337; trans. Le Saint, *Tertullian, Treatises on Penance,* 33.

[45] Tertullian, *De paenitentia* 9.2, in Borleffs, ed., "Tertulliani *De Paenitentia*," 336: *satisfactio confessione disponitur, confessione paenitentia nascitur, paenitentia Deus mitigatur.* See also Le Saint, *Tertullian, Treatises on Penance,* 31.

ing as this kind of language may sound, it still reveals the author's view of an intimate and wholesome participation and cooperation between the individual sinner and Christ in the very act of penance. When Tertullian speaks of confession as giving birth to penance *(paenitentia nascitur)*, intentionally or not he does evoke notions of a parent-child relationship between penance and the penitent sinner. Thus his choice of expressions presents penance as both a liability and an object to which the sinner has to relate with great care. Moreover, one notices that Tertullian sees penance in light of the work of Christ. Despite all the efforts needed on the part of the sinner, in the end it is Christ who in and through the penitent person continues his own work of redemption by way of satisfying God for the sins of the world. For Tertullian "exomologesis . . . render[s] penitence acceptable . . . [and] in passing sentence upon the sinner it may itself be a substitute for the wrath of God."[46]

In his later years, when Tertullian developed closer affinities with the teachings of Montanism,[47] he shifted in his view of penance to a somewhat harsher position,[48] becoming more rigorous with regard to moral questions. In *On Modesty* Tertullian not only provided the first known instance of an author mentioning the triad of capital sins, which are apostasy, murder, and fornication, the last of which for him included remarriage in the case of widowed men and women, but he also expressed that he no longer thought these capital sins could receive forgiveness.[49] Thus he critiqued what he now thought were the overly liberal practices of individual bishops when they reconciled sinners. In his view capital sins necessitated permanent exclusion from the Christian church. Not even the intercession of the martyrs would be able to obtain forgiveness of such sinners.[50] Rather, these sins carried heavy

---

[46] Tertullian, *De paenitentia* 9.5, in Borleffs, ed., "Tertulliani *De Paenitentia*," 336; trans. Le Saint, *Tertullian, Treatises on Penance*, 32, translation modified.

[47] For a study of Tertullian's connections to Montanism see Christine Trevett, *Montanism: Gender, Authority, and the New Prophecy* (Cambridge: Cambridge University Press, 1996) 66–76.

[48] See Johannes Quasten, *Patrology* 2:313, who speaks of a "complete contradiction" between *De paenitentia* and *De pudicitia*.

[49] Tertullian, *De pudicitia* 9.20, in Eligius Dekkers, ed., "Q. S. Fl. Tertulliani *De Pudicitia*," in *Tertulliani Opera*, CCSL 2 (Turnhout: Brepols, 1954) 1281–1330, at 1299; trans. Le Saint, *Tertullian, Treatises on Penance*, 79.

[50] For a study that considers the phenomenon of obtaining forgiveness for sins through the intercession of martyrs see Ernst Dassmann, *Sündenvergebung durch*

and lasting punishment.[51] The option of a "second penance" that the *Shepherd of Hermas* had promoted now received explicit rejection and scathing critique from Tertullian's pen when he qualified the *Shepherd of Hermas* as having "been judged apocryphal and false by all the councils of the churches" and as being "adulterous [which explained why it] favor[ed] its associates."[52] Tertullian's writings on penance provide an excellent example of how a shift in a person's emphasis on theological truths impacts practical theology.

### c. Penitential Pedagogy in the East: Clement of Alexandria

The two most famous catechetical teachers in Alexandria in the late second and early third century were Clement and Origen. According to Eusebius of Caesarea both held positions at the local catechetical school.[53] While this information on the official character and structure of Clement's exercise of instructing newcomers to the Christian faith in a school setting has to be taken with some caution, nevertheless it is clear that both Clement and Origen dedicated much of their energy to educating both catechumens and more experienced Christians in the faith. Clement and Origen each developed his own distinct perspectives on penance.[54] This discussion will focus on Clement's contribution to the development of penitential theology.[55]

---

*Buße, Taufe und Martyrerfürbitte in den Zeugnissen frühchristlicher Frömmigkeit und Kunst*, Münsterische Beiträge zur Theologie 36 (Münster: Aschendorff, 1973).

[51] Tertullian, *De pudicitia* 5, in Dekkers, ed., "Tertulliani *De Pudicitia*," 1287–89; trans. Le Saint, *Tertullian, Treatises on Penance*, 62–65.

[52] Tertullian, *De pudicitia* 10.12, in Dekkers, ed., "Tertulliani *De Pudicitia*," 1301; trans. Le Saint, *Tertullian, Treatises on Penance*, 82.

[53] See Eusebius of Caesarea, *Church History* 6.3.1 and 6.3.6, in Eduard Schwartz and Theodor Mommsen, eds., *Eusebius Werke. Zweiter Band. Die Kirchengeschichte. [Including:] Lateinische Übersetzung des Rufinus. Zweiter Teil. Die Bücher VI bis X*, GCS 92 (Leipzig: J. C. Hinrichs'sche Buchhandlung, 1908) 524 (Origen) and 534 (Clement); trans. Roy J. Deferrari, *Eusebius Pamphili. Ecclesiastical History (Books 6–10)*, FC 29 (New York: Fathers of the Church, Inc., 1955), 8 (Origen) and 15 (Clement).

[54] See the discussion of their views of penitence in Poschmann, *Paenitentia Secunda*, 229–60 (on Clement) and 425–80 (on Origen).

[55] Aspects of Clement's thought on penitence are studied in Olivier Prunet, *La Morale de Clément d'Alexandrie et le Nouveau Testament*, Études d'Histoire et de Philosophie Religieuses 61 (Paris: Presses Universitaires de France, 1966)

The theological writings of Clement of Alexandria (ca. 160-215 C.E.) served and reflected his pedagogical and pastoral interests.[56] He composed a trilogy of texts that addressed the successive stages of the increasing knowledge and experience his students had and developed as they grew in their understanding of the Christian faith and its requirements of the moral life. In the *Protreptikos* Clement exhorted and attempted to attract unbaptized inquirers to action.[57] In his *Paidagogos* he laid out specific ethical duties and basic principles of the ethical life geared toward an audience of newly baptized Christians.[58] Here he emphasized the role of the Logos as teacher and educator toward the good life. Finally, in his *Stromateis* Clement attempted to guide more experienced Christians on the way to ultimate perfection while giving them pointers along the way that were grounded in higher ethical principles.[59] Clement's christological emphasis on Christ as educator was probably motivated also by his own role as instructor of Christians. This personal experience and role-identity left its mark on the way Clement developed his characteristic approach to penitential theology.

---

62–67; Carlo Nardi, *Il Battesimo in Clemente Alessandrino. Interpretazione di Eclogae Propheticae 1–26*, SEAug 19 (Rome: Institutum Patristicum Augustinianum, 1984) 133–35; and Benrath, "Buße," 456.

[56] For a recent consideration of the place of pedagogy in Clement see also Judith L. Kovacs, "Divine Pedagogy and the Gnostic Teacher according to Clement of Alexandria," *JECS* 9/1 (2001) 3–25. For a recent study of Clement's approach to pastoral care see Hildegard König, "Für sich und andere sorgen: Beobachtungen zum Seelsorgebegriff bei Clemens von Alexandrien," in Lorenzo Perrone, P. Bernardino, and D. Marchini, eds., *Origeniana Octava: Origen and the Alexandrian Tradition* (Leuven: University Press and Peeters, 2003) 1:385–95.

[57] Clement of Alexandria, *Protreptikos*, in Otto Stählin, ed., *Clemens Alexandrinus. Erster Band. Protrepticus und Paedagogus*, GCS Clemens Alexandrinus I (Leipzig: J. C. Hinrichs'sche Buchhandlung, 1905) 3–86; more recently see also Miroslav Marcovich, ed., *Clementis Alexandrini Protrepticus*, VCSup 34 (Leiden, New York, and Köln: Brill, 1995).

[58] Clement of Alexandria, *Paedagogus*, in Miroslav Marcovich, ed., *Clementis Alexandrini Paedagogus*, VCSup 61 (Leiden and Boston: Brill, 2002).

[59] Clement of Alexandria, *Stromateis*, in Otto Stählin and Ludwig Früchtel, eds., *Clemens Alexandrinus. Stromata Buch I–VI*, GCS Clemens Alexandrinus 2 (3d ed. Berlin: Akademie-Verlag, 1960); and Otto Stählin and Ludwig Früchtel, eds., *Clemens Alexandrinus. Stromata Buch VII und VIII, Excerpta ex Theodoto, Eclogae Propheticae, Quis Dives Salvetur, Fragmente*, GCS Clemens Alexandrinus 3 (2d ed. Berlin: Akademie-Verlag, 1970) 3–102.

Clement's work hardly ever hints at any elements of a structured, church-supported system of penance,[60] nor is penance considered to be a function of the sacramental life of the church. With regard to some aspects of his view of penance Clement is a typical representative of the general view of Eastern Christianity on the subject. He shares the position of those who think there is only one "second penance" after baptism. On the basis of 2 Cor 7:10, Clement sees this penance as a "repentance of which one does not have to repent (μετάνοιαν ἀμετανόητον),"[61] a phrase that more literally renders the idea of penance as an irreversible, and thus by implication a nonrepeatable act. This example illustrates that Clement saw penance as the last chance and exception to the rule, given the expectation that the Christian would live his or her life after baptism without blame. In the face of the unavoidable judgment everyone faces at the end of one's life, penance that cannot be repeated forces the Christian who had enjoyed its grace to continue in his or her life after having used that second chance of penance with careful attention to possible pitfalls leading to sin, perhaps even with fear in order to guard oneself against the onslaught of sin. For, as Clement explains, the person who after baptism sins again and repents, perhaps even does so several times, simply lacks self-discipline that could control and prevent falling into sin in the first place.[62]

In his famous sermon, *Who is the Rich Man Who Will Be Saved?* Clement taught his Alexandrian audience that the sinner would only be able to overcome the temptations of the passions if his or her supplications collaborated with God's power. Moreover, the sinner's constant efforts needed to be supported by the intercessory prayer of Christian brothers and sisters.[63] When individual Christians neglected to engage in acts of penitence in proper measure in their lives they had only one alternative opportunity to make up for works of penance otherwise required

[60] See Benrath, "Buße," 456.

[61] Clement of Alexandria, *Stromateis* 2.57.1, in Stählin and Früchtel, eds., *Clemens Alexandrinus. Stromata Buch I–VI*, 143.

[62] See Clement of Alexandria, *Stromateis* 2.58.3, in Stählin and Früchtel, eds., *Clemens Alexandrinus. Stromata Buch I–VI*, 144; trans. John Ferguson, *Clement of Alexandria. Stromateis Books One to Three*, FC 85 (Washington, DC: Catholic University of America Press, 1991) 198.

[63] Clement of Alexandria, *Quis dives salvetur?* 40.6, in Stählin and Früchtel, eds., *Clemens Alexandrinus. Stromata Buch VII and VIII*, 187; trans. Otto Stählin and Manfred Wacht, *Klemens von Alexandrien. Welcher Reiche wird gerettet werden?* Schriften der Kirchenväter, Vol. 1, ed. Norbert Brox (Munich: Kösel, 1983) 57.

of all sinners. If they lacked in penance but if they had given witness during times of persecution and if necessary had died as martyrs during such times of hardship, these sufferings counted as a penitential substitute.[64]

Clement shared these more common principles on how to view aspects of the penitential life with other early Eastern Christian teachers. Yet in his more developed ideas of penance he seems to have laid a different emphasis with regard to what the essence of penance in a Christian's life really was. For Clement the main function of penance in the life of the Christian was to contribute to the lifelong process of education, purification, and healing of the individual who was constantly tempted and threatened to give in to impure passions. Discernment of sins and thus knowledge of sins was essential for penitence. Clement knew that

> [i]f a person does not faithfully see that it was a sin to which he [or she] was previously prisoner, there will be no change of behavior at all. If a person does not believe that wrong behavior involves punishment, whereas salvation is for those who live by the commandments, there will be no conversion either.[65]

Given such an understanding of the human situation, Clement saw God as a loving and caring father or teacher who does not take revenge on sinners for their deeds. One of Clement's favorite ideas was to speak of human beings as children who are to be educated by Christ the Logos. The Logos is "educator of little children (παιδαγωγός νηπίων)"[66] and "the educator . . . who leads us children to salvation (παιδαγωγός . . . ὁ λόγος ὁ τοὺς σωτηρίαν ἄγων)."[67] For Clement, sin is to be seen as a deed committed by one's free will. Thus, the sinner is responsible for attracting God's punishment upon himself or herself. Given God's qualities as educator,

---

[64] See Clement of Alexandria, *Stromateis* 4.73.1-3, in Stählin and Früchtel, eds., *Clemens Alexandrinus. Stromata Buch I–VI*, 281.

[65] Clement of Alexandria, *Stromateis* 2.27.1, in Stählin and Früchtel, eds., *Clemens Alexandrinus. Stromateis Buch I–VI*, 127; trans. Ferguson, *Clement of Alexandria. Stromateis*, 176.

[66] Clement of Alexandria, *Paedagogus* 1.84.1, in Marcovich, ed., *Clementis Alexandrini Paedagogus*, 52.

[67] Clement of Alexandria, *Paedagogus* 1.53.3, in Marcovich, ed., *Clementis Alexandrini Paedagogus*, 34. See also Friedrich Quatember, *Die christliche Lebenshaltung des Klemens von Alexandrien nach seinem Pädagogus* (Vienna: Herder, 1946) 104.

Clement deduced that God punished sinners only for their own benefit. By administering punishments God pursued three goals with what one may call his penitential pedagogy. First of all, punishments were meant to be educational measures that worked toward the improvement of those being punished. Second, the punishment served as a warning for other sinners. Finally, it also protected those who were threatened by the evil of the sins being committed.[68] Clement saw God's justice as the ultimate ground and motivation for the punishment of sinners, given that in acting on this justice God desired what was best for the individual sinner. Alongside justice, Clement considered God's mercy and goodness to be two further sources from which challenges and tests for those with hardened hearts arose.[69]

For Clement, God was not only to be described as teacher and educator, but also as judge and healer.[70] Clement shared Tertullian's view that God functioned as judge. Thus Clement conceived of the Logos as one who judges sins,[71] but the Logos alone is qualified to do so, since he alone is without sin.[72] Yet Clement availed himself more frequently of the healing metaphor in the penitential context. For him penance could very appropriately be described as a process of healing. As much as a sick patient has to take the medicine the doctor prescribes for him or her, so also one may see penance as the necessary and good deed of faith the human person contributes.[73] Penance has a purifying effect on the soul.[74] As a person falls sick when diseases attack him or her, so also does the human soul become sick when it is being attacked by sin. In both instances the healing

---

[68] Clement of Alexandria, *Stromateis* 4.154.1, in Stählin and Früchtel, eds., *Clemens Alexandrinus. Stromateis Buch I–VI*, 316. See also Benrath, "Buße," 456.

[69] Clement of Alexandria, *Stromateis* 7.12.3-5, in Stählin and Früchtel, eds., *Clemens Alexandrinus. Stromateis Buch VII and VII*, 9–10. See also Benrath, "Buße," 456.

[70] See also Quatember, *Die christliche Lebenshaltung des Klemens von Alexandrien*, 116–17.

[71] Clement of Alexandria, *Paedagogus* 1.67.3, in Marcovich, ed., *Clementis Alexandrini Paedagogus*, 42; trans. Simon P. Wood, *Clement of Alexandria. Christ the Educator*, FC 23 (New York: Fathers of the Church, Inc., 1954) 61.

[72] Clement of Alexandria, *Paedagogus* 1.4.2, in Marcovich, ed., *Clementis Alexandrini Paedagogus*, 4; trans. Wood, *Clement of Alexandria. Christ the Educator*, 5.

[73] Clement of Alexandria, *Stromateis* 2.27.1, in Stählin and Früchtel, eds., *Clemens Alexandrinus. Stromateis Buch I–VI*, 127; trans. Ferguson, *Clement of Alexandria. Stromateis*, 176.

[74] Clement of Alexandria, *Stromateis* 4.143.1, in Stählin and Früchtel, eds., *Clemens Alexandrinus. Stromateis Buch I–VI*, 311.

process is similar. A sick body is healed if the person chooses proper diets, medications, and surgical operations to advance restoration to a wholesome, original state. When the soul is affected by sin it also experiences relief through the healing treatment of admonitions (ἡ νουθέτησις), blame (ὁ ὀνειδισμός), and public acts of revealing its wrongdoings (ὁ ἔλεγχος) that in the end lead to the conviction of the sinner.[75] Clement's rhetorical training comes to the fore in his description of these acts of penance as well. Medical imagery and rhetorical practices conjoin so much that Clement even speaks of these acts of penance the sinner has to endure as surgery that is being conducted on the passions of the soul.[76]

The distinction between normal Christians and those who had become more advanced in the Christian life, the true Gnostics, is characteristic of Clement's thought.[77] This differentiating classification of Christian believers also affected the way he viewed repentance and penance taken up by either one of these two groups. The penance of the Christian Gnostic was to be regarded as far superior to that of the normal Christian, since the latter was only concerned with doing penance for the individual sins he or she had committed. The true Gnostic, on the other hand, was someone who had gained insight into the very nature of sin. Guided by reason, he or she had become empowered systematically to desist from committing sins.[78] Thus eventually the Gnostic could achieve a state in which he or she was not only freed from sin but was also enabled to effect the forgiveness of sins for other Christians,[79] independent of any additional commissioning on the part of the church for that ministry.

### d. Penitence in the Desert: Examples from Egypt and Palestine

Despite the appreciation of the ministry of ordained clergy in bringing God's forgiveness to the faithful, in many instances Eastern Christians

---

[75] Clement of Alexandria, *Paedagogus* 1.64.4–1.65.2, in Marcovich, ed., *Clementis Alexandrini Paedagogus*, 40; trans. Wood, *Clement of Alexandria. Christ the Educator*, 58–59.

[76] Clement of Alexandria, *Paedagogus* 1.64.4, in Marcovich, ed., *Clementis Alexandrini Paedagogus*, 40: οἱονεὶ χειρουργία τῶν τῆς ψυχῆς παθῶν. See also Wood, *Clement of Alexandria. Christ the Educator*, 58; and see Benrath, "Buße," 456.

[77] See the classic study by Walther Völker, *Der wahre Gnostiker nach Clemens Alexandrinus* (Leipzig: Akademie-Verlag, 1952).

[78] See also Benrath, "Buße," 456.

[79] Clement of Alexandria, *Eclogae propheticae* 15.1-2, in Stählin and Früchtel, eds., *Clemens Alexandrinus. Stromateis Buch VII and VII*, 137–55, at 141.

followed Clement's view that the power of forgiveness was not limited to ordained ministers. Rather, it rested equally with spiritual guides to whom Christians entrusted the care of their souls. One of the primary groups of people who functioned as spiritual guides were ascetics, those who had withdrawn from the world, who often lived in the desert, and who through practicing renunciation of the desires of the world strove for Christian perfection.

Repentance and penance were essential components of the lives of ascetics.[80] Ascetics were called upon to guard themselves constantly against the attacks and stirrings of the passions of body and soul, movements that not infrequently were characterized as the work of demons. The very self-definition of ascetics was determined by the concern to avoid sin and to realize the necessity of penance in a spirit of returning to God.

The theology of penance was even part of the habit that monks wore.[81] One of the teachers of the ascetic life, Evagrius of Pontus, arguably the most influential fourth-century ascetic theologian in the desert of Egypt, explained in his *Praktikos* to those who were beginners in the ascetic life that "the belt which [monks] wear about their loins signifies their rejection of all impurity."[82] Moreover,

> to signify that they continually bear in their bodies the mortification of Jesus and check all the irrational passions, [these men] wear also a sheep-skin garment. Further they cut off the vices of the soul by their communion in the good, as also by loving poverty and fleeing from avarice, the mother of idolatry.[83]

---

[80] On the intersection of the themes of asceticism, authority, and penitence see the study by Karl Holl, *Enthusiasmus und Bußgewalt beim griechischen Mönchtum* (Leipzig: J. C. Hinrichs'sche Buchhandlung, 1898). The systematic collection of *Apophthegmata Patrum* lists compunction (κατάνυξις) as the third item of concern for ascetics. See Jean-Claude Guy, *Les Apophtegmes des Pères. Collection Systématique, Chapitres I–IX*, SC 387 (Paris: Cerf, 1993) 148–83.

[81] For a discussion of the garment of penitents see Bernhard Poschmann, "Bußkleid," in *RAC* 2 (1954) 812–14.

[82] Evagrius Ponticus, *Praktikos*, "Introductory Letter to Anatolius," 5, in Antoine and Claire Guillaumont, eds., *Évagre le Pontique. Traité Pratique ou Le Moine. Tome II*, SC 171 (Paris: Cerf, 1971) 488; trans. John Eudes Bamberger, *Evagrius Ponticus: The Praktikos, Chapters on Prayer*, CS 4 (Kalamazoo: Cistercian Publications, 1981) 14.

[83] Evagrius Ponticus, *Praktikos*, "Introductory Letter to Anatolius," 6, in Guillaumont, eds., *Évagre le Pontique. Traité Pratique*, 488–90; trans. Bamberger, *Evagrius Ponticus: The Praktikos, Chapters on Prayer*, 14.

Early reflections on the connection between baptism and penitence had developed into a direction of acknowledging penance as a one-time, additional opportunity to rid oneself of sins committed previously, thus imitating the effect of baptism. Within the earliest strands of ascetic literature one notices that the same view developed with regard to the connection between cleansing from sins and monastic initiation. Athanasius of Alexandria's *Life of Antony*, probably the most influential portrayal of an ascetic hero and founding figure of the ascetic movement at that, reflects the view that on entering the ascetic life the monk was given the opportunity to start afresh with a clean slate, so to speak. Antony's guides informed the demons, who prepared to attack him, that "[t]he Lord has wiped clean the items dating from his birth, but from the time he became a monk, and devoted himself to God, you can take an account [of the sins he may have committed since then]."[84] In later centuries this equation between the baptismal effect and the effect of monastic initiation with regard to their power of forgiveness of sins became a common understanding.[85]

Like Tertullian, who as seen above applied imagery taken from the realm of female experience to the process of obtaining penance, Evagrius of Pontus availed himself of language related to the experience of birthgiving and childhood when he reported on the prayers that were being said at the occasion of a monk's introduction to the ascetic life. Being advised to cultivate faith through growing in the fear of God and in continence, the newly initiated monks also learned that

> [p]atience and hope make this latter virtue [i.e., fear of God] solid beyond all shaking and they also give birth to *apatheia*. Now this *apatheia* has a child (τέκνα) called *agapē* who keeps the door to deep knowledge

---

[84] Athanasius of Alexandria, *Life of Antony* 65.4, in G. J. M. Bartelink, ed., *Athanase d'Alexandrie. Vie d'Antoine*, SC 400 (Paris: Cerf, 1994) 304–306; trans. Robert C. Gregg, *Athanasius. The Life of Antony and The Letter to Marcellinus*, CWS (Mahwah, NJ: Paulist, 1980) 79; also see the comments in Anitra Bingham Kolenkow, "Sharing the Pain: Saint and Sinner in Late Antique Egypt," in David W. Johnson, ed., *Acts of the Fifth International Congress of Coptic Studies (Washington, [DC], 12–15 August 1992)* (Rome: Centro Italiano Microfiches, 1993) 2/1:247–61, at 255.

[85] See also Holl, *Enthusiasmus und Bußgewalt*, 207–208 (John of Damascus, Eustathius of Thessaloniki, Symeon the New Theologian, and John of Antioch); and Benrath, "Buße," 458.

of the created universe. Finally, to this knowledge succeed theology and the supreme beatitude.[86]

Turning away from sin was understood as a process of turning away from all attachments to the passions. Patience when falling back into sin and hope that the future would bring one closer to God were the driving forces that kept the ascetic going on this path of conversion to God. The ascetic reached the ultimate goal of penitence by achieving access to the height of the ascetic life, namely *apatheia*, more fully understood in Evagrius as the simplicity of life that is unencumbered by physical pleasures and needs, a state of perfect joining of the fear of God with love of one's neighbor. Much practice, indeed, was needed if one was ever to attain that height.

The so-called *Apophthegmata Patrum*, or *Sayings of the Desert Fathers*, a collection of short episodes recounting the lives and words of ascetic men and women who had lived in the regions of Egypt and Palestine, preserves precious glances at how these ascetics treasured penance and viewed it as the task of their lives. For example, it was recounted "of Abba Sisoes that when he was at the point of death" and shared with other ascetics the visions he received while he was preparing for his coming end, he not only saw Abba Antony, "the choir of prophets," and "the choir of apostles" coming to him. Rather, "[h]is countenance increased in brightness" when he was allowed to speak with the angels, who were "coming to fetch [him]." Abba Sisoes "begged them to let [him] do a little penance" before they took him away. When one of his fellow ascetics remarked to him that he "ha[d] no need to do penance," Abba Sisoes responded that he "d[id] not think [he] ha[d] even made a beginning yet." This comment sufficed for his friends to know "that he was perfect."[87]

On the one hand the *Sayings of the Desert Fathers* shows how much ascetics had internalized the need to do penance. On the other hand these texts also reflect the sense ascetics had that God was willing to respond to the sinner with abundant mercy, even if one had merely started to step onto the path of penance. Stories are told about both

[86] Evagrius Ponticus, *Praktikos*, "Introductory Letter to Anatolius," 8, in Guillaumont, eds., *Évagre le Pontique. Traité Pratique*, 492; trans. Bamberger, *Evagrius Ponticus: The Praktikos, Chapters on Prayer*, 14.

[87] The quotes are taken from *Apophthegmata Patrum*, Abba Sisoes, Saying 14, trans. Benedicta Ward, *The Sayings of the Desert Fathers. The Alphabetical Collection*, CS 59 (rev. ed. Kalamazoo: Cistercian Publications, 1984) 214–15.

Abba Sisoes and Abba Poemen giving advice to sinners.[88] Confronted with a sinner who "wanted to do penance for three years," Abba Poemen told him that "[t]hat [wa]s a lot." He repeated this response when the sinner suggested he reduce the time of penance to one year, so that those present asked if perhaps the sinner should do penance for forty days only. Abba Poemen taught them "that if a man repents with his whole heart and does not intend to commit the sin any more, God will accept him after only three days."[89]

The teaching on penance in ascetic texts from early Christian times provides one of the rarer occasions to gain a glance at the sometimes quite prominent presence of female figures in early Christian literature, even if the reader may at first be suspicious of why women are depicted as examples of penitence.[90] The presumption that the emphasis on the need for repentance in the case of women was due to a perceived necessity for women to make up for the guilt brought on humankind through Eve in the Garden does not seem to be borne out by the texts. Rather, penitent women were chosen for illustration because they provided exemplary models for all, models that were to be imitated by both men and women.

A formidable example is the case of the young orphan girl Paëisa, otherwise known as Païs. Having expended all her resources on hospitality for the Fathers of the Desert of Scetis, Paëisa was at her wits' end about how to make ends meet, and had fallen into prostitution. Thus the Fathers sent Abba John the Dwarf to provide assistance for her. Expecting him to bring her pearls in exchange for sexual favors, Paëisa admitted Abba John into her chamber. Yet when Abba John spoke of Jesus against whom Paëisa was sinning and when he wept copiously, Paëisa was moved to ask him if "it [was] possible to repent." When Abba John confirmed for her that this option existed, Paëisa immediately made a radical change in her life. She left everything behind, "not mak[ing] any arrangements with regard to her house," but simply following Abba John into the desert.

[88] For the instance involving Abba Sisoes see *Apophthegmata Patrum*, Abba Sisoes, Saying 20, trans. Ward, *The Sayings of the Desert Fathers*, 217.

[89] *Apophthegmata Patrum*, Poemen (called the Shepherd), Saying 12, trans. Ward, *Sayings of the Desert Fathers*, 169.

[90] See also the collection of texts on Mary Magdalene, Mary of Egypt, Pelagia, Thaïs, and Mary the Niece of Abraham in Benedicta Ward, *Harlots of the Desert. A Study of Repentance in Early Monastic Sources*. CS 106 (Kalamazoo: Cistercian Publications, 1987).

When they reached the desert, the evening drew on. He, making a little pillow with the sand, and marking it with the sign of the cross, said to her, "Sleep here." Then, a little further on, he did the same for himself, said his prayers, and lay down. Waking in the middle of the night, he saw a shining path reaching from heaven to her, and he saw the angels of God bearing away her soul. So he got up and went to touch her feet. When he saw that she was dead he threw himself face downwards on the ground, praying to God. He heard this: "One single hour of repentance has brought her more than the penitence of many who persevere without showing such fervor in repentance."[91]

The more radical the conversion and penitence, the more perfect the lot of the former sinner. Thus ascetic teachers and spiritual guides from among the monks of Palestine likewise instructed those under their care to engage eagerly in acts of penance.

Abba Isaiah of Scetis was a prominent spiritual advisor of both lay-people and ascetics in Egypt and later on also in Gaza, Palestine. One of his 29 *Ascetic Discourses* is dedicated exclusively to the theme of repentance.[92] While much else in this treatise is of interest for a study of penance, one notices that Abba Isaiah also recommended to repentant sinners that they follow the example of women. He presents the example of the New Testament characters Martha and Mary. For him Martha and Mary were the example of "mortification and mourning before the Savior."[93] Mortification and mourning were two of the manifold ways in which early Christian ascetics in the East chose to live their repentant life of renunciation.[94] When

---

[91] *Apophthegmata Patrum,* John the Dwarf, Saying 40, trans. Ward, *The Sayings of the Desert Fathers,* 93–94, translation modified.

[92] Abba Isaiah of Scetis, *Asceticon* 21, trans. John Chryssavgis and Pachomios (Robert) Penkett, *Abba Isaiah of Scetis: Ascetic Discourses,* CS 150 (Kalamazoo: Cistercian Publications, 2002) 149–61.

[93] Abba Isaiah of Scetis, *Asceticon* 21, trans. Chryssavgis and Penkett, *Abba Isaiah of Scetis: Ascetic Discourses,* 161.

[94] Early Christian asceticism in the Syriac-speaking realm, for example, knew of the so-called *abîlê* (mourners) as a distinct type of ascetics. For some discussion of this aspect of Syrian asceticism with references to examples from the works of Ephraem the Syrian, see more recently Sidney H. Griffith, "Asceticism in the Church of Syria: The Hermeneutics of Early Syrian Monasticism," in Vincent L. Wimbush and Richard Valantasis, eds., *Asceticism* (New York: Oxford University Press, 1995) 220–45, at 234–35. The mortification practiced by monks and nuns, in the East and in the West, is grounded in the scriptural instruction to crucify

the Savior "untied and released Lazarus" from the burial clothes after his resurrection, "the zeal of Mary and Martha was shown. Lazarus found the others free from anxiety, reclining at table with Jesus. While Martha carries out her duty with diligence and joy, Mary carries the Alabaster jar of myrrh and anoints the Lord's feet."[95] These women provided the perfect example of how the hardship and weeping of repentance had as its ultimate goal and fulfillment *apatheia* as the fulfillment of joy in the Lord.

### e. Penitence as Boundary Marker: Aphrahat the Persian Sage

The early Christian church in the Syriac-speaking realm boasts of two outstanding writers and Christian theologians, Aphrahat and Ephraem. Their respective teachings on penance thus far have not entered the mainstream presentation of patristic teachings on penance. While both deserve careful attention, this discussion has to limit itself to Aphrahat, the earlier of the two.

Aphrahat, also known as the Persian Sage, is the author of twenty-three *Demonstrations*, which were written between 337 and 345 c.e. and today are our only source of knowledge about his theology.[96] While Aphrahat comments occasionally on penance in other places, particularly in *Demonstrations* 3 and 21,[97] it is the central subject of

---

the flesh (Gal 5:24) and to take up one's cross and follow Christ (Matt 16:24, Mark 8:34, and Luke 9:23).

[95] Abba Isaiah of Scetis, *Asceticon* 21, trans. Chryssavgis and Penkett, *Abba Isaiah of Scetis: Ascetic Discourses*, 161.

[96] A complete English translation of the *Demonstrations* is not yet available, but appears to be in progress. Modern translations into French and German have been published. See Marie-Joseph Pierre, *Aphraate le Sage Persan: Les Exposés*, 2 vols. SC 349, 359 (Paris: Cerf, 1988–1989); and Peter Bruns, *Aphrahat: Demonstrationes/Unterweisungen*, 2 vols. Fontes Christiani 5.1 und 5.2 (Freiburg, Basel, Vienna, Barcelona, Rome, New York: Herder, 1991). Individual *Demonstrations* have been translated into English in John Gwynn, "Aphrahat; Select Demonstrations," in *Selections Translated into English from the Hymns and Homilies of Ephraim the Syrian and from the Demonstrations of Aphrahat the Persian Sage*, NPNF, n.s. 13 (Grand Rapids: Eerdmans, repr. 1979) 343–412 (*Demonstrations* 1, 5–6, 8, 10, 17, and 21–22), as well as in selected academic journals.

[97] For a fuller discussion of penance in Aphrahat see P. Boulos Féghali, "Penance in Aphrahat [in Arabic]," in *Péché et Réconciliation hier et aujourd'hui. Patrimoine Syriaque. Actes du colloque IV* (Antelias, Lebanon: Centre d'Etudes et de Recherches Pastorales, Ordre Antonin Maronite o.a.m., 1997) 51–58. See also

*Demonstrations 7*,[98] where it follows a discussion in the preceding treatise on the so-called "Sons and Daughters of the Covenant," a group of Christians who practiced asceticism integrated into the practical demands of charity in everyday settings of parish life.[99] The phenomenon of the "Sons and Daughters of the Covenant" is a unique and characteristic feature of Christianity in the Syriac-speaking church during early Christian times.

For Aphrahat fasting was an important form of both ascesis and repentance. He used the account of the repentance of the Ninivites to highlight the quality and purpose of the fast of these people who were known to the Christian reader from the Old Testament. In line with the Old Testament examples of Abel and Moses as fasters, Aphrahat presented the Ninivites as a group that kept a pure fast in response to Jonah's preaching of repentance. As Aphrahat read the text of Scripture he commented that the Ninivites combined continuous fasting with acts of persistently imploring God that he might show mercy to them, while they themselves were sitting in ashes and sackcloth in order to underline their commitment to repentance.[100] Aphrahat was concerned to communicate to his audience that God responded to their pleas not because "he saw their abstinence from bread and water accompanied by sack and ashes," but because they repented and turned back from

---

Giuseppe Ricciotti, "La testimonianza di Afraate Siro sulla penitenza," *ScC* (1924) 48–50; F. Pericoli Ridolfini, "Battesimo e penitenza negli scritti del Sapiente Persiano," in Sergio Felici, ed., *Catechesi battesimale e riconciliazione dei padri del IV secolo* (Rome: LAS, 1984) 119–29; and Taeke Jansma, "Aphraates' Demonstration VII §§ 18 and 20. Some Observations on the Discourse on Penance," *ParOr* 5 (1974) 21–48.

[98] An English translation of *Demonstrations 7* has been published in F. H. Hallock, "On Penitents," *JSOR* 16 (1932) 43–56.

[99] The "Sons and Daughters of the Covenant" have attracted and continue to attract considerable attention among researchers, particularly with regard to their place in Aphrahat's broader view of the ascetic life. For a helpful initial bibliographical list see Pierre, *Aphraate le Sage Persan* 1:21–22; also see Cornelia B. Horn, "Frühsyrische Mariologie: Maria und ihre Schwestern im Werk Aphrahats des Persischen Weisen," in Martin Tamcke and Andreas Heinz, eds., *Die Suryoye und ihre Umwelt. 4. deutsches Syrologen-Symposium in Trier 2004. Festgabe Wolfgang Hage zum 70. Geburtstag,* Studien zur Orientalischen Kirchengeschichte 36 (Münster, Hamburg, Berlin, Wien, and London: LIT-Verlag, 2005) 313–32.

[100] Aphrahat, *Demonstrations 3.7,* in J. Parisot, ed., *Aphraatis Sapientis Persae Demonstrationes I–XXII,* PS 1 (Paris: Firmin-Didot et Socii, 1894) 112. Throughout, the translation is my own.

their evil deeds.[101] Thus greater value rests in the renunciation of evil deeds than in the renunciation of bread and water,[102] since the latter can be done for selfish reasons, e.g., in order to gain the praise and recognition of those who see these deeds.[103] It was also practiced, as Aphrahat knew, by Marcionites, Valentinians, and Manichaeans, for whom it was of no avail, according to him, because they followed erroneous doctrinal teachings.[104]

One notices in Aphrahat's treatment of questions of penance an emphasis on charitable works and a disassociation from heretical teachings as necessary components that had to accompany any act of fasting in order for the fast to be a true and effective expression of repentance. In Aphrahat's immediate environment the Christian church was a minority phenomenon and was still in the process of forming its social structures, also in parish life. The "Sons and Daughters of the Covenant" appear to have contributed significantly to the charitable outreach of the community. At the same time, as more definitive formulations of Christian orthodoxy were being developed, different religious groups competed with one another for the attention of the city's population. Thus a position of sheltering one's activities against outsiders was deemed necessary. The later liturgical development of the Fast of the Ninivites inherited this twofold emphasis on charity and orthodoxy.[105]

Besides this pronounced use of the image of the Ninivites as a reference, Aphrahat also commented on other Old and New Testament examples of people who repented when they were threatened with destruction, e.g., the Gibeonites (Josh 9:16-26) or Rahab, who according to Heb 11:31 was granted penance because she believed in the word spoken to her.[106] Employing biblical types, Aphrahat repeatedly stressed his point that if people repent and thus return to God, God will turn to them.[107]

---

[101] Ibid., 112–13.

[102] Aphrahat, *Demonstrations* 3.8, in PS 1, 113.

[103] Aphrahat, *Demonstrations* 3.8, in PS 1, 113–16.

[104] Aphrahat, *Demonstrations* 3.9, in PS 1, 116.

[105] See the discussion in Louis Sako, "Fasting and Penitence: the Fast of Nineveh" [in Arabic], in *Péché et Réconciliation hier et aujourd'hui*, 95–103.

[106] See Aphrahat, *Demonstrations* 3.11, in PS 1, 121–24; on the figure of Rahab in patristic exegesis see now also Anneliese Felber, *Ecclesia ex gentibus congregata. Die Deutung der Rahabepisode (Jos 2) in der Patristik*, Dissertationen der KFU Graz 85 (Graz: dbv, 1992).

[107] See Aphrahat, *Demonstrations* 3.11, in PS 1, 124.

Aphrahat saw clearly that with the exception of Christ no one from among the children of Adam "who entered the stadium [of the world] did not become injured or wounded; because sin rules ever since Adam transgressed the commandment."[108] Every human being was affected by sin and needed to find ways to rid himself or herself of its effects. One way was to seek healing. Thus when talking about repentance Aphrahat frequently employed medical imagery. He spoke of those wounded in the battle against sin as having available repentance as a remedy for the wounds of their sin. He also encouraged those in charge of the well-being of the Christian flock, a group of people he called physicians, to avail themselves of repentance as a medicine that is to be prescribed to patients for the healing of their souls.[109]

Aphrahat was confident that "God does not reject those who repent,"[110] a conviction for which he found support in the writings of the prophet Ezekiel.[111] Especially the person who had valiantly fought against sin, but then had succumbed, certainly would feel great pain in his or her soul. In such cases repentance was a formidable means of healing.[112] Yet healing could only occur if the sinner first accused himself or herself of having committed sin and thus requested penance to be administered. Aphrahat described this necessary connection as follows:

> Then one who was wounded in the battle does not feel ashamed to entrust himself to the hands of an experienced physician, since the battle overpowered him and he was wounded. Yet as soon as he has been healed, the king does not dismiss him; rather he counts and reckons him as a member of his army. Thus, also the person who has been wounded by Satan may not be ashamed to confess his or her sins and distance himself or herself from it, and to request penance as his or her remedy. For the one who is ashamed to show his or her abscesses becomes sick with cancer, so that the person's whole body becomes damaged. . . . The one who has been conquered in battle only has this one opportunity to receive healing, namely to say, "I have sinned," and to request penance.[113]

---

[108] See Aphrahat, *Demonstrations* 7.1, in PS 1, 313.
[109] See Aphrahat, *Demonstrations* 7.2, in PS 1, 316.
[110] See Aphrahat, *Demonstrations* 7.2, in PS 1, 316.
[111] See Ezek 3:11; 18:23, 32.
[112] See Aphrahat, *Demonstrations* 7.2, in PS 1, 316.
[113] See Aphrahat, *Demonstrations* 7.3, in PS 1, 317.

The Syriac tradition developed a rite of penance consisting of four steps: the self-accusation of the penitent sinner, the imposition of penance on him or her, the accomplishment of what is required in the act of penance, and the rite of forgiveness, *Ṭaksā d-ḥussāyā*, celebrated in the context of the Sunday liturgy. The passage just cited from Aphrahat's *Demonstrations* 7 is the earliest witness from the tradition for the first step of this penitential process.[114]

When Aphrahat was talking about repentance and penance he was rather fond of using military imagery. He recommended that spiritual directors encourage those who had sinned to reveal to them their sufferings caused by sin.[115] Yet Aphrahat warned that when such confessions took place one was not to make publicly known what damage sin had done. As in a military group, also in the case of those fighting valiantly against sin it was not wise to make known who had been wounded. Enemies would only take advantage of this knowledge and consequently the reputation of the whole battalion would be dishonored.[116] On the part of those harmed by sin who wished to repent for their sins, unrestricted openness about their condition was necessary unless they were willing to take the risk that their sins might grow into irreparable cancer.[117]

According to Aphrahat the opportunity for *paenitentia secunda* was in principle an option for the fallen Christian. Yet since healing is difficult in cases where scars have formed from previous wounds one should try not to have to avail oneself of it. The one, who has been harmed a second time by sin has taken on "the habit of being defeated," and thus is no longer fit for the battle against sin, which is a necessary part of being a Christian.[118]

The battle against sin in this life required wakefulness and decisiveness from the ascetic as much as from the nonascetic Christian in order to coun-

---

[114] Jacques Isaac, *ṬAKSĀ D-ḤUSSĀYĀ. Le rite du Pardon dans l'Église syriaque orientale*, OrChrAn 233 (Rome: Pontificium Institutum Orientale, 1989) 154–55, also provides evidence from the works of Narsai (399–502) and Išōʿyahb I (ca. 585) for early Syriac textual witnesses to the practice of this first step of accusation as part of the penitential process. I am grateful to Mrs. Ivanovska for having called my attention to Isaac's study.

[115] See Aphrahat, *Demonstrations* 7.4, in PS 1, 320.

[116] See Aphrahat, *Demonstrations* 7.4, in PS 1, 320.

[117] See Aphrahat, *Demonstrations* 7.5, in PS 1, 320–21.

[118] See Aphrahat, *Demonstrations* 7.6, in PS 1, 321.

teract Satan's cunning effectively.[119] Aphrahat marshaled the Old Testament examples of Adam (Gen 3:9), Cain (Gen 4:7), and the contemporaries of Noah (Gen 6:3 and 7:6) to show that those who refused to repent were on the wrong path.[120] In contrast to the Ninivites, who had listened to the prophet Jonah's preaching of repentance, many times the Israelites had resisted the prophets who had been sent to them for the same purpose.[121] Aphrahat warned his audience of such hardened resistance against repentance and admonished the sinners to have hope of forgiveness, so that they might indeed turn away from injustice.[122]

Nevertheless, a spiritual director whose task it was to provide the right medicine of repentance for the person he or she was advising should not show any arrogance to the sinner. Rather, they "who have the keys for the gates of heaven" were called upon to "open these gates for those who repent."[123] Christ himself, as Aphrahat emphasized, called the sinners to repentance and cared for their success on this chosen path.[124]

At the very heart of penance was confession of one's sins in a spirit of contrition, which brought about forgiveness of sins as a necessary consequence.[125] David, Solomon, Aaron, and Simon Peter were excellent examples of this attitude and practice, according to Aphrahat.[126]

Yet in the face of God's readiness to forgive sins the individual Christian could not become lax in his or her zeal to avoid committing sins. God's forgiveness in response to a person's repentance was to be seen as alms given to the poor who needed them.[127] The goal of the Christian had to be to be counted among the rich who have no need of these morsels. Aphrahat encouraged his listeners not to lose through sin what they possessed, so that they would not have to seek repentance while never knowing for certain whether they had gained enough of it or not.[128] The one who committed sins and repented was not to be seen as equal to the one who managed not to sin. Rather, relying again on his preferred

---

[119] See Aphrahat, *Demonstrations* 7.7, in PS 1, 321.
[120] See Aphrahat, *Demonstrations* 7.8, in PS 1, 324.
[121] See Aphrahat, *Demonstrations* 7.9, in PS 1, 325.
[122] See Aphrahat, *Demonstrations* 7.10, in PS 1, 328–29.
[123] See Aphrahat, *Demonstrations* 7.11, in PS 1, 329.
[124] See Aphrahat, *Demonstrations* 7.13, in PS 1, 332–33.
[125] See Aphrahat, *Demonstrations* 7.7, in PS 1, 321.
[126] See Aphrahat, *Demonstrations* 7.14-15, in PS 1, 333–36.
[127] See Aphrahat, *Demonstrations* 7.17, in PS 1, 337.
[128] See Aphrahat, *Demonstrations* 7.17, in PS 1, 337–40.

military and medicinal imagery, Aphrahat illustrated what he thought was the desirable behavior of a Christian by speaking of a soldier who skillfully uses his armor so as not to be wounded and thus not to need any medicine or any attention from a physician.[129] Based on his concern that the Christian not fall into sin, Aphrahat also made the case that only people who were resolved not to fall into sin and who were thus willing to take on the necessary life of asceticism ought to be admitted to baptism.[130] Aphrahat's theological reflections have been interpreted as evidence that in the Church of Syria a commitment to asceticism, specifically to virginity, was a requirement for baptism.[131] Nevertheless, under no circumstances should anyone who was harmed by sin despair, but rather he or she should incessantly ask for penance. It was seen as appropriate for the person to spend all of his or her days in contrition in order not to become haughty and in the end be condemned.[132] Aphrahat introduced the prodigal son, the sinful woman in Luke 7:36-50, Zachaeus the tax collector, and the apostle Paul (1 Tim 1:13, 16) as New Testament examples of sinners who knew about their sins, confessed them, and received forgiveness,[133] in order to emphasize through the variety of people represented that God did not wish that even a single person should be lost.

Aphrahat was concerned that his readers understand that the question of an individual person's need for repentance at the same time affected the life of the whole church. He called upon all to accept their responsibility not to punish the sinner but to render assistance toward healing.[134]

Aphrahat was confronted with concrete situations of a twofold nature. On the one hand, some individuals from among the "Sons and Daughters of the Covenant" in his community had sinned, but instead of confessing their sins and repenting of them they had tried to defend themselves for what they had done. Aphrahat warned those people not to risk their eternal salvation because of their misguided behavior.[135] On the other hand, Aphrahat

---

[129] See Aphrahat, *Demonstrations* 7.17, in PS 1, 340.

[130] See Aphrahat, *Demonstrations* 7.18-22, in PS 1, 341–49.

[131] See Arthur Vööbus, *Celibacy, a Requirement for Admission to Baptism in the Early Syrian Church*, PETSE 1 (Stockholm: Estonian Theological Society in Exile, 1951). This question was discussed rather vigorously in subsequent scholarly literature.

[132] See Aphrahat, *Demonstrations* 7.23, in PS 1, 352.

[133] See Aphrahat, *Demonstrations* 7.23, in PS 1, 352–53.

[134] See Aphrahat, *Demonstrations* 7.24, in PS 1, 353–56.

[135] See Aphrahat, *Demonstrations* 7.25, in PS 1, 356.

also encountered situations in his community in which individuals wanted to repent but were rejected and opportunities for penance were refused. In such instances Aphrahat's words of warning were directed against the leaders of the church. They also would be held responsible if a sinner was not admitted to the heavenly banquet and bridal chamber.[136]

According to Aphrahat "this world belongs to grace (*ṭaibuthā*)," and "until its perfection penance (*tyābutā*) is to be found in it."[137] Yet like the author of the *Second Letter of Clement*,[138] Aphrahat was also painfully aware, and wished to warn his audience, that the time during which penance was possible was coming to an end. He had warned the "Sons and Daughters of the Covenant" in the preceding *Demonstrations* 6 in reference to the Last Judgment that at that time when "grace passes by [in front of the righteous ones and] justice rules [there] is no longer any repentance."[139] Now he repeated that "the time has come near, when grace disappears and justice rules. At this time there is no more penance, and justice . . . surpasses the power of grace."[140] Thus it was of the essence for the believer to live as a penitent, at every moment, in order to be ready also at that very last moment.

### f. Conclusion

The discussion of the selected authors and texts, as much as any attempt to derive trajectories or even conclusions on typical generalities of "Western" and "Eastern" positions on penitence, has to be placed under a *caveat* that focuses on method and the significance of the historical background of the sources. Although the sample of Christian authors chosen for this discussion is relatively small, significant methodological and thus hermeneutical questions must be addressed. Each of these texts reflects the unique circumstances of a given author, historical period, and socio-cultural setting. Outlining in each instance a text's background is complex and would have gone well beyond the scope of this article. Terminological

---

[136] See Aphrahat, *Demonstrations* 7.25-26, in PS 1, 356–60.

[137] See Aphrahat, *Demonstrations* 7.27, in PS 1, 360.

[138] *Second Letter of Clement to the Corinthians* 8.1-2, in Bart D. Ehrmann, ed. and trans., *The Apostolic Fathers*, LCL 24 (Cambridge, MA, and London: Harvard University Press, 2003) 176: Ὡς οὖν ἐσμὲν ἐπὶ γῆς, μετανοήσωμεν . . . ἕως ἔχομεν καιρὸν μετανοίας.

[139] See Aphrahat, *Demonstrations* 6.6, in PS 1, 268.

[140] See Aphrahat, *Demonstrations* 7.27, in PS 1, 360.

distinctions within a text as well as across texts, understanding of all the challenges facing an author, the religious and social situation of his audience, and potential literary influences are some of the important areas that must be considered when attempting to compare texts as diverse as those of Christians in late antiquity. While these could not in each instance be explicitly examined here, they remain part of the overall considerations that underlie the investigation and presentation of this article.

There are three reasons why such information is more than mere "background," but rather constitutes an integral part of a sound method or hermeneutical framework. First, given that there is no *prima facie* relationship between, say, Aphrahat the Persian Sage and Tertullian of Carthage, the scope of the sources demands a unified investigation of each source in order to provide a basis for comparison of terms and theological ideas across texts of substantially different Christian provenances. Although Greek and Latin texts do share relatively more in common with respect to their position within the late antique social and religious milieu, even among these sources the pitfalls of uncritical comparison are many. Second, a method that accounts for such differences has a better chance of ascertaining whether parallels between a set of sources are the result of influence or merely coincidence drawn from similar religious and historical conditions. Finally, without critical appreciation for the historical backgrounds of the various sources the reader is left to wonder to what extent the researcher has imposed his or her own theological "unities" on this body of material. Given the extent of restrictions on the content and format of this study, not all the background relevant for the discussion of terms related to penitence and repentance could be presented and discussed. Further investigation by the reader is facilitated by references to studies that provide a more comprehensive approach to the literary and historical backgrounds of a given text. Arguably more important than seeing global differences between Eastern and Western approaches to penitence is in my view the realization that the personal background of an individual author—his or her level of education and professional training as in the case of Tertullian or Clement, his or her placement in a region of the world torn apart by constant military struggles between empires as in the case of Aphrahat, his or her position as pastoral leader within the community from which derives concern for the corporate effects of sins and the need to engage in penance for purification and sanctification of the body of the church as a whole as again in the case of Aphrahat, or his or her personal contact with sinners-turned-radical-penitents, as in the case of Abba John the Dwarf and Paëisa—that knowledge of this individual,

personal background is essential for understanding the emphasis someone chooses in his or her approach to the question of penitence.

## 2. Implications

A renewed Christian theology of penance can derive significant benefits from reconsidering the experiences and perspectives expressed and
reflected in early Christian sources from both the East and the West.
Although the material presented above does not provide comprehensive
coverage for the whole of early Christianity, important impulses are to
be gained from the spectrum of sources covered. Admittedly at times
the goal of penance emerges as one of punishing the sinner. Yet it is balanced by the concern to see the call to penance as an expression of the
quest for change, a change away from what has become decayed and
corrupted and toward a pristine state before the Fall, as some view it, a
renewed receipt of the grace of baptism, or a change toward the ultimate
goal of human existence: perfection in a state that consists of eternally
being with God. The overall trajectory of the role of penance in the life
of a person therefore is distinctly positive and uplifting.

Shared aspects of approaches to penitence in the East and in the West
allow one to recover a common theological tradition and thus aid in recon-
necting what has grown into different directions over the course of later
centuries. The discussion above has indicated that from the beginning
West and East have shared the emphasis on the need to embody penance
in rituals and physical expressions both of the individual and of the community. The whole range of rules for how to do penance witnesses to and
allows for the recovery of a wholesome view of the world, of the truly
human reality of acknowledging and realizing the necessity of a fine-tuned
interplay of the material and the spiritual/rational realm. Across the range
of examples discussed, concern for the involvement of the broader community of believers in the penitential process, ideally of the whole Christian community, emerges clearly. Penance is not the task of the individual
sinner alone. As much as individual sin affects community and thus church
reality, so also the process of penitence is to be carried and accompanied
by the congregation of believers, the church. Courageous engagement
with penitence therefore carries the promise of positively developing
community coherence, even of building up the body of Christ. Indeed, the
markedly christological dimensions of penitence manifest themselves in
the unity of Christ with his body, the church, when both join, intermingle,

even represent one another in their intercession on behalf of the sinner(s) before God the Father. Penance invites to an intimate cooperation between human and divine, and becomes an act of participation in the very work of redemption. Penance teaches the preciousness of salvation.

The exercise of penance clearly has societal and political implications, as Tertullian's ready use of legal terminology suggests. Not only does penance aid the transgressor in avoiding potentially eternal punishment. It also calls upon the individual to accept personal responsibility for his or her actions. More than ever before, in the modern global but anonymous world it is an absolute necessity to act upon such a call.

Repentance is a process. It carries educational benefits, but therefore also defies expectations of immediate fulfillment. Aiding Christian believers in developing a repentant spirit contributes toward overcoming the impact of a world seemingly built on expectations of immediate gratification. By contributing to the furtherance of the virtue of patience, the cultivation of an attitude of penance in the body of Christ may in fact provide one of the tools necessary to overcome crises that threaten the life of the Christian community. Instead of death and destruction, penance brings restoration, healing, and purification. The best climate in which penitence can grow is one that emphasizes God manifesting Godself as a loving and caring parent, concerned about the well-being of his or her children. The authors surveyed express that lifegiving quality both in language that references God as Father and in emphasizing the persistent and lifegiving realities of giving birth and women's zeal in the service of God. This perhaps unexpected dimension of penitential language reveals rather clearly that penance in Christian theology deserves to be admired and appreciated for its truly lifegiving quality, both to the individual and to the whole church.

The teachers and practitioners of a Christian life in the desert demonstrate that entering upon the process of penitence requires receiving direction, spiritual guidance. As the Christian essentially is a member of the body of Christ, one who is part of a community, so also the exercise of penitence has to be directed toward the reconciliation with others and has to be facilitated and made possible by others. Aphrahat's expositions demonstrate this point very well.

# 3. Further Reading

Bitton-Ashkelony, Brouria. "Penitence in Late Antique Monastic Literature." In Jan Assmann and Guy G. Stroumsa, eds., *Transformations of the Inner Self in*

*Ancient Religions.* Studies in the History of Religions 83. Leiden, Boston, and Köln: Brill, 1999, 179–94.

Burns, James Patout. "Confessing the Church: Cyprian on Penance." *StPatr* 36 (2001) 338–48.

Chryssavgis, John. *In the Heart of the Desert: the Spirituality of the Desert Fathers and Mothers.* Bloomington, IN: World Wisdom Books, 2003.

De Clerck, Paul. "Pénitence seconde et conversion quotidienne aux III$^{ème}$ et IV$^{ème}$ siècles." *StPatr* 20 (1989) 352–74.

Fitzgerald, Allan. *Conversion through Penance in the Italian Church of the Fourth and Fifth Centuries. New Approaches to the Experience of Conversion from Sin.* SBEC 15. Lewiston, NY: Edwin Mellen, 1988.

Mathews, Edward G. "The rich man and Lazarus: almsgiving and repentance in early Syriac tradition." *Diakonia* 22/2 (1988–1989) 89–104.

Paikatt, Mathew. "Repentance and Penitence in Mar Aprem of Nisibis." *Christian Orient* 12 (1991) 135–48.

Stroumsa, Guy G. "From Repentance to Penance in Early Christianity: Tertullian's *De Paenitentia* in Context." In Jan Assmann and Guy G. Stroumsa, eds., *Transformations of the Inner Self in Ancient Religions.* SHR 83. Leiden, Boston, and Köln: Brill, 1999, 167–78.

Tilley, Maureen A. "Theologies of Penance During the Donatist Controversy." *StPatr* 35 (2001) 330–37.

Ward, Benedicta. *Harlots of the Desert. A Study of Repentance in Early Monastic Sources.* CS 106. Kalamazoo: Cistercian Publications, 1987.

# 4. Hermeneutical Reflections

The process of engaging in researching, reflecting upon, and exchanging results concerning the theme of penance in the Judeo-Christian theological tradition, which provided the framework for the present article, in a way has functioned hermeneutically for me also like a penitential process, shaped by precisely these two dimensions. On the one hand there was a debt to be paid to biblical theology on the one end of the spectrum and systematic, modern-day practical theology on the other end. More recent historical studies of theological topics do not always make the insights they can provide readily available to other neighboring theological disciplines. At times also concern for social, cultural, philosophical, or political perspectives takes over and does so at the price of a serious engagement with theological questions, which are and should be at the heart of the matter. On the other hand, the place of historical theological inquiry into questions of penance is not one that is readily acknowledged as self-evident by all theological disciplines involved in the enterprise. Of the sixteen different voices heard in the consultation, only two contributions from the field of historical theology were deemed necessary, and one of them was a latecomer to the project. Perhaps one needs to join with Aphrahat in calling out to the community of theological professionals, academic and otherwise, to provide opportunities for repentance, and thus for making known to the theological world the treasures of the tradition more readily and more often. In light of the riches of the early Christian historical tradition revealed above, such a change of heart toward greater willingness to hear the voice of history is certainly called for.

Nine

# Private Confession in the German Reformation*

*Ronald K. Rittgers*

## 1. History

"Catholics confess, Protestants do not." While this stereotype about the practice of private confession may be largely true for the modern context,[1] it would be very problematic if applied to the early modern period. From the sixteenth through the eighteenth century at least one of the larger Protestant churches, the Lutheran, practiced a modified version of private confession that was an integral part of its piety and identity vis-à-vis other Protestants, none of whom had such a rite.[2] Lutheran

* Portions of this article appeared under the title "An Apology for Evangelical Confession," in *Crux: A Quarterly Journal of Christian Thought and Opinion published by Regent College* 35/1 (1999) 2–11.

[1] It should be noted that private confession has of late experienced something of a renaissance within some Protestant mainline churches, most notably among Episcopalians.

[2] While Ulrich Zwingli and John Calvin thought private confession could be salutary as a voluntary practice, neither pushed for the development of a

private confession is one of the most interesting and, until recently, under-studied practices of the Reformation era.[3] The task of this essay is to trace the development of Lutheran private confession from its origins in the thought of Luther to its actual implementation and practice in the late sixteenth and seventeenth centuries. It is hoped that this brief sketch will provide the reader with a helpful introduction to the Lutheran version of private confession and also reveal some of the unique challenges this practice presented to the leaders of the German Reformation. Before we turn to consider Luther's views on private confession, a word about the late medieval sacrament of penance is in order.

### a. The Late Medieval Sacrament of Penance

Private confession had been practiced in the Christian West since at least the early seventh century when Celtic monks made it a defining feature of the piety they sought to spread throughout Europe.[4] Prior to the appearance of Celtic pilgrims on the continent, penance and confession had been largely public affairs. This was certainly the case in the early church, which knew nothing like the later sacrament of penance. The unique contribution of the Celts was to "privatize" both penance and confession, and also to allow for repeated penances even for serious sin, something that was also unknown in early Christianity. (The Celts may have been influenced in their predilection toward private penance and private confession by the pre-Christian Celtic tradition of

reformed rite the way Luther did. Private confession was not part of Reformed Protestant piety. Similarly, English Reformers were supportive of the practice early in the Reformation, but it never became an important feature of Anglican piety. On the plight of private confession among non-Lutheran Protestants see Mary Collins and David Power, eds., *The Fate of Confession* (Edinburgh: T & T Clark, 1987).

[3] For a recent treatment of Lutheran private confession see my book, *The Reformation of the Keys: Confession, Conscience, and Authority in Sixteenth-Century Germany* (Cambridge, MA: Harvard University Press, 2004).

[4] On the contribution of the Celts to the history of penance in the Christian West see John T. McNeill and Helena M. Gamer, *Medieval Handbooks of Penance: A Translation of the Principal Libri Poenitentiales* (New York: Columbia University Press, 1938) 23–50. For more general treatments of penance in the Western church see Henry Charles Lea, *A History of Auricular Confession and Indulgences in the Latin Church*, 3 vols. (Philadelphia: Lea Brothers, 1896), and Oscar D. Watkins, *A History of Penance*, 2 vols. (London: Longmans, Green, 1920).

the *anmchara,* or soul guide, who would dispense spiritual advice on an individual basis.)[5]

While many medieval church leaders became strong supporters of the practice introduced by the Celts—Carolingian reformers sought to make it a prominent feature of lay piety, though without much success[6]—prior to the early thirteenth century lay participation in private confession was governed by local or regional custom. This changed at the Fourth Lateran Council (1215). According to Canon 21 of this landmark meeting of church leaders, all Christians who had reached the age of discretion had to confess all of their sins at least once a year to their own priest and perform the penance imposed on them. Lay people were also to receive the Eucharist annually, at least at Easter. Those who refused to confess and communicate annually were to be barred from entering a church while alive and denied Christian burial upon death. The canon instructed confessors to inquire into the "circumstances both of the sinner and the sin," so that they would know how best to offer healing to the sin-sick soul. The encounter between penitent and confessor was to be strictly confidential; priests who broke the seal of confession were to be deposed from office and confined to a "monastery of strict observance," where they would do penance for the remainder of their lives.[7] This canon formally instituted the requirement of annual confession and communion as a mandatory universal rite in Western Christendom.

While Lateran IV established an official standard for frequency of confession, it did not provide a theology of the sacrament of penance. There soon emerged an enormous literature on the working of sacramental confession that included a variety of theological perspectives. This diversity of viewpoints continued well into the later Middle Ages: there was no one official theology of confession on the eve of the Reformation.[8] Rather, there were numerous attempts to define the four elements of the

[5] McNeill and Gamer, *Medieval Handbooks,* 29.

[6] Joseph H. Lynch, *The Medieval Church: A Brief History* (London and New York: Longman, 1992) 82.

[7] D. C. Douglas, general ed., *English Historical Documents,* Vol. 3 (London and New York: Oxford University Press, 1953) 654–55.

[8] See Thomas Tentler, *Sin and Confession on the Eve of the Reformation* (Princeton: Princeton University Press, 1977), Part Two: The Teaching On Sacramental Confession At The End Of The Middle Ages; W. David Myers, *"Poor Sinning Folk": Confession and Conscience in Counter-Reformation Germany* (Ithaca and London: Cornell University Press, 1996), Prologue: Theology of Confession before

sacrament—contrition, confession, absolution, and satisfaction or penance—and to explain how they were related to one another. For example, some theologies stressed that true sorrow for sin (contrition), motivated by the love of God, was necessary for forgiveness, while others maintained that imperfect sorrow (attrition), motivated by the fear of punishment, was sufficient. There were also disagreements about the relative roles of human and divine agency in the sacrament. Some theologians argued that human beings could produce contrition of their own accord, while others insisted that divine agency (grace) was necessary at every stage of the process to quicken and strengthen the human will. Consensus about priestly absolution was also difficult to achieve. Some theologians ascribed great efficacy to clerical absolution, seeing it as actually mediating divine forgiveness, while others maintained that priests only "showed" or "declared" to penitents the absolution God had already pronounced.

Just as there were numerous theologies of confession on the eve of the Reformation, so there were also numerous experiences of the sacrament in the later Middle Ages. Confession manuals and summas for confessors called for exhaustive interrogations of conscience and this certainly happened in some cases, but more often than not the actual experience fell short of the theory outlined in clerical handbooks. While the sacrament of penance was available throughout the year, the laity typically went to confession in Lent. Especially in urban contexts this meant that confessors did not have the opportunity—and perhaps the training—to conduct thorough confessions. The Lenten experience may have also been anything but private. The confessional booth was not introduced until the late sixteenth century. In the later Middle Ages confessions took place in an open space within a church, usually before the altar, with the confessor seated on a chair and the confessant kneeling before him. Penitents waiting to be confessed were supposed to keep their distance, but there is evidence to suggest that they did not always do so.[9]

This lack of theological precision coupled with the problems of actual practice need not suggest that the sacrament of penance had only a minimal impact on lay piety. Most scholars would agree that the church was very effective at communicating the basic theological assumptions behind

---

the Reformation; and Anne T. Thayer, *Preaching, Penitence, and the Coming of the Reformation* (Aldershot: Ashgate, 2002).

[9] On the actual practice of confession in the later Middle Ages see Lawrence G. Duggan, "Fear and Confession on the Eve of the Reformation," *Archive for Reformation History* 75 (1984) 153–75, and Myers, *"Poor Sinning Folk,"* ch. 1.

the sacrament to the laity: God is just and punishes sin in this life and the next; human beings are sinful and need to acknowledge their sins to God and the church in order to avoid or reduce this punishment; God is merciful and desires to forgive sinners, but also requires satisfaction for sin (i.e., penance)—usually more than the church actually demands—before he is willing to do so;[10] penitents must contribute in some measure to the rendering of satisfaction for sin; the clergy, and not the laity, possesses the authority from God to retain and remit sins. These basic assumptions directly informed the myriad forms of lay piety that flourished on the eve of the Reformation. Processions, pilgrimages, buying indulgences, fasting, self-flagellation—each of these expressions of lay piety and countless more were infused with a penitential outlook that may ultimately be traced back to the sacrament of penance. From one point of view this burgeoning of lay piety may be seen as a sign of the health of late medieval Christianity. From another point of view it may be taken as a sign of a deep fear that no amount of penance could ever be enough to satisfy the divine Judge.

## b. Luther and the Sacrament of Penance

Luther certainly had a difficult time believing that late medieval piety was good and salutary. He frequently found the sacrament of penance to be especially burdensome. Luther's largely negative experience with confession was determined in part by the fact that he was subjected to an especially rigorous version of the sacrament, particularly during his earliest days as a monk. He came to believe that God demanded true sorrow for sin and that human beings had to produce this contrition of their own accord. There was very little room for divine initiative—for grace—in his understanding of confession. The assurance of forgiveness that he desired so intensely continually eluded him because he could never believe that he had achieved true sorrow for sin or confessed enough transgressions. In time Luther found a spiritual director, Johannes von Staupitz, who presented him with quite a different version of confession, one that stressed divine agency, divine love, and the importance of faith.[11]

---

[10] It should be noted that most late medieval theologians held that God forgave the guilt of sin as an act of sheer mercy, but remission of the penalty for sin—or at least a portion of it—required a human contribution in the form of works of satisfaction.

[11] David Curtis Steinmetz, *Misericordia Dei: The Theology of Johannes von Staupitz in its Late Medieval Setting* (Leiden: Brill, 1968) 101.

This experience set the young monk on the road to his Reformation breakthrough. Though Luther was well aware of the diversity of views in the church with respect to confession, by the time he had developed his mature evangelical soteriology he would come to reject all late-medieval attempts to explain the sacrament. In his mind they all required a human contribution to the reception of forgiveness—some more than others—rather than seeing God as the sole actor in salvation. For Luther, God and God's promises were the only reliable grounds for assurance of forgiveness. Human beings simply received by faith—itself a gift of grace—the salvation that God freely gave through Christ.

It is well known that in the early years of the Reformation Luther objected strongly to the sacrament of penance. In *The Babylonian Captivity of the Church* (1520) he asserted, "The promise of penance . . . has been transformed into the most oppressive despotism, being used to establish a sovereignty which is more than merely temporal."[12] For Luther and his early followers the sacrament of penance represented all that was wrong with late medieval Christianity: works righteousness, man-made doctrines, oppressive and intrusive clericalism. The reformer attacked what he saw in sacramental confession as an attempt by the church to make lay consciences accountable to a purely human judge. Confession became for him a symbol of the spiritual oppression he believed was inherent in late medieval Catholicism. In his 1521 treatise *On Confession: Whether the Pope has Power to Command It,* Luther accused the pope of using the sacrament of penance to invade vulnerable lay consciences with his false gospel of works righteousness. The Wittenberg reformer insisted that Christ alone was to dwell in the human conscience; the Word was to be its one true standard. He castigated the pope as the Antichrist who "breaks open the bridal chamber of Christ and makes all Christian souls into whores."[13] Luther wanted to eject the pope from the inner sanctum in order to reunite consciences with their true Husband.

Luther and his early followers loathed the late-medieval version of private confession. However, it is important that we understand the source of their animosity. Luther and his fellow reformers attacked confession not because they opposed the practice as such, but because they believed it had been corrupted. They saw in private confession—in the

---

[12] WA 6: 544, lines 12–13; LW 36: 83.
[13] WA 8: 152, lines 7–8.

individual application of the Word to the believer—the most effective way of preaching the Gospel to troubled souls. When one of Luther's colleagues in Wittenberg, Andreas Bodenstein von Karlstadt, sought to abolish private confession, Luther responded in a 1522 sermon,

> I will allow no one to take private confession from me and would not give it in exchange for all the wealth of the world. For I know what consolation and strength it has given me. No one knows what it can give unless he has struggled much and frequently with the devil. I would have been strangled by the devil long ago if confession had not sustained me.[14]

Luther wanted no one to be forced to confession, but neither would he allow anyone to deny him access to it. "We must have much absolution," he argued, "so that we may strengthen our fearful consciences and despondent hearts against the devil. Therefore no one should forbid confession."[15] He conceded that those with strong faith had no need of private confession: they could simply receive absolution directly from heaven. But he observed that few, including himself, possessed such unwavering trust in God. Luther wanted to redeem confession, not abolish it. As he later observed in his *Large Catechism*, "when I exhort a person to confession, I am doing nothing else than exhorting him to be a Christian."[16] In time, Luther would do more than exhort people to go to confession; he would require it.

From the beginning of the German Reformation the overwhelming majority of its leaders, both lay and clerical, wanted to retain some form of private confession. In their minds there was nothing inherently un-Protestant about the practice. Most were convinced that the Bible offered support for it. They took Christ's giving of the keys to the apostles seriously, and believed the binding and loosing of sins was a necessary part of a truly evangelical church. While leaders of the Reformation acknowledged there was no specific warrant in the Scriptures for private confession, neither did they think the practice violated either the spirit or the letter of the Word.

The first Protestants also believed that unworthy participation in the Lord's Supper elicited divine wrath. The apostle Paul had warned

---

[14] WA 10 III: 62, lines 1–2.
[15] WA 10 III: 62, lines 9–10.
[16] BSLK, 732.

that those who partook of the sacred wine and bread unworthily ate
and drank judgment to themselves (1 Cor 11:29). Lutheran clergy and
magistrates took this warning to heart, believing it extended to whole
communities. In contrast to followers of Zwingli, Lutherans maintained
that Christ was physically present in the Eucharist, though they rejected
the Catholic belief in the Mass as a sacrifice. Because they wanted laypeople to communicate more frequently than they had in the old church,
it became all the more important for communicants to approach the
sacrament worthily. Some sort of preparation was appropriate. Private
confession seemed a good option. Though most reformers supported
lay confession and absolution, few thought the practice provided either
the discipline or consolation communicants required. Theologically they
were committed to lay confession, because the authority to forgive re-
sided in the Word, not in an ordained cleric. But pastorally the reformers
preferred private confession.[17]

The goal of Luther and his fellow reformers, then, was to reform
private confession so completely that common laypeople, who were
admittedly dubious about the practice, would neither feel threatened
by it nor see it again as a good work necessary to salvation. They
wanted to ensure that laypeople would see confession as a source of
unparalleled consolation. On the other hand, the reformers also wanted
a ritual that would provide the discipline they believed was necessary
to pious reception of the Lord's Supper. The result was a new ritual
designed to protect and console lay consciences as well as to discipline
and inform them.

### c. Lutheran Private Confession

By the early 1530s there was widespread agreement among the leaders of the evangelical movement about both the value of private confession and how it should be reformed.[18] The 1533 Nürnberg-Brandenburg
Church Order, one of the most influential new guides for worship and

---

[17] For Luther's comments on the validity of lay confession and absolution
see *Sermon on the Sacrament of Penance* (1519) (WA 2, 716 and 722). Luther supported lay confession and absolution throughout his life but never wished for
the practice to supplant private confession to a pastor, which became the norm
in Lutheranism.

[18] Nearly every sixteenth-century Lutheran church order contained an article
on confession. ER 1, 403.

belief in the German Reformation,[19] reflected this consensus. In keeping with the Augsburg Confession, a defining statement of Lutheran belief that clearly supported private confession,[20] the order stipulated that anyone who desired to participate in the Lord's Supper had to register *(anzaigen)* with his pastor beforehand and undergo an examination of faith *(Glaubensverhör)*.[21] Luther had required the same of Wittenberg laity already in 1524.[22] Communicants were to know and understand the Ten Commandments, the Apostles' Creed, and the Lord's Prayer. They were also expected to know what the sacrament was and how one could receive it worthily. Clergy were to avoid shaming laypeople in the examination of faith—especially the very young and the very old—lest they give them cause to avoid the sacrament.[23] Those whose knowledge of the faith was well known to the pastor did not have to be examined each time.[24]

This emphasis on understanding doctrine was a hallmark of Lutheran private confession from the beginning. It was a logical outgrowth of evangelical soteriology: salvation by faith assumed a certain level of familiarity with basic theology. Lay and clerical leaders of the Reformation believed the examination of faith far less intrusive than the traditional interrogation of conscience. To be sure, both were designed to enforce discipline, but the examination of faith did not penetrate into the conscience, which for Lutherans was the most essential and most vulnerable

[19] Most of the major Franconian cities, towns, and principalities adopted the 1533 Brandenburg-Nürnberg Church Order. It also influenced church orders in Swabia, Württemberg, northern Bavaria, Mecklenburg, and Saxony. Based on its widespread influence, one scholar has written of the 1533 Brandenburg-Nürnberg Church Order, "one may properly refer to it as the stem-mother *(Stammutter)* of a very important family of clearly Lutheran church orders." Sehling XI, 125.

[20] Article 11 of the Augsburg Confession reads "our churches teach that private absolution should be retained in the churches. However, in confession an enumeration of all sins is not necessary, for this is not possible according to the Psalm [19:12] , 'who can discern his errors.'" In article 25 the creed stated that only those "who have been previously examined and absolved" would be allowed to participate in the Lord's Supper. Leif Grane, *The Augsburg Confession: A Commentary* (Minneapolis: Augsburg Publishing House, 1987) 127, 226.

[21] Sehling XI, 186.

[22] Luther had made the same allowance for the "intelligens" in his *Form for the Mass and Communion (Formula Missae et Communionis)*, WA 12: 215, lines 30–31.

[23] Sehling XI, 186.

[24] Ibid.

part of the human psyche. As a later Nürnberg church order explained, "the exploration—the account of faith which everyone must give to his pastor before he may go to the sacrament—is no confession, but an instruction, which one may not make into auricular confession where all sins must be confessed."[25]

The 1533 church order further required lay people to acknowledge their depravity and confess any public sins they had committed that threatened the harmony among Christians figured in the Eucharist. The church order mentioned only enmity and wrath.[26] Those who either performed poorly in the examination of faith or lived in open sin were denied access to the Lord's Supper. The confession of secret transgressions, no matter how serious, was a strictly voluntary matter. The church order absolutely forbade pastors to probe the souls of the laity in search of hidden sins. Lay people were encouraged to confess any transgressions that burdened their consciences, but they were to do so in order to receive guidance and consolation, not to earn forgiveness. The order assailed as "unchristian" and "superstitious" the traditional belief that one had to confess all one's mortal sins in order to be forgiven.

Because of its great value for troubled consciences, pastors were to exhort their parishioners to seek out private absolution frequently. Clergymen were to teach their congregations how to examine their consciences so that they could know when they required instruction or consolation.[27] They were also to warn their parishioners about the dangers of not asking for the encouragement of clerical absolution when they needed it. Satan could easily tempt them to believe that their sins were too great to be forgiven by God, and thus lead them into despair. The church order portrayed the devil as a master of deception who possessed a full arsenal of weapons with which to tempt, discourage, and frighten human beings. Private absolution was the believer's most effective defense against "the great storm winds of Satan."[28] It was for this reason that Christ had instituted the keys. "He knew for certain that we would sorely need such consolation."[29]

---

[25] Veit Dietrich, *Liturgy Booklet for Pastors in the Countryside (Agendbüchlein für Pfarrherren auf dem Land)*, Sehling XI, 549.

[26] Sehling XI, 186.

[27] Ibid.

[28] Ibid.

[29] Ibid.

According to the church order, once a layperson had acknowledged her depravity, confessed any public sins she had committed, and proven her knowledge of the Lutheran catechism, she could expect to receive absolution from her pastor. The absolution itself became efficacious when the layperson placed her faith in the divine promise of forgiveness her pastor set before her:

> The Almighty God has had mercy on you and through the merit of the most holy suffering, death, and resurrection of our Lord Jesus Christ, his beloved Son, forgives you all of your sins. I, as a duly called servant of the Christian Church, by order of our Lord Jesus Christ, pronounce to you this forgiveness of all your sins in the name of the Father, Son, and Holy Spirit. Amen. Go in peace! May it be to you as you believe! *(Dir geschehe, wie du glaubst!).*[30]

As was true of the Augsburg Confession, absolution was nowhere referred to as a sacrament in the church order.[31] Melanchthon specifically called private absolution a sacrament in his Apology for the Augsburg Confession.[32] Luther was always ambiguous on the issue. Throughout *The Babylonian Captivity of the Church* he treated private absolution as a sacrament, but then reversed himself in the conclusion to this work, reasoning,

> it has seemed proper to restrict the name of sacrament to those promises which have signs attached to them. The remainder, not being bound to signs, are bare promises. Hence there are, strictly speaking,

[30] The order provided a second form for absolution that was identical to the first up to the "Amen." It then concluded, "Go forth and sin no more; rather, better yourself without end! May God help you in this! Amen." Sehling XI, 187.

[31] Private absolution did, however, appear immediately after the sections dealing with baptism and the Lord's Supper in the Augsburg Confession.

[32] Melanchthon stated, "Wherefore the voice of the one absolving must be believed not otherwise than we would believe a voice from heaven. And absolution properly can be called a sacrament of repentance, as also the more learned scholastic theologians speak." Ibid. 81. Later Melanchthon asserted, "[t]herefore Baptism, the Lord's Supper, and Absolution, which is the Sacrament of Repentance, are truly sacraments. For these rites have God's command and the promise of grace, which is peculiar to the New Testament." *Concordia or Book of Concord. The Symbols of the Ev. Lutheran Church* (St. Louis: Concordia Publishing House, 1922) 94.

but two sacraments in the church of God—baptism and the bread. . . .
The sacrament of penance, which I added to these two, lacks the divinely instituted visible sign, and is, as I have said, nothing but a way
and a return to baptism.[33]

Luther wanted confession retained because it was "a cure without equal
for distressed consciences."[34] Nevertheless, he accorded it a pseudo-
sacramental status only. His equivocation meant that Lutherans could
never speak confidently of a sacrament of absolution.

Evangelical private confession, what contemporaries simply called
*Beichte* (confession), thus had two parts: the examination of faith and a
voluntary private confession. It was a confession in both senses of the
word: a confession of faith and a confession of sin. The examination of
faith and conduct was designed to enforce discipline; the giving of instruction and absolution were intended to offer consolation. As we have
seen, both were essential to the new ritual.[35]

### d. Problems of Implementation and Definition

The actual implementation of the new version of private confession
was accomplished at an uneven pace. In Luther's Saxony the practice was
enforced by the 1520s. However, in areas of Germany where Reformed
Protestantism had a significant influence, especially in Württemberg, it
took until the late sixteenth or early seventeenth century for private confession to become a reality.[36] Even in some of the more staunchly Lutheran
cities of Germany it could take some time to match actual practice to the
theory set out in the new church orders. In Nürnberg, one of the leading cities of the German Reformation, there was a fifteen-year delay between the
appearance of the 1533 church order and the implementation of Lutheran

---

[33] WA 6: 572, lines 10–34; LW 36: 124.

[34] WA 6: 546, lines 13–14; LW 36: 86.

[35] I have borrowed the rubric of discipline and consolation from Tentler. He
argued that the sacrament of penance sought to discipline and console penitents,
something I believe Lutheran private confession also endeavored to do, but offering a very different theological justification.

[36] Ernst Bezzel, *Frei zum Eingeständnis: Geschichte und Praxis der evangelischen
Einzelbeichte* (Stuttgart: Calwer, 1982) 48 n138 (the note appears on p. 210). See
also my forthcoming article in *The Sixteenth Century Journal* entitled "Private
Confession and the 'Lutheranization' of Sixteenth-Century Nördlingen."

private confession in 1548.[37] As in other cities, opposition to the practice among burghers coupled with concern among city council members that the practice signaled a resurgent sacerdotalism frustrated the Lutheran clergy's attempts to implement private confession, at least for a time.

Lutheran reformers also encountered theological difficulties as they sought to implement their new version of private confession. During the 1530s a prolonged debate took place in Nürnberg about the relationship between private absolution and general absolution (i.e., the absolution spoken by a pastor to his congregation following its common confession of sin).[38] The debate involved several leading reformers—Luther, Melanchthon, the Schwäbisch Hall reformer Johannes Brenz, and the Nürnberg preacher Andreas Osiander—and ultimately revealed some important problems in the evangelical approach to private confession. When Osiander pressed Luther about the difference between private absolution and general absolution, the latter maintained that both were simply means of preaching the gospel, the only real difference being one of venue. Like Luther, Osiander was a strong supporter of private confession, but unlike the Wittenberg reformer he thought there was a qualitative difference between private confession and general confession: the former was a sacrament while the latter was not. In fact, Osiander wanted general confession abolished because he observed in Nürnberg that it was deterring lay people from coming to private confession. Burghers clearly preferred receiving absolution in a crowd over seeking it from their pastors in a personal encounter. Osiander thought this state of affairs both deprived lay people of the consolation only private absolution could provide and prevented confessors from properly examining confessants to determine whether they should be absolved and admitted to communion. The Nürnberg preacher thought evangelical pastors bore a responsibility before God to use the power of the keys responsibly, which meant being as sure as possible that their decisions to bind and loose sins corresponded to the will of heaven.

All of this sounded far too Catholic to Osiander's opponents, who opted for Luther's position, which was that both private and general absolution were to be retained in evangelical churches—both were valid means of preaching the Word to troubled consciences. Osiander had attempted to force a more precise theological explanation of the new rite,

---

[37] See Rittgers, *Reformation of the Keys*, ch. 8.
[38] See ibid. chs. 6 and 7.

especially regarding its status as a sacrament. But owing largely to his sacerdotal tendencies and rather difficult personality—Osiander was abrasive, to say the least—his opponents ignored his call for greater theological clarity. This meant that the justification for the new rite rested largely on pastoral grounds and the move to make it mandatory was finally based on political authority: city councils and princes ordered lay people to go to private confession.

### e. Conclusion

Despite these difficulties of implementation and theological definition, Lutheran private confession eventually became an accepted and important reality in evangelical religious life. The practice received a great deal of attention in popular devotional works of the late sixteenth and seventeenth centuries.[39] It also served as an important tool for establishing a Lutheran worldview among the laity during the so-called "age of confessionalization," when political and religious leaders became increasingly concerned about planting distinctive confessional identities in the common folk.[40] The private examination of faith provided an ideal opportunity for evangelical clergy to conduct one-to-one catechization.

Lutheran private confession was ultimately Luther's version of private confession. It benefited from his deep pastoral sensitivities and must have been a great source of consolation to many troubled souls. But the new rite also suffered from Luther's inability to provide a finally satisfying theological rationale for its existence, especially as a mandatory practice.[41] Lutheran private confession was not the first rite in the history of the church to enjoy widespread support and to serve a valuable function while lacking an adequate theological foundation.

## 2. Implications

Perhaps the most important implication of my article for a Christian theology of penitence is that private confession is part of the original

---

[39] Laurentius Klein, *Evangelish-Lutherisch Beichte: Lehre und Praxis.* Konfessionskundliche und kontroverstheologie Studien 5 (Paderborn: Bonifacius-Drückerei, 1961) 174.

[40] On this point see Susan C. Karant-Nunn, *The Reformation of Ritual: An Interpretation of Early Modern Germany* (New York: Routledge, 1997) 100.

[41] See Rittgers, *Reformation of the Keys,* Conclusion.

Protestant birthright. Protestants can confess! Though I note important theological problems with the early modern Lutheran version of
private confession, it is possible for modern Protestants to overcome
these difficulties and benefit from the rite today. As a *voluntary* practice
evangelical private confession has great promise for Protestant piety. As
I have argued elsewhere, private confession could be a very effective
means of limiting the influence of the secular therapeutic culture on
Christian pastoral care.[42] The very presence of a rite like private confession signals that not all guilt is false or neurotic guilt—there are things
we do for which we ought to experience real guilt, because we have
transgressed a divine commandment, not simply violated a societal or
familial taboo. Confession would also signal that the church—and the
church alone—has access to real forgiveness, by virtue of its possession of the keys, a topic Protestants tend not to discuss. The church has
more to offer than release from neurotic burdens, as liberating at that
can be. The church has divine absolution via the Word! Private confession is no panacea, but it could encourage greater faithfulness to the
true healer of souls, Christ, and thus help us protect ourselves from the
secularizing influence of the contemporary therapeutic culture. Private
confession, informed by a biblical theology of the keys, could greatly
assist us in withstanding the "great storm winds" of the Adversary in
our own generation.

## 3. Further Reading

Collins, Mary, and David Power, eds., *The Fate of Confession*. Edinburgh: T & T
    Clark, 1987.
de Boer, Wietse. *The Conquest of the Soul: Confession, Discipline, and Public Order
    in Counter-Reformation Milan*. Leiden and Boston: Brill, 2001.
Firey, Abigail, ed., *The New History of Penance*. Leiden and Boston: Brill, 2006.
Lea, Henry Charles. *A History of Auricular Confession and Indulgences in the Latin
    Church*. 3 vols. Philadelphia: Lea Brothers, 1896.
Lualdi, Katharine Jackson, and Anne T. Thayer, eds., *Penitence in the Age of Reformations*. St. Andrews Studies in Reformation History. Aldershot, England;
    Burlington, VT: Ashgate, 2000.

---

[42] Ronald K. Rittgers, "An Apology for Evangelical Confession," in *Crux:
A Quarterly Journal of Christian Thought and Opinion published by Regent College*,
35/1 (1999) 2–11.

Ozment, Steven. *The Age of Reform, 1250–1550: An Intellectual and Religious History of Late Medieval and Reformation Europe.* New Haven: Yale University Press, 1980, 204–22.

Rittgers, Ronald K. *The Reformation of the Keys: Confession, Conscience, and Authority in Sixteenth-Century Germany.* Cambridge, MA: Harvard University Press, 2004.

Tentler, Thomas. *Sin and Confession on the Eve of the Reformation.* Princeton: Princeton University Press, 1977.

Thayer, Anne T. *Preaching, Penitence, and the Coming of the Reformation.* Aldershot, England; Burlington, VT: Ashgate, 2002.

Watkins, Oscar D. *A History of Penance.* 2 vols. London: Longmans, Green, 1920.

# 4. Hermeneutical Reflection

In this hermeneutical reflection I would like to comment on one important issue that emerged as a result of my interaction with the other authors in this volume: the tension between personal and communal notions of sin, penance, and reconciliation. Several of the authors observe that for their texts sin, penance, and reconciliation are conceived communally, having as much to do with relationships between human beings in human communities as between individual souls and God. My sense is that these authors see something positive in this communal emphasis, as it reveals a concern for the "other" that may be lacking in some versions of Christianity. The charge of hyper-individualism is typically leveled against Western expressions of Christianity, especially those that emerged out of the Reformation. There is something to this charge, but I would like to offer some reflections that seek to challenge the assumed connection between the Reformation and the rise of individualism. The penitential thought and practice of the late medieval and early modern period tells a much more complicated story.

If we consider first the late-medieval sacrament of penance we find that the church was just as concerned with social sins and reconciliation within communities as it was with personal—especially sexual—sins and reconciliation between souls and God. John Bossy has argued that medieval Europeans came to confession not so much to gain absolution from God as to seek reconciliation with their church and neighbors. Their focus was on mending human relationships and only secondarily on making amends to God. Bossy is impressed with the amount of space given over in medieval confession manuals to discussions of restitution. According to these sources, he maintains, the ideal confessor "was called to be a counselor and diplomat, dealing with the interests of the community at large and procuring the peace of the church, as well as a guardian of the secret passage between the soul and God."[43] Similarly, if a person chose to abstain from the sacrament it was more likely due to an outstanding disagreement with a neighbor than to some inward sin against God. For Bossy this behavior expressed the belief "that sin was a state of offence inhering in communities rather than in individuals."[44] Bossy, a social historian, has overstated his case, but his observations about the communal understanding of sin, penance, and reconciliation in the medieval period are still important.

Bossy believes that as the Middle Ages wore on, a more interiorized sense of sin came to the fore, a trend that became especially dominant in the Reformation with its alleged emphasis on personal sin and personal salvation. Again, there is something to this statement, but it ignores clear evidence to the contrary in Protestant penitential literature and also contradicts Bossy's own earlier statements on Luther's reformation of penance.[45] We should first point out that far from being individualistic, Luther's theology was marked by a strong emphasis on love of neighbor. For Luther there was an essential connection between justification by faith and love of the other. He put it this way in *The Freedom of the Christian*, as part of an extended reflection on the Christ hymn in Philippians 2:

> See . . . the good things we have from God should flow from one to the other and be common to all, so that everyone should "put on" his neighbor and so conduct himself toward him as if he himself were in the other's place. From Christ the good things have flowed and are flowing into us. He has so "put on" us and acted for us as if he had been what we are. From us they flow on to those who have need of them so that I should lay before God my faith and my righteousness that they may cover and intercede for the sins of my neighbor which

---

[43] John Bossy, *Christianity in the West, 1400–1700* (Oxford: Oxford University Press, 1985) 48. For an earlier statement of this argument see Bossy's "The Social History of Confession in the Age of the Reformation," *Transactions of the Royal Historical Society,* Series 5, Vol. 25 (1975) 21–38.

[44] Bossy, *Christianity in the West,* 47.

[45] Bossy had earlier argued that Luther tried to recapture the social understanding of sin. In Luther's version of the confessional one had only to confess sins that had a direct impact on the life of one's community. Bossy concluded that, with respect to confession, "Luther was a backward-looking figure." See Bossy, "The Social History of Confession," 26–27.

> I have taken upon myself and so labor and serve in them as if they
> were my very own. That is what Christ did for us. This is true love
> and the genuine rule of the Christian life.[46]

A few lines later Luther asserted, "We conclude . . . that a Christian lives
not in himself, but in Christ and in his neighbor. Otherwise he is not a
Christian. He lives in Christ through faith, in his neighbor through love.
By faith he is caught up beyond himself into God. By love he descends beneath himself into his neighbor."[47] These are hardly the reflections of a introspective mystic who wishes to free himself from the burdens of human
relationships so he can contemplate the divine without distraction.

This concern for the other also influenced the Lutheran reform of
penance. As I noted in my essay, one of the reasons Lutherans retained
private confession was because they saw themselves not as so many individuals before God striving for personal forgiveness, but as Christian
communities that needed to receive forgiveness on a collective basis
before they participated in the Lord's Supper. More to the point are
the instructions in the Lutheran church orders about the kinds of sins
evangelical penitents were to confess. The 1533 Brandenburg-Nürnberg
Church Order lists enmity and wrath, that is, social sins that affected the
whole community and thus threatened the harmony between Christians symbolized in the Lord's Supper. Confession of personal sin was
a voluntary matter and may well not have taken place at all unless the
penitent needed spiritual counsel for some specific struggle.

There are counter-examples one could raise to the thesis I have briefly
defended here. For example, there was no official rite of reconciliation
between estranged members of the community in early modern Lutheran
churches, aside from renewed access to the Lord's Supper (there was such
a rite in Calvin's Geneva).[48] I have simply wished to note that the story
of Western individualism is rather complicated, and that the Reformation occupies a somewhat ambiguous place in this story, especially with

---

[46] WA 7: 69, lines 1–10; LW 31: 371.

[47] WA 7: 69, lines 12–18; LW 31: 371.

[48] Robert Kingdon, "A New View of Calvin in the Light of the Registers of
the Geneva Consistory, " in William H. Neuser and Brian G. Armstrong, eds.,
*Calvinus Sincerioris: Religionis Vindex: Calvin as Protector of the Purer Religion*, Sixteenth Century Essays & Studies 36 (Kirksville, MO: Sixteenth Century Journal
Publishers, 1997) 21–33. See especially pp. 30–33.

respect to penitential thought and practice. As we have seen, concern for the other was a prominent part of Lutheran private confession.

I am indebted to my colleagues in this project for renewing my appreciation for the myriad ways in which the Judeo-Christian tradition has sought to deal with issues of sin, penitence, and reconciliation. The contributions of biblical scholars, theologians, and other historians to this volume have greatly enriched my understanding of my own field, Reformation Studies, and helped me see larger connections between early modern Christian penitential practices and those of Christians who lived in both the pre-modern and modern worlds. We need much more of this interdisciplinary dialogue and work in theological education.

Section Three

# Theological Traditions

Ten

# "Life in Abundance":
# Eastern Orthodox Perspectives on
# Repentance and Confession

*John Chryssavgis*

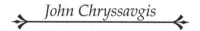

## 1. Tradition

### a. Repentance and Resurrection: Introductory Remarks

Most Christians intuitively understand a connection between repentance and resurrection.[1] Many appreciate how repentance and forgiveness can lead to new life. What is harder to discern, however, is the *equation* between repentance and resurrection, that repentance is resurrection unleashed. Repentance not only prepares us for, but is itself the beginning of the "passover" into life—the lifting up of the inner being in anticipation of the raising up of the total being. We have become so accustomed to thinking of repentance as an unpleasant though necessary rejection of sin that we have tended to lose sight of repentance as a fundamentally

---

[1] This paper draws upon material in previous studies, including *Repentance and Confession in the Orthodox Church* (Brookline: Holy Cross Press, 1990) and *Soul Mending: The Art of Spiritual Direction* (Brookline: Holy Cross Press, 2000).

joyous, restorative return to life in its abundant fullness. To repent is to awaken from the sleep of ignorance and to rediscover the soul.

Yet the mystery of repentance may be said to conceal four paradoxes that lie at the heart of the sacrament while at the same time causing some misunderstanding. Borrowing an expression from popular culture, we might call the first "back to the future." While taking critical stock of failure, and courageously assuming personal responsibility, repentance focuses not on human imperfection but on the perfect love of a God who "is good and loves mankind."[2] In the mystery of repentance we confess not simply our faults but, more fundamentally, our *faith* in the One who is able to forgive sins. The primary orientation of repentance, in other words, is not toward the past—with which most people normally associate it—but in fact toward the future, which becomes brighter in the light of divine mercy and forgiveness offered in Christ.

Second, this lifegiving reconciliation in Jesus Christ occurs only, and paradoxically, by way of his death on the cross and our own acceptance and appropriation of this transforming death in ourselves. "For if we died with him, we shall also live with him" (2 Tim 2:20). Most of us imagine repentance as a way of resuscitation from "mere living," while in fact it is a way of surrender and dying. Curiously, it is this very dying that alone can lead to authentic living.

Third, the deepening of self-knowledge, which results from this process, occurs through a relationship with another person, specifically with one's spiritual mentor. To find ourselves we must give ourselves away, and the spiritual father or mother helps us achieve this. Once again, most people see repentance and confession as private or individual affairs. In reality they are the keys to personal opening and social relations.

Fourth, the healing relationship is set within the context of community. To be integrated into the body of Christ implies healing and reconciliation not only of our selves individually, but also interpersonally. While many of us believe that the healing process of repentance occurs on a personal level, the truth is that only the community of believers can restore wholeness and health.

## b. The Root of Repentance: The Sacrament of Baptism

In the Orthodox Church baptism marks a mystical death and rebirth into new life in Christ. Herein lies the first public moment of repentance.

---

[2] The concluding words to almost every Orthodox service.

It is by way of baptism that we mystically enter into the death of Christ as we are submerged into water. It is here that we begin to experience the new birth of eternal life. No wonder, then, that the early Christian church affirmed a close connection between the illumination of baptism and the light of *Pascha*. In the Passion and *Pascha* of our Lord we discern and celebrate the healing of all wounds and of all wounded relationships. Through baptism we enter into this healing mystery (Col 2:14).

In his remarkable treatise *On Repentance,* Mark the Monk (fl. ca. 430 C.E.) writes: "the person who knows reality does not repent for things done or wrongs remembered; rather he confesses to God about *things to come."* The mystery of repentance is not a backward-looking reflection upon evils committed in the past but a courageous forward-looking movement into life. It is an act of faith. "This one thing I do," writes St. Paul, "forgetting what lies behind and straining forward to what lies ahead" (Phil 3:13). When the Baptist John cries: "Repent, for the kingdom of heaven is coming" (Matt 3:2), he is alerting our attention ahead, to the future.

St. John of Sinai, whose *Ladder of Divine Ascent* has for centuries nourished Orthodox believers, particularly during the baptismal preparation period of Great Lent, defines repentance as "the renewal of baptism." "Repentance," he writes, "is a contract with God for a second life."[3] And in the words of the Orthodox rite of baptism, this sacrament "enables us to find life . . . and once again to rejoice in the world, that we may render praise to God."

The Orthodox Church understands this baptismal renewal as radical spiritual liberation. It speaks of *passover* from death to life, from darkness into light, from hopelessness to joy. This is a complete reversal of the "normal" but fundamentally *unnatural* movement we ordinarily experience in the opposite direction. We pray in the service of baptism: "Take away the death of the old Adam, and make this a child of your kingdom."

Much more than simply a social rite of initiation, baptism is understood to inaugurate an ontological transformation. It is a spiritual transition from *bios* to *zoē*, from mere biological survival to "life in abundance" (John 10:10). Baptism is the point of entry into the Passion and *Pascha* of the Lord, marking the beginning of ascension to the kingdom of eternal life. Baptism thus signifies a turn toward the newness and fullness of life given to the world once for all in Christ. It communicates the decision to

---

[3] Step 5, 1.

shake off all that is worn and dead in order to experience all the depth and intensity of life to which we are called. Baptism is not simply, then, an invitation to membership in the church. It means, or ought to mean, our affirmative reply and response to that invitation.

Mark the Monk sees this process of repentance as a progressive "revelation" and realization of the grace received originally at baptism. He prefers to speak not only of a renewal of baptism but especially of a deepening of the experience revealed and received at baptism:

> By the grace of Christ, you have become a new Adam. . . . The Lord came for our sakes and died for us. He delivered us from inherited death. He cleansed us and renewed us through baptism. He now sets us in the paradise of the church.[4]

The entire world is thus claimed by Christ, from "the least of our brethren" (Matt 18:40, 45) to the last speck of dust. The First Prayer in the baptismal service reads:

> The sun sings to you, the moon glorifies you, the stars meet in your presence, the light obeys you, the deep is filled by you. . . . We confess your grace; we proclaim your mercy; we do not conceal your benefits.

Through baptism, Nicholas Cabasilas writes in the fourteenth century, "God claims us for his own, and adopts us as divine children." We are God's own precious children. We know that "unless we become like little children we cannot enter the kingdom of heaven" (Matt 18:3-4). We believe, as Orthodox faithful chant in the Sunday vesperal *prokeimenon* of Great Lent, that God will "not turn his face away from his children." In the words of an early commentator on baptism: "Our sins cannot surpass the multitude of God's mercy; our wounds are not greater than his healing power."[5]

### c. The End: Resurrection Through Death

If baptism waters the seed of repentance, which the word of God has planted within us, it remains for us to nurture this seedling. If the

---

[4] *On Baptism,* in J.-P. Migne, *Patrologia Graeca* (henceforth PG) 65:1025.

[5] Cyril of Jerusalem, *On Repentance,* ch. 6.

pledge of the kingdom is offered to us from the very outset of our life, as in the case of infant baptism, the revelation of this promise demands response on our part. Nevertheless, there is a paradox in this corresponding action. Just as repentance does not begin with our determination to make changes in our lives, but with God's determination that we come to repentance (cf. Matt 9:13), so also repentance is not a matter of achievement, but of surrender. Repentance, like baptism, implies an act of faith. It requires unlearning self-centered behavior, undoing willfulness, and relinquishing self-conceit. It, too, is an act of risk and trust, a sacrifice and form of death.

This is precisely the reason why the Orthodox baptismal service begins with a series of exorcisms. In the past these marked the final act of the catechumenate; today they have become the prerequisite for those who desire the light and life of resurrection. Again the return is to the root of evil in the world and the renunciation of diabolical forces. Evil is not merely the absence of good. And exorcism is not simply a matter of clearing "negative" feelings. Evil is far more potent and important, requiring far more than merely positive thinking. It cannot be reduced to manageable proportions to be analyzed and addressed in therapy.

It is fitting that the word "evil" in English is the reverse of "live." Evil opposes life and the source of life. We must detect it in order to reject it; we must recognize it if we are to repent of it. It is true, of course, that Christ has shattered the gates of death and hell. Fundamentally, the war against evil has already been won; life has overcome death, good has triumphed over evil, "Christ has—truly—risen!" The final outcome is already known. Still, the enemy has not been annihilated and he continues to wreak havoc and inflict damage. The battle is not "against flesh and blood, but against principalities, against powers, against the rulers of the darkness of this age, against spiritual hosts of wickedness in the heavenly places" (Eph 6:12). The first step, then, is to confront evil at its source:

> The priest turns the person who is coming to baptism toward the west . . . and says: "Do you renounce Satan, and all his angels, and all his works, and all his services, and all his pride?" And the catechumen [or sponsor] answers, saying: "I do."

One cannot belong to Christ until one has renounced evil. In the Orthodox understanding this initial step should be taken as early as possible in life. Even toddlers know how to say "no." Their innate ability to say "no" is given so that one may learn to reject evil. Being involved personally in the struggle against evil in the world is one of the most radical ways by which a Christian grows in likeness to God. Christianity is not simply a life of spiritual comfort; it is a path of spiritual combat (Eph 6:11). It is this reality of evil that the church feels and faces as it stands before a new human being who has just entered this life in Christ, and on whom evil lays a claim not only in the soul but in one's entire being. The first act of repentance in baptism, then, is confrontation. Conversion is the next:

> The priest, turning [literally, "converting"] the catechumen to the east, says: "Do you unite yourself to Christ? And do you believe in Him?"

Confrontation and conversion are the necessary conditions for the third step, which is confession. The confession of faith is the last act of preparation for baptism. It testifies to one's thoughtful acceptance and willing obedience to the faith of the church and to Christ: The priest concludes: "Bow down before Christ, and worship Him." And the catechumen replies: "I bow down before the Father, the Son, and the Holy Spirit."

### d. Spiritual Direction: One Plus One Equals Infinity

One does not, however, achieve resurrection through death on one's own; one can neither confront evil nor confess God's grace alone. In order to receive healing grace, one needs to open up to at least one other person. In order to allow the divine Other into our life, we must allow another human being into the deepest recesses of our heart and mind, sharing every thought, emotion, insight, wound, and joy. This is not always easy in a world that teaches and encourages us from an early age to be self-sufficient and assertive, if not aggressive. Yet, in Orthodox spirituality, individual self-sufficiency is not the way of life. To the contrary, it resembles more the way of the demons.

People are relational, communal beings. We need one another, even to repent. Sin ruptures the "I-Thou" relationship with God and among human beings, and this same sacred relationship is the only way of return. The community of the church exists for this very purpose. In the sixth century Abba Dorotheus used an illustration of a compass to describe how our bonds with people affect our bond with God:

Suppose we were to take a compass and insert the point and draw
the outline of a circle. The center point is the same distance from any
point on the circumference. . . . Let us suppose that this circle is the
world and that God is the center; the straight lines drawn from the
circumference to the center are the lives of human beings.

In order to move toward God, says Dorotheos, human beings must
move from the circumference to life's center:

The closer they are to God, the closer they become to one another; and
the closer they are to one another, the closer they become to God. . . .
Such is the very nature of life. The more we are turned away from
and do not love God, the greater the distance that separates us from
our neighbor.[6]

"Human beings are God's language," according to a Hasidic saying.
In the spiritual elder the Orthodox Church offers someone with whom we
can share our heart, a benevolent companion who accompanies us on our
spiritual journey. The spiritual father or mother is a fellow traveler, not a
tour guide. The bond that forms can be very intense, the relationship very
intimate. When one mortal consults another in total sincerity and complete
openness, the depth of immortality is revealed to both. To paraphrase St.
John Climacus: "One [mortal] and one [mortal] make —not just two mor-
tals, but— immortality." In the spiritual life, one plus one equals infinity.
There is something healing and life-giving in the simple act of verbally
sharing one's private burden with one's elder. The rule in Orthodox spirituality is that doing by sharing is always better than doing alone.

So we learn repentance from another person, and such learning is
not optional. Salvation depends on it. Through consultation we learn to
let our burdens be borne by another person and, in the process, to bear
the burdens of others. We learn to be forgiven, and thereby also to forgive. We learn to be loved, and thus begin also to love others as well as
ourselves. Learning to accept the repentance of others is as critical and
healing as learning to repent ourselves. We are, after all, members one of
another. Clearly, repentance involves much more than simply remembering the past. Let us now consider how repenting implies "remembering"
in the sense of becoming again members of one another in God.

---

[6] See Eric P. Wheeler, trans., *Dorotheos of Gaza: Discourses and Sayings* (Kalamazoo: Cistercian Publications, 1977) 138–39.

### e. Community: Repentance as Re-membering

The church is the place where we confess and celebrate the fact that we are called, in our imperfection, to become merciful, "even as our Father who is in heaven" (cf. Matt 5:48, interpreted in the light of Luke 6:36). The church is the place where we are accepted as who we are and adopted as children of God. The church is the place, in our culture of individualism and loneliness, where dependency is validated and inter-dependency is valued. The church is the place with room enough for all, where all our faults are validated. Here we are welcomed and affirmed as children of God. Here we are encouraged to dwell "in the same space with one another," the literal meaning of the Greek word *syn-choresis*, forgiveness. Here earth becomes as roomy and spacious as heaven.

In the community of the church we learn to share weaknesses and shed tears, to love and to be loved. We recognize that we do not have to be perfect for people to welcome us. Repentance is the act of our reintegration into the healing body of the faithful, our way toward reconciliation with the "communion of saints." "Therefore," St. James encourages us, "confess your sins to one another . . . that you may be healed" (Jas 5:16). Forgiveness needs to be sought as well as given, accepted as well as offered.[7] In community we feel at home, speaking openly and freely. We begin to make sense of the voices of our parents and of our past. If we are wise enough to understand our limitations, and generous enough to share, and strong enough to forgive, then we are in a position to achieve wholeness. By widening "the gates of repentance" we can open the doors of paradise.[8]

This healing aspect of community further invites a sense of responsibility from us all. Interdependence acknowledges not only our dependence on God and on one another, but also God's reliance on us. We are required to assume responsibility as agents of forgiveness, as ministers of divine healing in the world. Forgiveness through repentance does not alienate us from the weaknesses of others, but in fact welcomes such weaknesses, for we are all responsible one for another. The author of *The Ladder of Divine Ascent*, John of Sinai, is quite clear on this:

> I have seen an infirm person who has, through faith, healed another's infirmity. . . . And as a result of the other's healing, his own

---

[7] Cf. C. S. Lewis, *The Problem of Pain* (New York: Macmillan, 1944) ch. 8.
[8] Hymn from the Sunday Matins of the Lenten or pre-Paschal period.

soul too was healed. . . . If God has redeemed you, then redeem others. . . . One who wipes away and cleans the impurity of others through the purity given to him by God . . . becomes like a coworker of the angels.[9]

St. Anthony expresses this succinctly when he says: "Our life and death lie with our brother and sister." A more recent saint, Silouan of Athos (d.1938), puts it more concisely: "Your brother is your life." We are saved together, by working out our salvation together as members of the body of Christ and as members of one another. How we relate with one another has everything to do with how we relate with God. As imperfect, perfected people, we have our only hope in the forgiveness God has made possible for us in Christ, and in offering that forgiveness to one another. As we recite in the Lord's Prayer: "Forgive us our debts as we forgive our debtors." We repent, ultimately, by forgiving.

### f. Repentant Sinners: Resurrection With Wounds

Repentance is the joy of the resurrection spilled over into our life. Yet it is not a way that is without complexity and pain. In this, we have—as the fifth-century *Sayings of the Desert Fathers* remind us—"Christ as our pledge, our example, and our prototype."[10] When Jesus appeared to Thomas after the resurrection, he did not show Thomas any healed and antiseptic scars. He said: "Put your finger here and see my hands. Reach out your hand and put it in my side. Do not doubt, but believe" (John 20:27).

The paradox of the crucified and risen Lord is that, when Jesus rose, he rose with his wounds; the paradox of repentance and healing is that we, too, rise with our wounds. We are not called to ignore our wounds in repentance; we are inspired to illumine them through the light of resurrection. In repentance, then, we are able to realize a resurrection of the heart before the final resurrection of the dead. The key to this mystery is given at the moment of our baptism, where we learn that repentance is not a denial or a disparagement of our past wounds and vulnerability. It is not a rejection of our own past, no matter how painful and broken this may have been. Resurrection is not abandonment of the cross, but reintegration of all crosses, reconciliation of all sinners, and incorporation

---

[9] *Treatise to the Shepherd,* chs. 76–79.
[10] Amma Theodora, *Saying* 10.

of all suffering. Where, before, we could only see a wasteland of pain, we can now witness crops watered by the grace of God.

God's grace is sufficient, his mercy infinitely greater than our sin. The light of his resurrection is able to dispel any darkness in our heart and in our world. The power of the resurrection alone can finally change this world. Christ's resurrection is the seed of new life, a life that is greater than sin, corruption, and death. This divine life can transform the cosmos into heaven. Repentance is at once the first steps and the first fruits of this process of transfiguration.

### g. To Repent is to Rejoice

Repentance precedes reconciliation and renewal. The whole host of reconciled sinners which form Christ's broken body cry in one voice with the Psalmist: "Have mercy upon me, O God, in accordance with your great mercy; according to the abundance of your compassion blot out my offense . . ." (Psalm 50). It is through the faith not simply of the repentant sinner but of the repentant community of sinners that the individual is readmitted and forgiven: "When Jesus saw their faith he said, 'your sins are forgiven'" (Luke 5:20). Repentance is a continual enactment of freedom, a bold movement forward leading toward greater spiritual liberty. To repent is "to accept with joy," in St. Isaac the Syrian's words, "the humility and humiliation of nature." The aim of repentance is not self-justification, but reentry into that consuming fire of love where all sin and imperfection and selfishness wither.

Yet one repents not because one is virtuous, but because human beings have the freedom and the power and the will to change with the help of God. What is impossible for us is possible for God. In the way of repentance, passions are conquered by greater passions, and desire by stronger desire. Just as the power of God is revealed in the extreme vulnerability of the Son on the Cross, so also the greatest strength and glory of the human being is manifested when one embraces one's weakness: "My strength is made perfect in weakness. Most gladly, therefore, will I render glory in my infirmities, that the power of Christ may rest upon the world" (2 Cor 12:9).

The Greek term for repentance, *metanoia*, denotes change of mind, reorientation, fundamental transformation of one's entire self-image and worldview. Repentance means a new way of loving. It involves not mere regret of past wrong but also recognition and reversal of a darkened vision and version of our own condition. As we repent we begin to see how sin, by dividing us from God and also from God's creation, has reduced us to a separated, pseudo-autonomous existence, depriving us of true freedom and divine glory. "This life," observes John Chrysostom, "is in truth wholly devoted to repentance, *penthos*, and tears. Thus it is necessary to repent, not merely for one or two days, but throughout one's life."[11]

In some mysterious way, my weakness, my helplessness is itself part of God's grace, a shadow that reveals the light of his countenance, a mask that conceals his very intimacy. Perhaps this is the reason for the wide variety of joyful expressions in which the words "Lord, have mercy" are chanted in all Orthodox services (once, thrice, twelve, and even forty times). These words are always chanted in joyful notes. By repeatedly singing *"Kyrie eleison"* we learn to be thankful instead of resentful, to express gratitude for who we are, to cease obsessing over ourselves, and to begin glorifying God, who alone can finally heal the wounds of sin and undo evil itself.

### h. The Two Dimensions of Repentance: Divine and Human

God in Christ has already assumed the initiative for reconciliation, but the fulfillment of Christ's sacrifice in our lives depends on our response. Openness to God is the precondition for God's dwelling within us. It marks our willing presence before God in the abundance of divine mercy, and God's willing presence before us in the abyss of his compassionate weakness: "Set your compassion over against our iniquities, and the abyss of your loving kindness against our transgression."[12]

We often ignore the connection between the confession of sins and the compassion of God. However, the Greek word for "confession" (*ex-omologesis*) suggests something more than accepting or acknowledging something. Beyond admitting a hitherto unacknowledged sin, to confess means to accept and submit to the divine Logos (*ex-omo-logesis*), who is beyond and above the nature and condition of humanity.[13] To repent and confess is not so much to recognize and expose a failure as it is to respond from within to the call of God in whose image and likeness every person is created.

---

[11] *On Spiritual Perfection* 4, PG 31:636. *On Compunction* I, i, PG 47:395 and I, ix, 47:408.

[12] First Prayer of Kneeling, Vespers at Pentecost.

[13] Cf. Archbishop Stylianos Harkianakis, "Repentance and Confession," *Akropolis Newspaper* (in Greek), Athens (April 10, 1980) 6.

"God is love" (1 John 4:8, 16), the Theologian John declares, implying simultaneously that love is the true being of humanity as well, created in the very image and likeness of God. "Out of extreme erotic love . . . the creator of all . . . moves outside Himself . . . burning with great goodness and love and eros. He . . . is the fullness of erotic love," Dionysius claims,[14] while St. Maximus notes that "As Lover, He creates; and as Lover He attracts all toward Himself."[15] "As mad lover," St. Nilus adds, "God desires the beloved human soul."[16] God is, therefore, not only at the end of the journey of repentance but also at the beginning (Rev 1:8). "In my end is my beginning," says the poet.[17] One seeks whom one already possesses. In all one's sinfulness, one is still loved by God. In the words of the Psalmist, "the mercy of God runs after us all the days of our lives . . . for His mercy endures forever" (Ps 26:6 and 135).

### i. The Sacrament of Tears

"Passion or [longing] for God gives rise to tears," teaches Theodoret.[18] There is an intimate link between repentance and tears. There are other criteria,[19] but *penthos* is essential. *Penthos* consists in mourning for the loss of God's presence. It entails sorrow at his absence and thirst for him. Etymologically, the terms *penthos* (mourning) and *pathos* (passion) stem from the Greek verb meaning "to suffer." Just as passion is subsumed in God, so is mourning. "Like a woman suffering in childbirth,"[20] the repentant soul cannot but mourn in the midst of regeneration. Gregory the Theologian considers tears an integral part of repentance: "All must shed tears, all must be purified, all must ascend."[21] Symeon the New Theologian is categorical: "Remove tears and with them you remove purification. Without purification no one is saved."[22]

Humanity is in a state of grief. Orthodox liturgy speaks of Adam sitting opposite paradise in mourning over his estrangement from God.

---

[14] Dionysius, *On the Divine Names* 4, 2, PG 3:712.

[15] Maximus, ibid., and *De Ambiguis*, PG 91:1260.

[16] *PG* 79:464.

[17] T. S. Eliot, *Four Quartets* (East Coker, 209).

[18] Theodoret of Cyrus, *Philotheos History* XXX, Domnina 2, *PG* 87:1493.

[19] John Climacus, *Ladder* 7, 25 and 48, PG 88:805 and 809.

[20] John Climacus, *Ladder* 7, 60, PG 88:813.

[21] *Oration* 19, 7, *PG* 35:1049–52.

[22] *Catechesis* 29.

The *Macarian Homilies* say that humanity must "weep its way back" to paradise.[23] Tears demonstrate the frontier between present and future. In the longing to return home from exile, tears are a sign of welcoming, a pledge of return, and a first fruit of its joy. In the Orthodox understanding this is conveyed by the expression "joyful sorrow," often used to characterize the quality of compunction in Orthodox icons, music, and worship. Joyful sorrow is the theological expression of resurrection through crucifixion, of life through death. "Blessed are they that mourn, for they shall be comforted," says our Lord (Matt 5:4). In a surprising way, those who fall into sin and then mourn are almost preferred to those who neither sin nor mourn. In the words again of the *Ladder* by John Climacus:

> I consider those fallen mourners more blessed than those who have not fallen and are not mourning over themselves; because as a result of their fall, they have risen by a sure resurrection.[24]

Repentance takes time; it moves at glacial speed. This is why the Orthodox Church connects repentance and baptism to ascetic toil and spiritual tears. Nonetheless, "blessed are those who mourn" (Matt 5:4). As in the case of St. Peter who broke down and "wept bitterly" (Matt 26:75), tears are a sign that we have begun to cross the frontier of repentance and enter into the vast expanse of holiness. Tears of repentance are a symbol both of mourning and of comfort. They are a sign at once of sins repented and of forgiveness received. We repent; therefore, we weep. We mourn; therefore, we heal.

### j. The Sacrament of Confession

Repentance is a dynamic act of responsibility to God and to others. Although it implies self-knowledge and self-examination, it is not a matter of pining away in narcissistic self-absorption. Sin itself is a relational rupture, a fissure in the "I-Thou" relationship. When the prodigal son "came to himself" in the gospel parable (Luke 15), he did so in recollection and in relation to his father: "I will arise and go to my father, and will

---

[23] Homily XV, 17. Cf. *Kontakion* and *Oikos* of Cheesefare Sunday in *Triodion Katanyktikon* (Rome, 1879) 105. Cf. also the prose poem by Staretz Silouan in Archim. Sophrony, *Wisdom from Mt Athos* (London: Mowbrays, 1974) 47–55.

[24] Step 5,5; *PG* 88: 776B.

say to him, 'Father, I have sinned against heaven and before you'" (v. 18). We repent in the face of God and in communion with others. Repentance in the early church was a solemn public act of reconciliation, through which a sinner was readmitted into the worshiping community (cf. Matt 3:6; Acts 19:18). Confession, therefore, takes place *within the church*.

The supreme act of community is the Eucharist, the communal sharing in Christ's broken body and spilt blood, which he offers "unto the forgiveness of sins and life eternal." The Eucharist celebrates, manifests, and advances the reconciliation of all in Christ. So the eucharistic prayers contain penitential elements in preparation for communion.[25] Conversely, many Christian writers, as, for example, the influential third-century Alexandrian theologian, Origen, emphasize the significance of the Eucharist for the forgiveness of sin.[26]

Perhaps the eucharistic aspect of repentance and confession was more apparent in the early church when penance constituted a public rather than a private act.[27] It was only after the fourth century that private confession was widely practiced.[28] Even then, penance lacked the legalistic and ritualistic character it later acquired.[29] Very few church fathers make reference to absolution as a formal procedure. What is even more unheard of in patristic literature is the reduction of sin to a punishable legal crime inviting a penalty.[30] St. John Chrysostom is typical in this regard. "Have you committed a sin?" he asks, "Then enter the Church and repent of your sin. . . . For here is the Physician, not the Judge; here one is not investigated but receives remission of sins."[31]

---

[25] Cf. Franz Nikolasch, "The Sacrament of Penance: Learning from the East," *Concilium* 1,7 (1971) 65–75.

[26] *On Prayer* 28, PG 11:528–29.

[27] See *Apostolic Constitutions* 8, 8-9; Gregory of Neocaesaria, *Canon* XII. For confession before a spiritual father, cf. Socrates, *Ecclesiastical History* 5, 19 and 7, 16; John Chrysostom, *Sermon 4 on Lazarus*, PG 48:1012.

[28] For a detailed description of this order see Nicholas Uspensky, *Evening Worship in the Orthodox Church*, trans. and ed. Paul Lazor (New York: St. Vladimir's Seminary Press, 1985) 22.

[29] The earliest extant order of confession, ascribed to John the Faster, Patriarch of Constantinople, is of relatively late origin (10th century). This text may well be the source of later Greek and Slavonic services of Confession.

[30] Cf. John Meyendorff, *Byzantine Theology: Historical Trends and Doctrinal Themes* (New York: Fordham University Press, 1974) 195.

[31] *On Repentance* 3,1, PG 49:292.

Unfortunately confession has sometimes been used—or rather, mis-used—in a way that undermines genuine inner repentance. Perhaps this is a result of the sacrament being narrowly and juridically reduced to a matter of "absolution." The concept repentance is not some forensic idiom, with the emphasis on the priest's power to absolve. In the Or-thodox tradition the priest is seen as a witness of repentance, not as a detective of misdeeds or a recipient of private secrets. The minister is not some power-wielding, forgiveness-dispensing authority. Such mis-conceptions externalize and distort the function of the confessor and the sacrament of confession, which is to be an act of reintegration *of penitent and priest alike* into the Body of Christ.

The declaration, "I, an unworthy priest, by the power given unto me, absolve you," is unknown in the penitential rites of the Orthodox Church. The practice is of later Latin origin, and was adopted only in certain Russian liturgical books in an era when Franco-Latin thought and practice unduly influenced Russian Orthodox theology.[32] The emphasis on "power" served to bring confession into disrepute, turning it into a procedure of justification and exculpation with respect to otherwise punishable offenses. By contrast, the typical Orthodox prayer of absolu-tion witnesses to faith in the mercy and forgiveness of God. Absolution or forgiveness is not "administered" by the priest or the bishop. It is a freely given grace of God, offered within and through the Body of Christ, "for the life of the world."

The most significant effect of confession is due neither to the penance itself nor to the penitent, but to God who "heals the brokenhearted and binds up their wounds" (Ps 147:3). It is not a matter of clearing any moral debt. It is about making the penitent whole and holy. Such healing can only come as a gift. "Let us apply to ourselves the saving medicine of repentance," says Chrysostom. "Let us accept from God the repentance that heals us. For it is not we who offer it to Him, but He who bestows it upon us."[33] This is conveyed in the Greek word for confession, *exo-mologesis*, which further implies an act of thanksgiving (cf. Matt 11:25; Luke 10:21): "I shall confess to the Lord with my whole heart, and tell of all his wonders" (Ps 9:11).

[32] Cf. Alexander Schmemann, *Confession and Communion: A Report* (New York: 1972) 13–16.

[33] John Chrysostom, *On Repentance* 7, 3, PG 49:327.

## k. Repentance and Guilt: Concluding Remarks

Reference has been made to the cloud of *guilt*, which at times shrouds the sacrament of confession. Guilt is part of the human condition and tragedy. We all experience guilt in the wake of mistakes and in the face of appalling misery for which we all share a degree of responsibility. Yet in the specific context of repentance, guilt is a highly misleading emotion.

There is no mention in Scripture of the word "guilt" *(enochē) per se*, although the adjective "guilty" *(enochos)* is occasionally used. Instead of "guilt," Scripture and the church prefer to speak of sin *(hamartia)*, which implies failure, loss, a breakup in relations. Even the root verb of the term for "guilty" *(enechomai)* implies, in the Greek, a positive bond of holding fast within, or cherishing, as distinct from being ashamed in the face of a deity who inflicts retributive punishment.

The distorted emphasis on guilt originated within a hypertrophied, individualistic culture, with its self-regarding view of sin and repentance and its attendant, legalistically oriented penitential system. Orthodoxy, when it has been most true to itself and to the gospel, has always resisted any form of individualism and legalism whether in repentance or in confession or canonical application. The Orthodox Church eschews both undue confidence in one's achievement or merit and the overharsh sense of guilt for one's failures. The latter is another way of being centered upon oneself and seeking for some means to propitiate a wrathful deity. The Christian view of humanity is largely a social one. Where there is a breakdown in personal love and a rise in impersonalism or institutionalism, one finds a thickening of the atmosphere of guilt.

According to the spiritual teaching of the Orthodox Church, God declares His love for human beings alike at their greatest extreme and worst disgrace, indeed perhaps especially at their most extreme weakness: "While we were still sinners, Christ died for us" (Rom 5:18). God does not turn from our sins, but rather meets us precisely there. Thus God's identification with humanity and loving acceptance of us makes repentance and confession not a desperate bargaining for forgiveness but a personal celebration of what God has already accomplished for us in Christ and of the life abundantly shared with us by Christ:

> There is therefore now no condemnation for those who are in Christ Jesus, who do not walk according to the flesh, but according to the Spirit. For the law of the Spirit of life in Christ Jesus has made me free from the law of sin and death. (Rom 8:12)

## 2. Implications

Orthodox Christians may not always be aware of the depth of the central spiritual dimensions of repentance and confession within their tradition. Over the centuries Orthodox Christians have sometimes been overwhelmed by legalistic elements pertaining to this sacrament, such as the validity of forgiveness or the precise definition of particular sins. This has created a barrier with regard to proclaiming the importance of repentance through confession, since people have avoided or even dreaded the ritual of confession, considering it at best a pious obligation on several occasions of the year, especially Great Lent.

At other times they have been distracted by peripheral elements of the sacrament, such as the number of times one should confess prior to Communion or even the choice of person who should receive one's confession. They have been variously admonished by their priests about the frequency of confession or advised about the necessity of confession as a license to receive Communion. This has led to a fundamentalist attitude to repentance and confession, which has again restricted its general espousal by the faithful.

Nevertheless, the prevailing Pauline notion that "where sin increased, there grace abounded all the more" (Rom 5:20) provided the general framework for a tradition of Patristic emphasis on a divine compassion that embraces all people at all times. Even during periods when Orthodox Christians leaned toward a narrower understanding of repentance and confession, they continued to be a part of a celebration of divine grace that redeems through Jesus Christ and restores all creation.

## 3. Further Reading

Cabasilas, Nicholas. *On the Life in Christ.* New York: St. Vladimir's Seminary Press, 1974.

Chryssavgis, John. *John Climacus, From the Egyptian Desert to the Sinaite Mountain.* London: Ashgate, 2004.

_____. *Repentance and Confession in the Orthodox Church.* Brookline: Holy Cross Orthodox Press, 1990.

_____. *Soul Mending: The Art of Spiritual Direction.* Brookline: Holy Cross Orthodox Press, 2000.

Colliander, Tito. *Way of the Ascetics: The Ancient Tradition of Discipline and Inner Growth.* New York: St. Vladimir's Seminary Press, 1985.

*Philokalia: The Complete Text.* 5 vols. Trans. G. E. H. Palmer, Philip Sherrard, and
    Kallistos Ware. Boston: Faber and Faber, 1979– (4 volumes to date).
Schmemann, Alexander. *For the Life of the World: Sacraments and Orthodoxy.* New
    York: St. Vladimir's Seminary Press, 1973.
_____. *Of Water and the Spirit: A Liturgical Study of Baptism.* New York: St. Vlad-
    imir's Seminary Press, 1974.
Ware, Kallistos. *The Orthodox Church.* Rev. ed. London: Penguin Books, 1993.
_____. *The Orthodox Way.* New York: St. Vladimir's Seminary Press, 1980.

## 4. Hermeneutical Reflection

The neglected communal dimension of repentance is clearly evident in peoples of covenant, suffering, and song. It comes as no surprise that the communal element is a central part of the Torah, as indeed it is for the African/African American experience. There, in the people of the land, greater emphasis is placed on the divine initiative than on any human response. Divine compassion is underlined, while human confession is undermined. When you are convinced of God's love for a community—above and beyond your own weaknesses and shortcomings—what else can you do but sing? It is no wonder, then, that the people of Israel and the Africans of America define their roots in a loving God by singing psalms and spirituals.

In the long course of their distinct, yet parallel journeys, the Jews and the African Americans lost almost everything. Yet they knew that they could never lose their souls, irrespective of how far they had journeyed from God, irrespective of how unfaithful they had been to their God. The conviction was that God always loves, that God is always there, Emmanuel. So they never lost their hope. Perhaps that is why they always sang. This song of repentance was a tribute to their joys and sorrows, their peace and trials, their wandering and their wisdom, ultimately of their God. When you understand that, no matter how few or how small you are, you are never alone, all you can do is sing! Then, with all one's voice, one chants: "Have mercy on me, O God, according to your steadfast love; and according to your abundant mercy . . . wash me and cleanse me" (Ps 51:1-2).

The fact that repentance and confession are closely connected with the sacrament of baptism, in the Catholic and Reformed traditions alike, reveals that these have never been understood as a mere act, but as an attitude. Furthermore, from the very outset of the practice of the Christian rite of initiation, repentance and confession constitute not merely an end but a beginning. Finally, whether considered a return through self-examination or a renewal through a festival of tears (Johns, quoting an early Patristic text), confession and repentance are considered a journey and not simply a stage. The experience and expression of repentance and confession in monastic circles of the early church (Horn) and through the centuries only serves to underscore this truth.

These trajectories comprise the overarching link in the diverse conceptions of repentance in Scripture and through the ages. To me, the articles in this volume indicate that there is nothing unique about the way repentance is viewed in different traditions, whether by the prophets of the Old Testament or the Synoptics of the New Testament. Moreover, in spite of a tendency toward "distinctive confessional identities" (Rittgers), each tradition perceives repentance and confession as a radical change and a bearing of fruit. Each endeavors to render God's love and justice a reality and to reconcile this with the reality of human frailty and failure.

Whether there has been through the centuries a general disapproval or even a gradual "disappearance" (Smith, quoting Hestenes) of confession, whether there is a shift that has occurred in the scope of confession from the notions of conversion, penance, and forgiveness to the notions of confession as reconciliation (Del Colle), and even whether there is an emphasis on the distinction between various kinds of sin (mortal and venial), the Christian churches have struggled to discern and discover ways of responding to God's grace (Purves). Both the medieval development of the sacrament of confession as rite and the Protestant reaction to extremes thereof are reflections of a church continually struggling to keep together the two poles of the individual and the communal within a world that is "already" a part and yet "not yet" a part of the heavenly kingdom.

Eleven

# Life as a Holy Penitent:
# The Catholic Call to Conversion

*Ralph Del Colle*

## 1. Tradition

It is no accident that the indulgence controversy that sparked the Protestant Reformation had much to do with the notion and practice of penance in the Catholic Church of the late Middle Ages. The reforming Council of Trent was mindful of this as well. In its efforts to clarify Catholic doctrine, reform ecclesiastical structures, excise abuses, and renew the practice of the faith, penance and its associate notions— cooperative grace, merit, contrition, satisfaction—were strongly affirmed and set the framework for Catholic doctrine and practice. In essence it promoted the integrative understanding of penance as essential to the salvation of the just. This requires the engagement of human agency in the transformation effected by grace, which is initiated in justification and bears fruit in sanctity either in this life or, if necessary, in the life to come, viz., the Catholic doctrine of purgatory.

I begin with this reference to the Tridentine account of Catholic doctrine in order to underscore the distinctive Catholic understanding of penance when it was most sharply contested in the Western church. This is not to deny the progress that has been made in ecumenism, most notably since the Second Vatican Council, or the advances in doctrinal understanding that have emerged. I am especially mindful of the Catholic/Lutheran *Joint*

*Declaration on the Doctrine of Justification,* which attempts to find common ground on that doctrine and which was the object of Protestant critique and Evangelical reform in the sixteenth century. However, especially in regard to penance a recent event in ecumenical relations is particularly instructive.

The refusal by the World Alliance of Reformed Churches (WARC) to attend the Great Jubilee 2000 celebration in Rome soon after the signing of the Joint Declaration because of the promulgation by the Roman Curia of a new document on indulgences (granting them for the Holy Year Celebration)[1] was at the time an unexpected blow to ecumenical relations. Subsequent meetings between the two communions (along with Lutherans) were held to clarify the matter. My intent here is not to be polemical or to engage in classic controversial theology over confessional differences. It is simply to illuminate the Catholic understanding of penance so as to avoid these misunderstandings. Therefore I will draw primarily upon magisterial documents rather than the work of theologians. If the Joint Declaration does not obviate the Catholic practice of indulgences, as perhaps WARC thought it should have, then the post–Vatican II Catholic understanding of penance—consider the postconciliar liturgical reforms of the Rite of Penance—does not undermine the Tridentine decree and canons on the sacrament either. Therefore, my purpose in this essay is to examine the Catholic theology of penance using the sacrament of penance/reconciliation as a focus. I will also take into account non- or extra-sacramental expressions of penance that inform Catholic ecclesial and Christian life.

The sacrament of penance presupposes the penitential dimensions of Christian and ecclesial life. The fourteenth session of the Council of Trent, meeting in 1551, dealt in part with the sacraments of penance and extreme unction. Introducing the latter, the Council had this to say:

> It has seemed good to the holy council to add to the preceding doctrine on penance the following concerning the sacrament of extreme unction, which was considered by the Fathers as the completion not only of penance but also of the whole Christian life, which ought to be a continual penance.[2]

[1] The Apostolic Pentitentiary issued the indulgence according to the will of Pope John Paul II as expressed in the *Bull of Indiction of the Great Jubilee of the Year 2000, Incarnationis Mysterium,* November 29, 1998. I shall return to the indulgence and its relationship to penance later in this essay.

[2] *The Canons and Decrees of the Council of Trent,* trans. H. J. Schroeder, o.p. (Rockford, IL: Tan, 1978) 99.

The call to "continual penance" is the continuation of the conversion that takes place in baptism or, as the *Catechism of the Catholic Church (CCC)* puts it, the "conversion of the baptized."[3]

In designating the sacrament of penance (its most common designation in the *Catechism*) the CCC also calls it the *"sacrament of conversion,"* the *"sacrament of confession,"* the *"sacrament of forgiveness,"* and the *"sacrament of reconciliation."*[4] Each is intended to illuminate a dimension of the sacrament relevant to its understanding and practice. Penance "consecrates the Christian sinner's personal and ecclesial steps of conversion, penance and satisfaction." Conversion "makes sacramentally present Jesus' call to conversion." Confession, which entails the "disclosure or confession of sins to a priest," is also an "acknowledgment and praise . . . of the holiness of God and of his mercy toward sinful man." Forgiveness "grants the penitent pardon and peace," while Reconciliation "imparts to the sinner the love of God who reconciles."[5] Each of these constitutes an aspect of penance in both its sacramental and nonsacramental expressions. I shall initially concentrate on conversion, since this links the sacrament of Penance and the penitential life to both baptism and Christian life. It is also essential to the development of any Christian spirituality.

Baptism is the initial site of conversion, "first and fundamental conversion."[6] In a tradition that does not exclude exterior signs of repentance the emphasis is first on the interior. Conversion of the heart embraces what "the Fathers called *animi cruciatis* (affliction of spirit) and *compunctio cordis* (repentance of heart)," in other words, that conviction by which the need for a new heart is understood to be the only solution to a heart "heavy and hardened" by sin.[7] It is described as "a radical reorientation of our whole life, a return, a conversion to God with all our heart, an end to sin, a turning away from evil, with repugnance toward the evil actions we have committed."[8] Such conversion of heart is not possible apart from the christological and pneumatological dimensions of conversion. Looking upon the one whom our sins pierced grants repentance, the

---

[3] All quotations are taken from the *Catechism of the Catholic Church with modifications from the Editio Typica* (New York: Doubleday, 1995, 1997). Paragraph rather than page numbers are given. Henceforth, as in this reference: CCC, 1427.

[4] CCC, 1423–1424.

[5] Ibid.

[6] CCC, 1427.

[7] CCC, 1431–1432.

[8] Ibid.

grace of which is given by the Consoler.[9] Only then may we speak—and interior conversion urges this—of "visible signs, gestures and works of penance."[10]

Clearly the model here is of adult conversion to the faith. Methodologically this is the primary way to examine conversion and the theology of grace. Not only does the *Catechism* employ this model, it has also been instantiated liturgically in the priority now given in the theology of baptism to the Rite of Christian Initiation of Adults (RCIA). This is not new. Treatises on grace presupposed its operation in adult Christians, and the Council of Trent in its *Decree Concerning Justification* entitled one of its chapters "The Necessity of Preparation for Justification in Adults and Whence it Proceeds."[11] Therefore we have the more precise description of how by God's "quickening and helping grace" one is able to convert oneself to one's own justification. This passage deserves more attention in regard to the theology of grace that underlies conversion and penance. Before we proceed further, however, a brief commentary on the priority of the adult model for theological explication is necessary.

The explanatory regime is clearly broader when our subjects are adults rather than children, especially infants. We can describe the working of grace relative to human response in reference to the former more easily than to the latter. This indeed we shall do precisely to illustrate how both divine and human agency are involved in the Catholic practice of penance. However, this is not to deny that grace is operative in all baptisms, including padeo-baptism. I say this to emphasize that such grace is indeed the grace of regeneration. Therefore children already cleansed of original sin will undergo conversion and penance through the ongoing catechesis they will experience along with the reception of the sacraments at the appropriate age—usually in the order of Penance, First Communion, Confirmation. This does not mean, as in some other Christian traditions, that the first conscious experience of conversion is the grace of regeneration for the Christian who was baptized as an infant. Rather, it may be a restoration to grace or simply a deeper consecration to the Lord and his service. With this clarification I now return to the theology of grace underlying justification and ongoing conversion in the Christian life.

---

[9] *CCC*, 1432–1433.

[10] Ibid. 1430.

[11] *The Canons and Decrees of the Council of Trent,* 31.

The passage to which I earlier referred is best quoted in full.

> It is furthermore declared that in adults the beginning of that justifica-
> tion must proceed from the predisposing grace of God through Jesus
> Christ, that is, from His vocation, whereby, without any merits on
> their parts, they are called; that they who by sin had been cut off from
> God, may be disposed through His quickening and helping grace to
> convert themselves to their own justification by freely assenting to and
> cooperating with that grace; so that, while God touches the heart of
> man through the illumination of the Holy Ghost, man himself neither
> does absolutely nothing while receiving that inspiration, since he can
> also reject it, nor yet is he able by his own free will and without the
> grace of God to move himself to justice in His sight.[12]

The following chapter in the decree continues with the specific manner of preparation for first conversion. The decision to receive baptism
and begin a new life in obedience to God's commandments must be
preceded by repentance, a process by which the sinner moves freely
toward God and in recognition of one's sinfulness turns from fear of
the divine justice to hope and trust in God's mercy.[13] What begins in
the movement of the heart, initiated by grace and free in its cooperation
with grace, issues in the exterior acts of repentance and the reception of
baptism, the instrument through which God justifies.[14]

The same pattern continues throughout the Christian life. The movement of God's grace—that is, God's action in the Holy Spirit—quickens
and helps our human faculties and thereby enables our assent and cooperation. Between doing nothing and moving oneself by free will alone

---

[12] Ibid. 31-32.

[13] Ibid. 32.

[14] Chapter VII of Trent's *Decree Concerning Justification* lists the various causes
of justification. Its final cause is the glory of God and Christ. The efficient cause
is the merciful God who washes and sanctifies with the Holy Spirit. The meritorious cause is the Lord Jesus Christ in his satisfaction made to the Father upon
the cross. The instrumental cause is baptism, the sacrament of faith, and the
formal cause is the justice of God by which he makes us just, thus receiving justice within us "according to each one's disposition and cooperation." The point
relevant to our purposes is that human agency is taken up by divine agency
in the mode and extent to which the sinner is actually made just. "Justification
. . . is not only a remission of sins but also the sanctification and renewal of the
inward man." Ibid. 33.

lies the supernatural organ of the divine economy in human salvation. God moves one so that one in grace is able to move oneself to justice—by grace preceding, accompanying, and following one's actions. Justification establishes the rectitude of divine love in the heart of the new believer, imparting faith, hope, and love (the theological virtues) and in so doing grants obedience to the divine will.[15]

In classical scholastic treatises on grace much is made of the distinction between actual grace and sanctifying grace. For our purposes we need note only several points relevant to the practice of penance that embraces human agency as salutary for the believer. Actual grace is that transient divine assistance that quickens and helps the believer in pursuit of the supernatural end of salvation. By strengthening and enlightening the human faculties it enables one to perform those acts that constitute the repentance of first conversion. Sanctifying or deifying grace is the designation for this divine working that heals and makes holy, and may be defined as "an habitual gift, a stable and supernatural disposition that perfects the soul itself to enable it to live with God, to act by his love."[16] In other words, as a habit it renders the person pleasing to God—the inhering righteousness that justifies the sinner—at the level of a person's being. In this respect actual grace serves as a means relative to the end of sanctifying grace, that permanent disposition by which the believer is actually made holy in fulfillment of the divine call and one's salvific end.

As we shall see, penance is intended to have a sanative and reparative effect in the believer's life in personal sanctification and in the communion that is the church. The theology of grace just rehearsed ensures from a Catholic perspective that the supernatural end of the divine economy is attained by the supernatural means of grace transforming the human subject in being and actions. Only within this framework can we understand the importance of penance in the ongoing life of discipleship and holiness. Sanctification strictly speaking is the increase of justification. Having been justified, one advances from virtue to virtue, increasing the inhering justice of sanctifying grace through the theological virtues of faith, hope, and love, leading to the cooperation of the person with grace in good works. Trent even links this with the doxological posture of the church, again with the operation of grace manifested in virtue:

[15] *CCC*, 1991.
[16] Ibid. 2000.

"This increase of justice holy Church asks for when she prays: 'Give unto us, O Lord, an increase of faith, hope and charity.'"[17]

It is perhaps the concept of merit in the Catholic doctrine of justification that historically has presented the most difficulty to Protestants. However, it is entirely consistent with the notions of the increase of justification and human cooperation in grace. Citing St. Augustine, the *Catechism of the Catholic Church* clearly understands merit as a further and more magnificent instance of God's grace: "You are glorified in the assembly of your Holy Ones, for in crowning their merits you are crowning your own gifts."[18] Merit is the increase of justice in the believer by cooperative grace. Being "[m]oved by the Holy Spirit and charity, *we can then merit for ourselves and others the graces needed for our sanctification, for the increase of grace and charity, and for the attainment of eternal life.*"[19] This does not deny the gratuity of salvation. In fact, it increases it since "*God has freely chosen to associate man with the work of his grace.*"[20] Such collaboration highlights the efficacy of divine grace and still requires in all human meritorious work "the predispositions and assistance given by the Holy Spirit."[21] In light of this understanding of grace we turn more directly to the practice of penance in the Catholic tradition.

The practice of penance has a focal point in the sacrament of Penance but it permeates many if not all dimensions of Catholic life. Spiritual and liturgical expressions of penitence abound along with the sacramental. Interior repentance, the conversion of the heart already referred to, is essential to penance and generates various forms of outward expression. In fact, the principle of sacramentality that so informs Catholic ecclesiology and spirituality presupposes the integral nature of the human person. The enactment of spiritual realities in and through our psychosomatic existence bespeaks a foundational anthropology derived from the formative Christian doctrines of creation, incarnation, and the resurrection of the dead. Protology, soteriology, and eschatology require that the efficacy of grace find expression in creaturely modalities. Sanctifying grace can also be described as a created supernatural entitative habit. To refer again briefly to the theology of grace, we should distinguish between the efficient and formal causes of justification, recalling also that sanctification is

---

[17] *The Canons and Decrees of the Council of Trent*, 36.
[18] *CCC*, 2006.
[19] Ibid. 2010.
[20] Ibid. 2008.
[21] Ibid.

the increase of justification. The Holy Spirit is the efficient cause and sanctifying grace is the formal cause. The Holy Spirit (or uncreated grace) is not to be identified with sanctifying grace, the gift that the Spirit imparts. Because the latter really inheres in the soul—the Holy Spirit inhabits or indwells the soul—the person is justified because it is that inherence that actually and in reality makes the person just. All of this is to suggest that the actions of the graced person, of which penance is a premier example, are indeed created (but also supernatural) expressions of the divine life offered in salvation. Human agency is taken up into divine agency as the person works out one's salvation in fear and trembling because God is at work in us (Phil 2:12).

With these caveats in mind we may say that the expressions or enactments of penance—the latter ensuring the notion that operation of grace effects created dispositions and operations—are varied and extensive. A nonexhaustive list from the *Catechism of the Catholic Church* is quite instructive. It includes fasting, prayer, almsgiving, efforts at reconciliation with one's neighbor, tears of repentance, concern for the salvation of one's neighbor, the intercession of the saints, the practice of charity, gestures of reconciliation, concern for the poor, the exercise and defense of justice and right, admission of faults to one's brethren, fraternal correction, revision of life, examination of conscience, spiritual direction, acceptance of suffering, endurance of persecution for the sake of righteousness, and the taking up of one's cross each day and following Jesus.[22] The habits of the spiritual life—"every sincere act of worship and devotion"—such as prayer and reading Sacred Scripture "[revive] the spirit of conversion and repentance within us and [contribute] to the forgiveness of our sins."[23] Additionally, there are liturgical times of penance that are intended to intensify penitential practice. Primary among these are the regular annual season of Lent and the weekly observance of each Friday as a day of penance in which the death of the Lord is remembered.[24] Most especially there is a close association between the Eucharist and penance. Not only does the Eucharist begin with a penitential rite (as do other liturgical rites) but "[d]aily conversion and penance find their source and nourishment in the Eucharist" wherein the sacrifice of Christ is made present.[25]

[22] Ibid. 1434–1435.
[23] Ibid. 1437.
[24] Ibid. 1438.
[25] Ibid. 1436.

I have leaned heavily on the *Catechism of the Catholic Church* in order to illustrate the scope of penance that is intended to be communicated to the faithful, which if anything is more descriptive of practices prevalent in the Catholic tradition than providing a new prescription. Nevertheless, its catechetical intent should not be downplayed and the renewal of Christian life depends on it. One could add other Catholic penitential expressions as well. They include two in particular. First, many traditional devotional practices possess a penitential cast. They seek to express penance or reparation in the act of devotional attention to Christ, Mary, the saints, or some dimension of salvation history. In other words, they are intended to foster through prayer a posture and attitude of virtue in the Christian life. One example may suffice. Devotions to the Sacred Heart of Jesus sometimes include an act of reparation, "a prayer with which the faithful, mindful of the infinite goodness of Christ, implore mercy for the offences committed in so many ways against his Sacred Heart."[26]

Second, some spiritualities in the history of the church are particularly penitential in character (even though any Christian spirituality must of necessity include a penitential dimension). The penitential acts of many a saint are part and parcel of the tradition and penitential practices have often been embraced and mandated for those in consecrated life. Classical spirituality has also emphasized the purgative way as the first stage in the spiritual life, eventually leading to the illuminative and unitive dimensions. However, the emphasis on penance by some can be quite distinctive, especially for those whose charism focused on union with Christ crucified, the most obvious examples being those who bore the name: the reformed Carmelite, St. John of the Cross, and St. Paul of the Cross, the founder of the Passionists.

In the sacramental economy of the church the sacrament of penance has emerged as the preeminent liturgical act for ongoing conversion and encounter with Christ in the specificity of forgiveness and reconciliation. This is not to deny that such is the case in an even more preeminent manner in the Eucharist through the real and substantial presence of Christ in sacrifice and communion. It is simply to acknowledge the particularity of the grace that is imparted in the sacrament of reconciliation or penance. While we need not review the entire history of the sacrament, it is

---

[26] *Directory On Popular Piety and the Liturgy: Principles and Guidelines* promulgated by the Congregation for Divine Worship and the Discipline of the Sacraments (Boston: Pauline Books & Media, 2002) 123 (#171).

important to realize that its present structure reflects an emphasis that moves from the public practice of penance before a bishop—Penance as "the second plank [of salvation] after the shipwreck which is the loss of grace"[27]—to the private but still ecclesial confession of sins to a priest followed by absolution and a penance or satisfaction that is required of the penitent. I shall concentrate on the present form of the sacrament while highlighting some of the reforms in the ritual since the Second Vatican Council.

It is important to distinguish between the canonical requirements of the sacrament and its wider use as an instrument of devotion and ongoing conversion by the faithful. The strict obligation of Penance demands that one confess one's grave sins at least once a year, and if there is any grave sin it is necessary to confess when possible before the reception of Holy Communion.[28] All Catholics are required to receive Holy Communion at least once a year, usually during the Easter season.[29] Needless to say, a more frequent reception of both sacraments is encouraged and for the most part practiced by the devout. I will presume the latter in order to explicate the nature and benefits of the sacraments for a healthy and fruitful spiritual life.[30] I will begin with the nature of sin and the distinction made by Catholics between mortal or grave sins and those that are venial.

The sacrament of penance is intended to deal with sins committed after baptism. All sins are forgiven in baptism, both original sin and personal sins. The former, contracted from Adam, is cleansed in baptism, meaning that the loss of original holiness and justice is restored through the washing of regeneration as well as the guilt of original sin being remitted. Likewise all personal sins are forgiven along with all punishment due to sin. The latter must be explained, since this effect of sin is important for the sacrament of penance.

In the tradition this is known as the temporal punishment of sin and is to be distinguished from the eternal punishment of sin. The latter may be described as the guilt of sin that is remitted when forgiveness is offered, true for both Baptism and Penance (as we shall see). The former, however, while forgiven in Baptism, remains after the absolution in

---

[27] *CCC*, 1446 (quoting Tertullian).

[28] Canon 989 of the *Code of Canon Law*.

[29] Canon 920.

[30] In fact, Canon 988 of the *Code of Canon Law* recommends the use of the sacrament for the confession of venial sins. Also *CCC*, 1458.

Penance (to which we shall return). Eternal punishment deprives one of communion with God and therefore makes one incapable of eternal life.[31] Temporal punishment, on the other hand, consists of the effects of sin, that which by the commission of sin distorts a person's habits and reinforces the tendency to sin known as concupiscence. Concupiscence, which remains after baptism, is not sin itself—tendencies toward sin require the assent of the will to sin—but becomes the site for growth in holiness summoning one to spiritual battle.[32] Temporal punishment as an effect of venial sin does not deprive one of communion with God but certainly hinders it, or at the very least, inhibits a life in grace and growth in virtue. The need here is not forgiveness but purification, to allow God's grace to heal the person of these effects of sin.

The distinction between mortal or grave sin and venial sin is therefore quite important.[33] Mortal sin destroys charity, kills the supernatural life that grace imparts, and is therefore deserving of eternal punishment. It always concerns a grave matter and must be committed with "full knowledge and deliberate consent."[34] Therefore, while culpability may vary depending on the coalescence of these factors, the possibility exists that a believer may so sin that eternal life is lost even though faith may remain.[35] In these instances the confession of sins in the sacrament of Penance is necessary for salvation. Venial sin, on the other hand, by way

[31] *CCC,* 1472.

[32] Ibid. 405.

[33] The distinction between mortal and grave sin is not always clear. The *Catechism of the Catholic Church* only distinguishes between mortal and venial sins. *Reconciliatio et Paenitentia,* Pope John Paul II's Post-Synodal Apostolic Exhortation "On Reconciliation and Penance in the Mission of the Church Today" (henceforth *RP*), mentions that some Fathers at the Synod Assembly of Bishops had recommended a threefold distinction of sins into venial, grave, and mortal. The Pope's response was to suggest that this "might illustrate the fact that there is a scale of seriousness among grave sins," but that "it still remains true that the essential and decisive distinction is between sin which destroys charity, and sin which does not kill the supernatural life: there is no middle way between life and death." *RP* 17.

[34] *CCC,* 1857.

[35] Trent's *Decree Concerning Justification* is very clear on the matter. Canon 28 states: "If anyone says that with the loss of grace through sin faith is also lost with it, or that faith which remains is not a true faith, though it is not a living one, or that he who has faith without charity is not a Christian, let him be anathema." *The Canons and Decrees of the Council of Trent,* 45.

of contrast with mortal sin (in the words of Pope John Paul II) "does not deprive the sinner of sanctifying grace, friendship with God, charity, and therefore eternal happiness, whereas just such a deprivation is precisely the consequence of mortal sin."[36] It nevertheless "weakens charity . . . manifests a disordered affection for created goods . . . impedes the soul's progress in the exercise of the virtues and the practice of the moral good . . . [and] merits temporal punishment."[37]

The distinction of sins is significant not only because it sets the parameters for the necessity of the sacrament of penance, but also because it helps inform both penitent and confessor of what direction the celebration of the sacrament is to take. In the best instances the priest/confessor is a doctor of souls who, through listening to the penitent's confession, in judgment applies the most appropriate clarifications, counsel, and penance to the person in light of his or her sins, spiritual needs, and the call to holiness.

The diagnostic, which the sacrament entails, is intended to mediate the necessary grace for the penitent's conversion of life. In the renewal of the *Rite of Penance* following the Second Vatican Council emphasis is placed, as it says in the introduction, on "The Mystery of Salvation in the History of Salvation."[38] The invitation to repentance extended by the prophets, John the Baptist, and Jesus in his public ministry is now proclaimed by the church in light of Christ's death and resurrection, his victory over sin, and the power to forgive sins that he gave to the church.[39] The ecclesial mediation of reconciliation is the logical consequence of the sacramentality of the church as a whole,[40] where Christ is encountered and his work made present by the Holy Spirit. This is stated eloquently in regard to the forgiveness of sins when the *Rite of Penance* says (quoting St. Ambrose) that the church "possesses both water and tears: the water of baptism, the tears of penance."[41]

---

[36] *RP* 17.

[37] *CCC*, 1863.

[38] *The Rites of the Catholic Church as Revised by Decree of the Second Vatican Council and Published by Authority of Pope Paul VI*, English translation prepared by The International Commission on English in the Liturgy (New York: Pueblo, 1976) 341.

[39] Ibid. 341–42.

[40] *Lumen Gentium*, 1.

[41] *The Rites of the Catholic Church*, 342.

The ecclesial mediation of penance bespeaks both the holiness of the church and the relational and even social nature of sin. The ecclesial mark of holiness does not deny the need for purification, repentance, and renewal but demands it.[42] Sin harms not only the sinner but the church as well. It damages the graced state of the believer and disrupts ecclesial communion. Therefore, "[r]econciliation with the Church is inseparable from reconciliation with God."[43] Likewise, the embrace of human agency within the divine action, discussed in our review of the theology of grace, is especially present here as the words of absolution uttered by the priest convey the forgiveness of God and the penance put into practice by the penitent counters the effects of sin, i.e., temporal punishment, and helps heal and elevate the believer (the effects of sanctifying grace). By virtue of these effects of the sacrament communion with the church, that very communion harmed by sin, is increased.

Validation of human action in grace is best expressed in a phrase used by John Paul II. Mindful of Paul's declaration that "where sins increased, grace abounded all the more" (Rom 5:20), the Pope contrasts the *mysterium iniquitatis* and the *mysterium pietatis*. He is so bold as to suggest that if the latter "were not part of the dynamism of history in order to conquer man's sin," then "God's salvific plan would remain incomplete or even totally defeated."[44] Or, in reference to divine action and human response, he writes that "the *loving kindness of God* toward the Christian must be matched by the *piety of the Christian* towards God."[45] The *mysterium pietatis* is not just human response. It embraces both divine action and human action, the divine mercy and the reconciled life.[46] The mystery of Christ in us, the Savior as the "interior source of spiritual energy," means that piety is a "force for conversion and reconciliation, [and therefore] . . . confronts iniquity and sin."[47] As far as reconciliation is concerned the sacrament of Penance is the privileged place of the actualization of this mystery.

We can now turn to the structure of the sacrament itself, which sets the framework for the Catholic practice of penance even in its nonsacramental expressions such as prayer, penitential works, and other liturgical expressions of penance including nonsacramental penitential services. The sacrament of penance includes four distinct acts, three on the part of the

---

[42] Ibid. 343.
[43] *CCC*, 1445.
[44] *RP*, 19.
[45] Ibid. 21.
[46] Ibid. 22.
[47] Ibid. 21.

penitent and one by the priest: contrition, confession of sins, the act of penance or satisfaction—the acts of the penitent—and absolution by the priest. I will examine each in turn. Together they embody the full action of grace, from God to the penitent and in and through the action of the penitent.

Contrition is defined as "sorrow of the soul and detestation for the sin committed, together with the resolution not to sin again."[48] It is considered the primary and most important act in the sacrament and of itself is sufficient to remit venial sins. Again, the sacrament can still benefit one who confesses only venial sins but contrition is that spiritual affection and resolution—the heartfelt sorrow leading to an act of the will—that opens the person to receive forgiveness. In the case of mortal sin contrition must be present for the necessary communication of grace in the sacrament to restore the sinner to supernatural life.[49]

The tradition—and it is taken up in the *Catechism of the Catholic Church*—distinguishes between perfect and imperfect contrition (or attrition). The former, also known as the "contrition of charity," arises from the love of God. The latter, "contrition of fear," proceeds from the "fear of eternal damnation and the other penalties threatening," but is still a gift of grace and is prompted by the Holy Spirit. In itself it cannot obtain forgiveness, but rather disposes one to receive it in the sacrament wherein it is brought to completion.[50] The relationship between contrition and attrition is best illustrated in the common prayer many Catholics learn as children, the act of contrition:

> O my God, I am heartily sorry for having offended you, and I detest all my sins, because I dread the loss of heaven and the pains of hell [imperfect contrition or attrition]; but most of all because they offend you, my God, who are all good and deserving of all my love [perfect contrition]. I firmly resolve, with the help of your grace, to confess my sins, to do penance, and to amend my life. Amen.

Needless to say, both contrition and attrition require an examination of conscience in order to identify one's sins. There are various methods

---

[48] *CCC*, 1451 (quoting Trent).

[49] More precisely, such contrition "also obtains forgiveness of mortal sins if it includes the resolution to have recourse to sacramental confession as soon as possible." *CCC*, 1452.

[50] Ibid. 1453.

to accomplish this. Consideration of one's life in light of the Ten Commandments and the Sermon on the Mount are but two.

Although the notion of attrition has been subject to critique, especially at the time of the Reformation, it may be taken as a measure of the church's understanding of divine generosity. It takes account of where persons may be in their relationship with God—some are snatched out of the fire (Jude 23) —and with the intent of always moving them from a servile fear of God to a filial fear, it enables them eventually to become conscious of the love of God now violated by sin, viz., true contrition.

The confession or disclosure of sin is the next element of the sacrament of Penance. Here the *Catechism of the Catholic Church* is eloquent. One "looks squarely at the sins he is guilty of, takes responsibility for them, and thereby opens himself again to God and to the communion of the Church in order to make a new future possible."[51] All mortal sins must be confessed; confession of venial sins is also encouraged. This is all to be considered in light of the divine mercy and is also intended to give knowledge to the confessor of where the penitent is spiritually so as to facilitate the proper counsel and the appropriate penance.

Satisfaction or the acts of penance follow. The confessor imposes a penance that should "correspond to the nature and the gravity of the sins committed."[52] Prayer, works of mercy, a voluntary sacrifice, the patient acceptance of the cross are all possibilities. Their intent is to "help configure us to Christ, who alone expiated our sins once for all."[53] In other words, based upon the forgiveness offered in the sacrament and presuming the understanding of the effects of sin (temporal punishment) and created grace (the supernatural healing and elevation of our human nature in habit and operation), penance entails the real transformation of the believer in holiness. It is a necessary component of the sacrament of penance because it sets the penitent on the path of restoration, taking sin seriously but grace even more.

Absolution by the confessor/priest completes the sacrament of penance. Indeed, it is the Father of mercies who is the source of forgiveness. He commends to the church the power to forgive sins by the authority of the Risen Christ in the power of the Spirit (John 20:21-23). All of this is manifest in the formula of absolution in the *Rite of Penance* used by the Latin Church:

[51] Ibid. 1455.
[52] *CCC*, 1460.
[53] Ibid.

> God, the Father of mercies, through the death and resurrection of his
> Son has reconciled the world to himself and sent the Holy Spirit for
> the forgiveness of sins; through the ministry of the Church may God
> give you pardon and peace, and I absolve you from your sins in the
> name of the Father, and of the Son, and of the Holy Spirit.[54]

Finally, I return to the practice of indulgences mentioned at the beginning of the essay. Although not formally a part of the sacrament of Penance, it is related to the remission of temporal punishment that satisfaction in the sacrament addresses. Whether partial or plenary (remitting either part or all of the temporal punishment of sins already forgiven), indulgences underscore the ecclesial and pneumatological dimensions of penitential practice. In the Body of Christ and the Communion of Saints pious acts (including penitential ones) can enact for oneself and others (including the faithful departed in the risen Christ) the transformative work of the Spirit in purification, healing, and sanctification. Such is the abounding grace of God in Christ and his church, with the *"Church's treasury"*[55] being none other than "glory in the church and in Christ Jesus to all generations" (Eph 3:21).

It is also no wonder that in his millennial Apostolic Letter *Novo Millennio Ineunte* Pope John Paul II exhorts the church to "put out into the deep" (Luke 5:4) and behold the face of the Savior. This is not without a penitential character, for the exhortation continues by calling on the faithful to engage in the purification of memory as a church (an examination of conscience and asking the Lord for forgiveness), renew the practice of sacramental penance, while being rooted in prayer and confessing the primacy of grace, for "without Christ we can do nothing" (John 15:5).[56]

## 2. Implications

All Christian theologies of penance share a basic commonality rooted in the gospel. The divine mercy and the preeminence of God's grace in Christ are the foundations for penance in the Christian life both at conversion/initiation and in the ongoing pilgrimage of Christian discipleship. The Catholic contribution calls attention to four aspects of the theology

---

[54] Quoted in *CCC*, 1449.
[55] *CCC*, 1476.
[56] *Novo Millennio Ineunte*, 1, 6, 16–28, 32, 37, 38.

and practice of penance: grace and anthropology, its ecclesiality, and its liturgical/sacramental expression.

The theology of grace and theological anthropology are interconnected. The relationship between divine and human agency, grace and free will, and the modality of the human reception of grace were all broached in the preceding essay. Needless to say, I have leaned heavily on the Catholic doctrine of cooperative grace, a position that not all Christian traditions adhere to. A Catholic contribution to a Christian theology of penitence would nevertheless inquire about the efficacy of grace. Certainly doctrinal and theological configurations on this matter will differ. Nevertheless, how the grace of God transforms a believer is of interest and the relationship between the doctrines of justification and sanctification figure greatly in any theology of penitence.

The anthropological dimensions of penance must account for the sociality of the human being. Theologically speaking, the Christian believer is an ecclesial person. Therefore, since sin affects the church, its remedy is likewise ecclesially mediated in the church's proclamation and worship. Again, Christian traditions differ on the matter and may even take theological exception to the use of the phrase "ecclesial mediation." But that Christ acts in and through the church is a common Christian affirmation, thereby eliciting attention to the church's own enactment of penance that is formative for its members. In the same light liturgy is the singular although not exclusive site of such enactment whether or not it is understood in terms of sacramentality. In favor of the latter the Catholic contribution underscores (as in its theology of grace) the divine and human aspects of penance undertaken by the church and its members.

## 3. Further Reading

Coffey, David. *The Sacrament of Reconciliation.* Collegeville: Liturgical Press, 2001.

Dallen, James. *The Reconciling Community: The Rite of Penance.* New York: Pueblo, 1986.

Dudley, Martin, and Geoffrey Rowell, eds. *Confession and Absolution.* Collegeville: Liturgical Press, 1990.

Häring, Bernard. *Shalom: Peace. The Sacrament of Reconciliation.* Rev. ed. Garden City, NY: Doubleday, 1969.

Hellwig, Monika K. *Sign of Reconciliation and Conversion: The Sacrament of Penance for our Times.* Collegeville: Liturgical Press, 1982.

Pope John Paul II. *Reconciliatio et Paenitentia (On Reconciliation and Penance)*. Boston: St. Paul Editions, 1984.

Lutten, Eric. *Sacramental Forgiveness as a Gift of God: Thomas Aquinas on the Sacrament of Penance*. Leuven: Peeters, 2003.

Rahner, Karl. "Forgotten Truths Concerning the Sacrament of Penance." In idem, *Theological Investigations II*. New York: Crossroad, 1990, 135–74.

_____. "The Status of the Sacrament of Reconciliation." In idem, *Theological Investigations XXIIII*. New York: Crossroad, 1992, 205–18.

Speyr, Adrienne von. *Confession*. San Francisco: Ignatius Press, 1985.

# 4. Hermeneutical Reflection

Two aspects in the papers and discussion have struck me in this project: the interconfessional consensus on penitence, and the role of penitence vis-à-vis society and culture. After exploring each briefly I will argue that the introduction of an ecclesiological perspective necessitates moving from the former to the latter.

All Christian communions represented in this volume consider penitence to be an essential dimension of the Christian life. This is consistent with its place in the biblical traditions and, as with those, there is diversity in its expression. To a great extent these differences reflect the doctrinal patrimony of each ecclesial tradition, its understanding and practice of the Christian life, as well as its liturgical practices. Three areas of difference are of particular interest: the relationship between divine and human agency, how justification and sanctification are conceived relative to each other, and the difference between sacramental and nonsacramental expressions of penitence. As one might suspect, these reflect the Reformation divide in the Western church. Nevertheless, they also represent a fruitful interchange among the different traditions that might prove enlightening for the Christian practice of penitence. I will examine each in turn.

Although the Catholic doctrine of cooperative grace may not elicit agreement from all quarters, there is consensus that God's action precedes human repentance and that both are necessary for a robust sense of penitence in the life of the church. Orthodox and Wesleyan positions on divine and human synergy (how close Wesley is to the Orthodox requires further explication) are similar (certainly not identical) to the Catholic theology of grace, but even Reformation and Evangelical theologies do not exclude a place for human action.

Since the very nature of this project is ecumenical, as a Catholic I must take seriously the reasons articulated by the Protestant position. In this regard Reformation and Evangelical theologies argue that repentance is necessary for the Christian life and is the expression, fruit, or consequence of faith but not its condition. This is no marginal opinion, but lies at the heart of Evangelical Reform and by conviction believes that it arrives at the fruit of God's grace in the converted life in accordance with the gospel. In lieu of a more extended theological discussion it is worth noting that Evangelical faith is intended to issue in an evangelical life, a witness to the good news of Jesus Christ. With this I could not be more in agreement.

The same holds true for the relationship between justification and sanctification. Again the differences between our ecclesial traditions cannot be too quickly resolved, although the 1999 *Joint Declaration on the Doctrine of Justification* by the Catholic Church and the Lutheran World Federation does demonstrate the possibility of confessing a common faith with differences that are not church-dividing. My point is that all agree that repentance and the penitential life are essential for holiness whether one considers holiness integral to salvation (the Catholic position) or the fruit of salvation already received (the Evangelical position). I am not diminishing the importance of doctrine. Rather, the promotion of holiness through penitence is the desired common outcome of the grace offered in conversion or Christian Initiation. To this end our respective theologies of penitence are intended to contribute.

In sum, these first two concerns bear witness to a common faith and praxis that embraces the following affirmations. First, divine grace precedes and enables human response to the gospel in faith and repentance. Second, repentance is a feature of both conversion/initiation and the ongoing life of the believer. Third, ongoing penitence is an essential dimension of the pursuit of holiness, a universal call directed to all Christians by virtue of baptism or saving faith. The differing configurations between divine and human agency and how justification and sanctification are related must be situated amid the striving for "holiness without which no one will see the Lord" (Heb 12:14).

In light of the above, does it make any difference if there be a sacramental expression of penitence? Is it sufficient that repentance be a "nonsacramental, on-going feature of Christian life" (Andrew Purves' essay)? Again, space forbids further investigation into comparative notions of sacramentality. However, the church must liturgically mark itself as a penitent community if penance is to figure greatly in the lives of Christian disciples, and this with a degree of liturgical regularity. Christian life and community are subject to the Word of God. Therefore, the formative dimension of liturgy instantiates the assembly as called together under the sign of penitence. Whether sacramentally mediated or not, it is important that Christians not only maintain a penitential posture in their interior life but are formed together through life in community, itself a penitential way of conversion. In this respect the church ought to be able to confess with Paul that it bears the marks of Jesus on its body (Gal 6:17).

Ecclesiological marks of penitence are essential for the church's witness to society and culture. Politics and culture informed a good deal of the group's discussion at the November 2004 meeting of the American Academy of Religion so soon after the general elections in the United States. Since the place of religion was particularly evident in that campaign and the continued division of the nation into red Republican and blue Democratic states has provoked endless examinations of the relationship between faith and politics and the cultural and religious divide in the country, it is particularly important that one understand how the Christian message of repentance is relevant to the larger culture. Needless to say, wisdom is hard to come by in the matter and no wish for a present day Jonah will simplify things. In a "nation with the soul of a church" (G. K. Chesterton), and with churches themselves ambivalent and often divided in their witness, complications increase. My contribution in the face of this is limited to one point.

The call to repentance in a pluralistic culture and one that attempts (perhaps unsuccessfully) to hold a delicate balance between the separation of church and state and a public square from which religion is not banished must be a mediated venture. Moral proclamations, advocacy for justice, the promotion of peace, if based in the gospel, must presume a community that derives its life from the transformative grace enacted in penitence. In this respect the ecclesial embodiment of penance is essential for the Christian practice of penance. At its source is the Holy Spirit who continually renews the church and who intends its maturation in love, knowledge, and holiness (Eph 3:19; 4:15; 5:27).

Twelve

# A Confessing Faith:
# Assent and Penitence
# in the Reformation Traditions
# of Luther, Calvin, and Bucer

*Andrew Purves*

## 1. Tradition

What place is properly to be given to repentance/penance within the
theological traditions born from the German and Swiss Reformations?
The question, of course, is profoundly pastoral, for the subject matter is
a person's relationship with God, including the assurance of salvation.
The Directory for Worship of The Presbyterian Church (USA), for example, appropriately though briefly gives due place to confession of sin
both in corporate worship and in the practice of pastoral care. However,
present practices and trends may suggest an alternative perspective. To
give one illustration: a survey of texts in pastoral care published during
the last fifty years by authors representing so-called mainline Protestant
denominations in North America would indicate in the main an interest
in psychological wholeness with an attendant lack of interest in issues
of sin, penance, and forgiveness. This redirection signals a turn away
from the teachings of the founding theologians.

I write on the Reformation tradition's treatment of repentance/penance[1] as a pastoral theologian, not as a historian of doctrine. In so doing I follow the pattern of the principal reformers themselves, whose concern above all else was for the godly care of God's people. I present the tradition's perspective in order to raise questions for the practice of faith and ministry today; there is little point to a theology of repentance that is not guidance in the practice of faith and ministry. Because pastoral practice today is largely unaware of the Reformation's theological discussion of repentance, the result is a limit to the range, responsibilities, and competency of pastoral ministry. The discussion will follow a systematic structure: grounding the understanding of penance/repentance in baptism (with Luther), reflecting on repentance in the Christian life (with Calvin), and considering the consequences for Christian pastoral ministry (with Bucer).

The overall theological theme in Reformation tradition is that repentance is a response to God's grace, the consequence of the gospel at the specific point of forgiveness of sins; repentance is not the condition for grace. As a gift of grace, repentance is nevertheless required as a part of the reception of this grace of forgiveness of sins by faith, and as such marks the Christian life.

## a. Martin Luther on Penance in the Context of Baptism

The place to begin is with a brief reflection on Luther's views on baptism. Penance, in his mind, is closely linked with it.[2] Thus in the first edition of The Larger Catechism of 1529, for example, compiled from Luther's sermons, he wrote, "Here you see that baptism, both by its power and by its signification, comprehends also the third sacrament, formally called penance, which is really nothing else than baptism."[3] Penance, then, is interpreted as a part of baptism.

---

[1] *Poenitentia* is used by Calvin, for example, for both penitence and repentance. John Calvin, *Institutes of the Christian Religion,* ed. John T. McNeill, trans. Ford Lewis Battles, 2 vols. (Philadelphia: Westminster, 1960) 3.3.1 n1.

[2] Heiko A. Oberman, *Luther: Man Between God and the Devil,* trans. Eileen Walliser-Schwarzbart (New Haven: Yale University Press, 1989) 231.

[3] Robert Kolb and Timothy J. Wengert, eds., *The Book of Concord: The Confessions of the Evangelical Lutheran Church* (Minneapolis: Fortress Press, 2000) 465–66; The Larger Catechism 4:74.

Commenting on Mark 16:16, Luther insists that "the power, effect, benefit, fruit, and purpose of baptism is that it saves" (LC 4:24). That is, baptism delivers from sin, death, and the devil, admits into Christ's kingdom and eternal life with Christ. The efficacy of the sacrament lies in the conjunction of the Word of God, that is, God's institution and command, that which is done in the name of God, and water. Thus water placed in the setting of God's Word and commandment becomes God's water (LC 4:14), conveying all that is God's (LC 4:17). Citing Augustine, Luther states that "when the Word is added to the element of the natural substance, it becomes a sacrament," a holy thing and sign (LC 4:1).[4] In the case of baptism, it becomes Christ's baptism (LC 4:22), and therefore the actuality of life and salvation. Baptism, then, is God's work that calls forth faith whereby one believes and receives in the water the promised salvation (LC 4:36). God gives; faith accepts and holds firmly (LC 4:40), though note: faith does not make baptism valid; its validity comes from the Word of God (LC 4:53). Baptism, in Luther's view, brings "the entire Christ" (LC 4:41). This perspective on baptism can be summed up thus: in baptism, on the ground of the institution and command of God, a person receives the entire salvation given by Jesus Christ.

One further point is required to complete the context of Luther's statement that baptism, in its signification, comprehends penance. The Christian life is a daily baptism that, once begun, continues day by day (LC 4:65). When one has entered Christ's kingdom, the corruption of the Old Adam must daily decrease until it is finally destroyed (LC 4:71). "Where faith is present with its fruits, there baptism is no empty symbol, but the effect accompanies it" (LC 4:73). Repentance, then, is an earnest attack on the old creature as one more deeply enters into a new life (LC 4:75). "If you live in repentance, therefore, you are walking in baptism, which not only announces this new life but also produces, begins, and exercises it" (LC 4:75). In this case, according to Luther, penance is not a separate sacrament from baptism, but a daily living out of one's baptismal reality.[5] Heiko Oberman notes that what Luther attacks is the

---

[4] This citation is from Augustine, *Tractate* 80 on John 15:3.

[5] See also Calvin, *Institutes*, 3.3.2, where he refers to "a repentance that for the Christian man ought to extend throughout his life," though this is not set in the specific context of baptism, but is developed in view of our participation in Christ. This is expressed more fully in the next section.

undervaluation of baptism in Christian life in favor of penance and penitential good works.[6]

This contextualization of Luther's teaching—suggesting that penance, and with it repentance and confession, is an aspect of baptized living—means that penance is not to be understood as an occasional response by a sinner but as a way of life. This perspective is illustrated, for example, in the opening two theses of Luther's ninety-five theses of 1517.

> 1. When our Lord and master Jesus Christ said, "Repent" (Matt 4:17), he willed the entire life of the faithful to be one of repentance.
> 2. This word is misunderstood if it is taken to refer to the sacrament of penance that is received from time to time.[7]

A penitential life, therefore, is a response of gratitude, of acted-out love for God's grace given as a salvation already won; it is not a response of fear of hell.

Faith is the goal now for Luther.[8] But baptism, and the penitential life that follows, give content to this life of faith. Everything else comes from this—contrition as well as consolation.[9] The focus, however—of course! —is outward, toward what Luther often called an alien righteousness, righteousness as a gift from God. The baptismal font, in fact, is already the reservoir of this alien righteousness.[10] In *The Babylonian Captivity of the Church*, in which he launched a determined attack on the sacramental system of the Roman church, he warns:

> Beware then, of putting your trust in your own contrition and of ascribing the forgiveness of sins to your own remorse . . . . Thus we owe whatever good there may be in our penance, not to our scrupulous enumeration of sins, but to the truth of God and to our faith. All other things are the works and fruits which follow of their own accord.[11]

---

[6] Oberman, *Luther*, 231.

[7] Cited by Oberman, *Luther*, 164.

[8] *The Babylonian Captivity of the Church, 1520*, in Abdel Ross Wentz, ed., *Luther's Works 36, Word and Sacrament II* (Philadelphia: Muhlenberg Press, 1959) 83.

[9] *The Babylonian Captivity of the Church*, 84.

[10] Oberman, *Luther*, 230.

[11] *The Babylonian Captivity of the Church*, 85.

There is a place for confession; it is even necessary, says Luther. But remove it from the sacramental system and let it be confession to a brother (or sister) in the faith, for every Christian has the power to absolve sins.[12] What is required is the faith of a contrite heart.

This brief review emphasizes the important theological location of penance/repentance in the Christian life in baptism as event and persisting reality. This perspective brings to light the anemic practical theology of baptism that arguably is present in many mainline Protestant congregations, in which there is little or no sense that in the sacrament the whole shape and direction of Christian life has already been given once for all. Further, it invites us to bear in mind that Christian life, in the context of grace certainly, is properly construed in some significant way to be a penitential life. And finally, we might well consider what shape pastoral ministry must take in order to reflect these considerations.

### b. Repentance in the Christian Life in the Teaching of John Calvin

While Luther explicitly grounds repentance in the event of baptism, Calvin casts his discussion in terms of the relationship between the twin graces of repentance and the forgiveness of sins: forgiveness is given, repentance is required; yet even as required, it is a singular gift from God effected by the Holy Spirit.

The correct exposition of Calvin on this point requires the recognition of the place given to the practice of the Christian life, the life of holiness, in Calvin's ordering of his whole system of theology. Calvin does not offer an abstract account of Christian doctrine. Repentance and forgiveness are intimately interrelated (*Inst.* 3.3.1 and *Inst.* 3.3.19). Thus while repentance follows from forgiveness of sins, repentance is treated first because in the overall scheme of the *Institutes of the Christian Religion* Calvin is concerned to call attention to its effect on holiness. The sum of the gospel, in fact, is held by him to consist in repentance and forgiveness of sins. Calvin, however, leaves the strictly dogmatic discussion for later attention, treating the practice of holiness first.

To repeat for emphasis: in Calvin's theology repentance is consequential, the result of the grace of forgiveness; repentance is not the condition for forgiveness. Newness of life and free reconciliation with God are conferred on us by Christ and received by faith (*Inst.* 3.3.1). Note that repentance follows faith, as it is also born of faith. And both are the

---

[12] Ibid. 88.

fruit of grace. Calvin characterizes the imperative of Matt 3:2 to mean: Because the Kingdom of Heaven has drawn near, repent (*Inst.* 3.3.2). Thus at the first level of interpretation it is noted that repentance is a response to grace announced as the forgiveness of sins, not a condition for it, and as such, following Luther, it is to be understood as shaping Christian life in an ongoing manner.

Calvin defines repentance as "the true turning of our life to God, a turning that arises from a pure and earnest fear of him; and it consists in the mortification of our flesh and of the old man, and in the vivification of the Spirit" (*Inst.* 3.3.5). True turning to God is not in outward acts of works or piety, but is characterized by a transformation of the deepest self, in the inmost heart (*Inst.* 3.3.6). Such a turning is no trivial realignment of our mentality and disposition. It is aroused by reflecting upon God's judgment; we are, says Calvin, violently slain by the sword of the Spirit and brought to nought (*Inst.* 3.3.8).

Immediately upon stating that repentance involves both mortification and vivification, however, Calvin firmly asserts that "both things happen to us by participation in Christ" (*Inst.* 3.3.9). The reference is cryptic but critical: indeed, it is the center of Calvin's understanding of the Christian life and it forces us to a second, and deeper, level of interpretation. The whole of Calvin's central doctrine of our union with Christ through the Holy Spirit must be present in our thought in order to understand Calvin correctly at this juncture. Calvin means (1) that God has not only spoken the word of forgiveness, but has also provided the perfect response of vicarious penitence in the Lord Jesus Christ. We are accepted in the person of the one Jesus Christ who has already said amen for us to the divine condemnation of our sin. Calvin means (2) that this becomes ours in a personal and actual way through union with Christ. In this sense it is a twin grace. Our response of faith is, as it were, a response to the response by virtue of the grace of being so joined to Jesus Christ that we share in his perfect response of vicarious penance.[13] Rebirth in Christ, regeneration through the benefit of Christ and a personal sharing in his life for us, restores us into the righteousness of and communion with

[13] See James B. Torrance, *Worship, Community and the Triune God of Grace* (Carlisle: Paternoster Press, 1996) 45–46. This interpretation of Calvin is informed by John McLeod Campbell, *The Nature of the Atonement* (Edinburgh: The Handsel Press and Grand Rapids: Eerdmans, 1996; first publication Cambridge: MacMillan, 1856).

God from which we had fallen. The inner structure of Calvin's thought here is deeply christological, Trinitarian, and soteriological.

Believers, of course, are still sinners. "There remains in a regenerate man a smoldering cinder of evil, from which desires continually leap forth to allure and spur him to commit sin" (*Inst.* 3.3.10). Sin, however, has lost its sovereignty over us: it dwells in us still, but no longer reigns. By the gift of the Spirit the regenerate person is enabled to wage the battle against the vestige of sin that remains (*Inst.* 3.3.11). Far removed from perfection, for still there is the entanglement of vice, Christians nevertheless move steadily forward under the teaching of the Spirit, fighting daily against these entanglements (3.3.14).

> And indeed, this restoration does not take place in one moment or one day or one year; but through continual and sometimes even slow advances God wipes out in his elect the corruptions of the flesh, cleanses them of guilt, consecrates them to himself as temples renewing all their minds to true purity that they may practice repentance throughout their lives and know that this warfare will end only at death. (*Inst.* 3.3.9)

The fruits of repentance are grace-filled: "the duties of piety toward God, of charity toward men, and in the whole of life, holiness and purity" (*Inst.* 3.3.16). In other words, the fruits are the marks of the Christian life. Thus Calvin's initial consideration is to reflect on the effect of repentance upon holiness.

Now Calvin turns explicitly to the dogmatics. Drawing on Christ's teaching at Mark 1:15, he makes three brief but significant points: "First he declares that the treasures of God's mercy have been opened in himself; then he requires repentance; finally, trust in God's promises" (*Inst.* 3.3.19). The ordering here is important: repentance is not the condition or basis for our deserving pardon. Rather, God has determined to have mercy upon us *to the end that we may repent* (*Inst.* 3.3.20). God's mercy is the cause for repentance. Through the preaching of repentance we are taught that all of our thoughts, inclinations, and acts are corrupt. But that is immediately set in the context of God's goodness. Forgiveness of sins is preached when we are taught that for us Christ became redemption, righteousness, salvation, and life; by his name we are freely accounted righteous and innocent in God's sight. These twin graces—repentance and forgiveness of sins—are received by faith (*Inst.* 3.3.19). Or, to put it differently, now in a baptismal metaphor: "having been engrafted into

the life and death of Christ, he may give attention to continual repentance
. . . . For no one ever hates sin unless he has previously been seized with
a love of righteousness (*Inst.* 3.3.20). Repentance, then, is an expression
of faith, which is a gift from God that comes from the Spirit of regeneration. "Whomsoever God wills to snatch from death, he quickens by the
Spirit of regeneration. Not that repentance, properly speaking, is the
cause of salvation, but because it is already from faith and from God's
mercy . . . . This fact stands firm: wherever the fear of God flourishes,
the Spirit has worked towards the salvation of man" (*Inst.* 3.3.21).

Calvin's teaching may be summed up thus: "it is certain that the
mind of man is not changed for the better except by God's prevenient
grace" (*Inst.* 3.3.24). Prevenient grace, of course, is theologically identified
entirely by our union with the life, death, resurrection, and ascension
of Jesus Christ. So, while forgiveness of sins can never happen without
repentance, repentance is not the condition for or cause of forgiveness
of sins (*Inst.* 3.4.3). The sinner is not counseled to turn toward his or her
own tears, but to turn the eyes upon the Lord's mercy alone—to Jesus
Christ clothed with his gospel. Thus from Calvin's perspective it makes
a great deal of difference whether repentance is understood legally, so
that forgiveness of sins is deserved by full contrition, which the sinner
can never perform, or evangelically, so that the sinner hungers and thirsts
after God's mercy, trusts in that alone, and gives glory to God.[14]

### c. Considerations for Ministry:
### Pastoral Discipline and Repentance in Martin Bucer[15]

Martin Bucer's *Von der waren Seelsorge*[16] is the principal Reformation
text on pastoral theology. The book was published in Strasbourg in April,
1538 (90, 1). Bucer wrote it out of the conviction that pastors were losing their way in the care of souls and people were reluctant anymore to
submit to the yoke of Christ. The goal was the reforming of the ministry.

---

[14] See Torrance, *Worship*, 44.

[15] For a fuller treatment see Andrew Purves, *Pastoral Theology in the Classical
Tradition* (Louisville: Westminster John Knox, 2001).

[16] References are to Robert Stupperich, ed., *Martin Bucers Deutsche Schriften,
Band 7: Schriften der Jahre 1538–1539* (Gütersloh and Paris: Gerd Mohn, 1964)
90–241. References to *Von der waren Seelsorge* will give the page number and the
line on which the citation begins. Some references are to marginal headings in
the German text; these are similarly documented, but not otherwise identified.

On two fronts, from the Roman church and from the leaders of Protestant sects, Bucer felt that the true church of Christ was under attack. This "little book," as he called it, was an attempt to restore a proper understanding of the church of Christ with regard to order and ministry, with a special concern for faithful pastoral care that leads to the salvation of Christ's people (94, 13-14). To this end his intent was not to omit anything that leads to godly discipline in the administration of the church.

In a review of the history of pastoral care, William A. Clebsch and Charles R. Jaekle note correctly that different epochs of the church's life have emphasized one function as the organizing task around which the others revolved.[17] The Reformation, they suggest, is characterized by reconciliation as the dominant pastoral concern.[18] This is indeed the case, as we see from Bucer's theme verse, taken from Ezek 34:16, and which is cited in his brief introduction: "I will seek the lost, and I will bring back the strayed, and I will bind up the injured, and I will strengthen the weak, but the fat and the strong I will destroy. I will feed them with justice" (93, 1–2).[19]

Bucer's pastoral theology is appropriately wide-ranging. The one aspect that bears on the issue for our consideration is his perspective on pastoral discipline understood as submitting to the yoke of Christ.

For Bucer, Jesus Christ alone has and exercises all power and rule in the church, for he rules, feeds, and cares for it, and through the church he brings the gospel to those who are lost or have strayed away from the ways of God. He does this in order that his flock may be purified more thoroughly and liberated from sin and sin's consequences. Bucer's goal is that God's people may be saved and encouraged to grow in piety and blessedness. He notes two goals the pastoral office ministers exercise on behalf of Christ: the first is evangelism, whereby those God has chosen to

---

[17] William A. Clebsch and Charles R. Jaekle, *Pastoral Care in Historical Perspective: An essay with Exhibits* (Englewood Cliffs, NJ: Prentice-Hall, 1964) 4, 11–12, and 32–33.

[18] "In the Rhineland Martin Bucer, and after him John Calvin, developed systems of ecclesiastical discipline which worked out in detail the ways in which reconciliation of the believer with God involved reconciliation with his fellow believers." Clebsch and Jaekle, *Pastoral Care in Historical Perspective*, 27.

[19] Bucer mistranslates the end of the verse to read, "to guard/look after the fat and the strong and feed them rightly." McNeill makes note of this mistranslation: John T. McNeill, *A History of the Cure of Souls* (New York: Harper, 1951) 178. For Bucer's use see *Von der waren Seelsorge*, 93,1 and 141,35.

be part of Christ's flock, but who are not yet in the sheepfold, are brought in; the second is the care of those who have already been brought in so that they may continue to grow in godliness (116, 31–32). Pastoral work consists of seeking the lost and guiding the faithful through ministries of teaching, exhorting, warning, disciplining, comforting, pardoning, and reconciling people to God.

We are concerned here with Bucer's treatment of pastoral care as pastoral discipline, the care of those who are within the communion of Christ. This takes up half of *Von der waren Seelsorge,* where he gives a significant amount of space to the pastoral care of gross and notorious sinners, that is, those who turn away from Christ, disobey those in authority, engage in serious misbehavior against others, or are prey to immoderate habits.

As the sacrament of penance was abandoned by Protestants at the Reformation it fell upon the pastors and elders, through home visitation, to assist people in their personal lives of faith at the point where sin, especially habitual sin, had to be brought to repentance and life amended. Bucer begins in a low-key manner, expressing the view, from Matt 18:15-17, that anyone who sins is to be corrected by a neighbor or, if necessary, by the congregation (157, 15). His schoolmasterish tone should not obscure the recognition that the goal is reconciliation to God and the joy of communion with God. Bucer's underlying reason for pastoral discipline is that to live in continuous, conscious, and deliberate sin is to live opposed to God and to be wounded thereby. Bucer reflects the Reformation's concern to take sin seriously as an impediment to new life in Christ and to the proclamation of the forgiveness of sins as the basis for the Christian life. He nuances this stand with his pastoral concern for the need for penance on the part of sinners.

Bucer makes three introductory points concerning pastoral discipline: (1) it is the responsibility of all Christians to care for sinners, as noted above, but the pastor has a special responsibility (159, 4–5 and 18–19); (2) attempts to bind up the wounds caused by sin and heal them should continue for as long as a sinner accepts the voice of the pastor (159, 24–25); and (3) the treatment to heal the wounded parishioner should enable him or her to acknowledge the sin and be moved to true contrition and sorrow, to the end that the person is comforted and strengthened in hope of grace (159, 36–37). With Christ as the source, the process for dealing with sin sounds remarkably contemporary. It is not judgment from without that brings healing, nor the imposition of punishment, but the personal realization whereby one says for oneself: "I have sinned, and I desire grace." Bringing a person to such self-awareness requires, says Bucer, a gentle spirit and great love (160, 19), so much so that one must be prepared even to bear the sinner's burden oneself. Here Bucer follows Paul, who believed that he might have to bear the humiliation himself if sinners had failed to do so (2 Cor 12:21). In this way believers share not only in one another's joy, but also in their suffering. Penance is serious but, says Bucer, the pastoral practice by which it is called forth must be guided by moderation; the goals are renewal of life and faith, not punishment and despair. The danger is always that an undue or immoderate penitential burden may lead a person to leave the church, or be plunged into despair. Great wisdom is needed by a pastor who guides a penitent along the path of amendment of life, and frequently Bucer describes these pastors as "faithful shepherds," implying perhaps that faithfulness is not a designation appropriate to all.

The issue, says Bucer, citing Luther, is, in view of the fact that we keep sinning, whether we really want to be Christians (193, 28). If our answer is Yes, we need to listen to Christ and purge our sins, for they wound us deeply. Lesser sins (for a similar distinction see Calvin, *Inst.* 4.12.4) may be dealt with by daily confession and repentance, but for serious sins it is not enough to say, "I am sorry, and I won't do it again" (172, 28), for an outward show of piety and repentance can mask an inward resistance. A deeper response is called for, one that will root out the source of sin. Bucer suggests that, though the pastor is guided by moderation, the penitent's true repentance may be associated with weeping and lamenting, much praying, and fasting and self-discipline. Pastoral moderation, too, may be mitigated by the gravity of sin: it may be necessary, for a while, even to exclude a person from the Lord's Table when he or she is bound to a period of penance because of serious sin. Satisfaction is not the goal, however, but the prevention of present and future sins. Penitence is not an atoning work, and not a condition for salvation, but a process in sanctification and the amendment of life. Coming to a true knowledge of one's sins—as far as that is possible for us—leads to deep regret and profound repentance.

Bucer rooted his support for the necessity of penitential discipline in the Bible and in the early church. While he cites Old Testament examples, he relies primarily on the treatment of the Corinthian sinner (1 Cor 5:1-5) to show that penance is God's command. However, the casting out of a sinner from the community is mitigated by forgiveness in due course, lest the sinner be overwhelmed by excessive sorrow (2 Cor 2:7), a sorrow so deep, perhaps, that it leads to a depression. In any case, Bucer regarded penitential discipline as the Lord's command, through the Holy Spirit, who orders the church (170, 17–18). He calls it both "this order and correction of Christ" (*ordnung und zucht Christi:* 195, 24), and "a work and command of Christ" (*eyn werck und befelch Christi:* 197, 30). Without discipline, sin runs amok, yet as Christ's sheep, sinners listen to his voice.

For Bucer this ministry of care for sinners is above all else a ministry of love (224, 13). Neither being domineering (*herrisch*) nor unfriendly, the caregiver is to act humbly and like a mother (*muterlich*), like a nurse with her child (225, 11). This is a most interesting series of words to use in describing the appropriate attitude to take in pastoral care, suggesting that ministry is here at least construed in relational rather than hierarchical terms. Penitential discipline, it might also be noted, may be dangerous for parishioners when it becomes narrow and hardened. Degenerating into a deadening legalism that kills rather than quickens faith, discipline can be the cause of fear of God rather than love for Christ. Bucer is clear that pastoral discipline, the process of enabling repentance and penitence, must be exercised in love, with humility, and as an operation of grace designed to win people back to faithfulness.

Bucer saw sin for what he believed it was and what it is—an offense to God that can be rooted out by the means of grace and the care of Christian pastors and friends. To that end he saw a place for the instruction and admonition of the word of God, personally accepted mortifications, and, in the case of serious sins, exclusion of the sinner from the Lord's Supper until life was amended.

Bucer turns briefly to consider the pastoral care of the weak and the healthy members of the church. The proportionate lack of space given to this in comparison to pastoral discipline indicates where he saw his priority. Modern practice has almost entirely not followed him in this emphasis. Yet it is just this emphasis in Bucer that allows us to see a lacuna in pastoral practice today. The tendency of much contemporary Protestant pastoral care is to emphasize a God who cares,[20] often to the exclusion of God's judgment on sin as an issue to be dealt with in the lives of people. As noted at the beginning, Protestant pastoral theologians today, on the whole, have tended to avoid discussion of sin altogether or to see it as a developmental

---

[20] See, for example, John Patton, *Pastoral Care in Context: An Introduction to Pastoral Care* (Louisville: Westminster John Knox, 1993) 16. The index contains no listing under "sin."

problem requiring treatment.[21] Bucer reminds us that there remains still to be dealt with the issue of persons standing before God at the point of their sin and that we, pastors and people together, neglect dealing with this at our peril. His pastoral care was tailored to another age. Yet his insistence that the focus of pastoral care is the life of persons before God in Jesus Christ is for us both a word of judgment on a discipline that has become concerned largely only with inward states, and an opportunity to reform a most noble and holy occupation according to the Word of God.

## 2. Implications

The common thread in the three principal Reformers here examined is the recognition of repentance/penance as a nonsacramental, ongoing feature of Christian life. It is rooted in baptism; it characterizes discipleship; and calling it forth is a noted feature of pastoral care.

The case is made, following the founders of the theological tradition, for an understanding of the Christian life that is established by grace and marked by response. Grace means the love, mercy, and forgiveness of God; response means faith, repentance, and holy living. The logic of Christian faith in this tradition is that the indicative of grace calls forth obedience to the imperatives of discipleship. Response is always the consequence of grace and never its condition. The call to repentance is prefaced by the word of grace; penance likewise is not atonement but, in Calvin's word, "mortification," which means a dying to sin as a consequence of being alive in Jesus Christ.

Two points of emphasis open up recovered perspectives for consideration, namely the relation of grace to repentance/penance, and the responsibility this understanding of the Christian life thereby places on pastoral care. On the one hand, the shape of the Christian life is here profoundly determined by an ongoing relationship between the mercy of God to forgive sin and the recognition that the sinner is called to a penitential and amended life. On the other hand, the overemphasis on psychotherapeutic modes of thought and action in pastoral work today is called into question, to be replaced instead by a theological foundation grounded in the indicative of grace and the imperatives of response.

---

[21] See, however, the effort of Don S. Browning to introduce moral discourse into pastoral theology, in "Pastoral Theology in a Pluralistic Age," in Don S. Browning, ed., *Practical Theology* (New York: Harper & Row, 1983).

# 3. Further Reading

Calvin, John. *Institutes of the Christian Religion,* ed. John T. McNeill, trans. Ford
    Lewis Battles. 2 vols. Philadelphia: Westminster, 1960.
Campbell, John McLeod. *The Nature of the Atonement.* Edinburgh: The Handsel
    Press, and Grand Rapids: Eerdmans, 1996; first publication Cambridge:
    MacMillan, 1856.
*Luther's Works 36, Word and Sacrament II,* ed. Abdel Ross Wentz. Philadelphia:
    Muhlenberg Press, 1959.
Oberman, Heiko A. *Luther: Man Between God and the Devil.* Trans. Eileen Walliser-
    Schwarzbart. New Haven: Yale University Press, 1989.
Purves, Andrew. *Pastoral Theology in the Classical Tradition.* Louisville: Westminster
    John Knox, 2001.
_____. *Reconstructing Pastoral Theology: A Christological Foundation.* Louisville:
    Westminster John Knox, 2004.
Thurneysen, Eduard. *A Theology of Pastoral Care.* Richmond: John Knox, 1962.
Torrance, James B. *Worship, Community and the Triune God of Grace.* Carlisle:
    Paternoster Press, 1996.
Torrance, Thomas F. *The Mediation of Christ.* Grand Rapids: Eerdmans, 1983.

# 4. Hermeneutical Reflections

First of all, in a joint project such as this, and in company with such
expertise, one is struck by the beauty and rigor of theological analysis
and construction and the sheer awful messiness of sin. As an intellectual
activity in response to the gospel, theology is an attempt at coherent
and reasonable construction. It aims to make sense. There are rules of
discourse and argument to be followed. Tradition is engaged and trajectories of meaning are followed into the present that intend to guide
Christian understanding and practice. There is a nobility of purpose in
the theologian's attempt to give glory to God by bringing the gospel to
faithful expression. Even when the theologian's pride casts a shadow
upon the printed page, or when sloth weakens the presentation, making
it less than it should be, there is a special place in heaven, so we care to
believe, for "the queen of the sciences" and, by implication, we trust, for
those who pursue this calling.

Sin, like surgery, is messy. Unlike surgery, it has no inherent meaning.
It is by nature irrational, destructive, and harmful, breaking communion
with God and relations with one another. Sin is messy insofar, then, as
it cannot be understood on its own terms. It has "surd-like" existence. It
cannot be resolved. While we experience its consequences and play our

parts as sinners, an understanding of sin on its own terms also eludes us. We cannot get our minds around it or tie down its power over us. Like Paul, in a sense, we may want to do good, but we act evilly—and we know it; and we do not want to act evilly, but we feel trapped, often repeating the same, dull sins again and again and again. Whether we name it sin or attach some secular designation, this is the human experi- ence—apart from Christ, the Christian would say, and yet, perplexingly, also for those who claim to be Christian. The theological problem posed by post-baptismal sin, arguably, has never been properly resolved. It confronts us as a sad mystery.

It is in this context that one is compelled to be thankful that it is not theology that saves us, no matter how beautiful and coherent. Neither is the theologian any wiser than anyone else in providing a way out of life's sinful entrapment. Whatever else the gospel of Jesus Christ proclaims, it is that God in, through, and as Jesus Christ has entered into the messiness of the human situation and brought us the love, mercy, and forgiveness of God. The result is restoration to relationship with God and one another. God, we might say, entered into the incoherent messiness of the human condition to bring us the beauty and coherence of the gospel.

Second, in an interdependent world repentance/penance has a special complexity, perhaps. A person's complicity in sin is magnified exponen- tially, for example (and the point, of course, is political), by virtue of medi- cations and cosmetics tested on live animals, clothes made under labor practices that would not be tolerated in the United States, and dispropor- tionate use of the world's natural resources. Much of the time we might even be quite unaware of our accommodation to social and economic sin, when our benefits and apparent blessings are obtained unknowingly in the context of the exploitation of others. In a world such as this, repent- ance/penance surely means deepening economic and political awareness. The concept of a faithful penitential life is expanded to be a life of solidarity with and working for the benefit of the "least of them." A penitential life may well come to mean the practice of pious suspicion.

Third, we must ask what a penitential life means today for our com- mon worship. Worship means many things, of course, but thinking of penance in this context raises serious questions for what is now con- ventionally called contemporary praise worship, as well as for so-called traditional worship.

Contemporary praise worship is surely legitimate in its place. The prob- lem arises when it is the only expression of worship in which one partici- pates. For the issue is this: contemporary praise worship is characterized in part by its lack of a penitential expression. Attention to sin and penance are judged to be depressing, the antithesis of the upbeat, emotionally gratifying character of the new expression. The question arises: does contemporary praise worship leave people in their sin?

Traditional worship, however, is also not without its problems in the light of the teaching on repentance/penance. The point here is that the prayer of confession of sin is so highly generic in its applicability to everybody that in fact it really applies to nobody. Our sins are personal and particular rather than blandly general. That being the case, while we can go through the confession of sin, the reality of sin is not specifically brought to the fore, and next to no amendment of life is called forth. As the question was put to contemporary praise worship, so also it is put to traditional worship: are people still left in their sin?

At least two observations seem to be appropriate. First, a hard look once again needs to be taken at the content of worship regarding the corporate confession of sin. Second, Protestantism needs to find a place for private confession, not just to God but also, occasionally, to a minister or specially trusted (and trained?) spiritual friend.

Thirteen

# The Penitential:
# An Evangelical Perspective

*Gordon T. Smith*

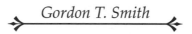

## 1. Tradition

### a. The Disappearance of Confession

In a typical Evangelical congregation of my youth we were regularly urged to confess our sins, and especially so when it came time for the celebration of the Lord's Supper. Indeed, this first-Sunday-of-the-month observance was for many of us first and foremost a time of deep soul-searching, "lest we partake unworthily." This manner of coming to the Table tended to be moralistic and one-dimensional, without much emphasis on joy and celebration, but there was no avoiding the call to confession. Later, my university years included participation in a chapter of the local Christian Intervarsity ministry where we were encouraged to approach our daily "quiet time" by a series of prayers, captured by the acronym ACTS: adoration, confession, thanksgiving, and supplication. And the confession component in our daily prayers tended to touch on those few things for which we feared God's judgment. Nevertheless, both in the Lord's Supper and in our daily prayers we recognized that confession was an integral part of Christian experience.

But even a cursory observation of the liturgical life of most Evangelicals at the beginning of the twenty-first century demonstrates what

Roberta Hestenes has aptly called "the strange disappearance of confession," especially within Evangelical and Protestant Mainline traditions. The practice of confession is now commonly viewed within these circles as either not necessary to the spiritual life or actually a detriment to piety and worship.[1]

This "disappearance" is perplexing because of the obvious witness of the Scriptures, which Evangelicals view as the primary source of Christian thought and piety. But it is equally strange because the penitential is such a vital dimension of the historic Evangelical spiritual tradition. While the moralism of my early years was inadequate, it nevertheless reflected an attempt to draw on this heritage and the biblical witness. Now, however, it is generally assumed that the penitential is best discarded.[2]

One sign of this lack of the penitential is the removal of prayers of confession from the Sunday morning liturgy of Evangelical churches. The reasons given for discontinuing the practice of confession are instructive. First, there are those who insist that the church needs to be more seeker-oriented in its worship and that this requires the removal of such "discouraging" acts as prayers of confession. In this perspective confession is a bit of a "downer"; it is not necessary for the spiritual life and may actually undermine a healthy and positive self-image, something that is viewed as a critical foundation for being a Christian.

Michael R. Linton observes, for example, the stark contrast between the way in which the crucifixion is remembered in Bach's St. Matthew's Passion (produced in 1727) and a contemporary version of Matthew's account, "The Glory of Easter" that is annually presented at one of the most famous of these seeker churches, the Crystal Cathedral. He notes that in

---

[1] The absence is not unique to Evangelicals, of course. Scott Hahn in *Lord, Have Mercy: The Healing Power of Confession* (New York: Doubleday, 2003) observes that many Catholic parishes have remarkably few times posted for confession and that many priests don't even go to confession, or if they do, it is only once or twice a year.

[2] While prayers of confession and teaching on confession is often discarded, it is noteworthy that in many Evangelical churches the practice of approaching the Lord's Supper through serious penitential introspection is still retained. Unfortunately, this tends to be a confession that arises more out of a "fear of unworthiness" than an eagerness for renewal and healing. It is also more individualist than communal, and moralistic rather than a means of attending to deeper disorders.

Bach's rendering, "in the liturgical readings, the congregation itself takes the role of the mob, forcing the congregants to recognize their culpability in the crucifixion." The performers stand not on a stage in front to be observed, but rather in and around the congregation. And as Linton puts it, "with performers ranged all around them, Bach's listeners found that they were not mere observers of a moving story, but the cause of the tale, participants in it, and its beneficiaries."[3] In contrast, for the "Glory of Easter" celebration at the Crystal Cathedral the members of the congregation are observers. They are only an audience to a spectacle: a sincere and perhaps moving spectacle, but one to which they are not responsible. Linton points out that in this version of the Passion the mob does not call for crucifixion. And at the Crystal Cathedral there is a noteworthy revision of the "Lord's Prayer." At the crucial section it reads: "Forgive us those who have wronged us. Lead us not into temptation, But deliver us from evil." The idea of personal responsibility for sin is removed from the ancient prayer. Thus there is no need for Good Friday and certainly no need for anything so "discouraging" as Lent. Confession, the pastor of the Crystal Cathedral is known to insist, is "self-demeaning" and inconsistent with a theology of self-esteem.

Second, other Evangelicals have dispensed with the practice of liturgical confession on the conviction that it is an actual violation of the gospel. The argument is often heard: we need to confess our sins when we become Christians; to feel "low" and guilty prior to our Christian faith is appropriate and something integral to what it means to become a Christian (thus a contrast to the "seeker-sensitive" approach). But to confess sins after that is a violation of the gospel. It is argued that in Christ a person's sins are forgiven, past, present, and future. These preachers proclaim that to confess after one becomes a Christian is to "nail Christ to the cross again!" Instead, they urge their followers to "live in the forgiveness they have already received."[4]

These two perspectives have differing levels of influence within the Evangelical community, and each may well be an understandable response to the ways in which confession has been practiced and understood. But

[3] Michael R. Linton, "Smoke and Mirrors at the Crystal Cathedral," *First Things* June/July (1997) 12–13.

[4] This is the conviction, for example, of popular radio host Bob George, whose message is based on the assumption that the "finished work of Christ" establishes once and for all that a Christian is "in fellowship with God" and that therefore confession is not needed because this "fellowship" cannot be severed.

to discard the penitential is to dispense with a practice that is integral to the Christian experience. And the Evangelical tradition at its best affirms (1) that confession does not demean a person but actually calls forth our best self, and (2) that the Christian is forgiven and in fellowship with Christ but also in need of continual healing, renewal, and reform.

### b. The Penitential in the Evangelical Spiritual Heritage

For the purposes of this essay the Evangelical spiritual heritage is the Christian tradition that in thought and practice arose largely in the seventeenth and eighteenth centuries as a renewal movement within the Protestant Reformation. This essay will focus on Puritan and Wesleyan influences that have had the most profound and lasting impact on the movement, but will also note the significant input of Anabaptist perspectives on confession and repentance.

It is helpful to locate the Evangelical perspective on repentance in the broader theological context in which it emerged. Evangelicals have consistently seen themselves to be the true heirs of the Protestant Reformation. The magisterial Reformers, John Calvin and Martin Luther, both had a marked emphasis on the place of repentance, though their doctrine was developed chiefly in response to Catholic teaching and practice on Penance, namely the practices and dispositions of contrition, confession, amendment, and satisfaction through penance. The Reformers accentuated the priority of faith—"justification by faith alone"—insisting that repentance is but an expression of faith, not necessarily integral to it. They were concerned that nothing "taint" faith as the sole means by which salvation is known and experienced. However, they continually stressed that repentance is vital to the Christian life. It was for Luther an essential means by which a Christian would enter into the grace of baptism, and by which the faith experience represented by our baptism is renewed. While rejecting penance, he maintained that repentance is necessary for the spiritual life while insisting that it was not to be included in "saving faith." Accordingly, there is no merit to be gained; repentance "follows" faith. For Luther any repentance prior to faith is a "work of the law," and thus not an authentic experience of the gospel. So then, as it is a fruit of faith, one could speak of evangelical repentance as integral to the daily experience of the Christian.

Calvin similarly asserts that repentance follows and is subordinate to faith. In some respects his is an even stronger call to repentance in the claim that repentance is not only the fruit of faith but the *necessary* fruit of faith. Without the inclusion of repentance, for Calvin, "any discussion concerning faith will be meager and defective, and indeed almost useless . . . repentance not only always follows faith, but is produced by it . . . ."[5] The call to a faith that effects repentance is reflected not only in the way in which one enters into Christian faith; it is intrinsic to the entire Christian experience, both as disposition and as a practice that we are obliged "to cultivate during the whole course of our lives."[6]

### c. Puritan Sources and Influences

It was out of this Reformed heritage that the Puritans nurtured their distinctive standpoint on repentance, insisting that repentance and confession are central to the gospel and thus to the experience of conversion—but more, that conversion is itself a gateway into a penitential life. This perspective was informed by two dynamics: on the one hand the deadly character of sin, and on the other the powerful goodness and mercy of God.

Through their preaching the Puritans sought to underscore that sin is horrific. They were masters of demonstrating how sin is sin, the destruction of life and all that is good and true, and how apart from conversion and repentance there is no life. This horror with sin blankets their writings with a heavy spirit, a soberness and a near feeling of terror in their writings, easily sensed, for example, in even a cursory reading of Thomas Watson's *The Doctrine of Repentance*. While some may conclude that the Puritans exaggerated the baseness of human wrong, or that they might have been more effective if they had made their message more palatable, we must appreciate that what prompted their concern was a deep awareness of the ramifications of sin.

Furthermore, the Puritans were fervent in stressing the horror of sin in contrast to and in comparison with the holiness of God. But they were equally keen to portray the compassion of God, so that their hearers and readers would see and ultimately experience the grace that God is eager, not reluctant, to forgive and restore. Consequently, Jonathan Edwards could even speak of repentance as a source of delight and pleasure. Though there is deep sorrow, it is for Edwards a "sweet sorrow" that

---

[5] John Calvin, *Institutes of the Christian Religion,* trans. Henry Beveridge (reprint Grand Rapids: Eerdmans, 1979) III, 3, §1.

[6] Ibid. § 18.

"clears the mind and makes it easy and serene," such that it is one of the sources of joy for the Christian.[7]

For the Puritans conversion is the fruit of a preparatory work of the Spirit: a season of humility and contrition for sin. Repentance ensued from this period of preparation. In some cases they were programmatic in their emphasis, insisting on a standard mode or pattern to repentance if it was to be accepted as authentic. The Puritans affirmed that, as acts of response to the prior work of the Spirit, both conversion and sanctification were leveraged by the cultivation of a "mind of repentance." As one Puritan divine, John Owen, has put it, "the vigor and power of spiritual life is dependent on mortification of sin."[8] This is reflected in the words of the Westminster Confession: "Repentance is of such necessity to all sinners, that none may expect pardon without it," and, "it is every [one's] duty to endeavor to repent of [one's] particular sins, particularly." Yet always a recurring theme for the Puritans, as for Calvin, is the affirmation of the priority of faith; repentance is the fruit of faith and is always twinned with faith. It is a faith that trusts in the compassion and mercy of God and rests on the proclivity of God to forgive. Thus what motivates repentance is not so much terror as an awareness of grace. As Thomas Watson puts it, "Sense of guilt is enough to breed terror. Infusion of grace breeds repentance."[9]

The Puritans also held that there is the possibility of false guilt and counterfeit repentance. Watson, for example, speaks of a "holy agony" as a way to capture the idea of a contrite heart (Ps 51:7), and then notes that not all sorrow leads to repentance.[10] Clearly repentance is an act of the human will; but for the Puritans this is nevertheless effected in one's life through the grace of the Word and Spirit. It is, consequently, only authentic conviction or guilt if its source is God, a God who is good and compassionate.[11] Thus the feeling of guilt is authentic (and transforming)

---

[7] Wilson H. Kimnach, Kenneth P. Minkema, and Douglas A. Sweeney, eds., *The Sermons of Jonathan Edwards, A Reader* (New Haven: Yale University Press, 1999) 18, 19.

[8] John Owen, "Of the Mortification of Sin in Believers," in Thomas Russell, ed., *Works VII* (1823) 350.

[9] Thomas Watson, *The Doctrine of Repentance* (Edinburgh: Banner of Truth, 1987 [original ed. 1668]) 15.

[10] Ibid. 20.

[11] It is important to mention this. Jean Delumeau is probably right to speak of "the emergence of a Western guilt culture" in Europe and there is no doubt that

if it is motivated not by terror but by an awareness of the goodness and mercy of God. This means, then, that confession is never forced or offered under compunction or a feeling of coercion; rather, it is voluntary and sincere, motivated by a love for Christ and a genuine love of holiness.[12] Second, though, is that this conviction of sin is only authentic, coming from God through Word and Spirit, if it leads to reformation of life.

When it is authentic, it is integral to the spiritual life, both as disposition and as a practice. The Puritans called for a disposition of "mortification," a mind set against sin and the pattern of sin. The whole of the Christian life, from this perspective, is a lifelong process of recognizing the presence of sin in its manifold expressions: superficial matters when one is younger and the deeper, more tenacious presence of sin as one grows older. Jonathan Edwards attested that a person who has genuine religious affections will be one in whom there is a tender spirit,[13] an inclination of heart that is heedful, actually open to the convicting ministry of the Spirit. When a person becomes a Christian, he or she embraces a habit of mind; such persons become attentive to the well-being of their souls and, since they have come to faith, are ever more conscious of their own sinfulness. Thus, Edwards insists, to be a Christian is to feel a "godly sorrow and mourning for sin."[14] It follows, then, that a true conversion leads to a tenderness of heart, a sensitive conscience. A false conversion puts "an end to convictions of conscience."[15]

A true penitential disposition is then expressed in a practice: the "mortification" evident in self-examination. One particular venue for this was the observance of the Lord's Supper. Thomas Watson, for example, claims that there is a need for ongoing and continuous confession while also indicating that the Lord's Supper is the hour of one's death and that one only approaches the Table as a penitent. He says that "a weeping

---

the Puritans were influenced by this broader cultural trend. See Jean Delumeau, *Sin and Fear: The Emergence of a Western Guilt Culture,* trans. Eric Nicholson (New York: St. Martin's Press, 1990). This is surely the saving grace of the Puritan vision of repentance: that it arises not so much from a fear of hell and judgment but rather from the love of God. But there is no doubt that much Puritan preaching on repentance was both threatening and consoling.

[12] Watson, *The Doctrine of Repentance,* 53, 57.

[13] Jonathan Edwards, *Religious Affections,* ed. John E. Smith (New Haven: Yale University Press, 1959) 363.

[14] Ibid. 366.

[15] Ibid. 364.

frame is a sacramental frame."[16] While the emphasis of the Puritans was on individual confession in personal prayer before God, some also acknowledged the place of confession to another.[17]

A contemporary example of this perspective on the Christian life can be found in the writings of J. I. Packer, who intentionally locates himself within the Puritan spiritual tradition. In one of his works he has an extended section on how spiritual maturity and growth in holiness requires what he calls "growing downward." If the Christian is to grow in faith, hope, and love it all depends on what Packer calls "a life of habitual repentance, as a discipline integral to healthy holy living," and he stresses this while affirming the language of Luther, whom he quotes as saying "that the whole life of believers should be one of repentance."[18]

Consistent with his Puritan mentors, Packer bases his call to "continual" repentance on a particular understanding of the deadly character of sin. Sin is an affront to the holiness of God, a violation of the creation and the Creator. And further, it is rejection of the goodness of God, a sign of ingratitude.[19]

Thus the Christian, Packer insists, instinctively longs to pray with the Psalms that God would search the heart and lead one in the way of life (Ps 139). He uses the image of the gardener who must always be about the task of weeding with the urging that what is evident on the surface requires an approach that routs not only the greenery but also the root system.[20] In so doing, he insists, we attend to the health of the

---

[16] Watson, *The Doctrine of Repentance,* 27.

[17] Watson, in *The Doctrine of Repentance,* speaks directly to the value of confessing sin to another. The Puritans were very wary of anything that struck them as "papist" or any suggestion that forgiveness was only experienced if there was formal confession/absolution in the presence of a priest. However, with reference to Jas 5:16 there is an acknowledgment of the value of confession to another, as a means by which the penitent would experience the freedom of conscience: the value of confessing to a "prudent, pious friend." Watson writes: "It is sinful modesty in Christians that they are not more free with their ministers and other spiritual friends in unburdening themselves and opening the sores and troubles of their souls to them. If there is a thorn sticking to the conscience, it is good to make use of those who may help pluck it out" (37).

[18] J. I. Packer, *Rediscovering Holiness* (Ann Arbor: Servant Publications, 1992) 121.

[19] Ibid. 135–36.

[20] Ibid. 137.

soul, and view spiritual health as a gift from God that we do not take for granted, but tend with care the garden that is our souls.[21]

Thus for the Puritans the Christian life is a penitential life. A genuine life of faith is evident in a penitential habit of heart: that is, disposition of contriteness as well as the practice of repentance and confession. The penitential disposition and practice are then for the Puritans the engine or primary impulse of spiritual growth. They use the language of death, that repentance is an act of dying to sin; but death to sin is overtaken by a "repentance toward God" (Acts 20:21); the dying is not the end. And it is both the disposition and practice of penitence that enables one to experience the transforming grace of God. This transformation comes slowly, at a rate or pace, as Puritan preachers were wont to say, that is determined by the grace and initiative of the Spirit. Thus the practice of confession is one of radical dependence on the Spirit.[22]

### d. Wesleyan Perspectives

John (1703–1791) and Charles (1707–1788) Wesley gave primary leadership to a movement that was heir to the Reformation but was also deeply influenced by their Puritan upbringing, the Lutheran pietism of the Moravians, and the Anglican communion of which John and Charles were a part. However, John Wesley's theological and spiritual vision of the Christian life was also deeply influenced by the piety of the late Middle Ages, evident, for example, in his perspective on perfection or maturity in the Christian life and the place of the Eucharist in worship (though his theology of the Eucharist is actually closer to that of John Calvin).

Repentance had a critical place in John Wesley's idea of the spiritual life. It arose, in part, from his own experience; the "heart-warming" experience of Aldersgate Street (1738) was, specifically, an experience by which he was assured that his sins were pardoned. His growing disaffection with the dry formalism and soft morality of the high-church Anglicanism of

---

[21] Ibid. 149.

[22] The penitential prayers of John Bradford illustrate this well. The prayers include not only the appropriate cry for mercy, "we beseech thee therefore of thy rich mercy," but also the longing for the work of the Spirit, "Endue us with thy Holy Spirit" and elsewhere ". . . by thy Spirit, power and grace, to humble, mortify, and fear my conscience for my sins to salvation . . . ." Aubrey Townsend, ed., *The Writings of John Bradford* (Cambridge: Cambridge University Press, 1848) 201, 210.

his day left him seeking a genuinely experiential religion that included an assurance that one had been forgiven. This assurance, the knowledge of God's justifying grace, was for Wesley the fruit of repentance. But authentic repentance led not merely to forgiveness but also to transformation. In agreement with his Puritan heritage, its authenticity was evident in the pattern of one's life (what Wesley called works of piety and works of mercy, evident most notably in love of one's neighbor).

Repentance then is essential to the experience of Christian conversion; but it is equally critical to the maturing life of the believer. In his sermon on the "The Repentance of Believers"[23] Wesley observes that it is commonly thought that repentance and faith are only the "gate of religion," a time-bound practice or disposition concurrent with coming to Christian faith. He notes that appeal is sometimes made to the line in Heb 6:1, "not laying again a foundation of repentance from dead works." Wesley insists, however, that while faith and repentance are certainly needed in coming to faith in Christ (the experience of justification and regeneration), "repentance and faith are fully as necessary in order for our continuance and growth in grace . . . ."[24] He counsels that though sin does not "reign" in the Christian believer, it nevertheless "remains" in the heart of the new Christian, thus necessitating ongoing repentance. The new believer is always prone to love the creature more than the Creator, to be "a lover of pleasure rather than a lover of God" and thus the need to be watchful and to guard over one's life. For Wesley, just as "sin remains in our hearts . . ." so it cleaves to all our words and actions."[25] He uses the image of sin as sickness in want of healing, and notes that unless "we are sensible of our disease, it admits no cure."[26]

Repentance, then, is a reflection of self-knowledge, particularly the humility in which we see ourselves for who we are. Christians recognize that they are not immune to sin or temptation, but vulnerable, especially to pride. Indeed, Wesley emphasizes that in repentance the Christian believer must give specific attention to pride: "We may therefore set it down as an undoubted truth, that covetousness, together with pride, self-will, and anger, remain in the hearts even of them that are justified."

[23] John Wesley, *The Works of John Wesley*, 3rd ed. Vol. V: First Series of Sermons, No. XIV, "The Repentance of Believers" (Grand Rapids: Baker Books, 1986) 156–70. (Subsequent references are to section and paragraph numbers.)

[24] Wesley, "The Repentance of Believers," Intro, § 1.

[25] Ibid., I, §§ 10 and 11.

[26] Ibid., Intro, § 1.

He goes on to speak of the ways in which pride infiltrates all our actions, and how fear or timidity leads us to sins of omission: the failure to do what we know we should do.[27]

This self-knowledge is also reflected in a keen awareness of one's need for grace, for the enabling of God. Thus Christian repentance, for Wesley, is necessarily complemented by faith: not only the faith to believe and trust that sins are forgiven in Christ, but also the faith that appropriates the grace of God in Christ by which hearts are purified. One is able to receive not only mercy but also the grace "to find help in every time of need."[28]

The Wesleyan perspective, of course, assumes the legitimacy and significance of personal responsibility. If one sins, one is accountable. Quite simply, for Wesley a person sins when he or she yields to temptation. The added tragedy is the betrayal of one's Christian identity and commitment. And yet what especially marks the Wesleyan vision for the Christian life is the possibility of genuine transformation, that is, the "perfection" of the Christian. Wesley had an extraordinary vision of the possibilities of grace, of the potential for a holiness that marked each dimension of human existence. Thus the act of repentance is a practice by which the Christian reembraces this goal of personal holiness; it is an act of personal responsibility for one's life, in response to the grace of God and as a means of actually embracing this transforming grace.[29]

Contemporary theologians within the Wesleyan Methodist tradition recognize that the spiritual practice of confession and repentance is neglected within Methodist circles and call for its recovery. Walter Klaiber and Manfred Marquardt, for example, emphasize that in the Wesleyan heritage repentance is not an event that is a once-for-all in the life of the Christian. Rather, because a believer has the possibility of falling back "under the dominion of sin," repentance is both a necessity and a possibility if one is to live in fellowship with God. However, they insist that the recovery of this practice must be rooted in a deep appreciation of the gospel. They note that there is a deep joy in repentance when the call to confession arises out of an emphasis on the love of God rather than the condemnation of the law. They reject the idea that there is one act of repentance that is determined

---

[27] Ibid., I, §§ 9 and 14.

[28] Ibid., II, § 6.

[29] Wesley, *The Works of John Wesley*, 3rd ed. Vol. V: First Series of Sermons, Sermon XIX, "The Great Privilege of Those That Are Born of God" (Grand Rapids: Baker Books, 1986) 223–33, II, §§ 2, 3, 4, 6, 7, and 9.

by the law and another that is determined by the gospel, but rather insist that Christians can only appreciate the character and gravity of sins when their situation is seen in the light of God's love.[30]

Contemporary Methodists are also highlighting an invaluable part of their heritage: that societies, classes, and bands formed the heart of the movement and that the experience of community within these "structures" was indispensable to spiritual formation. The small group provided the Christian with support and encouragement, but also a safe place for mutual confession and accountability.

A critical theme in the Wesleyan heritage is the call to holiness, specifically Christian perfection. Yet even against the backdrop of this powerful call and the insistence on both the necessity of holiness and the possibilities of divine grace, repentance is still a vital Christian practice. Sondra Higgins Matthaei observes that Wesley never affirmed a final perfection in this life, but rather emphasized the absolute need for an intentional response to the "perfecting process by the Holy Spirit that saves us from [the] ongoing encounter with sin."[31] Quoting Wesley, she observes that the tradition affirms that even in the "perfect love of God" one continues to grow in grace, and thus one acknowledges ignorance, frailty, and temptation.[32] To summarize, then, if we take Jonathan Edwards and the Puritans as one stream and Wesleyan Methodism as another, it is fair to conclude that the practice of confession and repentance has been integral to the Evangelical theological and spiritual tradition. The contemporary "disappearance" of confession represents a notable departure from a dimension of Christian spirituality that the early movement deemed necessary to Christian faith and practice.

---

[30] Walter Klaiber and Manfred Marquardt, *Living Grace: An Outline of United Methodist Theology,* trans. J. Steven O'Malley and Ulrike R. M. Guthrie (Nashville: Abingdon, 2001) 238–40.

[31] Sondra Higgins Matthaei, *Making Disciplines: Faith Formation in the Wesleyan Tradition* (Nashville: Abingdon, 2000) 50.

[32] Ibid. 51. Randy L. Maddox, in *Responsible Grace: John Wesley's Practical Theology* (Nashville: Abingdon, 1994) 165, profiles Wesley's observation that there is a difference between outward sin and inward infirmities, a reminder that Wesley did not assume that Christians would receive the divine gift of perfection in this life and that as such repentance remains an essential practice of the Christian. "Thus," Maddox concludes, "no matter how much transformation we may experience along our Christian journey, we never outgrow our need for . . . repentance . . ." (166).

## e. The Mennonite Spiritual Heritage

This disappearance would be equally anomalous for Mennonites and other Evangelical Christians who are heirs to the Radical Reformation. A comprehensive summary of the Anabaptist call to repentance is found in the "Five Fruits of Repentance," part of a letter by Pilgram Marpeck. What is noteworthy in this list of "fruits" is that though it is written as a counter to Protestant as well as Catholic perspectives on confession and repentance, the themes are remarkably congruent with those of the Magisterial Reformation and the leaders of the Evangelical renewal movements of the seventeenth and eighteenth centuries.

Marpeck outlines, on the one hand, the deadly consequences of sin, and on the other, the personal responsibility for sin. Sin is inexcusable and thus its presence is a cause of deep sorrow and anguish. As he puts it, the "fruit of repentance proves itself in suffering, sorrowing, fear and pain of conscience, in deep affliction . . . ."[33] And this sorrow for sin is not so much out of a fear of the consequences of sin as a grief for having acted in a manner that is inconsistent with the character of God.[34] As with both the Puritans and Wesley, repentance is "vain" if it does not lead to reformation of character.[35] What all of this presupposes is, of course, personal responsibility. Marpeck, for example, insists that one cannot blame another or one's circumstances. His language is specific and forceful; to blame another is to blame God: "Whoever therefore points to any creature in heaven and on earth as the cause of their sin, deceptiveness, and wickedness in order to excuse themselves, accuses God, the Creator . . . ."[36]

All of this finds remarkable expression in a Menno Simons exposition of the Twenty-Fifth Psalm, which is written in the form of a penitential prayer. Again, it is noteworthy that what motivates the penitent is not so much the terror of hell and death as, rather, the goodness of God. Simons, the penitent, deeply aware of his own failures, cries out to God, "Accept me in grace and give me your mercy, blessing and confidence, Lord, for the sake of your own goodness . . ." and later, ". . . I do come before your throne of mercy, for I know that you are gracious and good. You do

---

[33] Cornelius J. Dyck, ed. and trans., *Spiritual Life in Anabaptism* (Scottsdale, PA: Herald Press, 1995) 224.

[34] Ibid. 226 (see the "Third Fruit of Repentance").

[35] Ibid. 227.

[36] Ibid.

not desire that sinners should die but that they repent and have life."[37]
For Simons the goodness and mercy of God summon forth a profound
longing expressed through the imagery of sickness and healing. As in
Wesley's sermons, Christ is the healer. When Simons despairs before God
of his wanton failures and error-prone life, he recognizes that "Your word
alone can heal all things . . . I seek and desire this grace, for it alone is
the medicament which can heal my sick soul."[38]

This notion that the grace of God alone is the means of one's transformation and healing is central to Anabaptist spirituality: "You alone,"
Simons writes, "can aid me in times of temptation and rescue my feet from
being stuck in the net of sinfulness."[39] This radical dependence on God is
specifically an act of intentional responsiveness to the Spirit. The Spirit
is the Teacher and Counselor who illumines the mind and enables the
heart to feel grief for sin.[40] This penitential perspective is, however, first
and foremost a response to Christ, with a heartfelt acknowledgment that
forgiveness is ultimately found in the "sprinkled blood."[41] It is in response
to the cross that Simons implores: "Only this I pray for and desire with
all my heart, that you look upon me, a miserable sinner, with the eyes of
your grace and mercy, that you have mercy on me in my great need and
comfort me with your Holy Spirit, and take away my sins."[42]

And one cannot help but highlight that Marpeck writes to Christian
communities; Simons reflects on Psalm 25 not only as one who in coming
to Christ finds the grace of forgiveness, but as a penitent Christian. And I
incorporate the Mennonite and Anabaptist perspective to reinforce how
integral the penitential is to the Evangelical spiritual heritage. Together
with the Puritan and Wesleyan they give us a remarkably consistent perspective on what is for them a defining element of the Christian life.

## f. Conclusion

At its best the Evangelical spiritual tradition affirmed that the Christian lives in humble awareness of the goodness of God, who unfail-

---

[37] Daniel Liechty, ed. and trans., *Early Anabaptist Spirituality: Selected Writings*
(Mahwah, NJ: Paulist, 1994) 253.

[38] Ibid. 257.

[39] Ibid. 261.

[40] Ibid. 262.

[41] Ibid., 264.

[42] Ibid. 265.

ingly calls the believer from a disposition and pattern of behavior that is inconsistent with the Christian confession. A distinctive strength of the movement was its stress on the need for honest self-appraisal and understanding, and that the Christian had the capacity to take personal responsibility for one's life.

But this was all too easily couched in a culture of guilt and fear. And with the recurring emphasis on volition within the revivalism of the nineteenth and twentieth centuries, many Evangelicals lived with a perpetual sense of failure because they had not "surrendered (their) all." Further, the propensity was to focus on individual "sinful acts" rather than that which had been more central to the heritage: the realization that the greatest danger may well be that of autonomous humanity, that is, the subtle and comprehensive sin of pride and self-righteousness. Finally, *contra* the best of the heritage, confession was seen to be a purely individual act, with little if any communal contriteness or confession to another. Further, it came to be viewed more as duty rather than gift, and so, perhaps most significantly, it lacked the corresponding assurance of pardon.

As a result we might be somewhat sympathetic to the more recent inclination within Evangelicalism to dispense with confession and repentance altogether! But in so doing we lose the legitimate and essential insights of the tradition.

## 2. Implications

While Evangelicals have much to learn from the spiritual wisdom of other Christian traditions and even, perhaps, from other religious traditions, we can begin by drawing on the insights of our own heritage.

First, it would mean a renewed appreciation of the vital place of repentance in the spiritual life. While repentance is not synonymous with conversion, it is so integral that the Scriptures often speak of conversion by speaking of repentance. The Evangelical tradition has consistently maintained that there is no conversion without repentance and, further, that there is no growth in faith, hope, and love without repentance and confession. The call to repentance is inherent in the gospel; the gospel is not preached unless there is a call for repentance. This call is not demoralizing news but, ultimately, good news; it is a declaration that there is hope in the midst of failure and brokenness.

The Evangelical tradition has affirmed, then, that confession is intrinsic to the very structure of the spiritual life; the Christian life is one of continuous repentance and conversion. Embracing the life of God requires a repudiation of the life that is anti-God so that, in this sense, repentance is a catalyst for spiritual renewal and growth.

Here is where John Wesley's and Menno Simons' image of sin as sickness is particularly pertinent. The Christian is welcomed and accepted by God, *fait accompli*. Yet it is nevertheless the case that baptism does not result in sinless perfection. It is, rather, the sacramental act by which the Christian is set on a penitential way, seeking the healing of God. However, the call to repentance has always been distorted within the Evangelical heritage when it was not rooted in the context of the love and acceptance of God. Contrary to the common language of my upbringing, the Christian does not repent in order to "make things right with God," as a kind of self-justification before God. Rather, the act of confession is located within a mindfulness of one's justification. While there is no doubt that some Evangelicals are inclined to think that if one sins, one is in a kind of suspended salvation (pending "making things right with God"), the tradition is at its best when it has affirmed that the Christian makes a confession from a personal knowledge of the love of God.

Further, the Evangelical heritage rightly calls for confession as a means of enabling Christians to live whole rather than fractured lives. Confession in this perspective is an act by which the believer acknowledges a disconnection between orthodoxy and "orthopraxis." The longing for consistency serves as motivation for approaching confession as a renewal of one's baptismal vows. The Christian seeks a realignment in thought, word, and deed around an awareness and conviction of the call of God to be holy.

The tradition is at its best when the approach to confession highlights the goodness and mercy of God. There is something deeply troubling in an Evangelical propensity to choose a posture of judgment toward the world and culture, toward those of other religious traditions, and toward their children.

Further, the tradition is at its best when repentance is clearly twinned with faith. As such, confession is an act of humble and radical dependence and trust in God. The Christian is able to live with greater integrity in the world largely and primarily because one is graced in the awareness that one's life is anchored in the mercy of God. Confession, then, is never merely the righting of wrongs or misdeeds. It is an acknowledgment that the Christian as yet bears the flesh *(sarx)* and that as humans we are prone to prideful self-sufficiency rather than trust in God. Confession, then, enables the Christian to be more thoroughly centered in God rather than self. This means, it must be stressed, that there is nothing gained by a perpetual feeling of guilt. To remain mired in guilt is nothing but narcissistic self-absorption and self-preoccupation, another form of pride. Rather, for the Evangelical tradition joy is the fruit of repentance and the evidence that one has truly experienced what it means to be forgiven. Confession arises out of an awareness that the kindness of God leads the Christian to repentance (Rom 2:4) and that the experience of forgiveness is expressed in joy. The practice of confession is badly skewed when the driving motivation is a fear of hell and judgment rather than an awareness of God's love and compassion and God's capacity to make one whole. It is God's love and capacity to heal than motivates repentance.

Evangelicals love to sing, and within the tradition no hymn writer more effectively captured these themes that Charles Wesley. Of his various penitential hymns surely one of the most treasured is "Depth of Mercy! Can there be." Notable in the hymn is the dynamic tension when the lyrics acknowledge the horror of sin and the "wrath" of God, but the driving force and grace-filled resolution is found in divine love:

> Depth of Mercy! Can there be
> Mercy still reserved for me?
> Can my God his wrath forbear?
> Me, the chief of sinners, spare?

> I have long withstood His grace,
> Long provoked Him to His face,
> Would not harken to His calls,
> Grieved Him by a thousand falls.

> Lord, incline me to repent;
> Let me now my fall lament,
> Deeply my revolt deplore,
> Weep, believe, and sin no more.

> Still for me the Saviour stands;
> Shows His wounds, and spreads his hands;
> God is love, I know, I feel.
> Jesus weeps, and loves me still.

# 3. Further Reading

## a. Anabaptist Perspectives

Dyck, Cornelius J., ed. and trans. *Spiritual Life in Anabaptism*. Scottsdale, PA: Herald Press, 1995.

Liechty, Daniel, ed. and trans. *Early Anabaptist Spirituality: Selected Writings.* Mahwah, NJ: Paulist, 1994; see particularly the meditation on Psalm 25 by Menno Simons.

### b. Puritan and Reformed Perspectives

Helm, Paul. *The Beginnings: Word and Spirit in Conversion.* Edinburgh: Banner of Truth, 1986.
Kimnach, Wilson H., Kenneth P. Minkema, and Douglas A. Sweeney, eds. *The Sermons of Jonathan Edwards, A Reader.* New Haven: Yale University Press, 1999.
Packer, J. I. *Rediscovering Holiness.* Ann Arbor: Servant Publications, 1992.
Watson, Thomas. *The Doctrine of Repentance.* Edinburgh: Banner of Truth, 1987 (original ed. 1668).

### c. Wesleyan Methodist Perspectives

Maddox, Randy L. *Responsible Grace: John Wesley's Practical Theology.* Nashville: Abingdon, 1994.
Wesley, John. *The Works of John Wesley,* 3rd ed. Vol. V: First Series of Sermons, No. XIV, "The Repentance of Believers," and Sermon XIX, "The Great Privilege of Those That Are Born of God." Grand Rapids: Baker Books, 1986.

# 4. Hermeneutical Reflections

The colloquium on the penitential in the Christian theological traditions was a conversation across disciplines as well as theological and spiritual traditions. At least two things emerged from this that are noteworthy for those who come to this discussion from the Evangelical tradition.

First, there is a tension inherent in the Christian experience of the penitential that Evangelicals have always struggled to maintain, and not always effectively. On the one hand, the Scriptures clearly speak of a God who is angry in the face of sin; there is no avoiding the language of judgment that runs through the Scriptures. And from this perspective it would seem that repentance is called for under threat of horrific consequences. We cannot speak of the penitential without at one and the same time recognizing that sin and disobedience are the violation of the holy character of God and the covenant God has established with his people.

Yet on the other hand repentance is based on a covenant relationship; it is the kindness of God that calls forth the repentance of the church, and it is the enabling of God that makes it possible for the community of faith to turn from sin to righteousness. Repentance is motivated by a love for God rather than a fear of judgment.

And it would seem that one generation of Evangelicals will emphasize one side of this equation at the expense of the other. Those within the tradition struggle to sustain a vision of the holiness of God and God's judgment upon not just the world, but indeed the church, while simultaneously celebrating and declaring the gospel in the face of wrong, evil, and disobedience. Unfortunately, one stream of Evangelicals has reacted against the moralism of a previous generation and now hardly mentions sin, judgment, and confession. And repentance has no place in liturgies where the sole agenda seems to be to stress how "nice" God is. Yet it is not that God is not holy, for Evangelicals are all too easily prone to indicate how they are accepted by God while at one and the same time condemning the society in which they live (often quite comfortably).

Surely the capacity to sustain the tension will come through a clear articulation of the deadly character of sin, but with an appreciation that the heart of the matter is dependence on God: that sin is first and foremost a matter of faith and that disobedience finds expression in thought, word, and deed, in both individual as well as social behaviors. But then, just as quickly, the community of faith will insist that sin and death do not have the last word; the call to repentance is a call to hope in response to the gracious initiative of God. Thus any discussion of sin is always in the context of the actions of God in Christ Jesus. Preaching will certainly include the pronouncement that sin is deadly, but also and always within the context of the grand narrative of redemption.

Second, however much the Evangelical spiritual heritage has emphasized the importance of repentance and confession, what is often missing for the contemporary Christian is a rite or practice that sustains confession within the rhythms of the spiritual life. Here is where many Evangelicals will draw on the more historic, sacramental, and liturgical traditions to find practices and prayers that can be incorporated into both individual and corporate spirituality. Part of the value of not just the cross-disciplinary discussion but also the exploration of this theme across traditions is that those within this tradition can appreciate how fundamental to the rhythms of worship is the practice of confession in these other communions.

However, some Evangelical Christians are still very hesitant to bring formal, liturgical prayers and rites into their worship. They are, at least for the time being, drawn to a more charismatic chorus-based worship. For them worship is the enthusiastic if not actually ecstatic celebration

of the goodness of God in songs of praise. Yet the joyful acknowledgment of the holiness of God is not, in turn, reflected in penitential songs
of worship. This is telling. Surely those who write and lead the songs of
worship for this tradition need to give attention to the composition of
sung prayers of confession and the integration of these into worship.

At its best the Evangelical heritage has within it a wonderful appreciation of the priority of God's initiative and grace and the indispensabil-
ity of human agency by way of response. Thus the practice of confession
can be a means of empowering Christians to act and refuse to succumb,
as though it were a matter of fate, to their predicament. They can be encouraged to respond to the awareness of God's goodness and the call of
God to turn from what is inconsistent with the character of God. While
responding with compassion to the failures of others, pastoral leadership
can include compassionate instruction that fosters genuine conversion,
ongoing and continuous conversion.

Fourteen

# Yielding to the Spirit:
# A Pentecostal Understanding of Penitence

*Cheryl Bridges Johns*

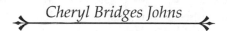

## 1. Tradition

The recent turn in Protestant churches toward celebratory worship has its roots in the North American Pentecostal/Charismatic movement. Many churches are now incorporating into their liturgy praise and worship music, enthusiastic hand-clapping, and liturgical dance. While this turn toward the experiential offers a needed corrective to the rational nature of Protestant worship, it fails to incorporate the inherent penitential aspects of Pentecostal liturgy. For this reason Pentecostalism's influence on the Christian churches within North America has been narrowed to adding a bit of spiritual vitality to worship. However, the movement's ecumenical witness includes a vision of penitence that counterbalances its more jubilant side.

Historically, Pentecostal worship has not only created space for contrition but also embodied a deconstructive vision of the Christian faith. This form of Pentecostalism is sometimes frightening and messy to those who value order and decency in worship, a category that would include most middle-class Pentecostals.[1] In the messier version persons do not come into

---

[1] Richard Shaull noted the tendency to reduce Pentecostalism's contribution to the Christian churches to vibrant forms of worship. He warned: "Our churches

the kingdom of light out of the kingdom of darkness without struggle, and repentance is often a desperate call for deliverance from the power of sin. Throughout the Christian journey penitence is fueled by ongoing yielding to the Holy Spirit that may be characterized by times of great crisis.

It should be noted, however, that while many North American Protestants are rejecting this messy paradigm for a more socially polite version, the majority of the world's Pentecostals continue to maintain a paradigm of worship that is able to incorporate both the celebratory and the penitential aspects. Most Pentecostals live in the forgotten parts of the world where violence and poverty mark daily existence. They are known to bring pathos into the sacred space of worship. For them, worship is frequently a "festival of tears."[2] All around the world, the floors and prayer altars of Pentecostal churches are often awash with the tears of both sinners and saints. Boxes of tissue are common liturgical items that adorn church sanctuaries.

It is this messier and broader version of Pentecostalism that will be offered within the space of this chapter. While not seen in the media and promoted in middle-class North America, it reveals the dominant Pentecostal vision of the Christian life. Hence it offers a truer version of a Pentecostal understanding of penitence.

It is the thesis of this chapter that a Pentecostal vision of repentance is fused into the heart of the Christian journey and finds its expression as an essential ingredient in the worshipful, Spirit-filled life. Repentance is therefore holistic. It involves the whole person in submission to a holy God. A Pentecostal understanding of repentance is grounded in

---

will not be revitalized, and much less reformed, if we simply appropriate some elements of Pentecostal worship and experience without subjecting our heritage and present existence to the sort of radical questioning that comes from a serious encounter with Pentecostalism. If in this encounter we limit ourselves to adding, to what we now have, some of the outward expressions of it without entering into the historical experience of suffering and struggle out of which it has evolved and without seeking to understand what God is doing in the midst of all this, we may create a bit of vitality to our superficial spirituality and sterile worship but will never open our whole being to God who can fill our lives with compassion." Richard Shaull and Waldo Cesar, *Pentecostalism and the Future of the Christian Churches* (Grand Rapids: Eerdmans, 2000) 133–34.

[2] The phrase "festival of tears" is borrowed from the ancient story of bishop Nonnus (448) whose night spent in prayer and tears resulted in the conversion of the notorious sinner Pelagia. She was also known for her life of prayer and penitent tears.

a distinctive worldview. It is exhibited in a particular understanding of salvation that is characterized as a journey. It is fueled by a passion for God and the kingdom of God.

## a. Worldview

Any discussion of a Pentecostal perspective on repentance should be framed within an exploration of the worldview that is common within the movement. In contrast to the scientific worldview that understands the world as operating out of laws and principles, Pentecostals see the world as God-centered, and thus centered in mystery. Jackie Johns observes that while this fusion of God with the phenomenological does not collapse God into creation, it is a predisposition to see the transcendent God at work in, with, through, above, and beyond all things.[3]

The belief that the natural world is joined dynamically to the supernatural not only creates an awareness of the presence of God in the most mundane; it also acknowledges the presence of the epiphanies of darkness that surround all knowing. The world is in a fallen state in which the powers of evil inhabit the created order. The devil, who is the "prince of this world," is a personal spirit-being who controls the powers of darkness. This world is not unlike the one portrayed within the Gospel of Mark: demon-infested and caught within a cosmic struggle between life and death.

Within this supra-natural worldview the traditional dichotomies that govern the Enlightenment are broken down. Reason and emotion are fused into a transrational vision of reality. While reason is valued, it is limited in its ability to truly know the world. The Spirit who knows all things can transcend it.

Time itself is systemically related to God. Pentecostal theologian Steven Land describes this view of time as a fusion in which all events, past, present, and future, are related to a single master plan of God that will be consummated at the second coming of Christ. Time is therefore a whole in which "space and time are fused in the prophetic reckoning created and sustained by the Spirit of the end. Here and now, there and then are telescoped and traversed by the Spirit."[4]

---

[3] Jackie Johns, "Pentecostalism and the Postmodern Worldview," *Journal of Pentecostal Theology* 78 (1995) 87.

[4] Steven J. Land, *Pentecostal Spirituality: A Passion for the Kingdom* (Sheffield: Sheffield Academic Press, 1993) 98.

Another fusion common to a Pentecostal worldview is that between body and spirit. This spirit-body correspondence allows for the body to be an instrument either of evil (demonic possession) or of God's grace. In redemption, the whole body is involved. It becomes a "temple of the Holy Ghost" through which God is worshiped and God's kingdom served. The body thus becomes sacramental and phenomena such as glossolalia signify the presence and activity of the Spirit.

### b. Salvation as Healing and Deliverance

Within this worldview salvation is understood as deliverance from the powers of evil and the kingdom of darkness. Under the effects of sin persons are held in bondage and are impotent to deliver themselves. Their lives are characterized by a pervasive brokenness: broken families, addictions, violence, and abuse. As a result people are not only guilty before a holy God; overwhelming shame alienates them. Salvation is healing from the brokenness created by sin. Broken bodies are renewed. Broken families are restored and broken dreams are reinvented. The shame that covers them is removed. Wholeness, therefore, is the result of salvation.

This image of salvation differs from the traditional Reformation emphasis on justification as declaration of righteousness. Within Pentecostalism, salvation is therapeutic. While guilt figures into a Pentecostal paradigm, it is not the dominant motive for repentance. Persons are driven to repentance because they are impotent to help themselves. In his research on Brazilian Pentecostals, Richard Shaull noted this sense of powerlessness:

> Human beings are poor, impotent, and condemned to insignificance. They are engaged in a desperate struggle for survival in a world falling apart around them. They and their world are "possessed," dominated by supernatural demonic forces who are agents of chaos and destruction. In their daily personal lives they are overwhelmed not primarily by the sense of sin and guilt, but by the painful realities of the life of the poor.[5]

[5] Richard Shaull, *Pentecostalism and the Future of the Christian Churches* (Grand Rapids: Eerdmans, 2000) 145. J. I. Packer has also noted this distinction among North American Pentecostals. He observed that many people in Pentecostal churches see themselves "less as guilty sinners than as moral, spiritual, and emotional cripples, scarred, soured, and desperately needing deliverance from bondages in their inner lives . . . ." See his "Pentecostalism Reinvented: The

Within this context salvation is the presence and power of the resurrected Christ as the source of life. Salvation is what Shaull describes as "the reconstruction of life." It is the experience of God to deliver persons who are condemned to their own death rows. This presence and power of God to bring life out of death and decay is not centered in the announcement of forgiveness and justification (although this is included). Rather, it is centered in a direct experience with the living Christ. By the power of the Spirit the resurrected Jesus is present to heal and deliver.[6] This experience of the resurrected Jesus brings about a newfound freedom. It is a freedom to begin a journey of faith. People find themselves being carried forward by the Spirit into a mysterious realm of the future. Where they once were imprisoned and impotent to deliver themselves, they are now encouraged to expect miracles and to find the courage and the energy to do the impossible.

### c. Salvation as Journey

Repentance within the context of Pentecostalism is not a one-time event. Rather, it is an action that initiates and maintains the Christian's journey from grace to grace. This way of salvation is not so much an *ordo salidus* as it is a *via salidus*. Pentecostals testify of their salvation in terms of a journey that involves "walking in the light as the Spirit shines that light upon your path." The image of salvation as a way or as a journey is rooted in the Wesleyan understanding of salvation as a synergy of grace and the human will that results in transformation of heart and life. Within this framework salvation is both crisis and development. It is both state of being and a journey. Justification and sanctification thus work together. Sin is not to reign in the life of the pilgrim. Therefore as one walks in the light, the blood of Christ, the Word, and the Spirit serve as agents of cleansing.[7]

---

Charismatic Renewal," in Harold B. Smith, ed., *Pentecostals from the Inside Out* (Wheaton: Victor Books, 1990) 147.

[6] It is a common misconception that Pentecostals emphasize the Spirit to the neglect of a Christ-centered faith. Early Pentecostals spoke of the fourfold gospel: Jesus as Saviour, Healer, Baptizer, and Coming King; or they spoke of a fivefold gospel: Jesus as Saviour, Sanctifier, Healer, Baptizer, and Coming King. Pentecostal testimonies are replete with references to experiences of the living Christ. So Christocentric was early Pentecostalism that its first major rift resulted in what are commonly known as "Jesus Only" Pentecostals.

[7] Land, *Pentecostal Spirituality*, 144.

Land, who centers Pentecostal spirituality within the affections,[8] understands the Pentecostal "way of salvation" as an ever-increasing passion for the in-breaking-coming kingdom. Passion is construed as ruling affection, with the heart of the affections being love.[9] The journey of the believer is therefore marked by a continual submission to God in confession and repentance. The journey is a continual yielding to the Spirit who knows all things, searches hearts, fills them with love, and sighs and groans for the kingdom. "When one sighs with the Spirit in longing expectation," observes Land, "then one is disposed rightly."[10]

This journey with God and in God is very serious, involving an ongoing process of overcoming sin and drawing closer to God. The God who liberates is also the God who exists in glory and holiness. The glory of God is the majesty worshipers feared to see lest they die (Heb 12:20, 21).[11] Fear of God is a common response in Pentecostal circles, for along with manifestations of healing and deliverance there are manifestations of God's glory. Consider the following:

> We pitched our tent near a place known as Albritton Mill on Bro. J. H. Lowery's place, on the fifteenth of October and began to tell the people that Jesus is just the same, and the Lord is working with us confirming the Word with signs following. Amen. . . . On Saturday night after a message was delivered, inspired by the Holy Ghost in obedience to the Spirit that reached the hearts of almost all the congregation of about 500, an altar call was made and there was about forty fell into the altar. The altar service had been going on for about a half hour, when the report was made under the tent that a large ball of fire was shedding its light on the side of the tent. The anxious crowd ran out from under the tent to see the wonder. The light passed upward, then fire began to pass through the elements as if it were raining fire, and great pillars of smoke would follow. It continued thus for an hour or so mingled with the praises of the saints and cries of lost souls as the sound of

---

[8] For Land, Christian affections "are objective, relational and dispositional. To say that Christian affections are objective means that affections take an object. In this case the object is also the subject: God is the source and object of Christian affections." *Pentecostal Spirituality*, 134.

[9] See ibid. 175.

[10] Ibid. 177.

[11] R. Hollis Gause, "Repentance as the Essential Element of Revival," unpublished manuscript.

many waters filling the elements. As the fire and smoke passed over several were saved and sanctified, while five were baptized with the Spirit. Glory to God. We are in the last days.[12]

The above testimony not only reflects the image of pilgrimage ("we pitched our tent"), but also indicates that early Pentecostals saw their "tents of meeting" as places where the *Shekinah* would come. The above testimony of a divine visitation contains a mingling of the cries of the lost, the praises of the saints, and the raining fire of God. Harvey Cox's description of the Azusa Street revival, which is commonly known as the birthplace of modern Pentecostalism, includes the same imagery: "they . . . sensed . . . that when the flames came, they would purge and purify as well as enliven and inspire . . . . There would be sulphur as well as balm. It would be the fearful as well as the wonderful day of the Lord."[13]

Within the context of this glory-filled eschatological journey converts are encouraged to seek sanctification.[14] Repentance thus continues as believers yield to the convicting Spirit who reveals the holdouts and areas of resistance within persons. As Land notes, "Sanctification was the center or heart of 'Bible Salvation' for the believers at Azusa and millions subsequently."[15] The desire for sanctification is a desire for the heart of God. It is a heart filled with purity and love. Compassion for those who are yet held captive within the kingdom of darkness marks the believer's journey. The sanctified heart is thus the missional heart.

In addition to sanctification, new believers are encouraged to be baptized with the Holy Spirit. This experience of the Spirit provides a

[12] A personal testimony submitted by V. W. Kennedy, *The Evening Light and the Church of God Evangel* 1:18 (1910).

[13] Harvey Cox, *Fire From Heaven: The Rise of Pentecostal Spirituality and the Reshaping of Religion in the 21ˢᵗ Century* (Reading, MA: Addison-Wesley, 1995) 46.

[14] It should be noted that the eschatological vision of the inbreaking of the Kingdom that so characterized early Pentecostals has waned in the Western world. Cox laments: "today many middle-class Pentecostal congregations appear very much at ease with the status quo. Now they seem confident not that Jesus is coming soon, but that He probably isn't, and that therefore nothing will interrupt their pursuit of success and self-indulgence." *Fire From Heaven*, 318. The ongoing repentance that is called for when believers understand themselves as signs of the end disappears when the end is no longer near.

[15] Land, *Pentecostal Spirituality*, 145.

radical change in perception of the world. It adds the dimension of life in the Spirit that allows for the victims to become the overcomers. The once impotent are now filled with a power not unlike the power that was present with Jesus. They are enabled to engage evil powers, evangelize, and pray for the sick. Persons are encouraged to live in the Spirit, walk in the Spirit, pray in the Spirit.[16] They are free to receive the gifts of the Spirit and serve as channels of grace to a hurting world. Most importantly, the baptism of the Spirit is a call to mission in the world. Passion replaces despair, and it is a passion for the kingdom.

### d. Orthopathos: The Passion of Repentance

A passion for the kingdom flows out of an experience of God as the One Who is filled with passion for lost humanity. This vision is contrary to the dominant Western image of God as apathetic, existing in a state of divine impassibility, free from passion, which has led to an impaired vision of repentance. The understanding of a passionless God is closely tied to a forensic view of salvation. God, as the impassionate judge, declares the repentant free of guilt, all the while never appearing to be moved by the plight of sinful humanity. We might say that Protestant Western Christianity offers "passionless" repentance in favor of a more reserved "decision for Christ."

Pentecostal theologian Samuel Solivan offers another vision of God as one who is full of pathos, the one who in the disclosure of Jesus Christ has borne human sorrows and iniquity. As such, God's *orthopathos* is an interlocutor between God and humanity. God is the God who suffers for creation and with creation.[17] Repentance is therefore a response to the passion of God for humanity. It is joining in God's sorrow as God addresses death and alienation.

---

[16] Pentecostal theologian R. Hollis Gause has developed a paradigm of redemption in which there is a unity of redemptive experiences. For Gause salvation, sanctification, and baptism of the Holy Spirit are unified under the rubric of "living in the Spirit." The Spirit of God is involved in every experience of redemption. Gause's paradigm avoids the misunderstanding that the baptism of the Holy Spirit is disjointed from salvation. Rather, it is a deepening and continuing of a life in the Holy Spirit. See his *Living in the Spirit: The Way of Salvation* (Cleveland, TN: Pathway Press, 1980).

[17] Samuel Solivan, *The Spirit, Pathos and Liberation* (Sheffield: Sheffield Academic Press, 1998).

Solivan offers *orthopathos* as the interlocutor between *orthodoxy* and *orthopraxis*. Because in the West *orthodoxy* has become a sterile term that "reduces the power of the Word to a set of faith statements posited by a given religious community," it has created an overemphasis on salvation occurring primarily through knowledge. It becomes merely a mental assent to rational propositions. Truth becomes propositional and revelation is dehumanized. Repentance in this context involves persuasion of the truth claims of the Bible.[18] The power of the human as the rational subject is retained. As a result, repentance is less a gift of grace than the logical choice. This sterile understanding of repentance leads to what Rogers and McKim call "faith without the Holy Spirit."[19]

While *orthopraxis* stresses the connection between knowledge and action, it fails to bridge the gap between the two. A *praxis* epistemology fails to break the dualism between matter and reason. Because of this dualism, *praxis* assumes an unbridgeable distance between the knower and the known. The objectification of others is thus an unavoidable aspect of this knowledge and the power of transformation is of necessity grounded in the "spirit" of the individual.

*Praxis* is, therefore, an insufficient means of knowing God and of achieving repentance. Human reflection-action may become distorted and self-serving. In order for true knowledge, and thereby true repentance, to occur there is a need for the human subject to be transcended and even negated. Transformation leading toward repentance calls for the knowing person to be known and exposed, thereby becoming an object as well as an active subject in the historical process. Mere activism is not repentance.

In speaking of the power of *orthopathy* Solivan notes: "Like the cross that stood between the incarnation and the resurrection, the possibilities of *orthopathos* stand between *orthodoxy* and *orthopraxis*."[20] In *orthopathos* the human affections are joined with the heart of God. It involves joining in God's sorrow as it addresses death and alienation. In *orthopathos* repentance is a response to God's passion for humanity. One is moved to grief by experiencing the pathos of God. The alienation of sin

---

[18] For an example of the overemphasis on the propositional nature of Christianity see Josh McDowell, *Evidence that Demands a Verdict* (San Bernadino: Here's Life Publishers, 1979).

[19] Jack B. Rogers and Donald K. McKim, *The Authority and Interpretation of the Bible: An Historical Approach* (New York: Harper & Row, 1979) 330–34.

[20] Solivan, *The Spirit, Pathos and Liberation*, 38.

is experienced as well as the great barrier of grief that exists between God and humanity. As the Holy Spirit broods over the penitent heart there is a fusion between the groans of the Spirit and the sighs of the human heart. They become one sigh and one groan.

### e. Healing Communities: The Context of Repentance

Within the context of Pentecostalism repentance is not solely an individual matter. It is at the same time deeply personal and highly communal. Individuals are called to repentance, but this call is expressed within the context of worshiping communities. Testimony becomes the means whereby the personal is made corporate. Believers testify to the church regarding God's convicting grace.

Much has been written about Pentecostal churches serving as "havens of the masses."[21] This analysis arises out of the classical Troeltschian sect/church typology in which churches of the lower class are understood to serve as buffers against the "chaotic impact of the urban-industrial milieu."[22] Within these safe havens people are thought to undergo the cathartic effects of ecstasy, making it easier to function in their new environment. In other words, Pentecostal communities among the poor serve as places of escape from the harsh realities of everyday existence. Pentecostal religion is no more than an "opiate of the masses."

As a consequence of these assumptions the communities created by Pentecostals have gone largely unnoticed and undervalued. More recently, however, researchers such as Walter Hollenweger and David Martin have called attention to the transformative character of these communities. For Hollenweger, Pentecostal communities serve as places with latent revolutionary quality, for they serve as zones of liberation for oppressed people.[23] Martin's research underscores the ability of Pentecostal churches to incorporate broken and scarred people, providing opportunities for persons to reinvent themselves. For Martin the Pente-

---

[21] In particular see Christian Lalive d'Epinay, *Haven of the Masses: A Study of the Pentecostal Movement in Chile* (London: Luttersworth Press, 1969); Robert Mapes Anderson, *Vision of the Disinherited: The Making of American Pentecostalism* (New York: Oxford University Press, 1979).

[22] Anderson, *Vision of the Disinherited*, 238.

[23] Walter Hollenweger, "The Social and Ecumenical Significance of Pentecostal Liturgy," *Studia Liturgica* 8/4 (1971–72) 207–15.

costal call to repentance is a call of migration and a call to "the loss of all the ties that bind, whether these be familial, communal or ecclesial."[24] When repentance means leaving behind an old life and a former way of existence there arises a need for the renewal of what was left behind in an atmosphere of "hope and anticipation rather than of despair." Within the context of a new cell or "free space" a "new faith is able to implant new disciplines, re-order priorities, counter corruption . . . and reverse the indifferent and injurious hierarchies of the outside world."

By incorporating chaos and pain into their life and liturgy these communities furnish not means of escape so much as places of confrontation and transformation. Here persons can migrate, renewing the ties that bind, re-ordering priorities, reversing the chaos and alienation of the outside world.[25]

### f. Worship

While Pentecostal communities serve as zones of healing and liberation, their primary function is worship. Worship is central to Pentecostal penitential life. It is the context in which faith is formed and expressed. Worship is constructed so as to facilitate the ever-deepening journey with God and into God. Worship is an event in historical time, but it also provides a window into eternity. It becomes what the Russian philosopher Nicholas Berdyaev described as "the quantitative depth of existential time."[26] In this dimension time is drawn as a vertical line as well as a horizontal one.

Frank Macchia notes that Pentecostal worship offers a form of sacramental spirituality that forges a third way between the typically Protestant emphasis on the freedom of the Spirit and the importance of divine initiative in religious experience (what Tillich referred to as the

---

[24] David Martin, *Tongues of Fire: The Explosion of Protestantism in Latin America* (Oxford: Blackwell, 1990) 284.

[25] The need for new converts to experience grace following initial repentance through integration into healing communities was part of John Wesley's paradigm of discipleship. His societies and bands were structured so as to enable persons to reinvent themselves in an atmosphere of hope and anticipation rather than despair. Wesley's understanding of "the penitential way" involved the critical role of healing communities.

[26] Nicholas Berdyaev, *Slavery and Freedom* (New York: Charles Scribner's Sons, 1944) 261.

"Protestant Principle"), and the Catholic emphasis on visible means of grace.[27]

Using Karl Rahner's definition of the sacramental in which the reality signified is made present in the process of signification, Macchia focuses on the sacramental nature of glossolalia as a "linguistic symbol of the sacred, which says 'God is here.'"[28] In the space of worship grace is experienced through the prophetic freedom of the Spirit. It is also experienced through the practices that serve as visible means of transformation.

Jackie Johns views a Pentecostal understanding of sacrament as rooted in the New Testament concept of mystery (Rom 11:25; Eph 1:9; 3:3-4). Mystery is thus a technical term for God's self-revelation as expressed in the incarnation of Christ. This revelation of God in the incarnate Christ is found in the resurrection and in the existence of the church. The church is, therefore, in its very existence the extension of the mystery. There is no true sacrament outside the communion of the church and the Holy Spirit. It is the presence of the Spirit in the church that makes the presence of Christ real. The Spirit is not subject to the church but is sovereign over the church. Within Johns' definition of sacrament, everything that happens in the life of the church that actualizes the presence of Christ by the Spirit is sacrament (mystery).[29]

In his research on Pentecostal worship Daniel Albrecht observes a variety of modes of sensibility.[30] Two of these are particularly pertinent to repentance: contemplative and penitent (purgative). Worship generally moves from a celebratory mode into a contemplative ritual mode that is characterized by a "deep receptivity and a sense of openness to God. . . ."[31] The contemplative mode frequently appears as the dominant congregational mode, fading in and out of the worship service. The contemplative mode has what Albrecht calls a "mediating

[27] Frank Macchia, "Tongues as a Sign: A Sacramental Understanding of Pentecostal Experience," *Pneuma* (1993) 61–76.

[28] Macchia, "Tongues as a Sign," 61.

[29] Jackie Johns, "Children and the Sacraments," 1997. Unpublished manuscript.

[30] Daniel Albrecht, *Rites in the Spirit: A Ritual Approach to Pentecostal/Charismatic Spirituality* (Sheffield: Sheffield Academic Press, 1999) 179–95. For Albrecht the modes of sensibility are not so much types of ritual or ties as *embodied attitudes, sensibilities, affections* with which ritualists perform and experience ritual" (179).

[31] Albrecht, *Rites in the Spirit*, 183.

function among the other ritual modes."[32] It "approaches the divine in a reverent interrogative mood."[33] This mode is a time of yielding to the Spirit. It involves "tarrying until," that is, a time of attending to and seeking the presence of God. It is the mode of attentive waiting. It seeks "the action and presence of the other, the one that cannot be controlled."[34]

The penitent (purgative) mode involves a sensibility characterized by "contrition, repentance, remorse, sorrow, lamenting or grieving."[35] It is often seen in the altar/response rite, but can be found at other times. For instance, during what may be construed as a celebrative mode in which there are rites of worship and praise, it is not unknown for persons to respond in contrition. They may kneel at their seats or come forward for prayer.

### g. Penitential Practices

Within the context of Pentecostal worship and life there are several rites or practices that facilitate repentance. These "rites in the Spirit" serve to reveal the mystery of the incarnate Christ. In particular, they provide opportunities for the intersection of human sinfulness and the transforming grace of God in Christ.

### (1) Baptism

Although Pentecostals practice "believers' baptism," meaning that repentance is to precede baptism, the dominant mode of baptism is penitent. Inasmuch as baptism is the immersion into the mystery that is in Christ, it calls for a total renouncing of the kingdom of darkness. It demands that the posture of the believer be that of repentance.[36] It serves to consummate the covenant to be members of Christ's body and citizens of his kingdom. As such, it is not merely symbolic of what has already occurred within the life of the believer. It serves to effectually initiate the believer into full participation into the new life that is in Christ. As Johns notes, "in water baptism personal union with Christ and his church are sealed; cleansing from sin, which was actualized by

---

[32] Ibid.
[33] Ibid.
[34] Ibid.
[35] Ibid.
[36] Johns, "Children and the Sacraments."

the Holy Spirit at the moment of true faith, is consummated as a shared inheritance of the Kingdom."[37]

### (2) Footwashing

The practice of footwashing, while not followed by all Pentecostals, is a sacramentally powerful penitential rite that signifies the continual need for post-baptismal cleansing.[38] John Christopher Thomas, in his excellent treatment of John 13, highlights the importance of footwashing as the key preparation for Christ's Passion. Thomas concludes that for the Johannine community footwashing "signifies the disciples' spiritual cleansing for a continued relationship with Jesus . . . footwashing functions as an extension of the disciples' baptism in that it signifies continual cleansing from the sin acquired (after baptism) through life in a sinful world."[39]

Thomas suggests that John highlights footwashing over the Eucharist in order to correct a quasi-magical view of the sacraments that had arisen within the church. Instead of magical rites, the sacraments are signs of God's gracious actions based upon the death of Jesus. These rites do not stand alone but must be accompanied by faith.[40]

Macchia, in his assessment of Thomas' treatment of John 13, calls for the integration of the significance of footwashing as a revelation of Christ's humility and humble servitude with the rite's significance for cleansing. In this light Macchia is interested in exploring the "various dynamics involved in footwashing as a drama that binds the communicant to the cross on many levels in order that Jesus' servitude can make its imprint on the communicant's life."[41] Macchia points out that footwashing serves as the bridge between baptism and Eucharist. The dramatic impact of foot-

---

[37] Ibid.

[38] Tom Driver offers this reflection on footwashing in the Pentecostal context: "Although Pentecostal churches are not known for their sacramentalism, this has more to do with word usage than with actuality, as anyone may be aware who has attended anything as powerfully God-present as a footwashing ceremony in old-time Pentecostal congregations." *The Magic of Ritual* (San Francisco: Harper & Row, 1991) 208.

[39] John Christopher Thomas, *Footwashing in the Johannine Community* (Sheffield: JSOT Press, 1991) 150.

[40] Ibid. 183.

[41] Frank Macchia, "Is Footwashing the Neglected Sacrament? A Theological Response to John Christopher Thomas," *Pneuma* 19/2 (Fall 1997) 239–49.

washing may help Pentecostals to approach baptism and Eucharist with the same expectations from which they approach footwashing. The same dramatic encounters with the living Christ that Pentecostals experience during footwashing, tongues, and the laying on of hands can be extended into baptism and Eucharist. The "sacramental actions of tongues and the laying on of hands would also gain their direction from the three-fold 'principal' sacraments of baptism, footwashing, and the Eucharist."[42]

Pentecostals practice footwashing as a rite of cleansing and reconciliation that brings about healing, not only between God and humanity but also between brothers and sisters in the body of Christ. Footwashing is a rite that conveys the power of the priesthood of all believers. As mutual confession is practiced, grace to heal and forgive comes through the cleansing hands of fellow believers. Participants in footwashing serve as agents of cleansing and healing as well as recipients of that grace. The way of salvation is a journey in which the pilgrims often find themselves bringing into the sacred space of worship the "dust of life." These pilgrims need the cleansing that prepares them to reenter the world with renewed strength.

### (3) Eucharist

Pentecostals practice the Eucharist as both remembering the atoning sacrifice of Christ (Passover) and celebrating the church's realized inheritance in Christ (Pentecost). The Eucharist, therefore, contains a fusion of *pathos* and joy. Celebration of the Eucharist often involves soul-searching penitent prayers. If footwashing precedes the Eucharist, the penitent mode has already been established as the dominant mode for the service. Sometimes, however, following footwashing, the Eucharist is more celebratory in its emphasis.

For most Pentecostals the real presence of Christ brought about by the power of the Holy Spirit makes efficacious the Eucharistic meal. I would concur, however, with Macchia that as to how Pentecostals experience this real presence of Christ, they are often uncertain as to how to fuse together the dynamics of yielding to the Spirit and the liturgical structure of the Eucharist.

### (4) Prayer

Don Saliers, in a key article on liturgy and ethics, states that "the relations between liturgy and ethics are most adequately formulated by

---

[42] Ibid.

specifying how certain affections and virtues are formed and expressed in the modalities of prayer and ritual action."[43] For Saliers, "how we pray and worship is linked to how we live—to our desires, emotions, attitudes, beliefs and actions."[44] Pentecostal affections are shaped by a life of prayer and worship and in turn these affections contribute to the nature of the practices. Prayer is the most common practice. It defines the nature of the "penitent way."

During the worship service penitent prayer usually follows the sermon and serves as a response to the prophetic call of the Word of the Lord. The altar-response mode of worship is a time in which orthopathy joins together orthodoxy and orthopraxis. The Word of the Lord has been experienced (orthodoxy) and its meaning has yet to be taken into the lives of believers (orthopraxis). Before right action can occur, believers need to tarry before the Lord, seeking transformation of the affections.

Orthopathic, repentant prayer involves "tarrying before the Lord." For Pentecostals tarrying implies "travailing, waiting, prostrating and submitting oneself before the presence of God in hopes that God's presence breaks forth in the mundane and profane circumstances of life."[45] Furthermore, "tarrying is a demonstration and embodiment of desire for God's very presence; in other words, this practice stems from a heart inclined in wonder to the life-transforming presence of God . . . it beckons eschatological time and in doing so focuses our lives on the in-breaking presence of the Spirit of God."[46]

Tarrying before the Lord involves inhabiting the pathos of the disunity between the world that is and the world that is coming. It takes seriously the holdouts and the places of resistance that are found in the human heart. Dwelling in the pathos, one mourns the brokenness resulting from sin. As this brokenness is embraced, the human is decentered as subject and becomes the object. As the self is eclipsed, words give way toward the speech of God and glossolalia may break forth. Tongues are sometimes followed by sighs and groans in the Spirit. Deeper still awaits the holy silence that signals that one has indeed "prayed through." Finally, there is the sheer wonder of beholding the beauty of God's glory.

[43] Don Saliers, "Liturgy and Ethics: Some New Beginnings," *Journal of Religious Ethics* 7/2 (Fall 1979) 173–89, at 175.

[44] Ibid.

[45] Daniel Castelo, "Tarrying on the Lord: Affections and Virtues in Pentecostal Perspective," *Journal of Pentecostal Theology* 13/1 (2004) 31–56.

[46] Ibid.

The posture of tarrying prayer is often that of falling prostrate before the Lord. Within the context of a Pentecostal worldview in which there is spirit-body correspondence, the body is sacramentalized. Speaking of the experiences of early Pentecostals being "slain in the Spirit," Grant Wacker notes that "the entire torso became a holy emblem. In those situations Christ's physical death and resurrection was re-embodied not just reenacted, but literally re-embodied."[47]

While tarrying before the Lord may occur within the altar-response mode of worship, it is also part of special prayer vigils. Pentecostals, especially those within the Two-Thirds world, frequently hold all-night prayer vigils. These may occur outdoors at a special place such as a "prayer mountain" or they may take place within homes or church buildings. These events are true "festivals of tears." They enact the need to pray through the darkness into the break of dawn. As believers pray through the dark night they come face to face with the epiphanies of darkness that surround their lives. The light once again overcomes the darkness and believers are strengthened in their journey of faith to continue onward.

## 2. Implications

The Pentecostal way of salvation is a complex and mysterious journey that offers healing and deliverance from the power of darkness. It is characterized by a yielding to the Spirit, who knows all things, searches hearts, and fills them with love and sighs and groans for the kingdom. The journey with God involves an ongoing process of overcoming sin and drawing closer to God. It involves a continual dialectic of crisis and development, with crisis serving as a means of deepening the journey.

At the heart of the Pentecostal way of salvation is a passion for the kingdom that is a response to the passion of God for humanity. As believers yield to the Spirit, their affections are joined with the heart of God. Worship is central to the life of believers and is constructed so as to facilitate the ever-deepening journey with God. The rites of baptism, footwashing, Eucharist, testimony, and prayer serve to facilitate the penitent life. Because Pentecostalism is predominately an oral tradition, there is little written regarding the movement's spirituality and theology. As a consequence, the tradition faces the loss of its distinctive

---

[47] Grant Wacker, *Heaven Below: Early Pentecostalism and American Culture* (Cambridge, MA: Harvard University Press, 2001) 108.

theological gifts and callings. The vision of penitence that is inherent in the movement is in danger of being discarded for a more socially acceptable "positive" self-image. Currently there is a need for catechetical and theological material that reflects an awareness of the multiple dimensions of Pentecostal spirituality, including the penitent dimension.

# 3. Further Reading

Albrecht, Daniel. *Rites in the Spirit: A Ritual Approach to Pentecostal/Charismatic Spirituality*. Sheffield: Sheffield Academic Press, 1999.

Anderson, Robert Mapes. *Vision of the Disinherited: The Making of American Pentecostalism*. New York: Oxford University Press, 1979.

Berdyaev, Nicholas. *Slavery and Freedom*. New York: Charles Scribner's Sons, 1944.

Castelo, Daniel. "Tarrying on the Lord: Affections and Virtues in Pentecostal Perspective," *Journal of Pentecostal Theology* 13/1 (2004) 31–56.

Cesar, Waldo, and Richard Shaull. *Pentecostalism and the Future of the Christian Churches*. Grand Rapids: Eerdmans, 2000.

Cox, Harvey. *Fire From Heaven The Rise of Pentecostal Spirituality and the Reshaping of Religion in the 21ˢᵗ Century*. Reading, MA: Addison-Wesley, 1995.

Driver, Tom. *The Magic of Ritual*. San Francisco: Harper & Row, 1991.

Gause, R. Hollis. *Living in the Spirit: The Way of Salvation*. Cleveland, TN: Pathway Press, 1980.

Hollenweger, Walter. "The Social and Ecumenical Significance of Pentecostal Liturgy," *Studia Liturgica* 8/4 (1971–72) 207–15.

Johns, Jackie. "Pentecostalism and the Postmodern Worldview," *Journal of Pentecostal Theology* 78 (1995) 87.

Kennedy, V. W. *The Evening Light and the Church of God Evangel* 1:18 (1910).

Lalive d'Epinay, Christian. *Haven of the Masses: A Study of the Pentecostal Movement in Chile*. London: Lutterworth Press, 1969.

Land, Steven J. *Pentecostal Spirituality: A Passion for the Kingdom*. Sheffield: Sheffield Academic Press, 1993.

Macchia, Frank. "Is Footwashing the Neglected Sacrament? A Theological Response to John Christopher Thomas." *Pneuma* 19/2 (Fall 1997) 239–49.

_____. "Tongues as a Sign: A Sacramental Understanding of Pentecostal Experience," *Pneuma* 15 (1993) 61–76.

Martin, David. *Tongues of Fire: The Explosion of Protestantism in Latin America*. Oxford: Blackwell, 1990.

McDowell, Josh. *Evidence that Demands a Verdict*. San Bernadino: Here's Life Publishers, 1979.

McKim, Donald K., and Jack B. Rogers. *The Authority and Interpretation of the Bible: An Historical Approach*. New York: Harper & Row, 1979.

Saliers, Don. "Liturgy and Ethics: Some New Beginnings," *Journal of Religious Ethics* 7/2 (Fall 1979) 173–89.

Smith, Harold B., ed. "Pentecostalism Reinvented: The Charismatic Renewal." In *Pentecostals from the Inside Out*. Wheaton, IL: Victor Books, 1990.

Solivan, Samuel. *The Spirit, Pathos and Liberation*. Sheffield: Sheffield Academic Press, 1998.

Thomas, John Christopher. *Footwashing in the Johannine Community*. Sheffield: JSOT Press, 1991.

Wacker, Grant. *Heaven Below: Early Pentecostalism and American Culture*. Cambridge, MA: Harvard University Press, 2001.

# 4. Hermeneutical Reflection

Joint projects, especially those that are multidisciplinary in nature, create opportunities for profound truths to be dialectically engaged. Niels Bohr, the Nobel Prize-winning physicist, aptly observed: "The opposite of a true statement is a false statement, but the opposite of a profound truth can be another profound truth."[48] This multilateral conversation created space for deep to call to deep and for the wisdom found in seemingly opposite spectrums of the body of Christ to emerge in paradoxical conversation. From this vantage point we can see the beauty of the whole.

I am struck by the profound truth of the all-encompassing, destructive nature of sin. The marred beauty of the earth and the marred face of a methamphetamine addict both mirror the tyranny of evil. Yet every tradition agrees that the grace found in Christ by the power of the Holy Spirit is indeed "amazing" in its ability to restore beauty from ashes.

The necessity for human repentance is highlighted in this project. On one side of the continuum there is the Reformation and Evangelical insistence that repentance is a necessity to live a converted life. On the other side there is the Catholic and Orthodox offering of the profound truth that is found in a grace-filled sacramental journey.

The lack of self-knowledge and the need for ongoing revelation is another area of agreement in this project. Humans exist in social constructs that blind us to the power of sin. Pentecostals, Evangelicals, and

---

[48] These words are attributed to Bohr. See Avery Dulles, *The Reshaping of Catholicism* (San Francisco: HarperSan Francisco, 1989). I am using Parker Palmer's reference to Bohr. See Palmer, *The Courage to Teach* (San Francisco: Jossey-Bass, 1998) 62.

the Black Church tradition offer the deeply disturbing and convicting voice of prophetic preaching. The power of the Word to reveal, convict, and transform is necessary in overcoming the numbing effects of sin.

On the other hand, Evangelicals and Pentecostals can learn from those traditions that offer the ancient penitential paths that are marked by contrition, confession of sins, and acts of penance. These paths offer revelation that is also deeply disturbing, prophetic, and convicting. They provide rites that shape the affections of the human heart.

This project highlighted the need for communities of grace where those broken by sin can find restoration and healing. It is a profound truth that the penitent life cannot be lived apart from the transformative grace found in the church. The living waters of grace flow through the liturgically constructed life of believers.

On the other hand, there is the profound truth of the necessity for individual confession. The penitent life is deeply personal. It is often marked by solitude and times of loneliness.

My own tradition highlights the need for the radical inbreaking of the power of the Holy Spirit to liberate persons who are bound by the power of sin. Radical divine action is not limited to the pages of Hebrew history or the gospel narratives. It is found in the testimonies of those who encounter God in dramatic ways. On the other hand, there is the profound truth that transformation occurs in the steady day-to-day journey of a grace-filled life. This project highlights the need to maintain the crisis-development dialectic, where grace comes in transforming moments and in the sometimes mundane tasks of daily life.

Finally, at its best the penitence project should contribute to a deeper appreciation for the penitent way as the way of the cross. The cross stands at the intersection of profound and deeply moving truths: Human sinfulness, the love of God that he would send his beloved Son as redeemer, and the suffering-beauty of redemption. It is at this cross that we all stand on level ground.

Fifteen

# Middle Eastern Perspectives and Expressions of Christian Repentance/Penitence

*Wafik Wahba*

## 1. Tradition

### a. Middle Eastern Christianity

Middle Eastern Christianity traces its roots to the day of Pentecost. According to the book of Acts several Middle Eastern communities were present on that day:

> [6]When they heard this sound, a crowd came together in bewilderment, because each one heard them speaking in his own language. [7]Utterly amazed, they asked: "Are not all these men who are speaking Galileans? [8]Then how is it that each of us hears them in his own native language? [9]Parthians, Medes and Elamites; residents of Mesopotamia, Judea and Cappadocia, Pontus and Asia, [10]Phrygia and Pamphylia, Egypt and the parts of Libya near Cyrene; visitors from Rome [11](both Jews and converts to Judaism); Cretans and Arabs—we hear them declaring the wonders of God in our own tongues!" [12]Amazed and perplexed, they asked one another, "What does this mean?" (Acts 2:6-12, *NIV*)

Like the early church, contemporary Middle Eastern Christianity is multilingual and multiethnic. A visit to the ancient city of East Jerusalem is a powerful reminder of the immense diversity of Middle Eastern Christianity today. Syriac, Greek, Latin, Coptic, along with Anglican, Lutheran, and Reformed churches exist side by side in this historical city. Today there are more than twenty million Christians living in the Middle East. By remaining indigenous to the area where Christianity began, they link the world church historically with its origins. They lived under several cultural, social, and religious circumstances that have shaped their own lives as well as their attitudes toward the world around them. To continue to survive is not an easy task in itself, yet the challenge is not simply to survive but also to be transformed by the message of the gospel and accordingly to actively live their Christian faith.

The purpose of this paper is to explore the different perspectives and expressions of Christian repentance/penitence in contemporary Middle Eastern Christianity. I hope that this theological study will provide a framework for transformation in the life and witness of Middle Eastern churches today. I also hope that this study will help the global church to understand and appreciate the life and witness of contemporary Middle Eastern Christians.

It should be noted that when we speak of contemporary Middle Eastern Christianity we refer to several Christian traditions: Orthodox, Catholic, and several Reformed and Evangelical traditions. While they differ in their theological orientation and their perspectives on repentance/penitence, the emphasis here will be on the common and most dominant forms of repentance expressed by contemporary Middle Eastern Christians.

## b. Middle Eastern Expressions of Repentance

Worship and salvation are central themes in understanding the context and expressions of repentance in Middle Eastern Christianity. The whole Christian life revolves around worship and salvation. The clearest expression of the ethos and life of the Orthodox Church (the dominant church in the region) is found in its liturgy, in which those in heaven and on earth are held to be united in their common acts of worship. However, the central focus of the earthly worship is to gain salvation and unity with Christ the Lord. The presence of Christ, primarily in the sacraments, becomes the focal point of worship. The understanding of the act of salvation, therefore, differs from that of the reformed tradition, which tends to focus on the justification of sinners, with the church being essentially the community of those who are justified by faith through grace. In Orthodoxy salvation is a process; it involves several steps and a journey of a lifetime. Pope Shenoda III, the current Patriarch of the Coptic Orthodox Church of Egypt, argued that baptism is the first step toward salvation; however, it is only sufficient for the removal of original sin. Then he added three other major steps in the process of Christian salvation. The second is a true and genuine faith in Christ who died for our sins and was raised for our salvation. These two basic steps will put the Christian on a journey of a lifetime in which salvation will be completed through the observance of church sacraments, primarily the sacraments of Holy Communion and Confession. Finally, salvation will be attained through good works, which are a natural outcome of Christian salvation.[1]

It must be noted that Orthodox theology makes a distinction between salvation and redemption, with salvation being the larger category that includes sanctification. Redemption, however, is included in this larger category, affected by God alone, through the work of Christ and the power of the Spirit.

Standing outside this earthly life with its pain and suffering, worship for many Middle Eastern Christians provides the crucial event for empowering and renewal. At the core of this process of renewal are several expressions of repentance.

### (1) Baptism

Baptism is one of the rich and diversified experiences in the Christian tradition. There are different baptismal practices in the Middle East. While the Orthodox and Catholic practice and understanding of baptism dominate the landscape of the Middle East, Reformed and Evangelical baptismal traditions are also present.

For the Orthodox and Catholic churches baptism is the sacrament that brings entry into the church. It is the first step in the process of salvation and results in the remission of original sin. It should be noted, however, that according to this view salvation is not complete. Baptism is only the first step in the process, not the whole. Baptism is the work of the Holy Spirit initiating people into the church. It unites the Christian with Christ's death and resurrection. Infants should be baptized in order to be guaranteed entry into heaven.

---

[1] Pope Shenoda III, *Salvation in the Orthodox Understanding* (Cairo: St. Mark Publications, 1985) 20–52.

Contemporary Orthodox theologian Matthew the Poor emphasizes not only the removal of original sin in baptism but the full participation in Christ's death and resurrection that leads to committed Christian life. At baptism the sign of the cross is made over the baptized and he or she is invited to join the fellowship of the resurrection and to share the burden of Christ's suffering.[2]

It should be noted that, according to Orthodox theology, baptism is not a rescue measure from the consequences of original sin because there is no belief in concupiscence or the passing on of original guilt to the infant in Orthodoxy. Infant baptism is central to the Orthodox tradition because the infant's personhood is fully recognized; that is why infants also participate in communion from the moment of their baptism.

On the other hand, Middle Eastern reformed churches believe that baptism is a sign of the covenant of grace. God's promise of grace is the basis for justification and salvation and justification is the act of faith by which we are brought into that covenant and therefore experience its benefits. The assumption is that believers will often be reminded of their baptism. The fact that one has been baptized and therefore is united with Christ in his death and resurrection will be a constant source of empowerment and inspiration to live a committed Christian life. It should be noted that the baptized child in both traditions does not participate in any form of repentance at the moment of baptism. As the first step in the Christian life, baptism becomes a point of reference where the Christian lives the benefits of God's salvation initiated in the practice of baptism. Some Middle Eastern Evangelical churches practice believers' baptism, in which repentance precedes baptism. The believer in that case is aware of the need for repentance from sin and the urgency to start a new beginning in Christ. Baptism, therefore, will serve to initiate the believer into full participation in the new life in Christ.

Baptism is a clear form of repentance because it summarizes the whole gospel, which is God's accepting and forgiving people through the blood of Christ. The forgiveness of sins becomes the center out of which the full Christian life will flow.

Baptism of Middle Eastern children or of believers is rarely seen as a public proclamation of allegiance to Christ. But for Middle Eastern non-Christians who come to proclaim faith in Christ, baptism becomes an

---

[2] Anba Matta El-Miskeen, *Baptism* (Wadi El-Natrun, Egypt: Anba Makar Monastery Press, 1989).

unavoidable test of the person's commitment to live for Christ. It reveals the depth and seriousness of the convert's intentions. Baptism signifies the rejection of previous religious affiliation and acceptance of Christ's death and resurrection as the basis for salvation. Baptism in that context reflects true repentance and change in the person's lifestyle; it is the beginning of a true transformation. At the same time, it sets the believer on a true path of participating in Christ's suffering. The consequences of following Christ in that case might vary from facing death to persecution or at least being cut off from the family and the community.

### (2) Preaching

Preaching provides a significant opportunity for repentance in contemporary Middle Eastern Christianity. From the second half of the nineteenth century onward, preaching became instrumental for explaining the need for repentance as the first step toward salvation. An emphasis on the necessity of repentance was the highlight of preaching during the second half of the nineteenth century. The nineteenth-century missionaries who introduced several reformed traditions (i.e., Presbyterian, Lutheran, and Anglican) to the Middle East were influenced by the renewal movements within the Protestant stream of Christianity.[3]

The eighteenth-century revival movement in the eastern United States and many parts of Britain known as the Great Awakening was the driving force in the teaching and preaching of many missionaries to the Middle East in the nineteenth century. Following the reformed tradition, they emphasized the priority of faith as the sole means by which salvation can be attained *(Sola Fides)*. They emphasized that repentance is the first step toward salvation; however, it is God's grace that finally counts in accepting and redeeming sinners. During the nineteenth-century period of Middle Eastern reformed theology emphasis was on repentance versus penance. According to Middle Eastern reformed theology, penance focused on what people can do in order to pay for their sins either through the reciting of certain prayers, good works, or other sacramental practices. By contrast, true repentance brings forgiveness and salvation. While penance always leaves the sinner powerless and imprisoned, repentance

---

[3] Middle Eastern Reformed theology, preaching and practices represent a mix of several Protestant traditions. One might find great emphasis on the Wesleyan holiness theology in a Presbyterian church in Egypt or Lebanon, but one of the most celebrated events among Presbyterians in Syria and Lebanon is Martin Luther's publication of his Ninety-Five Theses on Indulgences.

liberates and brings freedom from the bondage of sin. Repentance seeks the forgiveness provided through the blood of Christ once and for all. It should be noted that nineteenth-century Middle Eastern reformed theology was developed outside the Middle East, mainly in Europe and the United States; nonetheless, many of the issues pertaining to repentance and salvation in the Middle Eastern context were similar to those at the time of the early Reformation. This is not to suggest that Middle Eastern Orthodox churches share the same theological problems of medieval Christianity. However, the core issue Middle Eastern reformed theology faced during the nineteenth century was the role of faith in salvation versus good works and the authority of the church.

During the second half of the twentieth century two major developments took place. A wave of revival meetings with great emphasis on repentance characterized the evangelical movement during the 1960s–1990s in several Middle Eastern countries. The Baptist, Pentecostal, and Methodist churches led the current movement. On the other hand, starting from the 1980s, preaching became central to the liturgies of several Middle Eastern Orthodox and Catholic churches, most notably the Coptic Orthodox Church of Egypt. Along with preaching, repentance and salvation were emphasized. These new developments are very significant because on the one hand they provided for deeper understanding and appreciation among the different Middle Eastern traditions where Protestant, Catholic, and Orthodox churches see their traditions as complementing one another rather than contradicting one another. It also provided for new understanding and expressions of repentance that are indigenous to Middle Eastern culture and context.

Repentance today is emphasized in relationship to the overall realities of suffering and persecution that characterize the Middle Eastern context, where confessing sins and asking God for forgiveness provides for a renewed hope for the future. There is a deep sense that repentance is an essential step before God intervenes to transform the current state of suffering, despair, and confusion that dominates the landscape of the region. Contemporary preaching is vital in helping people to understand the roots of sin and alienation from God, directing them to seek God's forgiveness and ushering in a process of repentance that is crucial for moving toward a holistic redemption for the individual and for society as a whole.

### (3) Prayer

Along with preaching, prayer represents a significant occasion for repentance. Through the centuries the Orthodox liturgy emphasized repenting prayers. The most frequently repeated prayer in the liturgy of the Coptic Orthodox Church, which is also a doxology, reflects the continuous need for repentance as well as deep understanding of the holiness of God:

> Holy, Holy, Holy, O Lord of sabaoth, heaven and earth are full of Thy Glory and Thy dignity. Have mercy, O God the Father Almighty. O Holy Trinity, have mercy on us. O Lord God of powers be with us, for we have no other helper in our tribulations and adversities but Thee. O God, release, remit, and forgive us our transgressions which we have committed voluntarily and involuntarily, we have committed knowingly and unknowingly, the concealed and the apparent. O Lord, remit it for us, for the sake of Thy Holy Name, which is called upon us according to Thy mercy, O Lord, and not according to our sins.[4]

Prayers in the liturgy of the Orthodox Church provide for a comprehensive expression of repentance and renewal. Prayers are usually framed in a way that reflects God's glory and holiness as well as God's compassionate love and forgiving mercies. Liturgical prayers also balance the personal and the communal dimensions in the relationship with God. One of the common prayers in the Coptic liturgy emphasizes the purification of the believer (personal dimension) as well as the unity of faith (communal dimension):

> Have mercy on us O God, and have mercy on us. O Thou, who at all times and at every hour Art adored and glorified in heaven and on earth. O Christ our God the Good, Long-suffering, full of mercy and full of compassion. O Thou that loves the just, and has pity upon sinners among whom I am chief. Who desires not the death of a sinner but rather that he returns and lives. O Thou that calls all people to be saved through the tidings of the good things to come. O Lord, receive our supplications at this hour and at every hour. Order our life to do Thy commandments.
>
> Sanctify our souls; purify our bodies; rectify our thoughts; cleanse our consciences, heal our sickness, forgive us our sins and deliver us from all evil affliction and heartache, surround us with Thine holy Angels, that we, under the shield and guidance of their worship, may attain the unity of faith, and the knowledge of Thine incomprehensible glory; for blessed art Thou unto the ages of ages.[5]

---

[4] *Coptic Liturgy: The Seven Prayers of the Agpeya* (Cairo: St. Mark Publications, 1990) 91.

[5] Ibid. 98.

Individual and corporate prayers are vital expressions of repentance among Middle Eastern Christians. Repentance prayers often serve as a response to preaching; however, prayer meetings constitute a significant part of weekly worship services in many Middle Eastern churches today. The role of prayer in purifying the believer and maintaining a balanced Christian life is constantly highlighted. There is also an increasing awareness of the need for repentance, which is expressed in corporate prayers, in order for God to heal the land, to bring peace and stability in the region, and to give wisdom to political leaders. Repentance through corporate prayers is also perceived as an instrumental tool in transforming the society at large and in calling people to the saving knowledge of Christ.

### (4) Fasting

Prayer and fasting go hand in hand in the worship services of many Middle Eastern churches. Fasting occupies a significant portion of the liturgical calendar of the Orthodox Church; several weeks are dedicated to fasting. The fasting before Christmas, during Lent, the fasting of the Apostles, and St. Mary are examples. In the Orthodox tradition, fasting means complete abstention from food or from certain types of food. It is a powerful expression of repentance, an essential weapon in fighting against the devil and a source of victory, and is linked to Christ's death for our sin and his resurrection for our salvation. Fasting brings sins to light so that they can be dealt with. It is a comprehensive spiritual exercise.

Fasting is seen as a continuation of a rich biblical tradition in which biblical figures fasted in order to subdue carnal desires and seek God's face. The former Coptic Orthodox Patriarch, Pope Kyriollos VI, indicated in one of his sermons during Lent:

> Fasting, my children, is the first commandment that God has delivered unto mankind, when He commanded our fore-parents Adam and Eve that they should not eat certain fruits in the Garden. And fasting was the first deed that our Lord and Master Jesus Christ did after being baptized, even before He started His preaching ministry among the people. And fasting was the first deed that our fathers the Apostles did when the Bridegroom was taken from them. And while they fasted and prayed the Holy Spirit spoke unto them (Acts 13:2). . . . Fasting is a weapon the Prophets have used, for Moses, Elijah, David, Ezra and Nehemiah have all fasted. [6]

---

[6] Pope Kyriollos VI, *Sermon Delivered During Lent 1968* (Cairo: St. Mark Publications, 1982) 7–8.

From a Middle Eastern perspective, repentance is one of the main purposes of fasting. It is a spiritual exercise in which the spirit has victory over the desires of the flesh. This will lead to purity of heart, strength, and liberation in Christ.

> Fasting must be accompanied by repentance, compunction and confession of sins. When the Ninevites fasted, they put on sackcloth and they turned from their evil ways and from the violence that was in their hands. And they cried unto God. And God saw their repentance and showed mercy unto them. The importance of repentance to accompany fasting is expounded for us fully in the Book of Joel, where the Lord exhorts us, "Turn ye even to me with all your heart and with fasting and with weeping and with mourning . . . sanctify a fast, call a solemn assembly" (Joel 2:12-15). In the same manner did Daniel the Prophet fast, "And I set my face unto the Lord God, to seek by prayer and supplication, with fasting and sackcloth and ashes. And I prayed unto the Lord my God and made my confession" (Dan 9:3, 4). In the like manner did Nehemiah, Ezra and David. God desires this repentance while fasting, when the spirit has victory over the flesh, when we subdue the flesh and crucify it with all its affections (Gal 5:24). So, make your fast, my children, pure and holy, that it may be acceptable before God like the fasts of the saints. Preserve your purity in the land of your sojourn. Live the life of repentance that is pleasing to God. Let this season be a season for confession of sins and communion of the Holy Mysteries, that ye may abide in the Lord and He abides in you, even as the living branches that bear fruit abide in the True Vine. And the God of all mercies preserve, confirm and strengthen you.[7]

### (5) Confession

Confession is an essential expression of repentance in the Orthodox and Catholic churches. In both traditions confession of sins to the priest is an essential step toward the remission of sin that is usually associated with penitence. Confession of sins makes the person worthy of God's grace and forgiveness. People are encouraged to confess all their sins in order to receive full liberation from the burden of sin. The analogy used here is that just as people need to disclose all their physical pain and concerns to the physician in order to receive proper treatment, the shame of the soul must be shown to the priest in order to obtain spiritual medicine.

[7] Ibid.

It should be noted that the role of the priest is to direct the person to the proper treatment. However, the priest does not forgive sins; only God does. Confession has to be made with a true sense of repentance, humility, and willingness to turn away from sin.

In Middle Eastern reformed tradition confession of sin is also an essential expression of repentance; however, there is no need for confessing sins to a priest or a pastor. The argument made by Protestants all along has been that since salvation is by faith alone there is no work or penitence that will atone for any sin. The price has already been paid on the cross once and for all. This does not mean that the reformed tradition is less concerned about the need for confession as a significant form of repentance. However, the emphasis here is on the direct relationship between the person and God.

Confession of sin is encouraged in the reformed tradition through different expressions. Sometimes a call for the confession of sin follows preaching or comes as a natural consequence of the sermon. Some churches incorporate certain prayers of confession in their liturgy that direct the worshipers and help them focus on the necessity and need for confessing their sins. Usually the celebration of communion is used to highlight the need for confessing sins and asking for forgiveness before participating in communion.

Whatever expression is used, confessing sins is a vital expression of repentance. It reflects maturity in Christian growth and awareness of the need for repentance as a significant step toward freedom in Christ. Confession has to come from the heart with humility and willingness to turn away from sin. This brings joy and liberation.

### (f) Eucharist

The celebration of the communion or Eucharist is the focal point of what Christ has done on the cross to redeem humanity from the bondage of sin. It is the most celebrated expression of repentance in all churches in the Middle East. It should be noted that Orthodox, Catholic, and all reformed churches in the Middle East celebrate Easter according to the Eastern calendar, calling this holy day "Resurrection Sunday," not Easter. Contrary to Western emphasis on Christmas, Resurrection Sunday and Good Friday are the most celebrated events in Middle Eastern Christianity. This explains the importance of celebrating communion, as it is also tied to Christ's crucifixion and resurrection.

For the Orthodox and Catholic churches, participating in the Eucharist brings into completion what baptism and the confession of sin initiated. Without the communion there will be no complete participation in God's salvation. Repentance is a necessary step before participating in communion. Participating in the communion service is a confirmation of God's acceptance and granting forgiveness.

The Eucharist, according to the Orthodox and Catholic tradition, is a real sacrifice offered to God in the Mass. It is a service to atone for venial sins, a sacrifice offered by Christ on behalf of the worshipers. Therefore one should seriously examine oneself before participating in the sacrament of the Eucharist. This examination should lead to confessing sins before participating in the communion. The prayer before the Holy Communion in the Coptic liturgy explains the need for repentance and the unworthiness of the participant to receive the real body and blood of Christ:

> O Lord my God, I know that I am not worthy nor sufficient that Thou enter under my roof into the habitation of my soul, for it is all deserted and in ruins, and Thou hast not a fitting place in me to lay Thy head. But as from the heights of Thy glory Thou didst humble Thyself, so now bear me in my humility; as Thou didst deign to lie in a manger in a cave, so also come into my mute soul and corrupt body. . . . And grant that I may partake of Thine All-holy Body and precious Blood for the sanctification, enlightenment and strengthening of my weak soul and body; for the relief from the burden of my sins; for my preservation against all the snares of the devil; for victory over all my sinful and evil habits; for the mortification of my passions; for obedience to Thy commandments; for growth in Thy divine grace and for the inheritance of the kingdom. . . .[8]

Middle Eastern reformed churches hold that Christ is present in the Lord's Supper, but not physically or bodily. Rather, his presence in the communion is spiritual or dynamic. Repentance is an essential step before participating in the communion. It provides an opportunity for self-examination and thanksgiving for what Christ has accomplished for our salvation on the cross, and is a reminder of the responsibility of sharing and proclaiming the good news of salvation until he comes. Communion is a comprehensive event in which repentance and renewal lead to service and ministry. It is a powerful expression of unity between the Christian and Christ and among Christians in the fellowship of the church.

---

[8] *Coptic Liturgy: The Seven Prayers of the Agpeya,* 103.

Middle Eastern expression and experience of the Lord's Supper is linked to the death and resurrection of Christ. On the cross, Jesus' life and mission as the incarnated son of God reaches its fullness and purpose. Jesus' death is an integrated part of his total mission of bringing an alienated creation to experience God's grace, forgiveness, and redemption. On the cross Christ offers a holistic salvation. It starts with the personal experience of reconciliation but moves to wider circles that involve reconciliation with other people, communities, and nature. What we need to emphasize in the Middle Eastern context is that salvation is not limited to the private salvation of the individual soul but is a universal salvation that includes alienated creation as a whole.

Central to the Christian faith is the experience and affirmation of life. Resurrection is the heart of the Christian faith; without it there would be no meaning to Christ's suffering and death on the cross. Only in the light of Jesus' resurrection from the dead did his death gain that special, unique saving significance. Jesus' mission, life, death, and resurrection constitute an integral holistic event of God's salvation. To participate in it is to begin a process of renewal, personal and social wholeness, and reconciliation.

## c. Repentance: Islamic Perspective

Middle Eastern Christianity has lived with Islam for thirteen centuries; therefore it is essential for our discussion to provide an overview of the Islamic view of repentance. The Islamic understanding of human nature and the concept of sin differs from that of Christian theology. Whereas in Christianity the human fall resulted in creating a dominant state of sinfulness that pervaded all humanity, in Islam, Adam and Eve committed a mistake or a single slip that was completely forgiven by God after their repentance. The Qur'an does not refer to the fall as a sinful act; to the contrary, it is described as a mistake, disobedience, or an act of injustice. In *Sura* 14:34/37; 33:72 Adam's disobedience is referred to as "an unjust act" *(zulum)*. The Arabic word *(zulum)* is widely used today in reference to an act of iniquity, unfairness, or injustice in general. *Sura* 20:114/115 explains, "We (God) made a covenant with Adam before, but he forgot, and We found in him no determination." Muslims prefer to emphasize Adam's forgetfulness in reference to the Fall. The reason for emphasizing this is that Adam was a prophet, and by nature prophets do not intentionally sin or disobey God. Later on in the *Sura* it says "Adam rebelled against *(asa)* his Lord and went astray *(ghawa)*" (*Sura*

20:119/121). This later description gives a different perspective than the former description of forgetfulness. In any event, the consequence of Adam's act, according to the Qur'an, was Adam and Eve's descent from the Garden (which is believed to be somewhere outside the earth) to the earth, after which God turned toward them in mercy. "Then Adam received words (of guidance) from his Lord and He accepted his repentance: truly, He is the Acceptor of Repentance, the Compassionate" (*Sura* 2:34-37). It is important to note that God forgave Adam and Eve without the need for atonement or sacrifice. Contemporary Muslim scholar Isma'il al-Faruqi comments, "Islam denies that God had to ransom humanity by means of oblation and sacrifice."[9]

According to the Qur'an, Adam acknowledged that he had gone astray and sincerely sought God's forgiveness, which was granted to him unconditionally. Adam and Eve descended from the Garden to the earth because of their error, and yet none of their children inherited the blame for this error. It is inconceivable to Muslim thinking that humanity should be punished for wrong actions that others did. Thus the concept of divine forgiveness, featured strongly in the Qur'an, is centered on the idea that God accepts sincere repentance and forgives sins or mistakes.

Like Adam and Eve, people usually commit mistakes or act unjustly, sometimes out of ignorance; therefore Islam emphasizes the need for "guidance" (*hidayyah*), which is the core task of prophets and messengers. *Sura* 23:28 explains God's reaction to the human fall and emphasizes this central theme: "yet there shall come to you guidance from Me (God), and whoever follows My guidance, no fear shall be on them, neither shall they sorrow. As for the unbelievers . . . those shall be the inhabitants of the fire."

This concept of sin differs from the Christian concept, which emphasizes that the fall of the first humans resulted in distorting humanity's relationship with God and therefore created the need for a savior. According to Islam human beings are not "fallen" and therefore have no need of a savior. The idea of original sin has no place in Islam. A fundamental precept of Islam is that human nature is essentially good. The Qur'an teaches that people are born in a natural state of purity (*fitrah*). "So set your purpose for religion as a man by nature upright—the nature (framed) of God, in which He hath created man" (*Sura* 30:30). Al-Bukhari (810–870 c.e./ 194–256 a.h.) related that the prophet Muhammad said on this subject:

[9] Isma'il R. al-Faruqi, *Islam* (Niles, IL: Argus Communications, 1979) 10.

"No child is born except in the state of natural purity *(Surah)* and then his parents make him Jewish, Christian, or Magian."[10] Thus humanity begins with original righteousness, not original sin. People are created in a good condition, although not a perfect condition, since only God is perfect. Whereas Christians speak of the fallenness of humanity, Muslims believe one becomes a sinner through disbelief or disobeying God's law.

While the Qurʾan uses several terminologies in reference to human sin such as injustice (14:34/37; 33:72), boastfulness (11:9; 12:10/13) and rebelliousness (96:6), the Arabic word for sin *(khatiah)* is not the common word used in the Qurʾan or by Muslims in reference to sin against humans. The word *(khatiah)* is derived from *(khataa)*, which means to miss the target. It is equivalent to the Hebrew *hataʾt* and the Greek *hamartia*. *Khatiah* is the common word used in the Arabic Bible in reference to sin against God. In the biblical concept sin is committed against God. "Against Thee only have I sinned *(Akhataatu* in Arabic) and done that which is evil in Thy sight" (Ps 51:4; cf. also Gen 39:9; Lev 5:1; Isa 43:27). The only term used in the Qurʾan to describe the inward nature of sin is *ithm,* equivalent to the Hebrew *ʾAsham:* "Forsake the outwardness of sin *(ithm)* and the inwardness thereof. Lo! Those who garner sin will be awarded that which they have earned" *(Sura* 6:120). *Ithm* refers to a wrong attitude either toward God or toward human beings. The most unforgivable sin in Islam is *shirk,* which is associating other beings or deities with the only and one God. "Whoever associates anything with God has invented a mighty sin *(ithm)*" *(Sura* 4:48). While disbelief in God or the wrong beliefs are the grave sins in Islam, disobeying God's law is also considered a serious sin. The very word "Islam" means submitting to God and to God's will. Submission to God, therefore, is actualized by observing the five pillars of Islam: the unquestionable belief in the oneness of God and in God's prophet Muhammad, observing prayers, almsgiving, the fasting of the month of Ramadan, and the pilgrimage to Mecca.

The Qurʾan provides different explanations as to the source of sin. In one account it refers to external influences, mainly the influence of Satan on human beings. In the story of the Fall it says, "But the devil made them slip from it (the Garden), and caused them to depart from the state in which they were. And We (God) said, 'Down with you and be henceforth enemies unto one another; and you shall have in the land

---

[10] *Sahih al-Bukhari: Arabic-English,* trans. Muhammad Muhsin Khan (Beirut: Dar Al Arabia, 1985) 6:284 (chapter 230, tradition 298).

a state of settledness and necessities of life for a period'" (*Sura* 2:34-36). At the same time Muslims recognize that committing sins is a natural part of being human. It is narrated that the Prophet Muhammad said, "Every son of Adam is bound to commit sins and the best of those who commit sins are those who repent."[11]

According to Islam sin causes harm to the person who commits it, whether intentionally or out of ignorance. The person alone will bear the consequences of his or her mistakes or unbelief (*Sura* 16:35-36; 17:7). *Sura* 2:54-55 emphasizes that people do not wrong God, but themselves. People therefore are responsible for their own actions and are expected to bear their own burdens. Sin is breaking God's law, not breaking a fellowship with God (*Sura* 7:33). The harm is only against the person committing sin (*Sura* 7:22).

Repentance in Islam is understood as paying back what a person owes to God or to other people. Sin is regarded as a debt that can be compensated for by good deeds. The idea of substitutionary atonement is not acceptable in Islam. It is up to the individual to save oneself. Muslims place a great deal of emphasis on living the correct life, but this is not salvation by good works; it is more salvation because of good works. In other words, a Muslim is not saved because he or she follows the law, but rather following the law is an expression of commitment to God (one's being saved). Faith and good works go hand in hand. It must be noted, however, that the word "salvation" is never mentioned in the Qur'an in relationship to deliverance from sin. There is no need for salvation from sin in Islam; people seek God's favor instead.

This concept has to be understood in the larger context of the God-human relationship in Islam. On the one hand humans are required to submit to God and do God's will. On the other hand God is compassionate and merciful and accordingly God grants forgiveness to those who repent and obey God and his law. *Sura* 35:26 indicates that "Verily those who recite the Book of God, and are steadfast in prayer, and give alms of what We have bestowed, in secret and in public. . . . God may pay them their hire and give them increase of His grace." This concept is further expounded and emphasized in *Sura* 9:

> Do they not realize that God indeed accepts repentance from His ser-
> vants and receives freewill offerings? For God the merciful responds

[11] al-Tirmidhi, *al-Haddith,* in Arabic (Cairo: Dar-al-Aoloum, 1972) tradition 2423.

to penitence. . . . From the believers God purchases their very selves and their possessions, the price of the garden. They do battle in God's cause, they kill and are killed themselves. It is a pledge God undertakes in truth, in the Torah, in the Injil, and in the Qurʾan. Who is more true to covenant than God? So find joy in the bargain you have made with God: to do so is the supreme achievement. Such are they who repent, who worship, give praise, live as pilgrims, who kneel and prostrate in prayer, who enjoin what is right and repudiate what is proscribed, and who observe the limits God has set. So tell the believers the glad news. (*Sura* 9:104-112)

In Islam there are greater sins and lesser sins. Some traditions argue that lesser sins are forgiven automatically because of good works while greater sins require begging for forgiveness (*istighfar*) and the sin of polytheism requires repentance (*tawba*).[12] The conditions of forgiveness of sins are not very clearly stated. Sometimes the Qurʾan gives the impression that God forgives unconditionally: "Say, O My servants who have transgressed against themselves (by committing evil deeds and sins)! Despair not of the Mercy of God, verily God forgives all sins. Truly, He is Oft-Forgiving, Most Merciful" (*Sura* 39:53). Other Qurʾanic verses give a different impression: "God forgives whom he wills and punishes whom he wills" (*Sura* 3:124; 5:118); "God does not love evildoers" (*Sura* 2:276; 7:55; 42:40). At the same time the Qurʾan argues that if God wanted, God could keep people from sinning altogether (*Sura* 32:13; 13:31; 6:39).

In any case there is no assurance that sins have been forgiven in Islam; only at the Day of Judgment will people know their final destiny. Thus the ultimate question is whether one's good deeds are greater than one's evil deeds. Those whose scale of good deeds will be heavy will enter paradise. Those whose scale of good deeds will be light will go to hell (*Sura* 7:8-9). On the one hand it is ultimately one's own righteous deeds that determine one's eternal state. On the other hand, while good deeds are balanced against evil or bad deeds on the Day of Judgment, only God determines the final destiny of people (Sura 21:47, 25:70).

Some scholars argue that Islam was influenced by the Christian teaching of the seventh century, which emphasized penitence as key to gaining

---

[12] Samuel M. Zwemer, *The Moslem Doctrine of God* (New York: American Tract Society, 1905).

God's forgiveness.[13] Also there seem to be some similarities between the Islamic and Christian expressions of penitence such as prayer and fasting. However, it is interesting to note that Christian communities across the Middle East were not greatly influenced by the Islamic concept of repentance. Several things might have contributed to this. Christians through the centuries became aware of the fact that central to repentance and forgiveness of sin is Christ's death on the cross, a concept that is completely rejected by Islam and is considered to be the grave sin *(shirk)*. While different forms of Middle Eastern Christianity emphasized the concept of penitence, it has always been viewed in relationship to the person and work of Christ, which provides a different foundation for the forgiveness of sin than that of Islam.

## 2. Implications

Repentance is a holistic experience, expressed in an integrated form in which the biblical and historical dimensions are woven together to provide that experience. Contemporary Middle Eastern Christians see themselves rooted in that long history of biblical and historical foundation. Their perspective on repentance might take the form of seclusion and withdrawal from the world following a long history of monastic life. But they are also engaged in the realities of a sinful world that is characterized by suffering and alienation.

Middle Eastern Christians are often perceived as being inward-looking and isolated. The long history of suffering and persecution has generated a sense of suspicion and fear among them. This is central to understanding Middle Eastern spirituality. The long history of sporadic persecutions created a Middle Eastern spirituality that is eschatological in its orientation. With the exception of the Lebanese Maronite Christians, the majority of Middle Eastern Christians thrive in a spirituality that helps them to focus on their eternal life, which eventually will give them freedom from the bondage of this earthly life characterized by sin and suffering. One of the positive outcomes is a spirituality marked by a patient and forgiving spirit.

Middle Eastern Christian life revolves around worship. The central focus of earthly worship is to gain salvation and to be united with Christ the Lord. Repentance is the first and most significant step in reaching

---

[13] J. Windroe Sweetman, *Islam & Christian Theology* (London: Lutterworth Press, 1947) 2:194–220.

unity with Christ. Baptism summarizes the whole gospel, which is God's acceptance and forgiveness through the blood of Christ. The participation in Christ's death and resurrection marks the beginning of the new life in Christ (Romans 6).

Repentance is emphasized in relationship to suffering and persecution, where confessing sins and asking for God's forgiveness provides for a renewed hope for the future. Repentance is vital in helping people to understand the roots of suffering, sin, and alienation from God, directing them to seek God's forgiveness in order to move toward a holistic redemption for the individual and for society as a whole. Confessing sins reflects maturity in Christian growth. It has to come from the heart with humility and willingness to turn away from sin in order for God to heal the land and bring peace and stability (2 Chr 7:14).

The celebration of communion confirms the presence of Christ among the community and provides an opportunity for repentance, renewal, and thanksgiving that will lead to service and ministry. Communion is a powerful expression of the hope we have in Christ. The Christ who is to come in glory and power is present among his people in the fellowship of the church.

Our understanding of hope is both historical and transhistorical. If we view history with its conditions and potentialities as an open system we are bound to understand the creative power of God as a transforming and liberating power that is active through all history to open new possibilities for the future. A redeemed and liberated community that has experienced God's forgiveness is open to seize every opportunity to participate in this process of transformation. The hope we have in Christ is actualized when the community lives and witnesses to the love of Christ for a broken and alienated world.

Wars, conflicts, and instability continue to be the main features characterizing the Middle East today. Wars breed more wars, and the consequence of war is long-lasting hatred, animosity, devastation, and destruction. A forgiven and renewed community has a responsibility to be an instrument of peace and reconciliation in such a tragic and devastating context. The church's celebration of the death of Christ and his resurrection is not just a sacramental event; it is a transforming reality that has to bear fruit in real-life praxis. The cross of Christ and the power of his resurrection will transform any bitterness or hostility among contemporary Middle Eastern Christians into a renewed power of reconciliation and peace. Those who suffer have the capability to forgive. As South African Lauren van der Post observed,

Persons who really suffered at the hands of others do not find it difficult to forgive, nor even to understand the people who caused their suffering. They do not find it difficult to forgive because out of suffering and sorrow truly endured comes an instinctive sense of privilege. Recognition of the creative truth comes in a flash: forgiveness for others, as for ourselves, for we too, know not what we do.[14]

The Christian understanding and experience of forgiveness is based on God's reaching for us while we were sinners (Rom 5:8). God's forgiveness is not based on what we deserve, but on what God has done for us in Christ. This implies that a repentant and forgiven Christian is empowered to accept and include others, even those considered enemies. Whoever accepts the law of retaliation for the enemy falls into a vicious circle from which there is no escape. Love of the enemy, however, can never mean submission to the enemy's hostility. The concern becomes not to protect ourselves from the other's hostility, but to make him or her part of our responsibility. We cannot secure a just and peaceful society by the elimination of all threatening forces, but we may be able to overcome violence by nonviolent means. Justice alone creates a lasting peace—*Salam*, the Arabic equivalent of the Hebrew and biblical *Shalom*. God is just, because God creates rights for the people who are unrighteous. Our experience of God's justice, manifested in redeeming and accepting the sinners and the unrighteous, enables us to be an instrument for justice and peace in this world.

## 3. Further Reading

Bailey, Betty J., and J. Martin Bailey. Who *Are the Christians in the Middle East?* Grand Rapids: Eerdmans, 2003.

Cragg, Kenneth. *The Arab Christians: A History in the Middle East.* Louisville: Westminster John Knox, 1991.

*Coptic Liturgy: The Seven Prayers of the Agpeya.* Cairo: St. Mark Publications, 1990.

El-Miskeen, Anba Matta. *The Christian Tradition.* Wadi El-Natrun, Egypt: Anba Makar Monastery Press, 1978.

_____. *Baptism.* Wadi El-Natrun, Egypt: Anba Makar Monastery Press, 1989.

Etzioni, Amitai, and David E. Carney, eds., *Repentance: A Comparative Perspective.* Lanham, MD: Rowman & Littlefield, 1997.

[14] Lauren van der Post, *Venture to the Interior* (New York: William Morrow, 1951) 30–31.

Habib, Girgis. *The Sacrament of Repentance and Confession.* Cairo: St. Mark Publications, 1990.

Pope Shenoda III. *Salvation in the Orthodox Understanding.* Cairo: St. Mark Publications, 1985.

_____. *The Life of Repentance and Purity.* Cairo: St. Mark Publications, 1990.

Sweetmann, J. Windroe. *Islam and Christian Theology.* 4 vols. London: Lutterworth Press, 1947.

Watterson, Barbara. *Coptic Egypt.* Edinburgh: Scottish Academic Press, 1988.

Woodberry, J. Dudley, ed. *Muslims and Christians on the Emmaus Road.* Monrovia, CA: MARC Publishing, ©1989; fifth printing 2000.

# 4. Hermeneutical Reflections

The essays presented in this volume reflect rich biblical, historical, and theological understandings and expressions of repentance in the Christian tradition. The common theme that strikes me most is that there are multiple forms of experiencing and expressing repentance in the Christian faith. Even within a particular Christian tradition, e.g., Orthodox, Catholic, Evangelical, Pentecostal, there are varieties of theological understandings and practices of Christian repentance/penance.

A close examination of the Reformed understanding of repentance, for example, helps us to realize that confession is an integral component of the Christian life. While repentance is considered a necessary fruit of faith (Calvin), it is also an integral component of the Christian life as a whole. "It is a continuing response to God's grace" (Andrew Purves). For Pentecostals repentance is not a one-time event; rather, it is a journey. Salvation is understood as "a journey that involves walking in the light" (Cheryl Johns). In the Orthodox tradition repentance is perceived as the mystery that colors every aspect of the Christian life. "In the mystery of repentance we confess not simply our faults but, more fundamentally, our faith in the One who is able to forgive sins" (John Chryssavgis). Central to the Catholic understanding and experience of repentance is the sacrament of Penance. There are four common designations used to explain Penance: the sacrament of conversion, the sacrament of confession, the sacrament of forgiveness, the sacrament of reconciliation. "Each is intended to illuminate a dimension of the sacrament relevant to its understanding and practice" (Ralph Del Colle).

Many of my colleagues alluded to the fact that repentance/penance is individual as well as corporate and communal. Several articles emphasized the centrality of worship, liturgy, prayer, and preaching in directing people to seek forgiveness and the renewal of their hearts. Individual and corporate prayers are vital forms of expressing repentance in every Christian tradition. In the Orthodox tradition, fasting occupies a significant portion of the liturgical calendar and provides an opportunity for individual and corporate repentance. In the Catholic tradition, while the seasons of Advent and Lent are highly communal times when the whole community comes together to celebrate and worship, they also provide a great opportunity for personal searching and examining. Individual and communal confessions are encouraged in the Reformed, Evangelical, and Pentecostal traditions. Some churches incorporate prayers of confession in their liturgy in order to help the worshipers focus on the need for confessing their sins.

One area that needs to be highlighted and pursued in this project is the impact of repentance and forgiveness on Christian life praxis. We must ask how a renewed and forgiven community or individual might contribute to making a difference in the way we live. Considering the current state of mistrust, hatred, and conflict worldwide, can a forgiven and renewed community or individual be able to create an atmosphere where people are able to trust and accept one another? Will a reconciled community be able to become an instrument of peace and reconciliation among individuals, communities, and nations? The church's celebration of the death and resurrection of Christ is not a distant historical reality; it is a transforming power that is capable of creating renewed and liberated communities. Repentance, therefore, must be at the center of the way in which the Christian community lives and witnesses to the world today.

Sixteen

# Penitence as Practiced in African/African American Christian Spirituality

*Michael Battle*

## 1. Tradition

There is a profound impact of penitential practices within African/African American Christian spirituality. Because of the past two centuries, this essay focuses on penitential practices within both African and African American Christian spirituality. I provide such a focus because African American Christians have given the world penitential practices through the civil rights movement and African Christians have shown the world the extraordinary practice of the Truth and Reconciliation Commission. In this essay I seek to provide a general overview of the African and African American expression of penitential practice within the Christian tradition. By "penitential" I mean those practices within African Christian spirituality that encourage communities to respond appropriately to sin. Such practices can also be traced through the story of the Black Church within its various traditions and theologies. Herein we discover a crucial theological worldview of the Black Church and African Christians—that of God's nonviolence and forgiveness. I seek to peer through this worldview throughout this essay.

Theologians sometimes debate whether one can forgive another if that other does not repent. But we should also ask if one can repent without the prospect of forgiveness. Avengers do not much care about relating again to their enemies, but those who forgive often do the extraordinary—offer a future for all involved. Those who do the extraordinary are my focus in this chapter. Of course, we lack the space here to rehearse a substantial narrative of the Black Church regarding repentance and penitence, but we may gain glimpses of how such communities have responded to sin.

The tragedies of slavery and racism may cause the reader to wonder about the complexities around penitence and repentance within African Christian spirituality—namely, what does it mean for those who are oppressed to repent? Or do discussions of repentance and penitence really refer to appropriate actions that must be taken by those of European descent? Because of these questions we wander into the conundrum concerning what is exactly penitential about African and African American Christian spirituality. The complexities around the penitential movement as practiced in African/African American spirituality usually relate in some way to those of European descent. Because of slavery and colonialism there is now an inextricable link between black and white people. In other words, when dealing with African Christian spirituality one inevitably deals with white people and those of European descent. Further work needs to be done on this dialectic between black and white Christians so that we may see how those caught in abusive historical narratives make better sense of self and community. In this essay I focus more narrowly on the extraordinary practices developed by Africans and African Americans in response to their abusive historical narratives. When enticed to respond violently, African Christian spirituality has instead given the world the "best practices" of learning how to stop abusive historical cycles all together. In this thesis African Christian spirituality provides better and sustainable answers for the global conflicts we all face. In the end this essay seeks to encourage greater understanding of what penitence means in our complex and tragic histories in order to foster greater reflection on the "best practices" of the Christian faith.

In this display of how penitence continues to show the "best practices" of the Christian faith I highlight both important theological themes that undergird spiritual expression among African peoples and important sources from key Black Church texts and pastoral figures. This essay becomes a fairly unusual study in the Black Church, however, in which to focus on the theme of penitence/repentance because of the complexity named above in which it becomes difficult to describe penitence for those who have systematically suffered.

My primary thought regarding penitence within African Christian spirituality is that the penitential movement is understood more communally than personally. As stated above, this means that African Christians, when enticed to respond violently, have instead given the world the "best practices" of learning how to stop abusive historical cycles altogether. African Christian spirituality, however, does not lessen the uniqueness of persons. The person in traditional African spirituality is conceived not as an individualized self but as a unique person webbed in unique relationships. When such relationships are broken, a response of repair is needed. Such repair is vital because interrelatedness within community, past as well as present, constitutes personhood in many African cultures. This is why rites of passage are crucial to becoming a mature person in those cultures. Without increasing one's deeper formation in community, a person never matures. One could argue that such communal formation of individuals is not primarily an African sensibility. For example, David Blumenthal reflects on Jewish teachings on repentance and forgiveness and offers the insight that Judaism does not recognize confession of personal sin to a religious figure as part of the process of sin and repentance. In other words, there is no designated individual authority to whom a person goes to confess sins. He goes on to say that "sins are confessed privately, in prayer, before God." [1] In African Christian spirituality, however, one finds more public practices of remorse and repentance. Such practices of African Christian spirituality are ancient.

Ancient Christianity was not, as many think, a European religion. Christian communities were well established in Africa by the third and fourth centuries. In Egypt and Ethiopia, Coptic traditions of worship, monasticism, and spirituality have remained authentically African and authentically Christian down to the present day. [2] As Christianity became more associated with European culture and printing presses the practices of Christian spirituality also took on more European expression. In particular, Christian spirituality became more individualized and personalized. This becomes problematic in discussions of repentance and penitence in that the worldview of what needs to be repented from, or what practices of penitence need to be in place, becomes relative to the individual's definition of harm or injury done. As Ralf Wustenberg

[1] David Blumenthal, "Repentance and Forgiveness," *Cross Currents* 48 (Spring 1998) 75–82.

[2] Albert Raboteau, "African-American Orthodoxy." Reprinted from *Solia—The Herald* Diocesan Newspaper, issued by The Romanian Orthodox Episcopate of America at the following internet address: http://www.stmaryofegypt.net/afamorx.shtml.

reflects on the possibility of the miracle of South Africa's Truth and Reconciliation Commission ever happening in Germany, he believes that
communal and cultural differences become even more problematic in
understanding the scope of reconciliation.[3]

To illustrate my thesis that when enticed to respond violently, African
Christian spirituality has instead given the world the "best practices" of
learning how to stop abusive historical cycles altogether, I discuss three
themes below that help to identify the particularity of African Christian
spirituality. These three themes lead to the ultimate goal of restorative
justice.

## a. Invaluable Created World

Spirituality cannot be disembodied for African Christianity. African
spirituality values the material world as enlivened with spirit and makes
use of material objects that have been imbued with spiritual power.
These sacramental sensibilities lead to such practices as libation, dance,
laying on of hands, African rhythm, and testifying in the spirit. Worship
in African American tradition seeks to make the divine present and effective not for the sake of individuals, but for the sake of the community.
In ceremonies of spirit-entranced dance the human person becomes the
representation of the divine community and, through these intermedi-
ary dancers, divine power heals and transforms. One of the classical
liturgical expressions of this in African American spirituality is the *"ring
shout,"* a counterclockwise shuffling movement in which the shouters
move round in a circle to the driving rhythms of counter-clapping and
steadily repeated song that bring all present into one accord. The style of
movement and the religious impulse behind the ring shout go back to the
ancestral homelands of those Africans carried to America by the Atlantic
slave trade. The danced circle symbolizes the steadfast faith of African
peoples who survive slavery and hold on to the faith that all human
beings are created in the image and likeness of God. Ancient Christianity does not break that circle but brings it to amazing fulfillment in the
endless circle of love flowing continuously between the divine persons
of the all-merciful Trinity: Father, Son, and Holy Spirit.

[3] See Ralf Karolus Wustenberg, "Reconciliation with a 'New' Lustre: The
South African Example as a Paradigm for Dealing with the Political Past of the
German Democratic Republic," trans. Douglas S. Bax, *Journal of Theology for
Southern Africa* 113 (July 2002) 19–40.

These practices make use of created existence to join in the praise of God's created order. In light of the tragic past of African peoples used as slaves and impersonal objects in the created order, the context of communal sin becomes more apparent in creation. In other words, because of the suffering of African peoples it becomes all the more important to search for God's presence in created order. The context of African slavery in the Americas makes such a search difficult and deeply problematic. In 1866 the U.S. Congress passed a bill to grant 40 acres and a mule to all formerly enslaved Africans in America. This bill was vetoed by President Andrew Johnson and the Congress did not have enough votes to override the veto. Many feel that this was the last time anything has come close to giving Africans in America "closure" to the suffering of slavery. Commencing on November 30, 1989, Michigan's Democratic Congressman John Conyers began a series of introductions of an identical bill (which he has continued to introduce in every Congress since then). The bill is entitled:

> A bill to acknowledge the fundamental injustice, cruelty, brutality, and inhumanity of slavery in the United States and the 13 American colonies between 1619 and 1865 and to establish a commission to examine the institution of slavery, subsequently de jure and de facto racial and economic discrimination against African-Americans, and the impact of these forces on living African-Americans, to make recommendations to the Congress on appropriate remedies, and for other purposes.[4]

Such a bill reminds us all that Americans have not dealt well with the past and there must be a complete closure to human oppression and suffering.[5] In African Christian spirituality there is an understanding that God heals and restores whole communities that practice a healthy memory of the past. Perhaps this is why South Africa, and one could even say the United States, has not experienced the expected rebellion by people of African descent. Deeply instilled within the conceptual framework of African Christian spirituality is a direct correlation between the past actions of certain peoples and our present-day circumstances. To continue violent responses only exacerbates those circumstances. Within the African Christian worldview is the expectation that all of God's creation

---

[4] Bill H.R. 40, "Commission to Study Reparation Proposals for African Americans Act" found at http://www.house.gov/conyers/news_reparations.htm.

[5] See Desmond Tutu, *No Future without Forgiveness* (New York: Doubleday, 1999).

will be made whole again. For example, the future of Africa cannot be determined without factoring in the future of all people.

As demonstrated through the preaching of Martin Luther King, Jr., Richard Allen, and other prominent African American Christians, the created order cannot be restored until God's justice and mercy are tangibly displayed.

### b. Preaching and the Declared Word

To further illustrate my thesis that African Christian spirituality understands penitential movement as a healthy communal exercise, some attention must be given to the power of preaching and scriptural revelation. The following are some of the favorite pericopes pertaining to repentance preached in the Black Church.

> The Lord spoke to Moses, saying: When any of you sin and commit a trespass against the Lord by deceiving a neighbor in a matter of a deposit or a pledge, or by robbery, or if you have defrauded a neighbor, or have found something lost and lied about it—if you swear falsely regarding any of the various things that one may do and sin thereby—when you have sinned and realize your guilt, and would restore what you took by robbery or by fraud or the deposit that was committed to you, or the lost thing that you found, or anything else about which you have sworn falsely, you shall repay the principal amount and shall add one-fifth to it. You shall pay it to its owner when you realize your guilt. (Lev 6:1-5)

> The spirit of the Lord God is upon me, because the Lord has anointed me; he has sent me to bring good news to the oppressed, to bind up the brokenhearted, to proclaim liberty to the captives, and release to the prisoners; to proclaim the year of the Lord's favor, and the day of vengeance of our God; to comfort all who mourn; to provide for those who mourn in Zion—to give them a garland instead of ashes, the oil of gladness instead of mourning, the mantle of praise instead of a faint spirit. They will be called oaks of righteousness, the planting of the Lord, to display his glory. They shall build up the ancient ruins, they shall raise up the former devastations; they shall repair the ruined cities, the devastations; they shall repair the ruined cities, the devastations of many generations. (Isa 61:1-4)

> "Zacchaeus, hurry and come down; for I must stay at your house today." So he hurried down and was happy to welcome him. All who saw it began to grumble and said, "He has gone to be the guest of one

who is a sinner." Zacchaeus stood there and said to the Lord, "Look half of my possessions, Lord, I give to the poor; and if I have defrauded anyone of anything, I pay back four times as much." Then Jesus said to him, "Today salvation has come to this house, because he too is a son of Abraham. For the Son of Man came to seek out and to save the lost." (Luke 19:5-10)

As commonly understood in the Black Church tradition, the Law, the voice of the Old Testament prophets, and the teaching of Jesus in the New Testament speak often, both emphatically and parabolically, about repentance, restitution, restoration, and reconciliation. Preachers developed a cadence in which to personify the voice of the prophets. The morality behind much preaching in the Black Church tradition is that when something is stolen, obtained by deceit or through intentional or unintentional misdeeds, restitution plus "interest" must be made in order to restore the wholeness of the community. Wholeness of the community and a communal life that honors and glorifies God are the central themes in such preaching.

Also favored in Black preaching is the prophetic tradition. The prophets quite eloquently urge and plead for God's people to practice being in better community. Such a practice can be seen through a return to a focus on what God requires and a plea for God's people to heal the spirit of the oppressed and to do what is necessary to proclaim the day of the "Lord's favor." As noted in Isaiah 61 (repeated again in Luke 4:18 as Jesus' stated earthly mission and ministry focus), Isaiah summarizes God's request for God's people by calling for the rebuilding of (and advocacy for), a united and healed community that glorifies God, honors who God is and calls us to be. Isaiah describes this community as one wherein the ancient ruins both figuratively and literally are restored, and a place where prior devastation is reversed and despair is replaced by praise.

Likewise, Luke uses the story of Zacchaeus, denoted a "sinner" because of his oppression of and theft from the poor, to demonstrate how Zacchaeus' exposure to Jesus produced an act of repentance. Luke used this account of an acknowledged sinner's encounter with Jesus to demonstrate that systemic societal abuses will never stop until repentance, restitution, restoration, and reconciliation occur. Such biblical narratives provide obvious references for people of African descent who were forcefully stolen from Africa and forced to work without pay. But they were references for how to respond in such a way as not to perpetuate cycles of violence and abuse.

## c. Black Ecclesiology

To further illustrate my thesis that when enticed to respond violently, African Christian spirituality has instead given the world the "best practices" of learning how to stop abusive historical cycles altogether, an understanding of the beginning worldview of the Black Church proves helpful. Because of systemic prejudice and racism, three major denominations were formed—African Methodist Episcopal (AME) Church, African Methodist Episcopal Zion (AMEZ) Church, and Christian Methodist Episcopal (CME) Church.

The African Methodist Episcopal Church was founded by Richard Allen (1760–1831). At the age of seventeen Richard Allen had joined a Methodist society. When he was twenty-two years old he became a local preacher, and under the supervision of Bishop Francis Asbury, Allen began to travel widely in a preaching ministry. He purchased his freedom from his owner in 1783. Along with other African American Methodists and white Methodists, Allen attended St. George's Methodist Episcopal Church in Philadelphia. According to Allen, "When the colored people began to get numerous in attending the church, they moved us from the seats we usually sat on, and placed us around the wall." On April 12, 1787, the congregation's African American members met to protest slavery and to discuss the discrimination they experienced at the worship services. African Americans were forced to sit in church balconies and receive Holy Communion after their fellow white worshipers. Accordingly, Allen and other black Methodists walked out of St. George's to protest their treatment by whites.

In 1816 Richard Allen organized sixteen African American Methodist Congregations into a new denomination, the African Methodist Episcopal Church. The organizing conference elected Allen its first bishop, and he led the church until his death fifteen years later. The African Methodist Episcopal Zion Church was organized in 1796 by blacks protesting discrimination at John Street Methodist Church in New York City. The Christian Methodist Episcopal Church (originally the Colored Methodist Episcopal Church) was created in 1870 as the result of an agreement between white-and-black members of the Methodist Episcopal Church.

Lack of support and understanding on the part of the white church leaders, coupled with a strong desire by the African American Methodists for control of their own church affairs, led to the creation of these new denominations. Allen remained steadfast in his purpose and maintained a gentle spirit, answering hostile charges with soft replies. He wrote,

"We were filled with fresh vigor to get a house erected to worship God in."[6] Allen viewed the racial discrimination at St. George's Church as a manifestation of the decline in the religious fervor of American Christianity. He established the AME Church as a protest against racism and to preserve evangelicalism and egalitarianism in American Methodism. He introduced a broader debate on the nature of Wesleyan spirituality, envisioning African Methodism as a movement that emphasized a more communal spirituality more faithful to Wesley.

In 2000, United Methodists officially pledged to follow a path toward racial healing when the denomination's top legislative body, the General Conference, adopted the "Act of Repentance for Racism." The Act of Repentance calls for local congregations to engage in study sessions using the commission's study guide, Steps Toward Wholeness: Learning and Repentance, and for each annual conference to hold liturgical acts of repentance. The 2000 resolution, "Act of Repentance for Racism," points out that the United Methodist Church and its predecessors "have perpetuated the sin of racism" for years and need to make amends for that institutionalized racism, particularly against African Americans.[7]

Racism drove African Americans from Methodist churches. Even those who stayed were segregated further through the establishment of the Central Jurisdiction in 1939, a non-geographic jurisdiction that was abolished in 1968. African Americans were among the first Methodists in the United States, attending the early revival meetings and contributing major preachers such as Richard Allen to the church.

Richard Allen's hymn, *Spiritual Song*, is helpful in providing the early perspective of black ecclesiology. This hymn is actually a dialogue between two speakers. It is an antiphony or call and response. In some stanzas traditional historic styles of early African American worship are defended and affirmed. In other stanzas there are features of early African American worship that are exaggerated and decried.

---

[6] Richard Allen, quoted in Carolyn Henninger Oehler, *Steps Toward Wholeness: Learning and Repentance* (General Commission on Christian Unity and Interreligious Concerns, the United Methodist Church, 2000) 9–20, and "Methodism and the Black Experience," in Kenneth Cain Kinghorn, *The Heritage of American Methodism* (Nashville: Abingdon, 1999) 95–108.

[7] See the United Methodist Church's "Act of Repentance of Racism," http://www.umc.org/interior_print.asp?ptid=4&mid=1002.

### Fifth and Sixth Stanzas: The Third Speech of Richard Allen

Don't be so soon shaken, if I'm not mistaken,

Such things have been acted by Christians of old,

When the ark was a-coming, King David came running,

And dancing before it by scripture we're told,

When the Jewish nation had laid the foundation,

And rebuilt the temple at Ezra's command,

Some wept and some prais'd, and such a noise there was rais'd,

It was heard afar off, perhaps all through the land.

As for the preacher, Ezekiel the teacher,

Was taught for to stamp and to smite with his hand,

To shew the transgression of that wicked nation,

That they might repent and obey the command.

For scripture quotation in the dispensation,

The blessed Redeemer had handed them out,

If these cease from praying, we hear him declaring,

The stones to reprove him would quickly cry out.[8]

Obviously Allen is using this poetic means to respond to the patterns of historic African American Christian worship. The formation of the Black Church reflected the fact that even white Christians could not agree on issues of race and slavery. This became the touchstone for Methodism's founder, John Wesley, an outspoken opponent of slavery, as he denounced it as evil. This becomes all the more important for the early church in America as the Southern churches broke away in 1844. Wesley wrote: ". . . I am afraid, lest [the church in America] should only exist as a dead sect, having the form of religion without the power. And this undoubtedly will be the case, unless they hold fast both the doctrine, spirit, and discipline with which they first set out."[9]

---

[8] Quoted in Kenneth L. Waters, "Liturgy, Spirituality, and Polemic in the Hymnody of Richard Allen," *The North Star: A Journal of African American Religious History,* vol. 2, no. 2 (Spring 1999), reprinted in *The A.M.E. Church Review* 119/389 (January–March 2003) 29–41.

[9] John Wesley, *Selections From the Writings of the Rev. John Wesley, M.A.,* ed. Herbert Welch (Nashville: Abingdon, 1942) 205.

## 2. Implications

In light of the troubles of today, there are three key implications for how the Black Church and African Christians may teach us all to move from ambivalence to joyful practice. The first is reflected in the experienced suffering of Africans and African Americans. Instead of allowing negative circumstances to define human worth, black Christians maintained hope and a benign perspective on life. Those outside the black Christian experience can learn from the black experience that suffering is not the final definition of humanity for God's creation. Suffering humanity, following in the pattern of Christ and the saints, has been for African Christian spirituality a mark of the authenticity of faith. African American Christians have offered a prime example of suffering humanity and have understood their own tradition as an extension of the line of martyrs from the days of the ancient church. As described above, we learn from many African American spirituals that true reconciliation begins when victims abandon revenge and perpetrators abandon professions of innocence.

A second implication of authenticity follows from the ability to move beyond the limiting definitions of suffering. One may especially see how authenticity shapes a different pattern of worship among black Christians. There is more room for God's spontaneous interruptions. Christians must come to worship in a way that truly reveals God's inner and outer workings in their lives. Such worship can never be boring. Black Christians have key insights for stagnant liturgical practices that usually catapult people out of corporate worship or create a rite of passage for teenagers never to return to church. When we learn how to be authentic we experience a crucial spiritual practice in which we begin to see measures of growth. The concepts of justification and sanctification lose their dualistic debates within the Black Church because of the practice of spiritual authenticity. Needing to "be real" has always been a prominent assumption within African and African American spirituality. For so many Western churches struggling with their identity in relationship to secular culture, black Christians provide the insight that the greatest work in the Christian life is to make one's self available to the gift of God already given. Christian authenticity increases growth and maturity in what is already made available to us—God's complete love. How we are reconciled to such love is the last great benefit given by black Christians.

The last implication is a vital need for systemic practices of reconciliation. This is most crucial for the world's constant cycles of violence and abuse. The most eloquent example of such reconciliation is South Africa. The great lesson for the world is that public truth about past evil is essential to repentance and can only lead to healthier communities. This leads us back to the core thought presented in this essay—namely, that the essence of African Christian spirituality is communion. In establishing its Truth and Reconciliation Commission (TRC) in 1996, the South African parliament adopted the formula, "Amnesty for Truth." A black Christian headed this historical Commission, Archbishop Desmond Tutu. It took enormous courage to practice political forgiveness—setting aside questions of guilt and legal prosecution. All that the TRC demanded of its witnesses was that they tell the truth about what they had done to their victims. It did not demand an apology, though some did apologize. All that was demanded was that all feel safe in telling their stories. The benefit in doing so was the transition to a new civil society in which the truth about the past will lead to the end of abusive cycles of violence. Nation states that practice such creative penitential practices will always be healthier, suggests Canadian sociologist Nicholas Tavuchis in his remarkable book, *Mea Culpa*.[10]

In the end, how we deal with these three implications of suffering, authenticity, and reconciliation will determine the quality of the world's future. Of course, this is God's world, but black Christians teach us a crucial lesson—that God has created us to participate in creating a healthy past, present, and future. African and African American Christian spirituality teaches all of us that truthful and sincere engagement with situations of brokenness cannot take place unless victims and offenders have the opportunity to interact with each other for the sake of the future of human communities. This interaction must provide victims with the opportunity to express their pain and at the same time allows offenders the opportunity to seek forgiveness from the persons they have hurt. Desmond Tutu, in his discussion of restorative justice, states that its

> . . . central concern is the healing of breaches, the redressing of imbalances, the restoration of broken relationships, a seeking to rehabilitate both the victim and the perpetrator, who should be given the opportunity to be reintegrated into the community he has injured by his offense.[11]

[10] Nicholas Tavuchis, *Mea Culpa : A Sociology of Apology and Reconciliation* (Stanford, CA: Stanford University Press, 1991).

[11] Tutu, *No Future Without Forgiveness*, 54.

Tutu's words emphasize the importance that restorative justice places on helping the perpetrators of violence participate in the process of healing the communities they offend. Failure to offer these opportunities for healing will result in communities that remain fractured and broken. This is just the type of healing that many in African spirituality seek as they try to build a solid and secure future for God's children.

## 3. Further Reading

Battle, Michael. *Reconciliation: The Ubuntu Theology of Desmond Tutu*. Cleveland: Pilgrim Press, 1997.

_____. *Blessed Are the Peacemakers: A Christian Spirituality of Nonviolence*. Macon, GA: Mercer University Press, 2004.

_____, and Tony Campolo. *The Church Enslaved: A Spirituality of Racial Reconciliation*. Minneapolis: Fortress Press, 2005.

Fluker, W. E., and Catherine Tumber, eds., *A Strange Freedom: The Best of Howard Thurman on Religious Experience and Public Life*. Boston: Beacon Press, 1998.

Jones, Gregory L. *Embodying Forgiveness: A Theological Analysis*. Grand Rapids: Eerdmans, 1995.

McCormick, Patrick. "The Politics of Forgiveness." *U.S. Catholic* 62, no. 9 (September 1997) 1–5.

Tutu, Desmond. *No Future Without Forgiveness*. New York: Doubleday, 1999.

## 4. Hermeneutical Reflection

After reading the work of the other contributors in this book I have gained a better understanding for why a penitential theology is extremely important. From my colleagues writing in both biblical and historical traditions I have learned how traditions of penitence have always been vital for communities who suffer. This led me to address the problem of suffering and why black Christians refused any resulting negative definitions of identity. It is from those who reflect homiletically that I learned a key implication derived from African and African American spirituality. It is the implication of the need for authenticity—which I discuss below. Overall, I have learned in this project that African Christian spirituality understands the penitential movement through its communal practices, and that African responses to suffering often display a courageous and forgiving spirit more mindful of restorative justice rather than retributive justice. This leads me to make some autobiographical reflections.

Restorative justice is a vital concept for me, an African American who has chosen the Anglican/Episcopal tradition. I recently heard a story from a fellow African American Episcopalian who told me about his own difficulty in explaining why "a black man was an Episcopalian." The difficulty of this combination of being black and Episcopalian is seen through the colonial past of the Anglican Church in which many times the church simply followed vindictive governments and Anglo culture. The concept of restorative justice is important for me because it shapes my answer for why a black person may indeed be Anglican.

Such a spirit of restorative justice is difficult to understand, as illustrated by a question posed by a white woman, "Can the African American community forgive European Americans?" This question suggests the perception of isolated incidents of racial hatred that never seem to leave us. According to Peter J. Paris' book, *The Spirituality of African Peoples,* African people were able to overcome resentment and hatred toward Europeans because of their value of community.[12] In order not to misunderstand African Christian spirituality as "cheap grace," one must understand the value of building community, which in turn implies forgiveness becoming an important part of people's lives. Martin Luther King Jr. placed forgiveness and reconciliation at the core of the civil rights movement. This was not a struggle against white people, but a struggle for a better future for all people. African Americans, by granting systematic forgiveness to European Americans, were really seeking the presence of God in the created order. Such a search looks like reconciliation. For reconciliation to happen fully, European Americans will need to reciprocate the search for reconciliation and the presence of God.

One may see such a search for God's presence through African American spirituals that placed a strong emphasis on a tone of sad joyfulness. The following spiritual, "Study War No More," illustrates such ambivalence:

I'm going to lay down my sword and shield
Down by the riverside
Down by the riverside
Down by the riverside

---

[12] Peter J. Paris, *The Spirituality of African Peoples: The Search for a Common Moral Discourse* (Minneapolis: Fortress Press, 1995).

Going to lay down my sword and shield

Down by the riverside

Ain't going to study war no more

Ain't going to study war no more

Ain't going to study war no more

Ain't going to study war no more

Ain't going to study war no more

Ain't going to study war no more

Ain't going to study war no more

I'm going to put on my long white robe

Down by the riverside

Down by the riverside

Down by the riverside

I'm going to put on my long white robe

Down by the riverside

Ain't going to study war no more

I'm going to talk with the Prince of Peace . . .

The genius of African and African American penitential practice is in its ability to continue moving from ambivalence to joy. Instead of reveling in revenge or vindictive ideology, black Christians around the world have embraced their ambivalence to move to more positive ground and clarity. The very description "black Christian" displays the kind of ambivalence in which, for many, such a description would mean "negative Christian." The Black Church and African Christians, however, have sung a different song, not of negativity or evil, but of resolve and conviction that violence and revenge will not define God's people. It is with such conviction that we end this essay.

Section Four

# Reflection

Seventeen

# The Summons to New Life: A Reflection

*Walter Brueggemann*

## 1

The socioreligious environment of consumer culture in the United States makes penitence an urgent topic and, in general, as unwelcome as it is urgent. That environment is dominated by strident moral certitude, by unrestrained polemics toward those who think differently, and by an unashamed self-indulgence toward one's own autonomous way in the world, all of which makes our theme seem odd and incongruous. I have been thinking, moreover, that this self-indulgence, including the self-indulgence of moral certitude and rectitude, is not far removed from the "sale of indulgences" that triggered Luther's response in the sixteenth century. The parallel is more than the recurrence of the term "indulgence," for the religious-ethical pretense in both cases is the assumed capacity to purchase [!] well-being, to "purchase" by payment to the church as moral guarantor or as "purchase" to the mall, or to "get purchase" through ideological claim; all such "purchases" subvert the truth of God's rule and distort the true posture of each of us before that holy truth.

In such a socioreligious environment the theme of penitence is urgent and unwelcome because,

> a. The theme identifies our true position "before God" as dependent suppliants without resources, "without one plea"; we suppliants are

compelled by our true character to respond and come to terms with that holy reverence that exposes as a false way our presumed autonomy.[1] The theme of penitence defines all of us and each of us as answerable.

b. The theme calls attention to the profound alienation that exists between the holy God and us as needful suppliants. That profound alienation, of course, is a "discouraging word" that is never spoken in the illusionary culture of moral rectitude, "happy" consumerism, soft "therapeutic" culture, and "safe" militarism propelled by self-securing ideology. The depth of alienation exposes as fraudulent and inadequate all our culturally prescribed efforts at safety, happiness, and well-being.

c. The theme not only evidences alienation, but fixes that alienation as a burden and failure of the human self and the human community. Thus we are answerable before God not only in glad, praise-filled obedience as our proper destiny; we are answerable as well for the alienation that has refused God's gift of life. That refusal of the gift, moreover, is grounded in the passion for self-securing, for a gift of such depth undermines the illusion of a "can-do" culture that permeates the religious/moral dimensions of our common life.

d. The theme not only evidences alienation and places the burden of that alienation upon us, it also amounts to a steady summons and invitation that acts and gestures of redress are required. And while a can-do religious, moral environment may willingly undertake redress—because it is something to be *done*—the theme makes clear that the overcoming of alienation and the accomplishment of reconciliation before God are not assured by our best efforts at redress; rather, that reconciliation finally is not our work but the work and gift of God who wills the end of alienation. Such a double-edged reality asserts *responsibility* for redress, but finally that redress depends upon *holy initiative* toward us, which undermines the characteristically one-dimensional expectation of our environment that imagines a "quick fix."

On all these counts the matter of penitence is urgent because reconciliation with God—and derivatively reconciliation with our neighbor—is the deepest hope among us. The matter is unwelcome because in every way thinkable the claim tells against the religious-moral assumptions that propel our society. Thus the theme itself contains and

---

[1] See George Stroup, *Before God* (Louisville: Westminster John Knox, 2004).

articulates much that is most glorious and most subversive about the truth of the gospel.

This collection of essays is a wondrous and rich collage of historical and contemporary probes into the specific teachings and practices of penitence that have been undertaken in the several contexts of ancient Israel and the church. At the outset two matters in this erudite material are clear. First, it is clear that in every season and in every context the community of faith has devised procedures for penitence and has articulated teaching that gave imaginative depth and significance to these practices. Christian faith, and Judaism before it, are *religions of redemption* that are focused on the truth of alienation and the complementary truth of reconciliation. This theological claim, articulated in both liturgical, sacramental imagination and in ethical commitment, pervades the history of faith and no doubt testifies to the immense staying power of that faith and practice. This acknowledgment of alienation and this possibility of reconciliation attest that the human community is not fated to a life of deprivation and failure; rather the human community exists by the reality of God's grace that invites and compels always to new beginnings. The sum of these papers supports that affirmation.

We thus sense the commonality among these studies; the other inescapable awareness from them is the immense and imaginative diversity of practices and understandings that is evident in the long history of faith. In every specific context the faithful have been able and have been required to fashion understandings and practices that are quite context specific. Indeed, the variations seem to me to be so profound that one may conclude that in some instances the differences of understanding and practice are so great that there is nothing common to them except the use of the same word, "penitence." Thus, for example, we may note the contrast between the harsh "three strikes and you are out" motif in the early church and the pastoral concern of Martin Bucer who wants always to console and rehabilitate.

This awareness of a *commonly shared theme articulated in varied contextual specific ways* gives us access to this rich array of studies. It may also open a way to see that this collection is of much more than historical interest. For by the end of the collection the reader may be left, as is this reader, with the urgent wonderment: How in our context of late capitalist militarism in the greatest empire in the world does the church now take up this great theme of penitence in a way that is pertinent to a culture that is a mix of conformity and autonomy beset by nearly unimaginable and unbearable anxiety? This volume will not engage that question in any direct way, but it creates a venue in which that is the next question when we finish our study of the tradition in all its richness.

## 2

As these essays make clear, the common theme of penitence is given a variety of rich and imaginative articulations. Through all of them, however, we may identify four important tensions that seem always to be present in the practice of the community.

### a. Penitence concerns the individual and/or the community.

The scope of penitence, individual or communal, is crucial because it determines both the nature of sin and the requirement of redress. There is no doubt that the popular assumption of penitence, rooted in medieval sacramental practice and reinforced, even in the Reformation, in the private confessional, concerns the action of the intentional believer who must be absolved in order to "get right" with Jesus. The popular notion of penitence in the older practice of "indulgences" assumed that penitence concerned the individual. Derivative from that assumption, the character of sin was understood to consist in personal affronts and private violations that one would confess and of which one may be absolved. That dimension of penitence did indeed take seriously the individual reality of guilt, a reality made more acute in "The Tortured Conscience of the West."[2]

But of course Christian faith is characteristically communitarian, as is Judaism from which it emerged. In the tradition of Deuteronomy that stands at the head of one trajectory of penitence in the Old Testament, the imperative to repent is characteristically in the singular second person "you" that understands the community as a "corporate person." Thus the "heart" to be "circumcised" is the heart of the community, a circumcision that concerns each individual person as a member of the community (Deut 30:6). That ancient communitarianism, moreover, is front and center in much contemporary thought of penitence, especially among the communities of the marginated who understand sin primarily in terms of systemic exploitation in the exercise of economic and political power. Such an understanding is also primary in the major efforts of "liberation theology" to break out of

---

[2] The phrase famously comes from Krister Stendahl, "The Apostle Paul and the Introspective Conscience of the West," in *Paul Among Jews and Christians and Other Essays* (Philadelphia: Fortress Press, 1976) 78–96.

individualistic pietism that is rooted in older sacramental theology in order to see that the deep alienations to be addressed are alienations from neighbor through acquisitive systems that reflect alienation from God.

Thus if penitence focuses on the individual, the concern is perforce on smaller moral issues, whereas in a focus on the community the sin to be repented of concerns systemic issues. Penitence to be undertaken, moreover, in the latter case is more likely to be communal systemic reparations, whereas a focus on the individual more likely concerns a resolve to desist from affrontive personal practice. To be sure, the matter is best understood as a both/and, both individual and community, rather than an either/or. In the present context, however, I judge that in U.S. society—or perhaps anywhere today—the primal matter to be addressed is corporate sin that is expressed by participation in usurpatious economic and political systems. If the invitation to repent is offered to the powerful, the summons is to a reconfiguration of system power. If the summons to repent is to the powerless, perhaps the point of penitence is to desist from despairing collusion in a destructive system and a decision to become "an agent in one's own history." Of course such a latter repentance has to do not with self-abasement often linked to penitence, but rather a fresh embrace of entitlement assured by the creator God even to "the least among us."

### b. Penitence is constituted by a dramatic sacramental rite and/or by a changed life that is exhibited in transformed attitudes, behavior, and policy.

There is no doubt that the "rite of penitence," deeply rooted in Catholic sacramental theology, holds sway in much Christian imagination well beyond the Catholic Church. It consists in confession before a priest who hears confession and a response of absolution, sometimes accompanied by prescribed acts of reparation, restoration, or discipline. That rite is of course continued in much Protestant liturgical practice in the drama of "confession of sin and assurance of pardon," and in a somewhat less formal way in the intimacy of psychotherapeutic interactions. The performance of the rite itself is taken to be effective in forgiveness and reconciliation, precisely because the effective authority is invested in the large authority of the church and, more specifically, in the priest or pastor by way of ordination.[3] In this horizon both the confession and

---

[3] This authority has been taken as rooted in the dictum of Matt 16:19, an empowerment to preside over the process of forgiveness and reconciliation.

the absolution (assurance) are a "performance" so that what is said is, at the same time, done.

But of course all such traditions of penitence know that such liturgical enactment does not exist in a vacuum. Rather, it pertains to the life of penitence outside the venue of the rite. Thus such performative action is characteristically linked to a resolve for "amendment of life" and a commitment to live "a new, righteous, and sober life."

Thus not everything in all these several practices is staked on the performative aspect of the rite, for the obvious reason that such a verbal act as confession and a responsive verbal act of pardon do not assure any transformation of life in the world. All these liturgical traditions that invest the performative act with immense significance are wise enough to know that not every utterance of "Lord, Lord" is to be trusted. There is no doubt that a new life can only begin with the truth-telling that is the intent of confession. Such truth-telling, however, inescapably entails followup with new life in the world. Thus we may notice that the rite of verbal performance runs all the way from the ancient church confession to the Truth and Reconciliation Commission, but such truth-telling assures nothing without a changed life.

In many traditions, most notably the Deuteronomist, the rite of repentance is a weak component of the whole, if it was important at all. The summons to "seek YHWH with all your heart and mind and soul" had to do with changed life and a remembrance of Torah commandments, most notably those of Deuteronomy (Deut 4:29; 30:10). In the quintessential Deuteronomic act of penitence, King Josiah does "tear his clothes" (2 Kgs 22:11). And indeed Josiah is promised by Huldah a peaceable death, which he in the end did not receive:

> . . . because your heart was penitent, and you humbled yourself before the Lord, when you heard how I spoke against this place, and against its inhabitants, that they should become a desolation and a curse, and because you have torn your clothes and wept before me, I also have heard you, says the Lord. (2 Kgs 22:19)

What counts for the narrative, however, is Josiah's changed royal policy whereby he instituted reform, reasserted covenant, consolidated the practice of Passover, and purged the religious life of Judah (2 Kings 23). Josiah's "penitent" activity amounted to nothing less than the reorganization of public life according to the generative covenantal tradition of Deuteronomy that pertains to economic and political practices as much as liturgical. If that account of repentance is taken to be a postexilic act of narrative imagination, then the practice becomes the ground of reestablishing Jerusalem-based Judaism in a covenantal way after the destructive "spree" of royal self-aggrandizement. That reconstitution may have been initiated and triggered by a rite; but the practical, concrete followup is what mattered for the narrative report. The report of Neh 5:1-13 with the verb "restore" *(šûb)* in v. 1 is closely linked in the tradition to Josiah and exhibits "penitence" in public policy. There is no doubt that the intent of the Truth and Reconciliation Commission in South Africa, if not the performance itself, was designed to lead to a new righteous and sober life in the public domain of the republic. It is clear that *sacramental rite* and *changed life* are not an either/or, though one or the other may be more asserted in any particular context.

**c. Penitence is grounded upon and enacted on the basis of the generous grace of God and/or upon what we have called in this consultation "the human factor."**

All traditions of penitence studied in this collection are agreed that the overcoming of alienation from God and the restoration to fullness of life with God are possible because of the grace of God that is the context for all human penitence. Indeed, it is the grace of God that not only makes confession and repentance possible; it is that grace that even makes us aware of and under stress for sin. It is agreed, moreover, that such graciousness on God's part, in the gospel, is limitless. There is indeed a "wideness" in God's mercy that is like the wideness of the sea. All parties would agree that penitents never "earn" forgiveness, a point emphatically made in the prophetic assertion of Ps 50:8-13:

> Not for your sacrifices do I rebuke you;
>> your burnt offerings are continually before me.
> I will not accept a bull from your house,
>> or goats from your folds.
> For every wild animal of the forest is mine,
>> the cattle on a thousand hills.
> I know all the birds of the air,
>> and all that moves in the field is mine.
> If I were hungry, I would not tell you,
>> for the world and all that is in it is mine.
> Do I eat the flesh of bulls,
>> or drink the blood of goats?" (Ps 50:8-13)

Nonetheless, such a gift of God that invites reconciliation is not cheap or casual. As awkward as it is to credit "the human factor" as indispensable for reconciliation, it is simply essential pastorally and practically that the penitent give signs and gestures of a changed position and disposition toward God. Even the familiar text of Mic 6:8 that acknowledges that material offerings serve no purpose must "require" *(drs)* mercy, justice, and humility as either condition or sign of reconciliation. That teaching, moreover, is echoed in the remarkable invitation to "return" in Jer 4:1-2:

> If you return, O Israel,
>> says the LORD,
>> if you return to me,
> if you remove your abominations
>> from my presence,
>> and do not waver,
> and if you swear, "As the LORD lives!"
>> in truth, in justice, and in uprightness,
> then nations shall be blessed by him,
>> and by him they shall boast. (Jer 4:1-2)

Of course such a human ingredient in penitence is fraught with risk, for social action can be immediately transposed into notions of merit or bribery toward the Almighty. And while the "indulgences" of the sixteenth century amount to a crude exhibit of the human factor, there is no doubt that in much more subtle ways promised response to God's grace can be taken as leverage with the divine.

In some traditions, moreover, the exhibiting of a changed disposition seems almost to be a condition for forgiveness. In the best-loved psalm of penitence it is recognized that YHWH wants no sacrifices that in Israel had become too much a routinized gateway to reconciliation:

> For you have no delight in sacrifice;
>> if I were to give a burnt offering,
>>> you would not be pleased. (Ps 51:16)

The refusal of such "burnt offerings" is followed by an invitation to submit sacrifices not of ritual performance but of changed disposition:

The sacrifice acceptable to God
>> is a broken spirit;
> a broken and contrite heart,
>> O God, you will not despise. (Ps 51:17)

Given that, however, the final form of the text of Psalm 51 cannot resist a final invitation to "burnt offerings," the very ones excluded in v. 16:

Then you will delight in right sacrifices,
> in burnt offerings and whole burnt offerings;
> then bulls will be offered on your altar. (Ps 51:19)

Thus the tradition recognizes that such human acts are in themselves of no great import, except that the move toward new life must be sealed in such material and visible gestures. No doubt in this Psalm, as in the tradition generally, it is clear that such actions are responses to divine grace and not acts that themselves accomplish reconciliation—except, of course, that the human heart is capable of imagining other than unfettered acts of divine grace. Thus the human factor is secondary and indispensable. It is responsive at best, but surely in self-deceptive ways all too readily taken as definitional. It is easy and obvious that we critique "indulgences," except that such seduction is, I imagine, present everywhere in actual practice. Signs and gestures of new life are easily, perhaps inescapably, transposed in imagination and in intent to acts of purchase.

### d. Penitence is characteristically an act of discipline and/or nurture.

And indeed the central tradition of the church takes the "nurture and discipline of the Lord" as an indivisible practice. No doubt this is correct, because the God who grants reconciliation and new life is both an uncompromising master who sets the terms of the relationship and a mothering father God,

who knows how we were made,
who remembers that we are dust. (Ps 103:14)

It is evident in these several essays that a disposition toward discipline or toward nurture is variously the accent in specific practices. The interest of the early church in post-baptismal sin and the cautious question of "another chance after baptism" surely reflected a rigorous discipline precisely because all of the "chances" had been used up. On the other hand, the pastoral consolation featured in the work of Martin Bucer might suggest that penitence is an act of inviting the sinner to "reappear" in a bolder form.

I have the impression, in reading these essays, that when the reconciling authority and capacity of the church are aligned with centrist public authority, the accent is most characteristically on discipline, as though to assure that penitents are guaranteed to be responsible members of the community, perhaps with measures of conformity impressed upon the new life of the baptized. Conversely, where the pastoral capacity to forgive concerns communities of the marginal, there is a kind of gracious patience extended to those who have already been wounded enough, without the wound of starchy exploitation added to it. There can be no doubt that both nurture and discipline are present in the practice of penitence, and that they receive very different nuance in church practice. In current U.S. church practice it seems evident that churches aligned with dominant political opinion accent discipline in the interest of conformity, whereas churches more impacted by recent psychotherapeutic insight accent nurture, sometimes to the neglect of discipline. Partly these different accents are rooted in theological conviction, but they are also rooted variously in the felt nature of the community and in different notions of how it is that human persons are empowered to change and how they experience that change. No doubt there is a quite longstanding wisdom in church tradition and in church practice on these matters. Longstanding wisdom may be given varying nuance but also may be variously distorted in our several contexts.

In sum then, the church over time has had freedom in practice and has had decisions to make concerning:

(1) corporate and/or individual focus,

(2) accent on sacramental right and/or a renewed conduct of life,

(3) appreciation of divine grace and/or the human factor, and

(4) stress on nurture and/or discipline.

In negotiating these several possibilities we notice both the steadfast constancy of the tradition in its core claims and the rich variety and freedom available in different contexts.

## 3

There is no doubt that in the end the transaction of penitence and reconciliation is an intimate and hidden one between the believer and the God of the Gospel. It is clear, however, that our concern is the act of penitence that is mediated through the church, its teaching authority, and its pastoral capacity. Of course it need not be insisted that such a transaction is always mediated. But our concern in these essays is precisely such mediation through the exercise of human authority. And because of that reality of human mediation we may exercise a stretch of "hermeneutic of suspicion" about such human mediation that is inescapably freighted with temptations to social control and to the imposition of ideological passion.[4] (I should note at the outset that some members of the consultation are quite resistant to such questions; the matter nevertheless seems worthy of reflection.) I raise the question of *social control* and imposition of *ideology* amid the process of confession and reconciliation on two counts:

a. In my own field of study, the Christian Old Testament, recent scholarship has paid great attention to the force of ideology in the formation of the text. Largely at the initiative of Norman Gottwald, but with many other scholars after him, we have been made aware of the force of advocacy in the formation and transmission of the text, an advocacy that is not disinterested, but is propelled by a vested interest in socioeconomic and political dimensions.[5] Specifically it is argued that the "urban elites," those who clustered around the royal-temple concentration of power in Jerusalem, imposed their views on larger society and did so with acclaimed theological legitimacy. In the tradition of the Priestly holiness on the one hand, such urban elites devised a system of "graded holiness" that correlated with social class and controlled access to holy places in

---

[4] The notion of a "hermeneutic of suspicion" has been best articulated by Paul Ricoeur, *Freud and Philosophy: An Essay on Interpretation* (New Haven: Yale University Press, 1970). On his presentation of the theme see Dan R. Stiver, *Theology After Ricoeur: New Directions in Hermeneutical Theology* (Louisville: Westminster John Knox, 2001) 137–59.

[5] See especially Norman K. Gottwald, ed., *The Bible and Liberation: Political and Social Hermeneutics* (rev. ed. Maryknoll, NY: Orbis Books, 1983). James Barr, *History and Ideology in the Old Testament: Biblical Studies at the End of the Millennium* (Oxford: Oxford University Press, 2000), has reviewed the literature on ideology in Old Testament studies. Given Barr's modernist commitments, however, he does not much engage with or appreciate what is at issue in the theme.

their several gradations.[6] The upshot of such a social arrangement was that penitence expressed as the practice of holiness and purity meant conformity to the imposed system of holiness and, therefore, required qualification for access controlled by priests. On the other hand, the Deuteronomic tradition, with its accent on "repent" (šūb) enacted through the commandments of the corpus of Deuteronomy and given articulation in the Deuteronomic narrative of Joshua, Judges, Samuel, and Kings came to occupy a defining position in the formation of fifth-century Judaism.[7] Repentance in that tradition came to mean conformity to a particular interpretive trajectory among Jews that determined who were "real" and "qualified" Jews to the exclusion or downgrading of all others.

One does not need to accept the details of this sociopolitical analysis in order to entertain the notion that a summons to repentance and the establishment of the terms of reconciliation do not constitute an innocent or disinterested matter. *Mutatis mutandis,* it is at least credible to entertain the notion that in the ongoing tradition of the church specific characterizations of sin and alienation and procedures for reconciliation and forgiveness were not disinterested, but reflect the social interest of those who administered the process. Of course theologically we may say that it is God who forgives and reconciles and who is not a party to any of these impositions. The problem that concerns us here, however, is that such freely given divine forgiveness is mediated; the mediating structures and personnel are not automatons, but in fact are engaged and active agents in the process. Thus in my own field where the function of ideology is not in question, we may at least consider how the process of penitence and reconciliation has not been disinterested, but is in fact deeply interested in defining the sin to be forgiven and the procedures of reconciliation. This is easy to see in Ezra, where the breakup of "mixed marriages" served an agenda of the maintenance of the "holy seed" (Neh 13:23-30; see Ezra 9:2). Thus a major concern for future study might well be the *self-giving of the God* who accepts penitence and forgives and the *self-serving of mediating agents* who make the self-giving God available.

---

[6] See Philip P. Janzen, *Graded Holiness: A Key to the Priestly Conception of the World,* JSOTSup 106 (Sheffield: JSOT Press, 1992).

[7] On the motif of repentance in the Deuteronomic literature see Hans Walter Wolff, "The Kerygma of the Deuteronomic Historical Work," in Walter Brueggemann and Hans Walter Wolff, *The Vitality of Old Testament Traditions* (Atlanta: John Knox, 1975) 83–100.

b. In his book *Troubling Confessions*, Peter Brooks has explored the nature of "confessions" and has considered the ways in which they are "troubling."[8] It is clear that the adjective "troubling" points Brooks in the direction of a hermeneutic of suspicion; he considers why it is that we must be suspicious of the practice of confession.

His analysis begins with the confession of Rousseau, and with a great deal of attention to Dostoevsky's *Brothers Karamazov*. In the latter Brooks observes that "Mitya appears to enter wholly into a transferential bond with his interrogators, insisting on seeing them as kind companions."[9] In the end Mitya's "abjection" becomes "the guarantee of his full confession."[10] Thus Brooks shows the way in which the interaction of confession produces a confession of guilt that is not based in fact but in the tense, sometimes manipulative interaction with the one who hears the confession.

Brooks's analysis is primarily concerned with police interrogation and with the work of the Supreme Court—particularly with reference to the Miranda decision—in seeking to protect those who are interrogated. Brooks pays particular attention to the legal theory that was offered by Justices Frankfurter and Warren, and most notably Frankfurter's judgment that the will of the one interrogated was "overborne," that is, broken "by the process of interpretation."[11] Attention is given to the "bad cop/good cop" routine that characteristically produces confessions, in some small part because the police completely control the venue of the interrogation room, so that the one interrogated eventually comes to be dependent upon the police.

A discussion is also offered by Brooks concerning psychotherapy with the important observation,

> Psychoanalysis in this manner recognizes that the speech-act of confession is a dubious guide to the truth, which must rather be sought in the resistance to such speech; the confession itself may simply fulfill other purposes, be an avowal of dependency on and propitiation of the analyst. The need to confess speaks *of* guilt, certainly, but it does not speak *the* guilt, does not locate that psychic configuration that needs discovery and healing. It is not the "voluntary" confession that

---

[8] Peter Brooks, *Troubling Confessions: Speaking Guilt in Law and Literature* (Chicago: University of Chicago Press, 2000).

[9] Ibid. 56.

[10] Ibid. 57.

[11] Ibid. 80.

interests the psychoanalyst, but the involuntary, that which, we can almost say, is coerced from the analysand. For psychoanalysis, the claim of confession is necessarily of limited value and the object of suspicion, not a sure guide to the truth, and the test of voluntariness an utterly misleading criterion. The true confession may lie most of all in the resistance to confession.[12]

In the midst of the legal and psychological categories Brooks considers the practice of confession in religious tradition. Because he is especially attuned to the inherently coercive dimension in confession he makes an important point of the fact that the Fourth Lateran Council in 1215 both introduced an annual obligation upon the faithful to confess to a priest and instituted an inquisition toward the discovery of heresy.[13] The convergence of the two acts suggests to Brooks a crucial dimension of coercion in religious confession in the church tradition. Following the analysis of Michel Foucault, Brooks judges: "The religious model of confession, which, I will argue in the next chapter, appears fundamental to other, later, versions, itself includes an element of 'policing.'"[14]

On the basis of this threefold analysis of confession, Brooks appeals to Talmudic law that barred confession in the criminal case. Maimonides is quoted in the verdict that exposes the risks of confession: ". . . the principle that no man is to be declared guilty on his own admission is a divine decree."[15]

In appealing to the dimension of ideology in my own field in ancient interpretive method and to the interfaces suggested by Peter Brooks, I mean only to allow that the matter of confession needs to be treated with a kind of vigilance concerning its potential for coerciveness. I do not, of course, suggest that such a concern for coercion is primary. I note, moreover, that Brooks's analysis, only mentioned in our consultation, did not receive any response from members who contributed to the consultation.

# 4

I note one other dimension in current research in Old Testament study that I believe belongs on the horizon of our discussion. If I ask about the

---

[12] Ibid. 117.
[13] Ibid. 93.
[14] Ibid. 82.
[15] Ibid. 72.

dialectical alternative to "confession of sin" in Old Testament study, I judge it to be the psalms of lament and complaint, a subject to which I have given much attention.[16]

It is a domain assumption of the Christian tradition, reflected in these essays, that in the matter of alienation God is always in the right; it follows that the church, Israel, humanity are always on the erring end and must repent. This governing assumption is fundamental to the Christian gospel in its claim that the righteousness of God—contrasted with human righteousness—enacted in Jesus is the source of the saving power of truth.

While that general claim is a given in Christian faith, there is need and now impetus to reengage with Judaism. That reengagement does not have to do with "being nice to Jews," or even being careful not to be anti-Semitic, though of course anti-Semitism expressed in Christian theology through supersessionism is a source of shame in Christian theological tradition and practice.[17] Beyond that necessary prerequisite for reengagement, however, we are at a moment in the life of the church when we may relearn from Judaism an important theological recognition; Judaism has retained in its life and practice an awareness of its own entitlement that may on occasion put God in the wrong. This sensibility has been largely lost in Christian tradition.

The specific relearning from Judaism to which we may attend, given our theme of penitence, is that the overcoming of alienation from God is a dialogic transaction in which both parties may speak the truth. The particular insight of Judaism in this instance—perceived in the psalms of lament, complaint, and accusation and of course available in Christian Scripture though largely neglected—is that alienation from God is not in every case conceded to be the fault and failure of the human party.

The Psalter, to be sure, offers texts of confession and penitence, most widely identified in the seven so-called Penitential Psalms of which

---

[16] See Walter Brueggemann, *The Psalms and the Life of Faith,* ed. Patrick D. Miller (Minneapolis: Fortress Press, 1995). My focus on the laments has been steady over time, so much so that one of the editors of our repentance project has called it a "fixation"; see Mark Boda, "The priceless gain of penitence: from communal lament to penitential prayer in the 'exilic' liturgy of Israel," *HBT* 25 (2003) 51–75. I am not able to see how my focus on lament is a "fixation," whereas focus on repentance is simply pursuit of an important theological theme. But so it goes!

[17] See R. Kendall Soulen, *The God of Israel and Christian Theology* (Minneapolis: Fortress Press, 1996).

Psalm 51 is the best known and the most direct. Given those seven, however, we may notice two things. First, not even all of the seven are closely or primarily preoccupied with sin and guilt. And second, beyond the seven, of course, the large number of lament and complaint psalms are not preoccupied with guilt. Rather, they characteristically accuse God of failure in fidelity or they identify the "enemy" who has caused suffering. Fredrik Lindström, moreover, has shown that "the enemy" is capable of such damage only because of the absence, neglect, or indifference of YHWH, so that the intention of such psalms is to remobilize YHWH into activity.[18] When YHWH is active, however, the enemy flees, being able to function only in a vacuum that is left by YHWH's default.

The picture that emerges in these psalms that both accuse YHWH and appeal to YHWH is a lively dialogic transaction in which both parties can take initiative in the interaction and in which both parties may speak from strength and assertiveness, and in which Israel can address YHWH with a sense of entitlement, a conviction that Israel's legitimate claim to divine fidelity has not been properly honored.[19] Such an approach to YHWH, moreover, is characteristically addressed to YHWH in an urgent, insistent imperative, as though in the moment Israel is the commanding party who orders YHWH to act. Thus, for example, the imperatives include "hear," "rise," "rescue," "awake," to which YHWH is left to respond.

Now it may be concluded that such entitled speech is surely a practice of regressive rhetoric in a context of deep need and anxiety. The important point, however, is that Israel has rhetorical conventions for such articulation that reflect a conviction that on occasion YHWH has defaulted—has sinned against Israel—and is called to account. The fact that such speech occupies extensive space in the Psalter suggests, to my mind, that alongside penitence—the speech and gesture of YHWH's failed covenant partner—the themes of lament, complaint, and accusation differently position the suppliant before the throne of sovereign mercy. To be sure, the laments of Israel are commingled in the Psalter with hymns that attest to YHWH's generous, wondrous sovereignty and fidelity. Such hymns, however, evidently do not obliterate the sense of entitlement on Israel's part, so that the interaction upon which life depends is genuinely dialogical. My purpose in calling attention to this liturgical practice in

[18] Fredrik Lindström, *Suffering and Sin: Interpretations of Illness in the Individual Complaint Psalms*, ConBOT 37 (Stockholm: Almqvist & Wiksell, 1994).

[19] See the powerful and radical statement of David R. Blumenthal, *Facing the Abusing God: A Theology of Protest* (Louisville: Westminster John Knox, 1993).

ancient Israel is to caution against a kind of reductionism that takes penitence by itself as a defining theme. Because the interaction is genuinely dynamic and lively it is, in my judgment, important to allow for the interpersonal complexity of the transaction. While penitence will surely be, in Christian thought and practice, defining for the relationship, I suspect in time to come we will perforce continue to be instructed by Judaism in ways that may critique Christian understandings that are overly simple and reductionistic notions of the mystery of grace.

On both these counts concerning a *hermeneutic of suspicion* and *the practice of lament*, I suggest that the force field of interaction with the God of the Gospel requires critical attention to our easiness about familiar categories. The practice of hermeneutic of suspicion warns against a thoughtless coerciveness that lacks self-criticism. The citation of lament reminds us that an evangelical stance before the God of the Gospel cannot simply be reduced to guilt and forgiveness, alienation and reconciliation, because the mystery of this relationship is deeper and more wondrous, more subversive and more complex than that.

# 5

This collection of first-rate essays is of course an important contribution to our critical-historical understandings. But the collection intends to be more than historical reflection. It intends to make a contribution to the contemporary life of the church as we ponder a central and now deeply urgent theme of Christian faith and practice. At the end of the day we are left with two insights that bear upon our contemporary life and faith: First, that in every season of its life the church has of necessity engaged in penitence, because our stance before God is one of alienation. In our own time and place that constant of faith is surely true, that we now stand in need of penitence because of our alienation from God and from neighbor.

But second, we learn in these essays that the church, in every context, has of necessity defined its own faithful way of penitence. We must ask, consequently, what of penitence is now to be practiced among us? What follows is a reflection on the *constancy and contextuality* of penitence in the twenty-first-century U.S. church. As we think about this we can readily line out the issues and then ponder a faithful response:

- The penitence to be undertaken is commensurate with the sin that enacts and evidences alienation;

- The sense of sin that we repent is defined and characterized by the will and nature of God who is revealed in the gospel and who wills to be reconciled with us;

- It is the church as mediator and teacher, as it is led by the spirit, that testifies both to the character of God and to the consequent nature of sin. Thus the teaching, mediating function of the church, as it ponders the tradition and is led by the Spirit, is crucial, as in every context, for determining the substance of penitence.

Apropos the contemporary church, we attest that the God of the Gospel is a *God of purity* and a *God of justice.* The tradition, of course, attests to both claims. The claim of God as a *God of purity* is principally attested in the Priestly traditions of the book of Leviticus with the accent on the "holiness" and "cleanness" that pertain to every phase of Israel's life—public and personal, cultic and civic. And, of course, the theme of holiness has fed the "holiness traditions" that characteristically derive from Wesley and give accent to the ongoing process of sanctification, of becoming holy.

Conversely, the claim of God as a *God of justice* is primarily attested in the Deuteronomic tradition and the corpus of commandments in the book of Deuteronomy, with its focus on the "quadrilateral of vulnerability"—the widow, the orphan, the sojourner, and the poor. This accent has fed the ecclesial traditions that focus on the theme of justice and justification that has issued, among other things, in the liberationist trajectory of contemporary theology. Over the long sweep of tradition the church has managed to hold together these accents concerning holiness and justice or *justification* and *sanctification,* or at least it has held them together in a viable tension.

But now, so it seems to me, the church in the United States at the outset of the twenty-first century has divided the themes, so that different church traditions—or different parties in the same church traditions—have taken either purity or justice as the sum of the gospel mandate to the neglect of the alternative theme. The result is a deeply divided church that we may variously label conservative or liberal, or in current popular parlance, "Red" or "Blue."[20] These terms, in recent political discourse, refer to conservative-Republican (Red) and liberal-Democratic

[20] Editor's Note: This refers to media coverage of the 2004 U.S. elections.

(Blue) constituents, each of which is now powerfully reflected in ecclesial bodies that respectively champion the model of purity or of justice and, consequently, a notion of penitence that confesses *(Red) sins of impurity* or *(Blue) sins of injustice.*

Thus the "Priestly tradition" in the church now focuses singularly on *sins of sexuality,* now especially including abortion and gay/lesbian matters with an add-on of stem cell research; by contrast, the "justice tradition" focuses upon *economic sins,* most especially including taxes, wages, welfare provisions, and an add-on concerning the rights of immigrants. In each case, moreover, it is the determined, often shrill teaching of the church in these parts and practices that insists that these are exclusively the claims of God, that these are the sins of humanity, and therefore that these are the issues in penitence. Thus the matter of the *character of God* in relationship to the nature of sin cannot be understood apart from the interpretative, teaching, mediating function of the church that in many cases now is quite partisan, if not sectarian.

The outcome is the formation of sectarian church bodies that confess "preferred sins" to the neglect of all else. It is for this reason that I have commented at some length on a hermeneutic of suspicion and insisted on lament as a counter-theme. *A hermeneutic of suspicion* might make us duly cautious and skeptical about a theology of command and sin that is so partisan and exclusionary as to reflect the determined, almost visible self-interest of a church body. The accent on *lament* might remind us that our stance before God in confession is for truth-telling that is linked to pain, our pain as well as the pain that we cause. Such truth-telling of the elemental dimensions of our life—of our alienation—cannot be readily slotted to ideologies about which we have passion, either liberal or conservative.

It is not obvious or easy to see how the U.S. church, in its alienation that is to some extent divided into "Red" and "Blue," can go beneath slogans and mantras to the most fundamental alienations. Two thoughts occur to me:

First, authoritative confession of sin is profoundly *theocentric,* that is, committed to the God we name as Trinity:

> Against you, you alone, have I sinned,
>
> and done what is evil in your sight,
>
> so that you are justified in your sentence
>
> and blameless when you pass judgment. (Ps 51:4)

The guilt we carry does not have to do with enactment of ideology whereby we engage in partisan coercion. It has to do with the God who cares about justice (see Matt 23:23), who calls to holiness (Eph 4:23-24), and who calls to a life of intimate fellowship, invited as we are as sojourners in the world. Given that most elemental relational quality to communion and given the deception of that relational quality in alienated "Red" and "Blue," the church might notice that the God known in Jesus Christ cares only provisionally and not ultimately about our best passion. The most fundamental sin we have to confess is surely idolatry, the violation of the first commandment; we surely violate that commandment—along with the third—when we readily and lustily and uncritically equate our passion with God's caring, that is, when we imagine we know fully the mind of Christ on the issue of the day. The antithesis of ideology is surely trustful humility before the throne of mercy, trustful humility that does not translate into triumphalism or coercive institutional life.[21]

---

[21] Eberhard Busch, *Karl Barth and the Pietists: The Young Karl Barth's Critique of Pietism and Its Response* (Downers Grove, IL: InterVarsity Press, 2004) 289, has proposed ways of practicing humility in theological dialogue:

> In Barth's thinking there were two additional prerequisites for being able to talk to each other in the church of Christ, and these two are inextricably linked. First, such a dialogue between Christians, even if it has the form of an argument with each other, occurs in the brackets of the assumption that both are in the church of Christ. This gives the discussion its true seriousness but also marks the clear boundaries of the argument. Barth once said that the person we should drop completely could "only be an arch-heretic who is totally lost to the invisible church as well." But he adds, "We do not have the ability to ascertain such lost arch-heresy, we do not have this ability even in the case of Christians who are perhaps under strong suspicion." Barth concludes that this is true of two theologians with whom he especially took issue: "For me, Schleiermacher also belongs (in the community of the saints) and Bultmann does too; there is no question about that." This approach has some immediate specific consequences. As a Christian I can criticize other Christians only if I am also in solidarity with them. Furthermore, when I criticize others I can distance myself from them not on a tone of harsh indignation but only in a tone of sad dismay at a threat that had somehow turned into a temptation for me as well. And finally, believing that Israel's shepherd does not slumber or sleep even in the church, I have to keep myself open to the possibility not only that the "favorite voices" I like to hear testify to the truth of God in the church, but "that we need . . . totally unexpected voices even though these voices may at first be quite unwelcome."
>
> The other prerequisite for talking to each other and having an argument with each other is this: Even when I boldly stand up for my understanding of the truth, I can do so only by paying attention to the boundary that is drawn by the fact that God's truth and my understanding of it are always two completely different things. At the very

It may be that "Red" and "Blue" Christians together—all of whom have sinned and fallen short of the glory of God—might resolve to listen to the neighbor who is unlike us; we may further come to a generous resolve to confess not only the sins we "prefer" but the sins that are not on our screen as causes of alienation. "Reds" might take a second read on *public economic issues* where God's will is distorted. "Blues" might take a second read on the violations of *sexual fidelity* wherein God's will is distorted. In the twenty-first century, given the now ecumenical expanse of the church, it may be that what was, as with Luther, taken as private confession may desperately need to be communal confession alongside other Christians whose vision of alienation and reconciliation is other than our own. Specifically, it might be that privileged Christians in the United States who benefit from and are complicit in empire might confess alongside marginated communities of faith, and notice how these communities name differently the alienation and the prospect of reconciliation.

The remarkable model of confession and penitence in Ezekiel 18 may serve as an example of confession across ideological lines; that teaching identifies three characteristic dimensions of sin and alienation:[22]

First, the teaching names idolatry and the violation of the first commandment that is at the core of alienation:

> If he does not eat upon the mountains or lift up his eyes to the idols of the house of Israel. . . . (Ezek 18:6a; see vv. 12b, 15a)

This is the rubric that stands alongside Psalm 51:4 in staying focused on the truth of God who in majesty stands over against all of Israel's bland loyalty.

Second, as a first derivative from the primal alienation, the text speaks of distorted sexuality:

> . . . does not defile his neighbor's wife or approach a woman during her menstrual period. (Ezek 18:6b; see vv. 11b, 15b)

---

moment I forget this border, it will shift, and the border between my understanding of God's truth and other Christians' understanding of it will become absolute. At that very moment the other person and I no longer stand before our common judge, rather I become the judge of the other.

[22] The best discussion of this tricky passage is by Paul Joyce, *Divine Initiative and Human Response in Ezekiel*, JSOTSup 51 (Sheffield: Sheffield Academic Press, 1989).

We may take this terse command as an epitome for the entire range of personal distortions that stand under the rubric of purity, a category most congenial to the priest Ezekiel.

Third, as a second derivative from that primal command of idolatry, distorted economics:

> . . . does not oppress anyone, but restores to the debtor his pledge, commits no robbery, gives his bread to the hungry and covers the naked with a garment, does not take advance or accrued interest, withholds his hand from iniquity, executes true justice between contending parties. (Ezek 18:7-8; see vv. 12-13a; 16-17a)

This third component is remarkable in a priestly horizon. We may take this more elaborated statement on economic distortion as an epitome for the entire range of responsibilities the affluent have in society toward the weak and the vulnerable.

This triad in Ezekiel 18 is an adequate summary of the sources of alienation, the first directly from *Moses,* the second perhaps mediated through the Jew *Freud,* with his focus upon sexuality, and the third mediated through the Jew *Marx,* and his focus on economics. The triad precludes Ezekiel's listeners from limiting their horizon of sin, alienation, and confession to their preferred sin. The ground of unity in the church may be a conscious recognition that as we approach the God from whom no secret can be hid, no one occupies high moral ground that entitles to shrillness. The unity of the church and the drama of alienation and reconciliation is much more fundamental than the divisiveness of the church in its several ideological traits might indicate.

Ezekiel's pastoral conclusion is that preoccupation in all three modes of sin—concerning the *first commandment,* concerning *purity,* and concerning *justice*—are forgivable and in context are indivisible:

> Therefore I will judge you, O house of Israel, all of you according to your ways, says the Lord God. Repent and turn from all your transgressions; otherwise iniquity will be your ruin. Cast away from you all the transgressions that you have committed against me, and get yourselves a new heart and a new spirit! Why will you die, O house of Israel? For I have no pleasure in the death of anyone, says the Lord God. Turn, then, and live. (Ezek 18:30-32)

The accent is on *turn,* voiced in five imperatives rendered in the *NRSV* as "repent, turn, cast away, get, turn"; the consequence of these imperatives is Ezekiel's final word here, *"live!"* The assurance of the God of severe judgment indicates that the invitation to repentance is itself an act of generous consolation. That generosity is even more dramatic, as Jacqueline Lapsley has shown, when we move from Ezekiel 18 to Ezekiel 36.[23] In the first half of the book and particularly in chapter 18, Israel is under an imperative to repent. In the second half of the Book of Ezekiel, no doubt after the fall of Jerusalem and so addressed to the exiles, there is no more summons to repent. Now the word of God is promissory. No longer is Israel to "get" (make; *āśāh*) a new heart; now the new heart that permits restored relationship with Yhwh is a gift from the holy God who gives the gift, not for the sake of Israel, but for the sake of Yhwh's own reputation (Ezek 36:22, 32):

> A new heart I will give you, and a new spirit I will put within you; and I will remove from your body the heart of stone and give you a heart of flesh. I will put my spirit within you, and make you follow my statutes and be careful to observe my ordinances. (Ezek 36:26-27)

After all is said that can be said about penitence, the last word is one of divine grace that carries us well beyond our capacity to repent. In the final form of Ezekiel, as with the biblical text more generally, this assurance makes penitence no less urgent. It reminds us nonetheless that what we cannot "make" of new life for ourselves, we are given. In the twenty-first century, given an acquisitive cultural mindset, the gift of what we cannot make for ourselves is astonishing evangelical news, profoundly submissive, laden with Easter energy.

[23] See Jacqueline Lapsley, *Can These Bones Live? The Problem of the Moral Self in the Book of Ezekiel* (New York: de Gruyter, 2000).

# Eighteen

# Implications of This Book's Insights for Liturgical Practices

*Marva J. Dawn*

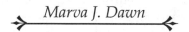

Reading the insights into biblical patterns and church practices concerning repentance and penitence as gathered by the sixteen scholars of this book caused me to yearn for better worship than is often offered by my own personal devotional life and by public, corporate services in churches across the denominational spectrum. What implications might we draw from this perceptive and stimulating research to deepen worship? What themes should shape worship practices? How might liturgical forms become more theologically grounded?

In this essay we gather together the prominent themes from the biblical and theological patterns studied and sketch some of their ramifications. Along the way many questions will be asked for various denominations to apply to their particular corporate and private worship forms. Then we can focus more specifically on additional suggestions and directions for the way forward in liturgical practices.

## 1. Biblical Patterns, Church Practices, and Their Ramifications

### a. General Themes

Three essays in particular establish clearly several general biblical themes that are echoed by most of the other chapters. First, Mark Boda's essay on the Torah delineates *return* as a major theme in Deuteronomy. Boda expounds this theme as a pattern of seeking ("a full engagement of the inner affections of the penitential community"), returning (*to* God, in a change of loyalty), and obeying (seeking and turning expressed in changed action). This threefold progression has substantial implications for Christian worship.

Liturgies should demonstrate that the search for God is most fruitful in a *community* of believers who speak and live the language of faith.[1] The liturgy ought also to call for the "full engagement" of each participant's whole person—not merely the emotions or an intellectual agreement with doctrinal propositions about sin. This full engagement, moreover, must lead to a genuine change of loyalty, a mindful rejection of the world's idols (and our personal favorite gods), and a commitment to serve God alone and truly. Furthermore, the liturgy should culminate in a genuine challenge to obey the Trinity faithfully.

To these major components Edith Humphrey's discussion of the Johannine writings adds a trio of elements from John 12:31-43. This text's recasting of Isa 6:10 (a key teaching passage in the early church) introduces the factors of God's economy (calling us to "seek" in the first place and providing a community that nurtures it), the miraculous nature of repentance (that God's faithfulness welcomes us back), and the mystery that God's own people still deny God's own Son. These elements highlight the grace of God drawing us to repentance and the Holy Spirit creating penitence in us, but also warn against our tendency to rebel and reject those gifts.

Thus we need another point from the epistles added by Stanley Porter, who underscores, through the epistles' display of repentance as both the initial turn to God and later remorse and contrition for sin, that both—faith and virtue—are God's gifts and not personal achievements. Dialectically, however, repentance must necessarily be a constant practice in the Christian's life.

Liturgies thus should emphasize the fullness of God's gifts that make our repentance possible, caution us against our willful nature, and remind us of the need for continued repentance.

To these biblical themes the essay by John Chryssavgis on Eastern Orthodox perspectives appends four crucial paradoxes. First, though in

---

[1] This notion of faith as a language is explicated in my *Talking the Walk: Letting the Christian Language Live Again* (Grand Rapids: Brazos Press, 2005).

repentance we take stock of past failures and accept responsibility for them, we do not dwell there, but in the future, for we focus not on human imperfection but on God's perfect love embracing all humankind. Thus the direction of liturgies is eschatological.

Second, the liturgy should inspire us to appropriate in ourselves Christ's transforming death, which alone makes possible genuine life-giving reconciliation. Thus public worship calls us regularly to death to ourselves and resurrection to God's future.

Third, as the Orthodox (and Roman Catholics) demonstrate particularly well, God makes possible a deepening of our own self-knowledge through spiritual mentors, though, fourth, such a "healing relationship is set within the context of community." Other Christian denominations need to make available liturgies for private confession, training for spiritual mentors, and a deeper sense of these paired relationships as part of Christ's whole Body and of private liturgies as taking place within the corporate practices of the entire Church.

### b. Focus on Divine Activity More Than Human Sorrow

Church leaders constructing new liturgies err when they focus on the human response of repentance instead of the divine activity making penitence possible. This is what overwhelmed Martin Luther and led to the Reformation. He mistakenly thought, Ronald Rittgers points out in his work on the German Reformation, that by his own efforts he should muster the true contrition God demanded. The whole Protestant world has Johannes von Staupitz to thank for guiding Luther toward "divine agency, divine love, and the importance of faith." Today we must guard against the same emphasis on our own "works righteousness" and the same "oppressive and intrusive clericalism" that characterized medieval churches.

Most biblical writers stress God's grace as foundational for repentance. Deuteronomy (see Boda) summons us to reflect in our seeking on God's covenant agreement and how Y$_{HWH}$ restores his people and returns them to the land. The Former Prophets, Terence Fretheim notes, divide God's word into both Law (judgment) and Gospel (in prophecy fulfilled by saving and forgiving), but also accent God's primary word to the exiles as declarative promise for them to cling to as they hear the imperatives of their responsibilities. Furthermore, not every prophetic judgment is necessarily fulfilled—the future is always open—for judgment is never an end in itself. Rather, it serves God's promises as "a refining fire for salvific purposes." Thus liturgies, too, should always make God's character (and not the depth of whatever contrition we can crank out) our basis in repentance for hope.

Edith Humphrey ascribes this truth to both the wayward and the "righteous remnant": repentance should concentrate on "what God has done, is doing, and will do—not on the compunction, turning, resolve, or satisfaction of the penitent." Similarly, Guy Nave recognizes that in the Synoptic Gospels Jesus decisively inaugurates God's reign and thereby "has created a situation that demands a fundamental change in thinking and living." Again, Stanley Porter shows the apostle Paul's insistence on God's kindness, forbearance, and patience as what leads sinners to repentance.

Do our liturgies paint God's gracious love and actions brightly enough so that worshipers are drawn to repentance? Do they emphasize the objective truth of God's interventions and restorations strongly enough so that subjective responses are roused? Or do participants in corporate worship or in the privacy of their own homes think they have to prod themselves into sufficient sorrow to deserve God's forgiveness? As Ronald Rittgers records, Luther insisted in the primary treatises that spurred the Reformation "that Christ alone was to dwell in the human conscience, the Word was to be its one true standard."

Of course, Catholics today, Ralph Del Colle demonstrates in "Life as a Holy Penitent," are much more aware than in the sixteenth century of God's grace as what "quickens and helps our human faculties and thereby enables our assent and cooperation." But Protestants would object to that language of "helping" us cooperate. Andrew Purves records Calvin strongly insisting that, though repentance is "required" of us, it is sheer grace, the consequence of the gospel and not a condition of grace, God's "singular gift" through the Holy Spirit.

All this does not mean, certainly, that we should not be sorry for sins. The Evangelical perspective on repentance, which Gordon Smith evaluates, recognizes both sin's "deadly character" and God's "powerful goodness and mercy." Do our various denominational liturgies remind participants that God in Christ initiates reconciliation with us, that God is both the beginning of our journey of repentance and its end (Chryssavgis)?

Moreover, what could other churches' liturgies incorporate to nurture the "yielding to the Spirit" Cheryl Bridges Johns describes in Pentecostal worship? How well do our services foster "tarrying until"? Are worshipers given time for "attending to" God's presence? Do our liturgies prepare us to wait mindfully and seek the workings of the Other who "cannot be controlled"?

Especially helpful is the word *orthopathos* Johns introduces as inclusion of human affections in God's heart. This word offers a way to be conscious of human sorrow for sins without losing sight of grace as the foundation; our sorrow expresses "joining in God's sorrow as it addresses death and alienation." Thus "repentance is a response to God's passion for humanity." We respond with a grief that exists in fusion with God's brooding. Our groans of sorrow arise within the Holy Spirit's.

### c. Baptism and Repentance

Several of this volume's writers comment that baptism marks the beginning of the process of repentance, though denominations' explications differ. The Orthodox call baptism the first public moment of repentance (Chryssavgis), though Catholics (Del Colle) and others would instead place penance as a continuation of the conversion of baptism.

Purves (quoting Heiko Oberman) emphasizes that what Luther attacked was the medieval focus on specific deeds of penance and good works that undervalued the *gifts* of baptism in initiating the Christian *way of life*. The radical liberation of baptism's mystical death and rebirth into new life in Christ could be better expressed in liturgies if all churches understood with the Orthodox that it "inaugurate[s] an ontological transformation," a "spiritual transition from *bios* to *zoē*," life in God's fullness (John 10:10). However, as Middle Eastern Christians know better than most because of centuries of adversities (Wafik Wahba), through baptism we not only join in the fellowship of Christ's resurrection, but also then share the burdens of his suffering as part of the Church's way of life.

How might it change Christians' participation in this world if liturgies insisted more on a continuing repentance that includes a readiness to join in our neighbors' sufferings? Could worship services avoid the consumeristic battles over musical taste if we knew more deeply baptism's radical spiritual renewal toward constant repentance and willingness to suffer?

### d. Repentance as Turning

This book's varied elaborations of the basic turning of repentance offer liturgists numerous images to welcome worshipers into deeper participation in it. The Former Prophets (Fretheim) provide a narrative inviting readers to "confess this story of unfaithfulness as their own story, to take personal responsibility for their sin that has brought this calamity upon them and to turn back to God." How crucial such an invitation is for the contemporary United States since its gluttony and militarism contribute greatly to the world's injustices and wars!

But Fretheim reminds us that the historian's telling of the story is itself a sign of hope. Hopeful, too, is the Latter Prophets' emphasis (Carol Dempsey) that God *desires* God's people to return to the mutuality of covenant relationship in spite of their infidelities.

The Writings, discussed by Richard Bautch, give us numerous models of confessions of sins that do not merely lament, but frankly refer to various aspects of human rebellion in specific "sins, iniquities, and transgressions." Such confessions would aid us in this present time to understand more deeply why God seems often to be absent. Do our liturgies make very clear how much damage our sins generate?

The Synoptic Gospels and Acts (Nave) offer models of the "turnings" of tax collectors and soldiers, characters in parables, disciples and the ill, men and women, who challenge our own way of thinking and call us to changes in attitude. Humphrey adds a remarkable list of verbs in John's gospel (stand, come, see, obey, hear, believe, turn, drink, be healed, follow, wash, be pruned, etc.) that bid us to enter the "divine drama" ourselves, to be rehabilitated, transformed, commissioned. Such "turning and returning ends in the glory of God (21:19) and in the encouragement of God's people." Similarly, Revelation (sharing with the Johannine gospel and epistles the theme of light and darkness) ignites us with a new perspective that enables us to "see reality from another, larger standpoint."

Do our liturgies make the perspective of the One True Light so clear that we look at the world and our daily lives in terms of God's kingdom reign? Do they show us that in repentance sin has lost its sovereignty over us (Purves) and that "passions are conquered by greater passions, and desire by stronger desire" (Chryssavgis)?

### e. Tears

In explicating African/African American practices, Michael Battle asks the crucial question, "what does it mean for the oppressed to repent?" Cheryl Bridges Johns answers partially in noting that Pentecostals (the majority of whom are poor) gather for prayer vigils—"festivals of tears" over the world's brokennesses—that activate energy to do what seems impossible.

Orthodox liturgy (Chryssavgis) expresses the brokenness in terms of "Adam sitting opposite paradise in mourning over his estrangement from God." In their eschatological orientation, Orthodox icons, music, and worship convey a "joyful sorrow" and prompt tears as signs of the distance between the present and the future. Could other liturgies more thoroughly remind the affluent of their own exile, too, so that all Christians in our longing to return home might know tears as "a sign of welcoming, a pledge of return, and a first fruit of its joy"? Perhaps wealthy whites, more than other peoples, do not experience such joy because we do not know deeply enough how alienated we are from our true home by our comfort in this one. How could our worship provoke a greater sense of this joyful sorrow?

### f. Pastors and Spiritual Mentors—Private and Public Confession

One aspect of repentance sometimes neglected in history by evangelical and mainline Protestants is private confession with a pastor or mentor, though the German Reformation (Rittgers) sought intensely to turn it from its oppressive medieval practices into a source of hope and comfort for believers. Martin Bucer, Andrew Purves shows, thought pastors were insufficiently caring for congregants' souls and, in turn, the people were less willing to submit to Christ's yoke. Indeed, this is also the case today.

How much more would church members be strengthened in a godly way of life if we understood discipline as the responsibility of all Christians and if we sought private confession in order to name our own sins more thoroughly and to be bolstered in our hope of grace! Such spiritual direction would renew our lives by binding up our wounds, increasing our true contrition, vanquishing our despair, and liberating us through submission to Christ and sharing in his sufferings for the sake of the Church and the world.

As John Chryssavgis remarks, the individual self-sufficiency characterizing our society is not the Christian way of life; rather, "it resembles more the way of the demons." My own experience with spiritual direction matches his mystical description; one's mentor is a fellow traveler (not a tour guide!), a "benevolent companion who accompanies us" as a spiritual elder and thereby brings about the miraculous faith growth that "One Plus One Equals Infinity."

Chryssavgis's vision is crucial for our liturgies, corporate and private, so that the priest or minister cannot become or be thought of as "some power-wielding, forgiveness-dispensing authority," a "detective of misdeeds" or a "recipient of private secrets," instead of "a witness of repentance," who welcomes us into the Church as the community of the

Physician. Confession's goal is to reintegrate both the penitent and the priest into Christ's Body.

### g. The Importance of Community

Repentance is not a solitary struggle. Both the Johannine epistles (Humphrey) and James (Porter) stress that Christians are responsible for each other to help those who stray from the truth turn from their errors and find healing in the faith community. As Boda shows, the Priestly stream in the Torah calls for the entire society's repentance for intragenerational sins committed within the present community (Leviticus 16) and for intergenerational sins committed by generations past (Leviticus 26).

African spirituality (Battle) reflects such a sense of corporate care, within a web of relationships (in contrast to most white cultures' focus on individualized selves). Only such a culture could make possible South Africa's Truth and Reconciliation Commission, which both freed victims to name the injustices and harm done them and enabled oppressors to confess.

Middle Eastern Christians (Wahba) link contemporary denominations with the Church's origins in a *community over time* through their history of early Fathers' theological reflection, the beginnings of monasticism, and a continuing endurance of persecution. Pentecostals (Johns) and Catholics (Del Colle) build the *community spatially* because their sense of themselves is more collective and universal. These denominations' orientation keeps repentance more thoroughly in its proper communal context. Do our worship liturgies foster such a communal sense and thereby nurture repentance as a healing act in the midst of Body life?

Eastern Orthodox, Chryssavgis explains, understand repentance as "re-membering," for it brings all the members of the church together as children of God, dwelling "in the same space with one another," so that "earth becomes as roomy and spacious as heaven." Imagine what such a sense of wholeness could do for righting the injustices of the present world order! How could our liturgies stir church members into making equal room for everyone on earth to live in genuine well-being? The Synoptic Gospels (Nave) offer precedent when John the Baptizer tells those in the crowd who have more food and clothing than their survival requires to share their excess with the needy.

### h. Healing of the Land

As Wahba reports, Middle Eastern Christians are increasingly aware that their community's special role is to pray corporately in repentance for God to heal the nations, to create true *shalom* and stability for their geographic setting, and to grant political leaders genuine wisdom. Could our liturgies of repentance be perceived also as tools to transform societies at large? Could they equip us with zeal to introduce people to Christ and his saving way?

Similarly, the suffering of African peoples, Battle observes, has spurred them "to search for God's presence in the created order," which "cannot be restored until God's justice and mercy are tangibly displayed." Historical events, such as Martin Luther King's campaign for civil rights and the South African Truth and Reconciliation Commission's work, demonstrate that social contenders must strive for a better future for both parties. Only when victims renounce resentment, hatred, and revenge and perpetrators discard their assertions of innocence can true reconciliation begin. Battle asks the crucial question: can an oppressor repent if there is no hope for forgiveness?

Can churches more thoroughly create through their liturgies such a context of public hope as models so that Christians can take the lead in societies to bring about public reconciliation and restoration in situations of oppression? We have learned, especially from 1 John 1, that God establishes such a confidence for us in his promises to receive us with grace and grant forgiveness.

### i. Fasting and the Eucharist

Two especially salutary liturgical rites can contribute to nurturing in believers a greater sense of the reconciliation in human relationships that is possible not only in the Church but on a larger social scale. Wafik Wahba introduces fasting as a way to "humiliate Satan [the perpetrator of divisions] and trample him under our feet as Jesus did." Fasting teaches us to live by the Spirit and not the flesh so that in our endurance according to Jesus' way Satan becomes powerless against us.

Wahba points to Pope Kyriollos VI, the former Coptic Orthodox Patriarch, who preached that God first commanded human beings to fast by prohibiting Adam and Eve from eating from one tree. Jesus' first deed after his baptism was to fast before beginning his ministry. Could more churches advocate fasting as a liturgical discipline that enables us to live in greater union with the Triune God?

Then, more deeply, could our liturgies call the wealthy to fast from their hoarding, urge the nations to fast from violence, inspire those who have too much to fast from their gluttony? Could we prepare sample liturgies to help families celebrate days of fasting in order to work for greater justice and reconciliation in the world?

Similarly, the Eucharist, a communal gift and not a sacrifice, is also a rite that propels us to contemplate issues of the rich and the poor. The apostle Paul rebukes those who have plenty and do not share their food with those who have less. He asserts that to act this way is to desecrate the Lord's Supper (1 Cor 11:17-34).

Do our communion liturgies call our attention to the importance of the Body as a community sharing equally in God's life? Do they welcome everyone, without any social barriers between us? Do they call us to repentance for our divisions and dislikes that tear us from each other and so crucify Christ anew? Do they invite us to the Eucharist as a foretaste of the eternal feast in which all people from every nation and tongue will enjoy God's heavenly bounty together equally?

### j. Repentance Leads to Obedience, Sanctification

Healing for the nations is possible only if repentance is not unfulfilled words or merely to avoid judgment (Boda). The doctrine of repentance in Deuteronomy especially summons us to the external response of active obedience as that springs from our internal self-examination.

Revelation is a crucially important text for our times because it pierces our hardened, "debauched, careless western ears" with God's "clarion call" to "Repent! Do the works that you did at first" (Humphrey). A chief problem with churches in our time is that worship too often makes us more comfortable and "uplifted" instead of igniting us to live in Jesus' way for the sake of the world!

Michael Battle sketches the latter in African worship. In black spirituality important texts call the people to a repentance fleshed out in redress, reparation, and reconciliation, beginning with God. The latter involves "a return to a focus on what God requires and a plea for God's people to heal the spirit of the oppressed, and to do what is necessary to proclaim the day of the 'Lord's favor.'"

In contrast, a main problem in contemporary society is the massive gap between what we know and how much we act on it. The technological society seems to have stolen from us an active "godly sorrow" such as Jonathan Edwards insisted on and the responsive conscience fostered by true conversion that, in turn, generates spiritual growth (Smith). In what ways could liturgies spur a closing of the gap and kindle a purifying sanctification that fires our participation in God's works of justice and mercy?

We need to realize how much contemporary "social, political, and economic factors can malform people and societies, enable sin in institutional and corporate contexts, and trap people in patterns of behavior from which they can hardly escape" (Purves). Good worship should be a megaphone to rouse us from our societal lethargy with a clear proclamation of what the Lord requires of us—namely, "to do justice, and to love kindness, and to walk humbly with [our] God" (Mic 6:8).

It is the lack of humility that prevents some from repentance, and we dare never lose sight of the biblical "sin unto death," which Humphrey defines as the refusal to repent. Some contemporary worship gurus like to make the call to repentance too soft and urge church leaders not to talk about sin because it is not "appealing," but in the Johannine writings, Humphrey insists, the contrast between light and darkness is extreme, the plight of sinners is grave, and God's summons to repentance is absolute and pressing. The possibility for repentance is always there in God's promises, but these "soft" alterable boundaries between the repentant and the hardened are also firm. People do ultimately choose darkness rather than light. Still, the Johannine epistles display great compassion for those trapped in sin.

How can liturgics be constructed so that the urgent call to cross over the boundary into the light is held dialectically with the bright promise of God's faithful reception? Otherwise people can fall too easily into a cheap grace or an expensive one rather than living in costly grace, in the penitential confidence of God working God's ways through us.

## 2. The Way Forward—Liturgical Suggestions and Directions

### a. Humility as the Source of Repentance

Since what our society lacks is "the humility of true self-knowledge of which repentance is the reflection" (Smith), one hope for this volume is that readers (and consequently their churches) might contemplate how such humility could be cultivated in worship. This is much more difficult than it might seem at first glance because liturgies must offset the entire cultural milieu of a consumerist society, which has for decades promoted narcissistic self-obsession, instant gratification, inflated whims, and escalating discontent by advertising to keep the economy flourishing on the basis of these traits.[2]

But the task is not impossible since the Triune God is infinitely greater than our enormous self-vaunting. The direction of liturgies must be to paint God's character and interventions as richly as achievable, as a mirror to reduce human beings to their proper size. In this matter worship services fail frightfully—using songs with little biblical and theological content, reducing liturgies to merely music and sermon, eliminating the full range of biblical texts from the First Testament, the Psalms, the Epistles, and the Gospels and often instead reading merely a few verses. How can people know both the hard boundary of God's judgment and the softness (Humphrey's terms) of God's promising grace if they hear and sing so little of God?

## b. Suggestive Sample Liturgical Excerpts

Several scholars in this book offer excerpts, from which lines are quoted here to highlight important elements that should be included in contemporary liturgies. As a model of penitential prayer, Smith presents Menno Simons' exposition of Psalm 25:

> Accept me in grace and give me your mercy, blessing and confidence, Lord, for the sake of your own goodness. . . . I do come before your throne of mercy, for I know that you are gracious and good. You do not desire that sinners should die but that they repent and have life. . . . Your word alone can heal all things. . . . I seek and desire this grace, for it alone is the medicament which can heal my sick soul.

Similarly, our liturgies should make very clear how much we need God's grace and how ready the Trinity is to offer it. Wahba's excerpt from Coptic Orthodox liturgy adds elements of doxology and Trinity, of God's holiness, and an inescapably broader list of how we fail:

> Holy, Holy, Holy, O Lord of Sabaoth. . . . O Holy Trinity, have mercy on us . . . be with us, for we have no other helper in our tribulations and adversities but Thee . . . forgive us our transgressions which we have committed voluntarily and involuntarily . . . knowingly and unknowingly, the concealed and the apparent. . . .

[2] See Albert Borgmann, *Crossing the Postmodern Divide* (Chicago: University of Chicago Press, 1992), and my *Unfettered Hope: A Call to Faithful Living in an Affluent Society* (Louisville: Westminster John Knox, 2003).

From the German Reformation Rittgers quotes an exemplar absolution that specifies Christ's merit through his holy suffering, death, and resurrection as the basis for forgiveness and his name as the order by which liturgical pardon can be pronounced. The absolution ends trinitarianly (too often totally missing in contemporary liturgies) and adds the comforting blessing, "Go in peace! May it be to you as you believe! *(Dir geschehe, wie du glaubst!)*."

Eastern Orthodox baptisms (Chryssavgis) not only begin with confrontation (exorcisms of other gods and powers), but also end with active submission to the only true, Triune God. The priest commands, "Bow down before Christ, and worship Him"; the catechumen replies: "I bow down before the Father, the Son, and the Holy Spirit." Bishop Kallistos Ware similarly stresses that repentance is "not a paroxysm of remorse and self-pity, but conversion, the recentering of our life upon the Holy Trinity" (Humphrey).

## c. Dangers to Avoid

Gordon Smith summarizes well the dangers of the "dry formalism and the soft morality of high-church Anglicanism" in Wesley's day. In overreaction to it, however, Evangelicals sometimes fall into these dangerous confessional habits:

- a surrounding culture of guilt and fear

- an emphasis on volition

- a "perpetual sense of failure" because one is not "totally surrendered"

- a focus on specific sinful deeds rather than the larger hazard of "pride and self-righteousness"

- solitary action rather than communal penitence or confession to another

- a sense of duty rather than gift

- no clear assurance of forgiveness.

Perhaps the rebuke in Hebrews that Christians should progress beyond elementary teaching toward solid food (Porter) should also stir many churches to repentance for the triviality of their worship services designed instead to "attract" and entertain!

## d. Gifts of Confession

The German Reformation sought to create confession that would not threaten lay people or be seen as "a good work necessary to salvation." Rather, the confession should be "a source of unparalleled consolation," a practice to prepare believers to receive the Lord's Supper piously, a ritual to "protect and console lay consciences, as well as discipline and inform them" (Rittgers). May the public and private liturgies we employ offer these gifts!

Eastern Orthodox perspectives (Chryssavgis) could guide us so that repentance offers healing for the oppressed and for nations. The liturgy is fundamentally joyous and restorative, "resurrection unleashed." It rouses us "from the sleep of ignorance" and enables us "to rediscover our soul."

Also, the liturgy does not ignore sufferings, but invigorates the "reintegration of all crosses, reconciliation of all sinners, and incorporation of all suffering." Moreover, joyful, repeated chanting of *Kyrie eleison* teaches thankfulness instead of resentment and expunges self-obsession in favor of glorifying God. Repentance that fulfills these goals could empower all believers, poor and affluent alike, to live as peacemakers. "May it be to [us] as [we] believe!"

# 3. Further Reading

Dawn, Marva J. *How Shall We Worship? Biblical Guidelines for the Worship Wars.* Wheaton, IL: Tyndale House, 2003.

_____. *Reaching Out without Dumbing Down: A Theology of Worship for this Urgent Time.* Grand Rapids: Eerdmans, 1995.

_____. *A Royal "Waste" of Time: The Splendor of Worshiping God and Being Church for the World.* Grand Rapids: Eerdmans, 1999.

Horton, Michael. *A Better Way: Rediscovering the Drama of God-Centered Worship.* Grand Rapids: Baker Books, 2002.

Long, Thomas G. *Beyond the Worship Wars: Building Vital and Faithful Worship.* Bethesda, MD: Alban Institute, 2001.

Malefyt, Norma deWaal, and Howard Vanderwell. *Designing Worship Together: Models and Strategies for Worship Planning.* Bethesda, MD: Alban Institute, 2005.

Mitman, Russell E. *Immersed in the Splendor of GOD: Resources for Worship Renewal.* Cleveland: Pilgrim Press, 2005.

_____. *Worship in the Shape of Scripture.* Cleveland: Pilgrim Press, 2001.

Torrance, James B. *Worship, Community, and the Triune God of Grace.* Downers Grove, IL: InterVarsity Press, 1996.

Webber, Robert, ed. *The Complete Library of Christian Worship.* Nashville: Star Song Publishing Group, 1994. Includes these seven volumes: *The Biblical Foundations of Christian Worship; Twenty Centuries of Christian Worship; The Renewal of Sunday Worship (Vol. IV in 2 books); Music and the Arts in Christian Worship; The Services of the Christian Year; The Sacred Actions of Christian Worship;* and *The Ministries of Christian Worship.*

# Conclusion

# The Jolly Penitent: Religious Leadership and the Practice of Confession

## Gordon T. Smith

The conversion narrative of the French mathematician and philosopher Blaise Pascal (1623–1662) typically and understandably focuses on his extraordinary "night of fire" *(la nuit de feu)* in which Pascal experienced a resolution to his many years of inner *angst*. It was an encounter of "fire" because it was an intense encounter with God. It was also an experience of integration between the intellectual and affective contours of his soul. Pascal met God, and the consequence was a deep and abiding joy. Prior to this night his manner of life was that of a devoted churchman, but one who was listless and despondent, lacking the joy for which he deeply longed. Following the encounter of that night, the outward form of his life was largely the same. But there was a notable change. Later his sister described the difference with a telling phrase: she spoke of him as a "jolly penitent."

The Pascal experience and his sister's description highlight something often missed in a discussion of the penitential dimensions of the Christian life. Frequently it is assumed that confession and repentance are about sorrow and sadness and the darker side of spiritual experience, and that joy and hilarity represent another, more positive experience. Yet Pascal's experience is a reminder that perhaps these seemingly contrary positions are so integrated that the Christian cannot have the one without the other. "Jolly penitent" is not an oxymoron; rather it is descriptive of the necessary relationship between joy and repentance.

Repentance is not an onerous burden whereby through self-examination we enter into darkness dealing with various unpleasantries so that we can, perhaps, justify the more celebratory and happy sides of the Christian life. Rather, the joy for which we so deeply long is experienced in and through the ancient Christian practice of confession.[1] And this is why it is so imperative that religious leaders view the practice of confession and repentance as an integral part of their pastoral ministry.

## 1. Confession and Religious Leadership

Following his encounter with Cornelius, the apostle Peter is challenged regarding his relationship with the Gentile community and forced to give an account of his behavior. Peter concludes his narrative by speaking of the realization that indeed he and his company "praised God, saying, 'Then God has given even to the Gentiles the repentance that leads to life'" (Acts 11:18).

What this account portrays, of course, is that repentance is a gift from God that makes possible the life of the community. It only follows, then, that the religious leaders of faith communities would enable the practice of confession and repentance. Life, healing, and joy are found through confession. To neglect to preach and teach in a manner that fosters the penitential life is an abrogation of pastoral duty. It is as absurd as the behavior of a physician who fails to provide a diagnosis and encourage a practice of good nutrition, fitness, and bodily health. To neglect this dimension of the spiritual life in preaching and pastoral care is to compromise the development of the Christian. It is a wholly inadequate form of pastoral care, a kind of pseudo-religious leadership, to declare that God is good and that God cares, without then also bringing instruction on the judgment of God on sin. We must speak of the deadly character of sin and provide the assembly of God's people a means for a constructive response. And the means, of course, is confession.

---

[1] As Fr. John Chryssavgis puts it earlier in this volume: "We have become so accustomed to thinking of repentance as an unpleasant though necessary rejection of sin that we have tended to lose sight of repentance as a fundamentally joyous, restorative return to life in its fullness."

There are at least three dimensions of pastoral leadership, apart from liturgical leadership itself, that are pertinent to the Christian practice of repentance: preaching, instruction in the practice of confession itself, and pastoral care and spiritual direction.

## a. Preaching

Preaching is a means by which the Christian community is called to repentance. To cultivate and foster the penitential life, preaching will need to have at least two features. It will need to profile the holiness of God against the backdrop of God's mercy, and it will need to cultivate faith—the necessary "soil" for authentic repentance—as the complement to repentance, in that true repentance arises from faith.

Preaching will include the declaration that God is holy. Yet it is always within the context of the mercy of God. The two are necessarily twinned. Preaching includes a call to repentance. It must. But true preaching is not castigating or reproving a congregation, nor does it arise from an assumption that the preacher knows for what the people should repent. The preacher is a penitent whose own experience of the mercy of God sustains a vital declaration of the holiness of God, the deadly character of sin, and the wonder of a God who delights to show mercy and forgive. It is the "kindness of God," as the apostle Paul puts it, that will "lead [one] to repentance" (Rom 2:4). In other words, the preacher does not genuinely proclaim the kindness of God if it is implied that this "kindness" tolerates sin. To the contrary, the preacher can confidently call sin what it is: *sin*. The exposition of Scripture must profile the ways in which the goodness of creation has been fragmented; this also means that we indicate how human actions have perpetuated this fragmentation. What is so crucial, however, is that preaching communicate that in all of this God is for us and not against us. God is the Divine Healer who longs to forgive and make all things well.

But then further, the proclamation of the holiness of God—a God who is full of mercy—is only meaningful if there is the reasonable certainty that it makes a difference. Therefore the call to repentance is a declaration of *hope*. Through this call we insist that sin, evil, and injustice do not have the last word. We celebrate that the status quo does not have to remain and that human actions and reactions matter. Indeed, the challenge of preaching is to demonstrate that no individual life or social situation is inherently hopeless. The grace of God is always greater than human sin.

Then also, for preaching to foster repentance it needs to be a means by which faith is cultivated. Repentance becomes not solely a resolution of the wrongs we have committed but also a reaffirmation and appropriation of the divine forgiveness that enables us to live in radical dependence on God and particularly on God's mercy. This is the grace and freedom of living in humility. The preacher who only focuses on misdeeds misses the point. The crucial issue is not obedience (or the lack thereof) but faith, from which obedience is derivative. Thus the critical task of preaching is to foster and cultivate faith—a deep and radical trust in a providential and good God. And the penitential dimension of the Christian life is one that enables us to live increasingly by faith. It is a faith that "sees" the inbreaking of the reign of Christ and chooses confidently to live under this reign. And it is a faith that is future oriented: experiencing forgiveness for the past, without doubt, but with its primary dynamic one that is oriented toward the future, choosing to look ahead to what will be.

And the fruit of this kind of preaching just might be "jolly penitents": women and men who live in the mercy of God, with hopeful hearts. Together, this awareness of mercy and this hopefulness establish the emotional contours that are consistent with the character of God's salvation.

### b. Instruction in the Practice of Confession

Preaching is more likely to foster the practice of confession if accompanied by instruction in *how* one is to repent. In some traditions this catechetical piece is inherent in the rhythms and rubrics of congregational life. But for many faith communities this is lacking, and thus a significant number of Christians are not sure how to repent. They have not been introduced to the spiritual practice of confession or how this practice can be incorporated into the routines and rhythms of their daily lives.

It is appropriate, then, to delineate this crucial spiritual practice. We can draw on the wisdom of those traditions that are explicit regarding the approach to confession, yet do so in a manner that provides Christians from a wide variety of spiritual traditions with a practice that is accessible: how to examine conscience and how to appropriate divine forgiveness and enabling for the Christian life. This is learned through instruction and then through regular practice.

The practice of confession will have at least five elements.

### (1) Acknowledgment of wrong.

The first element of confession is the acknowledgment that something is amiss, out of kilter, not consistent with what one knows to be true and right. It is the recognition of the presence of evil. We own or admit that something is wrong. But more, confession is also an act by which we declare that we do not need to acquiesce in evil, whether it be thought, word, or deed.

### (2) Responsibility and contrition.

The spiritual practice of confession includes the acknowledgment of wrong, but this is always accompanied by contrition; we accept responsibility. Confession means the refusal to deflect accountability or to claim extenuating circumstances; we may be victims, but we resolve that we will take responsibility for our actions and reactions. The penitent decries the sin for the simple reason that there is no excuse. And this contrition is expressed primarily toward God; we grieve for having failed to trust. We have not lived in a manner consistent with the call to trust God.

### (3) A plea for mercy (the **Kyrie Eleison**).

The sinner accepts responsibility, but just as quickly cries for mercy. Indeed, one cannot accept responsibility unless one knows that there is mercy and that one's guilt is not the final word. Nevertheless, the cry for mercy is an important and distinct element in confession. The first two (acknowledgment of wrong and contrition) are not in themselves confession; neither can we assume that they automatically lead to forgiveness. We approach confession knowing that God is obligated to us. And so we cry out: Lord have mercy; Christ have mercy; Lord have mercy on us all.

### (4) The appropriation of forgiveness.

Whether through absolution or the assurance of pardon pronounced by another, confession is only complete if the penitent receives mercy, accepts forgiveness and moves out from the burden of guilt. And this too cannot be taken for granted. All too many Christians live with a continual uncertainty of divine love and acceptance. Their confession is motivated by a fear of judgment and they live wondering if they did enough to appease the wrath. Few things are so necessary to the Christian life as the freedom of knowing that one is forgiven.

### (5) Resolution and turning.

Then also, confession includes conversion, a rejection of the way of sin and death and an embracing of those actions or choices that will enable the Christian to walk in the light. For some this will mean not only the personal, interior resolve to turn from sin, but also an accountability to a spiritual friend or mentor that will keep one focused on the life of faith.

No doubt there will be debate on the order in which I have outlined these. Some will insist that the appropriation of forgiveness cannot come until one has turned from the sin: A fair point. Others might counter that we cannot turn from sin until and unless we know that we are forgiven; that, indeed, the grace experienced through forgiveness is precisely the grace that enables the Christian to live in the truth.

Either way, even if there are distinct elements, confession is in the end a single act—each element only has meaning in light of the whole. And the centerpiece on which that whole rests is divine forgiveness. Confession is thus about accepting that God is one who forgives. Through the practice of confession we appropriate the mercy of God and live in gratitude for this mercy. And the practice is not reserved uniquely for those times of significant wrong; the Christian spiritual tradition suggests that there is value to the daily practice of confession.

### c. Spiritual Care and Direction

Pastoral leadership in the practice of confession and repentance will be exercised through preaching and instruction in the actual practice of confession. Further, we need to profile spiritual direction and pastoral care.

This dimension of the practice of confession is a reminder that sin is never solely a personal issue. The sinner is harmed by sin, but so is the community of faith (indeed, the whole of creation). Our sin is never solely about ourselves; it is also something that affects our neighbor. Further, our experience of grace and forgiveness is also shared. We learn repentance together; and we practice it together. And we learn to confess our sins to one another (Jas 5:16) so that together we know the grace of divine healing. The penitential is mediated to the individual through the community. This is why it is so crucial that the Sunday or weekly liturgy include the confession of sin and the assurance of pardon. While the confession may be a personal matter, it is as sinners that we are in community and it is in community that we receive pardon. Thus the liturgical life of the church must include the practice of confession, but this recognition also is a reminder of the vital place of spiritual direction and pastoral care.

Integral to the spiritual practice of confession is the capacity to speak with a fellow Christian who hears our confession. Whether it is a spiritual friend or a pastor, the one who hears our confession does so on behalf of the church community. Surely one of the most fundamental skills of pastoral leadership, ideally part of preparation for ordination within a religious community, is the capacity to hear a confession. But can we not also speak of this as a capacity for each maturing Christian, to hear the confession of a fellow believer? To be able to speak to one another of the trials and failures of life, work, and relationship and assure one another of the mercy of God? While some will have special training in pastoral ministry and in the hearing of confession, all Christians as fellow pilgrims on the road can view themselves as conversation partners on what matters most: what it means to live by faith, the struggle to do so, the failures and missteps along the way, and the mercy of God that restores us and enables us to walk in the light.

## 2. Divine Initiative and the Joy of our Salvation

While I have been suggesting that pastoral leadership plays a considerable role in fostering the penitential life within a community, it is always on the assumption that we sustain an awareness of the priority of divine initiative in the penitential. It is the Spirit who convicts of sin and grants an apprehension of the mercy of God. The Spirit and the Spirit alone can convict. God's grace precedes and enables confession. Confession and repentance are a Christian practice in response to the prior work of God, who invites and encourages the world to accept the offer of forgiveness and mercy and to participate in the life that is offered to the justified.

One of the implications of this is that we cannot confess *for* one another or assume that we know how the other should be confessing. And as religious communities we cannot presume to know how other communities should be repenting of sin. We can only know our own hearts, and only properly attend to how the Spirit is calling us to turn from sin to life.

On the one hand, then, this is an invitation to a practice, a spiritual discipline by which the Christian and the community of faith respond to the convicting ministry of the Spirit. And on the other hand it is an invitation to a disposition, a way of being and living. In confession we are not after some kind of emotional high or "release." Rather, through the regular practice of confession we maintain a dynamic awareness of hopefulness, that sin does not have the last word, and of the mercy of

God without which we cannot live. These in turn provide the emotional contours for a life lived in joy and humility. Confession is an act of humility, but it is also the vital way in which humility is cultivated and sustained. We are guarded from both arrogance and self-sufficiency.

As emphasized, confession sustains an awareness of the mercy of God. This is, indeed, the only possible posture from which we can begin to "process" the wrongs that have been done against us. If we are going to be reconciled to one another, in view of the wrongs we have experienced and committed, and if communities or peoples are going to live in peace, especially in those situations where there has been war and severe violence, the only hope is that we sustain an animating sense of the mercy of God, a mercy that is known and experienced through confession. Confession will keep us from judging our neighbor or from judging those who have wronged us, or those who disagree with us, for it is confession that keeps us aware of mercy. Confession is fundamentally an act of hope.

And hope opens our hearts to joy, a persistent and unshakable capacity to live in joy even in a fallen and broken world. It is a joy sustained by the mercy of God. Hope and joy are cultivated through the ancient practice of confession and repentance. In the grace of God we are jolly penitents. It only follows that pastoral leadership would make it a priority to encourage the penitential.

# List of Contributors

Mark J. Boda
Professor of Old Testament
McMaster Divinity College
McMaster University, Hamilton, ON

Terry E. Fretheim
Elva B. Lovell Professor of Old Testament
Lutheran Seminary, Saint Paul, MN

Carol J. Dempsey
Professor of Theology
University of Portland, Portland, OR

Richard J. Bautch
Assistant Professor of Religious Studies
St. Edward's University Austin, Austin, TX

Guy Dale Nave Jr.
Assistant Professor of Religion
Luther College, Decorah, IA

Edith M. Humphrey
William F. Orr Professor of New Testament
Pittsburgh Theological Seminary, Pittsburgh, PA

Stanley E. Porter
President, Dean and Professor of New Testament
McMaster Divinity College, Hamilton, ON

Cornelia B. Horn
Assistant Professor of Theology
St. Louis University, St. Louis, MO

Ronald Rittgers
Associate Professor of the History of Christianity
Yale University Divinity School
Associate Professor of History
Yale University, New Haven, CT

John Chryssavgis
Theological Advisor to the Ecumenical Patriarch on Environmental Issues
Greek Orthodox Archdiocese of America, New York, NY

Ralph Del Colle
Associate Professor of Systematic Theology
Marquette University, Milwaukee, WI

Andrew Purves
Hugh Thomson Kerr Professor of Pastoral Theology
Pittsburgh Theological Seminary, Pittsburgh, PA

Gordon T. Smith
President
reSource Leadership International
Adjunct Associate Professor in Spiritual Theology
Regent College, Vancouver, BC

Cheryl Bridges Johns
Professor of Discipleship and Christian Formation
Church of God Theological Seminary, Cleveland, TN

Wafik Wahba
Assistant Professor of Global Christianity
Tyndale Seminary, Toronto, ON

Michael Battle
Vice President, Associate Dean of Academic Studies
Associate Professor of Theology
Virginia Theological Seminary, Alexandria, VA

Walter Brueggemann
Professor of Old Testament (Emeritus)
Columbia Theological Seminary, Decatur, GA

Marva J. Dawn
Teaching Fellow in Spiritual Theology
Regent College, Vancouver, BC

# Subject Index

# Author and Name Index

# Index of Biblical and Extra-Biblical Citations